Stories of Struggle

Stories of Struggle

The Clash over Civil Rights
in South Carolina

Claudia Smith Brinson

THE UNIVERSITY OF
SOUTH CAROLINA PRESS

© 2020 Claudia Smith Brinson

Published by the University of South Carolina Press
Columbia, South Carolina 29208

www.uscpress.com

Manufactured in the United States of America

29 28 27 26 25 24 23 22 21 20
10 9 8 7 6 5 4 3 2 1

Library of Congress Cataloging-in-Publication Data
can be found at http://catalog.loc.gov/.

ISBN: 978-1-64336-107-9 (hardcover)
ISBN: 978-1-64336-108-6 (ebook)

This book was printed on recycled paper with
30 percent postconsumer waste content.

Contents

Introduction

This is a book of stories. Stories of arson, gunplay, abductions, murders, troops holding rifles with fixed bayonets. Stories of hate letters, death threats, bombs, and robed Klansmen parading, burning crosses, whipping, beating, knifing, and killing those who displeased them.

And stories of another kind—of devotion. Of deeply poor farm workers, sharecroppers, maids, and cooks who saved quarters to fund lawsuits defending constitutional rights. Of high school and college students who crashed to their knees under fire-hose spray, then peacefully followed a police officer to jail. Of women and children who marched down city streets, arms linked with celebrities and union officials. Of attorneys who tried more than fifteen thousand South Carolina civil rights cases in an effort to open lunch counters, restaurants, schools, hospitals, parks, playgrounds, beaches, colleges and universities; who lost almost every case in South Carolina—and appealed—and won and won and won.

All these stories are South Carolina stories.

This is a book full of people, lots of people. Not a cast of thousands, though, because activists require courage and perseverance and a deep understanding that all you have is one life, yours to live and, perhaps, yours to lose but, above all, yours to dedicate.

Stories of Struggle: The Clash over Civil Rights in South Carolina introduces you to black South Carolinians determined to attain full citizenship rights and white supremacists determined to stop them. Throughout my thirty-year reporting career in South Carolina, I made opportunities to find and write about black activists and the important events they participated in or led. In the natural course of my daily assignments, I also met and interviewed white officials who had worked to maintain segregation and, of course, ordinary white citizens who believed in segregation or thought little about it. In 2003 I began interviewing specifically for *Stories of Struggle*. Over the years I interviewed about 150 black activists and their spouses, siblings, children, and friends. The modesty, benevolence, and courage I encountered moved me, and it seemed so wrong that their stories might die with them. Many of the elders I interviewed had experienced the bleakest, cruelest side of South Carolina—a beating because deference was missing, an eviction from land and home in retaliation for a petition, a pitiful education lacking books and bathrooms and buses, a relative run out of town or lynched. Sometimes, because of time and place, such stories had to be secret. Sometimes they were just too sad to tell. I asked for those stories.

What is familiar to all, instead, is the false narrative of a benign and mannerly society. White officials I interviewed praised South Carolina as moderate in its day-to-day functioning and political responses to the civil rights movement—as if the terrorism of the everyday segregationist or member of the White Citizens' Council or the Ku Klux Klan was an aberration rather than daily life, as if denying a basic education or the vote could in any way exist as a moderate response to the humanity of your neighbors. South Carolina segregationists, particularly politicians promoting white supremacy, were just as malign as any others in the Deep South. They were propagandists, crafting a tale of a civil society that nobly preserved a way of life satisfactory to all, resisted destruction by wanton outsiders, and yielded reluctantly to undue intervention by the federal government.

Their endless creation of obstructions wasted energy and opportunity; much worse, it ruined lives. Their resistance to sharing even a crumb of the American pie was wicked in its repetitive undermining and destruction of people. That's part of the story too.

This book, then, is a collection of people and their stories. The location is South Carolina. The time period is the 1930s through the 1960s. The sights and sounds and feelings and happenings—the substance of the book—come from the people who were there. That information is reinforced by the reporting of local and national all-white and all-black newspapers, collected oral histories, and collected personal papers. While the five chapters proceed in chronological order and are best read that way, the book is written so that each can be read on its own in any order. To help readers make their way through the sprawl, people and organizations are repeatedly identified, as are important lawsuits. Think of Stories of Struggle as a collection of short and long stories both intertwined and independent.

The first chapter introduces Rev. James Myles Hinton Sr., the president of the South Carolina Conference of Branches of the National Association for the Advancement of Colored People (NAACP) from 1941 to 1958. Hinton and the NAACP seem one and the same, a man and an organization determined to obtain full citizenship for black Americans. He was an orphan, an artillery lieutenant in World War I, an executive with a black-owned insurance company, and an eloquent and sometimes wry letter writer, debater, and preacher. Bold, untiring, both practical and visionary, Hinton pushed for NAACP-sponsored lawsuits involving teacher pay, voting rights, public transportation, and equal access to public schools and colleges and universities. He challenged governors; he investigated lynchings; he hammered on the door of the U.S. Justice Department. He survived a Klan abduction; his wife survived a gunfire assault on their home. When Hinton said he would rather die fighting than live on his knees, he meant it.

The second chapter begins in Clarendon County, home to the immediate consequences of Hinton's demand that someone courageous sue for black schoolchildren's bus transportation. That challenge—taken up by Levi and Hammett Pearson, with the encouragement of Rev. Joseph Armstrong DeLaine—expanded and traveled from South Carolina to the U.S. Supreme Court. The resulting *Briggs v. Elliott* sought the end of segregation in public schools, becoming the first of five lawsuits making up *Brown v. Board of Education of Topeka, Kansas*. In 1954, in *Brown v. Board*, the court declared segregation in public schools unconstitutional. In 1955 the court set an ambiguous timeline for desegregation. Historians have explored *Brown v. Board* thoroughly and often but with a focus on presidents, governors, and attorneys doing political and legal battle. Instead, I offer the daily life of the Summerton children and adult petitioners as years passed. The children feared that their houses would burn down and their parents would die of poisoning. The adults endured shunning, a murder plot, a murder, Christmas firings, even the repossession of a mule. As one child said, though, the more they were threatened, the stronger they got.

The third chapter introduces Rev. Cecil Augustus Ivory, president of the Rock Hill branch of the NAACP from 1953 to 1961. The resurgence of a childhood spinal injury forced him into a wheelchair. Death threats kept him up at night with a pistol on the bedside table. Even so, he was a dynamo. In 1957 he started and ran a donations-funded bus company for black customers incensed by city drivers' abusive behavior. He persuaded the competitive adults of the NAACP and Congress of Racial Equality (CORE) to cooperate during Rock Hill sit-ins. His participatory leadership as the rare adult on the front lines accepting arrest fashioned local teens into the embodiments of nonviolent protest.

The fourth chapter moves sit-in by sit-in, college by college through 1960. South Carolina students endured more arrests than in other southern states, and several local leaders shaped the national movement. During Thanksgiving 1959, Charles Frederick McDew was arrested three times in two days: The freshman on holiday break from South Carolina State College was arrested for not saying "sir," refusing to ride in the baggage car of a segregated train, and walking in a whites-only park. On a freezing day in March 1960, he and others led a mass march in Orangeburg that ended with law enforcement soaking hundreds of students with high-pressure spray from fire hoses and confining them in an outdoor stockade. In April, McDew helped found the Student Nonviolent Coordinating Committee. In November he became its second chairman. In October 1960 in Sumter, when Mae Frances Moultrie and two classmates took a seat at a Kress lunch counter, the waitress screamed, "Oh, my God, they're here!" and the manager turned off the lights and called the police. Seven months later Moultrie, a Morris College student, boarded a Greyhound bus for the first Freedom Ride, recruited by James T. McCain Sr., a Sumter native and the CORE field secretary organizing the South. The violence the Riders met kept them riding through November 1961, forcing federal action that ended segregation in interstate travel.

Throughout, South Carolina officials vowed to crush the sit-in movement, called the students dupes and communists, arrested them for sitting quietly at lunch counters, charged thousands with breach of peace or trespass, locked them up with rapists and murderers, and, in 1961, sent several to a prison camp. The appeals by South Carolina students benefited all peaceful protesters. The Supreme Court affirmed peaceful demonstrators' rights to speech, assembly, and equal protection of the laws.

The final chapter covers the Charleston hospital strike in 1969. More than four hundred black women working for the Medical College and Charleston County hospitals went on strike. For more than a year, the women had tried to get a hearing from hospital officials regarding access to higher pay, higher-level jobs, and desegregated work bathrooms and cafeterias. Despite the 1964 Civil Rights Act and looming federal sanctions for discrimination, white leaders ignored them. On Mother's Day, 1969, nurse's aide Mary Moultrie and licensed practical nurse Rosetta Simmons led about fifteen thousand supporters down Charleston streets. The governor sent twelve hundred troopers and National Guardsmen, fully armed, while the nation awaited another summer race riot.

Cecil J. Williams, an Orangeburg native who began taking civil rights photographs as a teen, described *Briggs v. Elliott* and the decade-long Orangeburg Freedom Movement as "pioneering actions of South Carolinians who were really first to launch the era of extreme racial changes." These pages introduce you to the pioneers. They believed in the promises of the U.S. Constitution and wanted its words alive in their lives. Viewed one way, they are ordinary people like you and me, who got up in the morning for the ordinary tasks of cooking, cleaning, studying, working—with freedom on their minds. Viewed another way, they are remarkable, courageous, inventive, persevering people willing to give everything for first-class citizenship and, in that regard, the nation's saviors.

One

Fearless Leader

James Myles Hinton Sr.

They tied him to a tree. The men—those who kidnapped him, those
who were waiting in the woods—studied the blindfolded James Myles
Hinton Sr. in their flashlights' glare. Hinton heard one say, "This is not
the nigger." Perhaps that's why they didn't kill him. They beat him, head
to toe. After several cars drove off, Hinton found his way to a highway.
He walked barefoot for two hours, until he flagged down a bus.
It was spring 1949.

The Ku Klux Klan (KKK) used violence—abductions, beatings, mutilations,
and lynchings—to enforce subjugation. The KKK counted on its terrorism to
intimidate, silence, or run out of town any black person considered successful or outspoken, anyone who didn't know what was called his or her "place."
Among the twelve states with the most lynchings between 1877 and 1950,
South Carolina ranked seventh, with 185. The greatest number occurred in
Barnwell, Greenwood, Orangeburg, Laurens, and Aiken Counties, the last
just across the Savannah River from James Myles Hinton Sr.'s Augusta, Georgia, workplace.[1]

Activist Ida B. Wells-Barnett kept a tally. So did the National Association
for the Advancement of Colored People (NAACP); the Tuskegee Institute,
an Alabama school for black teachers; and the *Chicago Tribune*. The most
recent count, by the Equal Justice Initiative, is 6,500 lynchings, described
as "murders carried out with impunity." Wells-Barnett believed that white
men used lynching to enforce their economic and social supremacy. She described lynching as "an excuse to get rid of Negroes who were acquiring
wealth and property and thus keep the race terrorized and 'keep the nigger down.'"[2] Those lynched were hanged by ropes and chains, burned at the
stake, castrated, beheaded, their bodies dragged by people or horses through

the streets and blasted to shreds by hundreds of rounds of bullets. Those attending what were later called "public spectacle lynchings" often brought children, held picnics, posed for photographs, and carved away body parts as souvenirs. It's likely that every black person living in South Carolina during Jim Crow knew, knew of, and/or was related to someone who had been lynched.

Rev. James Myles Hinton Sr. knew he had narrowly escaped death. He knew exactly how dangerous South Carolina was. And if his captors had known who he truly was, the outcome surely would have been worse. They had abducted the president of the South Carolina Conference of Branches of the NAACP.

Hinton was born in Gates County, North Carolina, in 1891. His parents died when he was four years old, and an aunt in New York City took him in. There he attended public schools and a Bible teacher-training school. Upon graduation he worked as a postal clerk, was drafted into the U.S. Army, and rose to infantry lieutenant during World War I, ending his service at Fort Gordon in Augusta, Georgia. In 1919 Hinton joined the Pilgrim Health and Life Insurance Company and opened territory in Alabama, Florida, and South Carolina. In 1938 the widowed Hinton settled in Columbia, though he spent weekdays at the Augusta home office. By 1939—despite a full-time post, hours from home, and four children in the workweek care of housekeepers and then his second wife, Lula Hinton—he ran the Columbia NAACP branch.[3]

The Columbia branch was the biggest, and Hinton resisted a statewide organization, foreseeing a drain on local energy and funds. But Levi G. Byrd, a Chesterfield County plumber, wanted a means to keep branches alive and working. Unschooled but creative and determined, Byrd had decided to "fight the Brutal way thay doin our Race." In 1939 he pulled together representatives of seven branches to found the state conference. Hinton yielded, writing, "I'll go along with you, but if I can't run it, I'll tear it up." So Byrd employed that lure. In 1941 Hinton took over, following the first president, Rev. Alonzo Webster Wright. Within Hinton's first three years as state leader, NAACP membership reached fifteen thousand, and within the first seven years, the number of branches grew from thirteen to eighty.[4]

A year after that, Hinton was also executive secretary to the Colored Citizens' Committee, focused on police brutality, and then the Negro Citizens Committee, focused on the vote. He built partnerships with other fierce fighters: Rev. Eugene Avery Adams Sr., president of the Negro Citizens Committee and the Columbia NAACP branch; Modjeska Monteith Simkins, a founder of the State Negro Citizens Committee and corresponding secretary and publicist for the state conference; John Henry McCray, outspoken editor of Columbia's *Lighthouse and Informer* from 1941 to 1954, then a regional reporter and editor for other black-owned newspapers; Harold R. Boulware Sr., a U.S. Army Air Corps veteran, one of the state's five black lawyers, and the only one trained in civil rights law; and Osceola E. McKaine, a World War I infantry lieutenant, co-owner of a Belgium supper club, and executive secretary of the resurrected Sumter NAACP branch. Their energy and daring reconfigured South Carolina.[5]

In December 1940 Fort Jackson received its first black soldier. Just five miles from downtown Columbia, the fort's nearness allowed soldiers to jam city streets, restaurants, and clubs. In March 1941, because white military police frequently assaulted black civilians, male and female, Hinton met with the fort's provost marshal. Hinton correctly noted that federal law prohibited the military from arresting civilians or performing other police duties off the post without specific authorization, which the officer acknowledged but did not enforce. Hinton wrote the local papers that military police drove legitimate black customers from restaurants and places of business. He asked why city and military police employed "one treatment for one race and another treatment for the colored people." The answer: a deal with the mayor to rid the city of vice. Solicitor A. Fletcher Spigner asserted, "There are more killings, shootings, and cuttings among Negroes in the county and city than there are fleas on a dog's back." The brutality continued, particularly in the black neighborhood of Waverly and an area adjoining Washington Street's black business district. So Hinton wrote the army chief of staff and the U.S. secretary of war, whose assistant came to Columbia regarding affidavits that Hinton collected. Two investigations ended with the post commander reprimanded. While the results disappointed Hinton, he had made his presence and his persistence known.[6]

On August 21, 1941, the Klan received a police motorcycle escort across the Broad River Bridge before a meeting and parade on Senate and Main Streets in Columbia. Whether the men and women donned their robes in the police station, as they had in Charleston, was not announced. But up to two thousand heard the imperial wizard and South Carolina's grand dragon attack "the scum of Europe." In December 1942, during a Columbia NAACP meeting, word came that robed KKK were collecting in front of Hinton's and Reverend Adams's houses. The two returned to Waverly. "We went home, to find a line of cars parked in the street in front of the house. The Klan was lined up, in hoods, in considerable strength along the street," reported

Adams's daughter, Charity Adams. "Daddy got out his double-barreled shotgun and shells, gave instructions, and then he left to join Mr. Hinton." The KKK lurked throughout the night, restrained by neighbors standing guard. Police response was nil; they claimed they could do nothing about men parked on the street.[7]

"In the forties and early fifties, for a man to do the things he did—they were so strong, 'real' men, or they were crazy," said Noble Cooper Sr., a dentist, friend of Hinton's, and NAACP fundraiser. "What they thought of their lives was nothing, because you just didn't challenge the white authority. He was defying them on every level and succeeding at it." Hinton radiated calm and purpose, his hair cropped short, his eyes keen, cheeks full, shoulders broad, feet rooted to the ground. People frequently mistook him as white; he instantly corrected them. He said, "I'm not white; I'm colored." A fireplug of a man, five foot seven and stocky, Hinton didn't worry about stepping on toes but wasn't rash. "He believed in looking at all sides of everything. He would take that knowledge and test it for accuracy," said Stonewall "Stoney" M. Richburg, a principal in Columbia's segregated schools and Hinton friend. Hinton was stern; he was definite; when necessary, he was forceful.[8]

Hinton seemed determined to overcome each barrier—endless barriers— to full citizenship. He spoke every Sunday at black churches about rights and injustices, earning admiration for his fiery sermons. He served as chairman of the Negro Division of the American Red Cross War Fund drive and the Negro Defense Recreation Committee, acquiring a community center for black soldiers. He served as secretary-treasurer of the Richland County Interracial Committee, obtaining a park for black children. He demanded accountability from all and sundry. He wrote to a Bethune police chief about the beating of two black men. He wrote to Belk's department store about including black children in a youth radio program. He wrote to Columbia's mayor about the need for a school crosswalk after a driver injured a black child. He wrote to a WIS radio commentator, who had drummed up a mob by connecting a knifing to a voting rights case: "We request that you make a PERSONAL INVESTIGATION into the alleged attack and slashing of the white woman and see if you do not find that the alleged attacker WAS NOT A NEGRO."[9]

Hinton, Simkins, and McCray shared a frankness and ferocity. The trio spoke and wrote bluntly about the rights of black citizens, their voices as one, and the strength of their convictions and fearlessness startled the white power structure. Hinton's frequent letters and speeches announced a determined, fully present NAACP in South Carolina, but change had to be forced. That meant lawsuits, which were expensive, time consuming, and dangerous for plaintiffs. Equalizing salaries among black and white public-school teachers ranked high among early NAACP goals; pursuit began in the 1930s in Maryland and Virginia. In June 1940 the Fourth Circuit Court of Appeals, in *Alston v. School Board of City of Norfolk,* required the school board to equalize teacher salaries. The decision said that arbitrarily paying black teachers less than white teachers was "as clear a discrimination on the ground of race as could well be imagined," and the U.S. Supreme Court let the judgment stand.[10]

In November 1940, the Columbia NAACP asked Thurgood Marshall, counsel for the NAACP's Legal Defense and Education Fund (LDF), how to initiate a teacher pay case. At that early point, Marshall judged Hinton "exceptionally capable." The state conference publicly set expansive goals: voting rights, equalization of teacher pay, and equal school facilities. The all-black Palmetto State Teachers Association (PSTA) asked the legislature to equalize salaries voluntarily but also set aside money for a lawsuit. McKaine, an associate editor of the *Lighthouse and Informer,* described the slow PSTA approach as "shameful," pushed for support of an NAACP lawsuit, and collected vital statewide data on salaries.[11]

In 1943 Hinton vowed to sue. At the time white teachers' annual salaries ranged from $680 to $800 a year, black teachers' salaries from $360 to $480. When the PSTA decided not to spend its money, Hinton announced that "the fight is now the fight of the state conference of the NAACP." Simkins took on publicity and fundraising; her home became NAACP attorneys' way station. Charlestonian Malissa T. Smith volunteered as plaintiff. When school officials dismissed Smith, the NAACP turned to Viola Louise Duvall, filing *Duvall v. J. F. Seignous et al.* in November 1943. A February 14, 1944, consent decree by Judge J. Waties Waring ordered equalization of teacher salaries in Charleston.[12]

The state set up a grievance process as an impediment to salary complaints and lawsuits. The NAACP returned to court with Columbia teacher Albert N. Thompson. Between the case filing and Waring's decision on May 26, 1945, the state also created a recertification system requiring minimum scores on the National Teacher's Examination. This again limited employment and salaries of black teachers, who lacked state access to graduate education. Waring ruled, in *Thompson v. Gibbes,* that the school board must set a new salary schedule, but he accepted the legislature's means to determine pay. Duvall, avoided by fellow teachers and haunted by hate mail, left South Carolina in 1945. In 1946 Thompson lost his job when he didn't answer a complaint filed against him. This pattern—NAACP campaigns followed by retaliation, personal and systemic—dominated twenty years of Hinton's life.[13]

Always weighing on Hinton's mind was the right to vote, the true proof of citizenship. On April 3, 1944, the U.S. Supreme Court held in a Texas case, *Smith v. Allwright*, that primaries were part of general election machinery. Thus black citizens could not be denied participation through the use of white-only primaries—which South Carolina continued. In South Carolina voting was close to impossible for black citizens. Registrars could block a potential voter by requiring a person read or write any section of the state constitution or prove ownership of property worth more than three hundred dollars. Of two hundred thousand registered voters in South Carolina, only ten thousand were black. Evidently that wasn't restrictive enough. Immediately Gov. Olin D. Johnston initiated legislative repeal of all statutes governing primaries—150 statutes in six days-—leaving political parties free to make their own rules. In what was essentially a one-party state, only the Democratic primary mattered. Now party rules created a private club for whites only.[14]

McCray and McKaine shaped the founding of the biracial Progressive Democratic Party (PDP), a rebuttal to the state's all-white Democratic Party. On May 24, 1944, the PDP held its first state convention, with Hinton a featured speaker. "He is good enough to die," proclaimed Hinton of a son fighting in World War II, "but he is not good enough to vote in this hellish South Carolina." The PDP sent eighteen delegates—including Hinton, McCray, McKaine, and Simkins—to the Democratic National Convention. This first-ever challenge to the seating of any all-white delegation ended with a credentials committee disqualification. Undeterred, the PDP worked statewide: coaching voter registration, hunting black candidates, endorsing Franklin D. Roosevelt for president, enrolling forty-five thousand members, selecting McKaine to run against Johnston for U.S. Senate, and urging voters to "vote for freedom." Mysteriously unavailable PDP ballots contributed to McKaine's defeat.[15]

Since 1942 Adams and Hinton had been raising money—six thousand dollars—through the Negro Citizens Committee for a voting rights lawsuit. Attorney Marshall supported "knocking the white primary in South Carolina." Hinton, who went to the top regularly about what he called white legislators' "subterfuge, chicanery, and thievery," religiously documented obstruction. He sent affidavits to the U.S. Justice Department, sought federal intervention, and announced his actions in press releases. In July, Hinton and five other black Columbians appeared before the state Democratic Party's purging committee to protest the removal of all black voters' names from the rolls. Committee members informed them the political party was exclusively white; they were barred from voting solely because of race and color.[16]

In the midst of this, a black child was convicted of murder and sentenced to execution. George Junius Stinney Jr., fourteen years old, was accused in March 1944 of murdering two white children, Mary Emma Thames and Betty June Binnicker. Stinney's parents, a school cook and a mill worker, and three younger siblings fled, frightened by lynching threats in Alcolu. They did not attend his trial, where an all-white, all-male jury took ten minutes to convict Stinney in the death of Binnicker. Stinney's sisters, who said they and their brother only talked to the white girls and did so together, were not asked to testify. Arresting officers said the child confessed. Later reports said Stinney confessed after being denied food and visits from his family. Stinney's attorney did not present evidence or appeal the conviction and sentence, even though, in 1943, a white teen who pled guilty to the rape and murder of an eight-year-old girl was sentenced to twenty years imprisonment.[17]

Letters and telegrams—from Hinton, the national NAACP, state NAACP membership, ministerial alliances, Charleston unions, and several hundred citizens—objected to the speed of the three-month trial and the execution of a child. Johnston said he saw "no reason to interfere" with the June 16 electrocution, which required nightmarish adjustments as the five-foot-one-inch, ninety-pound, Bible-carrying child was too small for the chair and its straps.[18]

No Right So Basic as the Right to Vote

In December 1945 Hinton wrote the U.S. attorney general to demand investigations into voter registration: "Negroes are denied the right to vote in the Democratic Primary of South Carolina, and to deny them the right to register even for the General Election makes null and void all of their rights as citizens of the United States, for which they have fought and died like all other persons." A year later, when a U.S. Department of Justice spokesman denied awareness, Hinton replied that he had sent the department more than twenty-five sworn affidavits.[19]

Hinton had handpicked potential registrants in 1944. None succeeded. Efforts again underway in 1946 were again failing—until George Elmore tried. One afternoon, Hinton, McCray, and others waited on Columbia's Millwood Avenue. Four of the five men had crossed the street to a two-room store, only to be told the registration books weren't there. Enrollment clerks hid the books the second a black person appeared. The men could see into the store through its plate-glass windows and waited for the store clerk to register a white customer. At that moment they planned to rush over, according to McCray. Then Elmore arrived. The portly, chatty, light-skinned Elmore served as secretary of Richland County's PDP. He owned a five-and-dime and two liquor stores, drove for Blue Ribbon Taxi Club, and hired out as a photographer.[20]

Elmore volunteered, crossed the street, walked in, bought a Coke, and listened as the white woman complained about "them damn niggers" across the street. She told Elmore it was important for every white person to enroll and vote. She got the book and instructed Elmore in writing his name in the E section. When Elmore completed his address, a location recognizably in a black neighborhood, she yelled, "Then you're a damned nigger, too!" Elmore stepped out of the store and shouted across the street, "She says you other niggers might as well come on in and enroll, too." McCray lived in a different ward, but that's how Elmore, Hinton, Dr. R. W. Mance, Rev. E. A. Davis, and Rev. F. M. Young registered.[21]

On August 13, 1946, Elmore showed his poll tax receipt and was denied a vote in Richland County's Democratic primary because he was not white. The NAACP filed an injunction on behalf of Elmore and sixty others. In district court state attorneys argued that the Democratic Party was a "private voluntary association of individuals mutually acceptable to each other," so Elmore had lost no constitutional rights or privileges. "There is no right so basic as the right to vote," argued Marshall. He and assistant counsels Robert Carter and Boulware said that black citizens were deprived of their right to make political choices since the primary was South Carolina's "only meaningful election." Hinton called upon the Eighty-Seventh General Assembly to recall the "white supremacy EXTRA SESSION" whose circumventions "conspired to steal the ballot from forty-three percent of its electorate." South Carolina ran the nation's last all-white primary, and Hinton said it was time for the state to redeem itself by "producing some statesmen." On July 12, 1947, District Judge J. Waties Waring opened the primary with the observation, "It is time for South Carolina to rejoin the Union."[22]

Hinton immediately wrote the Democratic Party chairman to say the decision required "that the rules of the party be amended to include all qualified electors, and the word White to be stricken from the party rules," that all black citizens eighteen years old and older be permitted to participate in Democratic primaries, and, "in a democracy based on a judiciary," bitterness be forgotten. The PDP held a special convention five days after

Rev. James Myles Hinton Sr., fourth from right, voted in the 1948 primary
and general elections. The president of the South Carolina Conference
of Branches of the NAACP made possible black citizens' votes through
Elmore v. Rice, which ended South Carolina's all-white primary.
Courtesy of South Caroliniana Library, University of South Carolina, Columbia

Waring's decision. Elmore announced, "In the words of our other champion, Joe Louis, all I can say is 'I glad I win.'" He referred to the Brown Bomber, boxing's black world heavyweight champion from 1937 to 1949.[23]

South Carolina appealed. Hinton warned, "The Negroes who are determined to vote are not going to give an inch." The Fourth Circuit rejected the argument that black citizens had no more right to vote in the Democratic primary "than to vote in the election of officers of the Forest Lake Country Club," an exclusive whites-only club in Columbia. The December 30, 1947, decision, written by Judge John J. Parker, called the country club comparison a fundamental error: "An essential feature of our form of government is the right of the citizen to participate in the governmental process." On April 19, 1948, the U.S. Supreme Court denied review.[24]

On April 21, 1948, Hinton, McCray, and Elmore and wife Laura Delaney Elmore voted in a city primary. "I'm happy as a lark," Hinton told *The State*, the Columbia morning paper. Hinton often gave a pat on the back followed by a nudge, so he wrote a letter of congratulations to the party's executive committee, reminding them that black participants expected equality at precinct meetings. It might seem a man so focused on repetitively addressing infinite obstructions might be grim, but Hinton possessed an understated, wry humor. The Charleston mayor declared, "I'd rather die and go to hell before seeing Negroes vote in our primaries," and Hinton observed, when the man died, "A white man always keeps his word."[25]

In May, sure that Jim Crow still held sway, the state Democratic Party required that an aspiring voter had to swear belief in the social, religious, and educational separation of the races in order to qualify to vote. The NAACP sued on behalf of David Brown, a Beaufort County PDP officer and gas station attendant, whose name was struck when he wouldn't sign the oath. On July 20, 1948, in *Brown v. Baskin,* Waring ruled the court would not excuse further subterfuge, struck down the oath, ordered enrollment books open until July 31, and promised to jail anyone in contempt of his orders. Afterward thirty-five thousand black citizens registered.[26]

Segregationists burned crosses at Elmore's home, refused to supply his stores, and inundated his work and home life with death threats. In Calhoun Falls on August 10, Rev. Archie Ware cast his primary ballot and almost died for it. White men surrounded him, beat him with clubs, cut him with hawkbill knives, and left him for dead while two police officers watched. Hinton filed an affidavit for Ware, asked Thurmond to investigate, and asked the U.S. Justice Department to bring criminal prosecution. Ware identified the attackers and left for Illinois and safety. Seven weeks later the state constable only commented that investigations could take "three days, three weeks, three months."[27]

On the same day that Judge Waring listened to arguments about access to the voting booth, he also listened to arguments about access to the University of South Carolina (USC) School of Law. In the 1930s, guided by Charles Hamilton Houston, the NAACP had begun fighting segregation law by law, court by court, state by state. Houston, a World War I veteran and dean of Howard's law school, believed that challenging the 1896 "separate but equal" standard of *Plessy v. Ferguson* could force states that practiced segregation to provide actual equal educational facilities—a very expensive outcome. Houston began with law schools.[28]

In 1936, in *Murray v. Pearson,* Maryland's court of appeals agreed that equal treatment required that students be admitted to the one law school provided. Donald Gaines Murray graduated from the University of Maryland

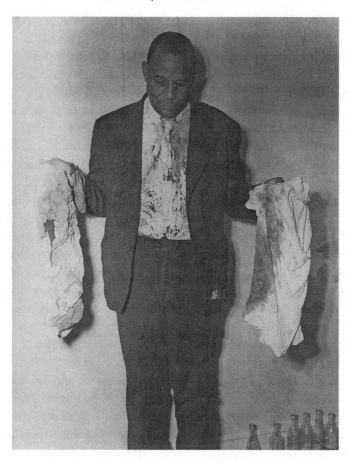

After Rev. Archie Ware cast his 1948 primary vote in
Calhoun Falls, white men stabbed him in the belly, back,
and thigh, beat him with clubs, and left him for dead.
Courtesy of South Caroliniana Library, University of South Carolina, Columbia

School of Law in 1938. That year, in *Missouri ex rel. Gaines v. Canada,* the
U.S. Supreme Court ruled that the Fourteenth Amendment's guarantee of
equal protection under the law meant that Missouri had to provide equal
access, admitting Lloyd Lionel Gaines to its only law school or building an
equal law school. Missouri briefly provided a law school in a beauty parlor.
Gaines never attended because he disappeared, certainly a warning to other
applicants. Also in 1938 Charles B. Bailey, a Columbia resident and graduate
of Atlanta's Morehouse College, applied to the USC School of Law. Houston

encouraged Bailey, saying the short-term goal was scholarship aid to other states, the long-term goal the right to attendance. Trustee and state representative Solomon Blatt assured white South Carolinians that the university remained for white students only. The NAACP put Bailey on hold for more promising cases.[29]

South Carolina took a turn again in 1946, when John H. Wrighten applied to USC. Wrighten grew up on Edisto Island, the eighth of nine children. He was drawn to law to right wrongs. His sister's husband was murdered at the behest of a white man; no investigation or arrest followed. At fourteen Wrighten left home to attend the private Avery Normal Institute in Charleston. Drafted in 1941, he returned two years later to finish secondary school and participated in the local NAACP youth council and the Southern Negro Youth Congress. Anticipating graduation, he applied to the segregated College of Charleston without success, then enrolled in the Colored Normal Industrial Agricultural and Mechanical College in Orangeburg, the state's only public college for black students. After completing prelaw and other college courses, he qualified upon graduation for law-school admission—except he was not white.[30]

Within four days of Wrighten's application, USC president Norman Smith answered that USC operated exclusively for white students. Wrighten appealed to the board of trustees, received no response, and contacted Hinton, who pushed Marshall. Hinton complained of the several NAACP lawsuits that "other states are getting action, but we are rebuffed each time." By now McCray, McKaine, and Hinton had persuaded attorney Boulware to "sue white folk" as NAACP local counsel. Hinton's leadership, increasing NAACP membership, NAACP attorneys, and Waring's openness to constitutional arguments made success seem likely. On January 6, 1947, an NAACP-supported Wrighten sued for admission. He asked for compensatory damages, not tuition for an out-of-state school, and a ruling that barring black students from the university on the basis of race denied Wrighten equal protection under the Fourteenth Amendment.[31]

South Carolina's constitution required separate schools for white and black students and prohibited those of one race from attending a school for the other race. In 1946, with Wrighten's lawsuit pending, the legislature provided all of sixty thousand dollars toward law and graduate schools in Orangeburg and teased Boulware with a deanship. In July 1947 Waring ordered the state to open, by September, an adequate law school, "satisfactorily staffed, equipped, and a going concern." If that wasn't accomplished, Wrighten had the right to enter USC, or the state had to stop providing law school to anyone. Upon its opening the Orangeburg law school had one classroom, one dean, two professors who had never taught, and almost no books.[32]

Hinton called it a "makeshift law school." Marshall, who opposed Wrighten's attending, called it a "Jim Crow dump" and asked why "the Negroes in South Carolina would accept a $10,000 law school in a $1.50 university." Hinton and Marshall took the long view: accepting tossed bones sustained segregation. Wrighten did sue again, maintaining inequality, but Waring terminated the lawsuit, saying the state had complied with his decree. Heman Sweatt got the same result in Texas. He was denied admission to the University of Texas School of Law. When he sued, the legislature created a "separate but equal" law school at Texas State University in 1947. But the NAACP did best in Oklahoma. Ada Lois Sipuel Fisher had sued Oklahoma when denied admission to its law school. In 1948 the U.S. Supreme Court agreed with the NAACP that she must be provided the same educational opportunities as other Oklahomans. The state tossed together a law school for her alma mater, Langston University, in senate rooms at the capitol. The NAACP argued the education was not equal and won. In 1949 Fisher was admitted to the University of Oklahoma College of Law, and Langston's was closed. She graduated in 1952. That's how this worked, state by state, year by year by year. That's why Hinton's energetic embrace of lawsuits mattered.[33]

Hinton moved to the next task; there was always a next task. "He had an objective, and that's what he worked for," said Cooper. That objective, as Hinton phrased it: first-class citizenship in our American democracy. To Hinton segregation was nonsensical. He told *Afro Magazine*, "You don't explain it. There is no rhyme or reason, no logic to racial segregation." At a women's club testimonial, professor and *Lighthouse and Informer* funder G. E. Nelson offered Hinton poetic praise: "You have fought all morning. Now it is noonday; the afternoon and evening are before you, and you are still fighting." And so he was. In 1948 the S.C. Sheriffs' Association adopted a resolution opposing civil rights proposals in the national Democratic Party platform. Their resolution supported the segregationist States Rights' Party and its presidential candidate, South Carolina governor J. Strom Thurmond, and predicted support of the Democratic platform would result in "chaos, hatred, lawlessness and bloodshed." Hinton wrote the association: "The talk of bloodshed is so frequently used by those fostering and running on the States Rights platform its only purpose must be to create bloodshed."[34]

Violence and death constantly interrupted the branch-building, dues-seeking, lawsuit-organizing, message-spreading work that Hinton undertook.

Sometimes the nation paid attention. On February 12, 1945, Sgt. Isaac Woodard Jr., a decorated World War II veteran, was riding a bus home to Winnsboro, South Carolina, and his wife. One of nine children of sharecropper parents, Woodard had been discharged from the military that morning at Fort Gordon. At some point the bus driver and the twenty-seven-year-old exchanged words. Woodard later said the driver cursed him, and Woodard replied in kind, insisting that the driver address him properly: "God damn it, talk to me like I am talking to you. I am a man just like you." At Batesburg, South Carolina, the driver fetched police. The driver and Police Chief Lynwood Lanier Shull described a drunk and disorderly soldier whom Shull subdued in defense. Woodard described a request for a restroom stop that resulted in Shull pummeling him, a struggle for the police blackjack, and an ensuing beating during which Shull likely rammed his blackjack's end into Woodard's eye sockets. The next morning, a bloodied Woodard couldn't see. Shull took him to court anyway. Mayor H. E. Quarles, also the judge, fined Woodard fifty dollars—police took forty-four dollars in cash from his pocket—before Shull drove Woodard to the Veterans Administration Hospital in Columbia. Woodard was permanently blind.[35]

Within the next two months, one of the veterans on Woodard's bus called Hinton about witnessing the start of the beating. Hinton and McCray investigated. Woodard told his story to the NAACP, signing an affidavit. The NAACP offered a reward of one thousand dollars for information and witnesses, the quest complicated by Woodard's misidentification of Aiken, South Carolina, as the site of his blinding. By July, Batesburg and Shull were identified. In August the state NAACP passed a resolution asking Gov. Ransome J. Williams to remove Shull from office and prosecute him. In July and August, actor and director Orson Welles devoted his ABC radio show to Woodard. His information came via McCray, who interviewed about fifty black Batesburg residents. Joe Louis announced an August 18 fundraiser in New York City. Singer and songwriter Woody Guthrie wrote and performed "The Blinding of Isaac Woodward" at the concert, which included such other luminaries as Paul Robeson, Billie Holliday, Cab Calloway, Welles, and Milton Berle.[36]

Growing concern over Woodard's maiming as well as a July lynching in Georgia of a veteran, his pregnant wife, and their married friends led the NAACP and other groups to create the National Emergency Committee Against Mob Violence and seek an audience with President Harry S. Truman. Walter White, NAACP executive secretary, described Woodard's blinding at the September 19 meeting. Truman, appalled that an American soldier was not only beaten but blinded, asked U.S. Attorney General Tom Clark what could be done since South Carolina had not acted. Clark filed a criminal information, which avoided a grand jury indictment and carried a maximum one-year sentence. It said that Shull violated Woodard's right "not to be beaten and tortured by persons exercising the authority to arrest." Asked to comment, Woodard said, "I had more sympathy for him than he had for me."[37]

On November 5, 1946, an all-white, all-male jury took twenty-eight minutes to acquit Shull. Marshall pointed out that the state attorney general didn't even ask the jury for a guilty verdict. In February 1947 Woodard also lost a fifty-thousand-dollar damage suit against the bus company, although three veterans testified that Woodard was neither drunk nor disorderly. In an editorial claiming Shull's "vindication," *The State* cited states' rights and objected to "intercession on the part of the central government." Hinton responded, "South Carolina has not shown any concern to bring to justice white officers of the law, or whites in general, who violate the rights or abuse Negroes, but will track down any Negro, who has in even a minor degree violated the rights or been accused of a crime against whites." His files were full of such stories. He compared states' rights to human rights: "Woodward was among these soldiers who fought for freedom, which has been denied to him, and if the federal government can send men beyond its borders to defend weak and helpless people, why should it be a violation of states rights to bring to trial those who abuse or mistreat citizens of any color?"[38]

Hinton, McCray, and Boulware frequently investigated police brutality and inquest neglect of murders of black men and women. McCray, whom Hinton called "the man most feared in South Carolina during our battle," secretly visited communities to interview victims and witnesses. Hinton reported findings to the national NAACP and the U.S. Justice Department. Most often ignored, they kept trying, as when James Walker Jr., a Charleston Navy Yard worker, was shot dead on August 12, 1946. Following words with white men at an Elko store, Walker visited his father and stepmother. As he talked to them, unarmed, on their porch, eight white men approached, and one shot Walker through the back. The white men insisted Walker had threatened the shooter. A hearing, held without notification to Boulware, ruled the shooting a justifiable homicide. Another assault by some of the same men followed Walker's death; using a car hand crank and other tools, the men seriously injured Fred Pryor. McCray investigated. Soon after, a third black man, a U.S. Navy veteran, was found dead across from the same store, on his knees, a noose around his neck. The death was ruled a suicide. Asked McCray, "While resting on his knees?" The U.S. Justice Department called the deaths purely a state matter.[39]

Beaten, Shot, Stabbed, Lynched

Months later a mob lynching yanked attention back to South Carolina. Around 4:30 A.M. on February 17, 1947, about thirty taxi drivers and businessmen drove to the Pickens County jail. Several entered the cell block, unlocked by the jailer, and abducted Willie Earle, a twenty-four-year-old black man arrested the day before as a suspect in the stabbing of a cabbie. Although Earle had not been charged, the drivers believed he had injured one of their own, Thomas Watson Brown. Around 6:30 A.M. someone called a black-owned mortuary to report Earle's body in a ditch near a Greenville slaughterhouse. At 11:40 A.M. Brown, who had described but not named a black assailant, died in a Greenville hospital. During those morning hours, an alerted Hinton called McCray. Hinton sent protest letters and telegrams to President Truman, Governor Thurmond, and Robert K. Carr, executive secretary of the president's Committee on Civil Rights. He talked to the NAACP's White.[40]

McCray and Hinton then drove, with photographer Elmore, to Greenville. They met with Tessie McKinsey Earle, Willie Earle's mother, at a funeral home. There Elmore photographed Earle's body. Earle had been beaten with fists and the butt of a shotgun and shot in the head three times. His left arm was sliced to the bone; his right thigh bore a similar slice; his forehead, chin, and stomach bore stab wounds, as did his chest, where the cut entered heart muscles. The *Lighthouse and Informer* and other newspapers published Elmore's photo of Earle's reconstructed skull and upper torso. An Associated Press photo showed Earle's body before the mortician's work, his neck cut ear to ear so deeply the windpipe was exposed, his skull so thoroughly shattered remnants of the brain showed.[41]

Thurmond quickly announced his objection to mob rule and lynching, enlisted state constables, and grudgingly accepted FBI participation. Hinton made public his letters, in which he criticized the failure to protect a suspect and called for arrests. He warned, "South Carolina is now on trial." The capital city's evening paper, the *Columbia Record,* also called for arrests but warned that congressional Republicans would see Earle's lynching and the stalled federal anti-lynching bill as "a regular pre-election Negro vote catcher." Although the jailer claimed he could not identify anyone—even though an in-law was a cab driver, even though the abductors didn't wear masks and asked if he knew them, to which he said yes—the dozens of investigators speedily located participants. By February 21 Greenville's city and county jails held thirty of thirty-one white men charged with Earle's murder; twenty-six confessed.[42]

A steady stream of national commentary followed, praising the quick investigation, arrests, and confessions and, in S.C. newspapers, carping about federal involvement. This might have seemed a good start. But Solicitor Robert T. Ashmore did not charge the jailer with complicity. The coroner's jury on Brown's death—despite Brown's generic description and inability to name an assailant, unrecovered robbery items, a truncated investigation, and Earle's denial of guilt until tortured—named Earle the assailant. The coroner's jury on Earle's death—despite confessions, with a shooter repeatedly named—refused to affix responsibility by name and ruled death by "party or parties of a mob." A *State* editorial placed the blame on Earle, who would "not have met such a horrible fate" if he "had not violated the laws of humanity." The editorial concluded, as if butchery were acceptable: "The way of the transgressor is hard."[43]

Fruit jars in area stores collected funds for the accused, who ranged in age from nineteen to fifty-eight. The thirty-one men faced charges of murder, conspiracy to commit murder, and accessory before and after the fact of murder. After indictment all were free on bonds of $2,500 each. On the trial's first day, the defendants crossed together from jail to court, rousing cheers from white onlookers. All pleaded innocent in the stifling heat of the brick courthouse, with more than three hundred white people crammed onto chairs on the lower floor: defendants' wives with their children, Brown's widow at the defense table, and an all-white, all-male jury. One hundred seventy-five black people observed from the gallery.[44]

During the first days of the trial, the prosecution read the defendants' statements into the record. Eight men had identified Roosevelt Carlos Hurd Sr. as the shooter; the cab dispatcher denied the act. At least three men had identified Hendrix Rector as cutting Earl; he denied doing so. While Judge J. Robert Martin Jr. allowed the confessions into the record, he ruled that each man's statement could be used only against himself, meaning no one would be convicted of the killing. He also ruled that photos of Earle's mutilated body could not be entered as evidence. After defense motions Martin directed the acquittal of three men on all charges and qualified acquittal of seven on charges of murder and accessory after the fact. Of the seven, five did not give statements, and defendants had named two of the five as leaders and assailants. Even so the prosecuting attorneys expected convictions at least on conspiracy charges. They were wrong.[45]

The defense did not present any witnesses. Instead they performed. Attorney Ben Bolt, criticizing the FBI's role, said, "Why you would have thought someone had found a new atomic bomb, but all it was was a dead nigger boy." Attorney John Bolt Culbertson proclaimed, "Willie Earle is dead, and I wish more like him were dead." Interrupted by the judge, he turned to the jury to add, "If a mad dog were loose in my community, I would shoot the dog and let them prosecute me." Rebecca West, who attended the trial for the *New Yorker* and had recently reported on the Nuremberg trials of Nazi war criminals, wrote that the defense attorneys revealed their "lack of regard for the values of civilization" in their lack of regard for black lives. She decided that Greenville's white citizens believed that "lynching is a social prophylactic." So, it seemed, did the jury.[46]

On May 20 prosecutors asked for conviction but not the death penalty. The defense asked for acquittal to punish northerners and the FBI's "meddler's itch." The penalty for accessory after the fact and for conspiracy ranged from three months to ten years imprisonment. But no one paid a price. On the evening of May 21, the jury acquitted all defendants of all charges. Attorneys and defendants stood on chairs and tables to celebrate with huzzahs and hugs. Newspapers nationwide called the verdict shameful, a national disgrace, a verdict for anarchy. The *Richmond Afro-American* called lynching an inexpensive "pastime," given that "not a single lyncher has ever been found guilty and made to pay the penalty for his crime."[47]

Afterward white men dragged from his cab and beat U. G. Fowler, who had refused to join the lynching and testified at the trial. Threatened with death, he made a complaint, the judge refused a warrant, and he left town. Tessie Earle protested the acquittals at National Negro Day in New York City. Hinton asked Attorney General Clark for a federal anti-lynching law "with teeth in it" and a federal trial of the thirty-one white men. "I personally viewed the body of Willie Earle," he wrote, "and the sight established the fact that the men who tortured, shot and cut his body were members of a blood-thirsty mob of depraved men whose minds are warped and who have allowed themselves to become as low in the sight of decent citizens as it is humanly possible." He asked the Speaker of the U.S. House for an anti-lynching law as "the only hope for justice in the South in general and South Carolina in particular." He asked the president of the U.S. Senate for an anti-lynching law because "Negroes in South Carolina in particular are not safe and may be shot down like dogs any time a blood-thirsty mob sees fit to unloose its depravity upon helpless, innocent Negroes." He voiced the outrage he and others lived with: those in "exalted positions see Negroes lynched, tortured, shot, discriminated against, disfranchised, segregated, Negroes who are part and parcel of this country."[48]

Hinton ended the decade as vigilant as ever. "Hinton was a man who felt it was his destiny, his responsibility because of the way he saw things," said his friend Richburg. Hinton got state constables to investigate the death of a black prisoner after a white prisoner wrote of murderous guards. He got another investigation after fifteen white men dragged a seventy-six-year-old West Columbia resident from his home, beat him, and left him naked in the rain. He publicly praised as "a fine demonstration of racial good will" white Democrats' reception of black participants in Columbia precinct meetings and the election of H. T. Marshall as a committeeman.[49]

All the while Hinton did more than create a statewide network of NAACP branches, more than push white officials to right wrongs, more than insist the national NAACP pursue lawsuits in South Carolina. He did more than preach on Sundays about justice. When he announced every single injustice that came to his attention, he modeled a refusal to be silent, to acquiesce. He also modeled practicality about what to announce, when to do so, and how far to push matters. "He had the courage to do what needed to be done, even to the point of personal risk," explained Richburg. But leavening that, Hinton believed that there was "no need to cross a bridge if it was going to be blown up when you got to the other side." He set an example and a tone that spread, partly because he recruited branch leaders with similar mettle and staying power. When Hinton and Joseph Lewis organized the Dunbarton branch in Williston, "I was told I was going to be killed," wrote Lewis. "The Klans was going to burn a cross at my door. I told them to burn it."[50]

"He wasn't afraid of anybody—white, black, blue, green," said Earl Matthew Middleton, a World War II veteran and Orangeburg entrepreneur active in the NAACP. Fearlessness seemed a job requirement. W. B. Hildebrand of St. Matthews wrote Hinton that "the masses of the negroes is satisfied and has been for fifty years, but if you are not stop from sowing discord and insulting our office holders, many of them will be made to suffer for your greed for power, and I hope you will have sence enough to stop before it is to late." A letter addressed to "My Dear Nigger Leader" and signed "Local Whites" began, "I suggest that you proceed to give your Tongue a vacation for if you keep Belly aching about the way your race is being treated you might be using the pick and shovel in your own behalf." The writer continued, "If you will put yourself to a little trouble in keeping your niggers in their places there won't be so much Lynching and the white people will not harm them. Every time you open your Trap you are pouring Powder into the drum of trouble and WOE TO 'YOU' when you get it full."[51]

In January 1949 Hinton asked Thurmond and Clark to investigate a dramatic threat: the writer of a postcard mailed from Greenwood invited Hinton to a cross burning at the State House. "We expect to have you as our guest on top of the cross," read the card, signed "KKK." Hinton's Augusta boardinghouse, across the Savannah River from Aiken, put him near some of South Carolina's most violent segregationists. Eugene A. R. Montgomery, hired in 1944 as the conference's executive secretary, described Aiken as a "hot bed of KKKism" when he and Hinton set up branches there.[52]

Hinton was in the news because he wanted the College of Charleston to accept black students. He wrote, "Negro taxes have aided in the support of this institution for years; now they desire to enter a school that is as much theirs as other people's." From 1944 on Avery Normal Institute and Burke High School students steadily applied for admission. Fifteen applicants in 1949 set off the powers that be, who said the city would close the municipal college rather than desegregate. Former applicant Wrighten, now a Charleston attorney, wanted the NAACP to sue. The city proposed Avery join Orangeburg's land-grant institution. Hinton wrote Marshall that he had made it clear the NAACP did not want an "extension school" continuing segregation. By the end of March, the city had guaranteed the College of Charleston would remain all white: the city council transferred property ownership to the college board of trustees. The legislature granted a private charter. Hinton labeled this proof that officials knew discrimination was illegal.[53]

A Whole Posse of Preachers

Around 10 P.M. on April 21, 1949, a white man knocked at the door of Hinton's boardinghouse, asking for the driver of Hinton's Ford, saying he was a law officer and Hinton's car had been hit by another vehicle. When landlady Annie Ball called to Hinton, he related in a letter to Marshall, "I arose, and without any thought of anything wrong, put on my house slippers, and went to the door." Hinton stepped onto the porch, and as he turned toward his 1936 Ford, parked beside the house, three men grabbed him, thrust him into a car, and pinned him to the floor with their feet. Hinton cried out. A white neighbor, witnessing the abduction, immediately called the police; Ball called allies, Hinton's family, and then the police.[54]

Hinton offered Marshall a bare-bones account: "One of the men asked, 'What is your name?' I did not reply at once, and he then said, 'Aren't you James M. Hinton?' I replied, 'Yes.' He further said, 'You want to place Negroes in the College of Charleston.' He said, 'Don't you know that cannot be done in South Carolina.'" When the cars stopped in distant woods, the men dragged Hinton out and blindfolded him. Others stood waiting. Hinton did not describe the assault. He did report hearing a man say, "This is not the nigger." Unnerved when a car radio broadcast reports of a police search, the men cleared out. Hinton reported that he was ordered to lie on the ground and wait; he followed the sound of the men's cars to a highway. For two hours he walked barefoot, in his pajamas, in a downpour, until he flagged down a Greyhound bus and persuaded the driver to let him board. Years later he told the *Washington Afro-American*, "They figured I was too hot to handle so they let me go unharmed."[55]

Hinton reached the boardinghouse at 3 A.M. In the hours before his return, the police, the FBI, and his friends had searched for him. He joked later that among those who set out to rescue him was "a whole posse of preachers," and it was good for their souls that they didn't find the abductors. No one else did, either. While Hinton obtained car license numbers and provided descriptions of six "rough White men," no one was arrested. The police found a revolver in the gutter at the boardinghouse but didn't trace it. Hinton didn't dwell on the near-death experience or the lack of an investigation; he concentrated on expressions of concern. He wrote Marshall that a hundred white people had called, leaving their names, to wish for his safety.[56]

At a meeting a few nights afterward, Hinton told NAACP members, "I counted the cost long ago when [I] entered this fight and decided that I had only one life to give. I am more determined than ever, God helping me, to carry on." While Hinton's accounts didn't acknowledge this, Waverly neighbors said he was horribly beaten, the assailants' fury visible on his body. They confirmed a KKK night ride, a deliberate echo of antebellum slave patrollers. Neighbors said that Hinton's kidnappers tied him to a tree and whipped him, that he returned to Columbia bruised, eyes swollen, skin broken. The very next day he was working. "He would just take it and go on the next day," said daughter Novella, an eighth grader at the time.[57]

Marshall stated the obvious in a letter to College of Charleston president George Daniel Grice, that Hinton ranked among the most courageous and effective officers of the NAACP. The state conference praised him with Shakespeare: "Cowards die many times before their deaths; the valiant never taste of death but once." An NAACP pamphlet fumed that "slinking elements of the opposition, in an effort to cool his fervor and quiet his searing tongue," had snatched Hinton and used "prolonged efforts to terrorize and intimidate him." The pamphlet proclaimed that "his name has flashed like a shuttle-cock through the halls of the General Assembly and across the state during political campaigns as the professional politicians denounced the man who has been a gadfly to them in their vain efforts to nurture and [perpetuate] the status quo." At a special testimonial on December 29, 1949, Simkins pre-sented Hinton a memory book of collected signatures and more than six hundred dollars.[58]

For Hinton the 1940s were distinguished by a series of hurdles cleared by lawsuits, no small investment in people and time. Fundraising for those lawsuits, with donations coming a nickel or a dollar at a time, was a tedious necessity. Hinton took pride that the state NAACP always paid its way. The national NAACP had found in the state conference an intelligent, deter-mined force that could, as White and Marshall wanted, attack segregation in all its forms—and win. Foremost loomed fraught and complicated chal-lenges to the South's remarkably unequal segregated public schools. Hinton had established in 1943 and then revived an NAACP branch in Clarendon County. There he inspired and fostered petitions for school buses for black children, who walked while white children rode. In 1949 parents agreed to ask for equal school facilities and, in 1950, for the end of segregation in schools. The petitioners of *Briggs v. Elliott* faced ferocious opponents. The petitioners' tenacity and the support of Hinton, Simkins, and local preachers sustained this first of five NAACP-sponsored cases opposing school segre-gation. Conversely South Carolina's remarkable contribution led to white supremacists salting the earth.[59]

In February 1950 Pilgrim Health and Life named Hinton a company di-rector. But—and there was always a but—on August 26, 1950, the KKK at-tacked Charlie's Place, a Myrtle Beach dance hall popular since 1937 with black and white fans of such Chitlin' Circuit artists as Duke Ellington, Ella Fitzgerald, Billie Holliday, and Little Richard. Around 8 P.M. robed Klans-men paraded through Atlantic Beach, a black-owned beach resort, and through Myrtle Beach and its black neighborhood, the Hill, their lead car adorned with a cross of red light bulbs. The Klansmen intended to strike fear and inhibit black voters' participation in the upcoming primary. A Hill caller warned police the Klan better not come back; the police passed that on to Grand Dragon Thomas L. Hamilton. Incensed by the threat and furi-ous that white and black patrons danced together at Charlie's Place, about sixty Klansmen returned. Hooded men swarmed armed-and-waiting owner

Charlie Fitzgerald, battering him and thrusting him into a car trunk. They shot up his club, firing three hundred rounds and wounding one patron. They broke windows and furniture. They beat male and female staff. Klansmen then drove Fitzgerald out of town, where they beat him again. During a debate about killing him, Fitzgerald escaped, shot in the foot, his ears sliced by a man sporting a sheriff's deputy star. Only a Klansman died, likely shot by his compatriots. James Daniel Johnston wore, underneath his robes, his policeman's uniform. He was buried by two thousand mourners offering six truckloads of flowers.[60]

Horry County sheriff C. E. Sasser held Fitzgerald in custody, whereabouts unknown. Hinton and White announced on August 30 that if Fitzgerald were charged with any crime, the NAACP would defend him. White appealed to the U.S. Justice Department. Marshall met with a Justice official. The state attorney general said the Klan was as free to operate within South Carolina as a "ladies' sewing circle."[61]

Sasser decided Fitzgerald was innocent of gunplay and worthy of protection. Within a week he cleared Fitzgerald in a radio address, preceded by a bomb threat; arrested and charged Hamilton and thirteen other Klansmen with conspiracy to commit mob violence; obtained the firing of state constable T. M. Floyd for participation in the Klan parade; and turned over confiscated Klan records to the FBI. Sasser also promised separate warrants for the dynamiting of one home and the defacing of another in a biracial Myrtle Beach neighborhood. Fitzgerald, released as a material witness on September 7, said, "I am a free man—and I am not a free man. I don't know who is and who isn't a member of the Klan."[62]

On October 6 a grand jury refused to indict Hamilton and four other Klansmen. Charges against nine others had been dropped the previous week. On November 5 Klansmen dragged Rufus Lee, a white Conway farmer, from his home and bullwhipped him for daring to criticize the club siege, not so popular with white residents after the resort lost one hundred thousand dollars in Labor Day tourism. Twenty-two union leaders, worried about nearby tobacco-belt productivity, asked the Justice Department to address Klan violence. On November 12 a green-robed Hamilton stood in the back of a truck in nearby Conway, addressing five thousand at a rally lit by a twenty-foot cross and guarded by armed Klansmen. He promised, "The lid is going to fly off." Sasser, battling Klan death threats and a smear campaign, lost reelection.[63]

The resurgent Klan focused on maintaining segregation. As Hamilton declared, "The Klan is fighting so that no Negro will ever sit in a classroom with white children." If the gubernatorial election of James F. Byrnes—formerly a champion of President Franklin Delano Roosevelt's New Deal, a U.S. Supreme Court justice, and a secretary of state to Truman—brought Hinton a flicker of hope in 1951, that was dashed by Byrnes's campaign and inauguration speech. He condemned "professional agitators" and promised "substantial equality of [school] facilities" while warning that the end of segregation could be the end of public schools. Hinton responded that a former member of the highest court could not possibly believe that seeking "relief through due process of law" was "interference."[64]

Of course Hinton was an agitator. After *Briggs v. Elliott* was heard in Charleston on May 28, 1951, attorneys Marshall and Carter issued a joint statement: "Many of us who sit in comfortable and safe homes in other sections of the country will never understand the courage of these people in Clarendon County, a rural prejudiced southern community, who dared the risks involved in their bold challenge to white supremacy. To their aid came James M. Hinton, who has never lost the will to fight for human rights, even after having been almost lynched himself." Hinton, who never lost his New York accent, tossed aside white politicians' constant charge of northern interference, pointing out that he was the only state NAACP official not born in South Carolina. He labeled segregation "unconstitutional, unchristian, and unmoral" and—pointing out that the state had valued white children's public schools at $74 million and black children's at $16 million—asked, "Who violated the law?"[65]

Recognition of his steadfastness continued. In 1952 the NAACP elected Hinton to its national board of directors, and in 1953 Pilgrim named him an agency director. But the work of desegregating South Carolina just got harder. Lawsuits elsewhere—Virginia, the District of Columbia, Kansas, and Delaware—also challenged the "separate but equal" doctrine and, with *Briggs,* were combined as *Brown v. Board of Education of Topeka.* As the cases made their way through lower courts and to the Supreme Court and back between 1951 and 1953, Byrnes predicted a win for segregationists. Hinton responded, "Segregation is on its way out. The harder the fight, the sweeter the victory, and victory will come." But he contended with a seesaw response among his constituents. Petitioners he supported said that they were fearful of their children attending school with white children and were satisfied with new, separate facilities. On the other hand, KKK activity in Horry County resulted in thirty-three teachers joining the NAACP.[66]

On May 17, 1954, in *Brown v. Board,* the Supreme Court decided that "in the field of public education, the doctrine of 'separate but equal' has no place.

Separate educational facilities are inherently unequal." On May 31, 1955, the court decreed that states must desegregate "with all deliberate speed." For Hinton, personally so pivotal, this was a glorious affirmation of constitutional rights followed by a plague of vengefulness of biblical proportions. And, with ill timing, rousing voices hushed. On March 20, 1954, McCray resigned from the *Lighthouse and Informer,* and Simkins briefly took over as acting editor and manager. George Bell Timmerman Jr., busy condemning the NAACP in his gubernatorial campaign, took out a quarter-page ad that month, focusing on "the communistic cunning" of the *Lighthouse and Informer* and Simkins as "known in Communist circles." McCray and Simkins had been feuding, and the paper was in hot water not only politically but also financially. Unable to pay its debts and taxes, the *Lighthouse and Informer* closed in July. In December, McKaine was buried in Sumter; he had returned to Belgium in 1946 but had stayed in touch and involved.[67]

Throughout the South white politicians decided the NAACP must go. After the 1954 *Brown* decision, segregationists in Mississippi founded the White Citizens' Councils (WCC), which quickly spread to South Carolina. Focused on making life miserable for anyone supporting desegregation, WCC members fired black workers, kicked sharecroppers off their land, denied credit and stock to black-owned businesses, and refused to sell to black customers everything from food to farm equipment. Instead of quelling the KKK, Byrnes took to comparing the group and the NAACP as an "equal menace." In August the Committee of 52, a group of prominent white businessmen, published a resolution that assailed the "pressure and propaganda" of the NAACP and called on the legislature to maintain separate schools and "to interpose the sovereignty" of the state between federal courts and local school officials.[68]

Hinton didn't back off. Defending the NAACP, he said, "It has never done more than go into courts and fight the issues out before white judges, using white men's laws. It has lost yet never has it become bitter. It has won, yet never has it become overbearing."He repeated what kept him going: "Justice and right will succeed." Before 350 peers at a regional NAACP meeting, he sounded those notes in less temperate fashion. Only six states had done nothing after the 1954 and 1955 *Brown* decisions, he said; only three were "acting like jackasses—Georgia, South Carolina and Mississippi." He warned, "There is nothing the white South can do to turn the Negroes back." The KKK, WCC, and states' rights groups would lose because they weren't fighting black citizens, they were fighting the U.S. government, Hinton said, always holding the Constitution close.[69]

On January 19, 1956, an unidentified gunman fired double-aught buck-shot, used to kill large game, into the Hinton home, piercing the frame house's front wall and interior plaster, shattering a mirror and houseplant pots. Police removed nine shotgun pellets from the walls, floor, and stairs. While no one was hurt, Lula Hinton was home and heard at least three other shots, likely into the air, before the blast into her home. "I can remember neighbors and others on rooftops around the block with guns to ward off people," said son Rodney Hinton.[70]

Byrd wrote Marshall that "the papers, The State has just Published about the Thugs shooting in Rev. Hintons Home Monday Night. People is so Dum at least some of them We will see just what The Gov. of S.C. Will do about this. Nothing of course." The state conference's treasurer, and, informally, a corresponding secretary since he kept Marshall and others apprised non-stop, Byrd had survived a severe beating by white men in 1933. He added a declaration that he and Hinton lived by: "AS LONG AS I AND SOME OTHERS THAT HAVE NINE LIVES THE N.A.A.C.P. WILL NEVER DIE IN S.C. RIGHT WILL WIN."[71]

On February 14, 1956, Gov. George Bell Timmerman Jr. signed an inter-position resolution. In theory the legislature placed the state's sovereignty between the segregated schools and the *Brown* ruling that segregated schools were unconstitutional. A revamping of John C. Calhoun's nullification the-ory, interposition clashed with the U.S. Constitution's Supremacy Clause that federal law prevails when in conflict with state law or state constitu-tions. Timmerman also signed an appropriations bill that included an order to close any state-supported college upon any court order to desegregate and to close state parks upon any litigation to desegregate. Hinton wrote Con-gress that black citizens comprised at least 42 percent of the state population, but not one black person was asked to appear before the General Assembly regarding these actions.[72]

On February 22, 1956, the state legislature asked that the NAACP be placed on the Justice Department's subversives list. "If resorting to due pro-cess of law is subversive, God help any other approach, aside from the courts," replied Hinton. The legislature claimed that fifty-three NAACP officials were associated with communist, communist-front, or subversive groups. Timmerman had used this during his 1954 gubernatorial campaign, in an obsessive focus on the NAACP. At that time Hinton had charged "political demagoguery" and urged the U.S. attorney general to go ahead and inves-tigate. When T. C. Callison, the state attorney general on the losing end of *Brown,* said the NAACP helped communists and replaced good will in South

Carolina with ill will, Hinton asked why fighting for first-class citizenship was termed subversive while white people who placed roadblocks to citizenship were called good Americans. Hinton always gave as good as he got. But this anticommunist campaign cost the state conference Simkins. She had worked with the Southern Negro Youth Congress, the Southern Conference for Human Welfare, and the Southern Conference Educational Fund, all targeted by the House Un-American Activities Committee, which kept a file on her. Replaced as state conference secretary, she blamed Hinton.[73]

Next Thurmond jumped in with his Southern Manifesto, commending states claiming interposition and condemning the *Brown* decisions as illegal, unconstitutional, and an "invasion" of states' sovereignty. The final Declaration of Constitutional Principles, signed by twenty-two U.S. senators and eighty-one House members on March 12, 1956, declared that the Supreme Court abused its judicial powers to frame a decision with no legal basis. Consequently southern states could and would use all lawful means to obstruct or overturn the decision.[74]

South Carolina's NAACP conference was acknowledged as the strongest in the South. Hinton seemed to be the calm in this unrelenting storm. "He believed God gave you a mind, and you should use it. He believed you should endure," said Richburg. When Hinton served as chairman of an NAACP regional meeting, an attending *New Yorker* writer marveled, "No one in the group seemed to question the chairman's authority, and I, too, in the course of the meeting came to be powerfully impressed by the strength and firmness of his character although I would have been hard put to it to say how he communicated these traits, for he never raised his voice and most of the time a mild, kindly smile lingered on his moon-shaped face." Responding to Timmerman's description of NAACP membership as "contrary" to the state's economic and social life, Hinton reminded the public of the state's primary shenanigans and its defeat, promising, "History will repeat itself."[75]

On March 16, 1956, Timmerman signed a resolution requiring an investigation of any NAACP activity at Orangeburg's black land-grant college, now called South Carolina State College. Students, supported by faculty, were demonstrating and employing countermeasures to WCC reprisals. The next day Timmerman signed legislation that banned city, county, school district, or state employment of any NAACP member. The act targeted black schoolteachers and administrators, the core of NAACP membership. Legislators claimed that the NAACP convinced black South Carolinians that they were the "subject of economic and social strangulation," thus challenging "the principles upon which the economic and social life of our State rests." As a

More than two hundred robed and hooded Klansmen formed a
human cross on the State House steps before marching up and down
Main Street, a day after five Klansmen were charged with dynamiting
the Gaffney home of Claudia Sanders. She had contributed
to a pamphlet urging better race relations.
Courtesy of Richland Library, Columbia, South Carolina

condition of employment, teachers had to reveal whether they or relatives
had ties to the association. Hinton pointed out that the intended punishment
of the state's 7,300 black teachers violated their constitutional rights. A joint
state and national NAACP press release noted that the NAACP's objective of
"first-class citizenship for Negro Americans" appeared to be "incompatible
with the South Carolina concept of Americanism."[76]

At Elloree Training School, seventeen schoolteachers sued, after eighteen resigned and three refused to answer statements regarding the NAACP
and integration. At trial on October 22, 1956, NAACP attorney Jack Greenberg said the law violated freedom of speech and association. The district

court decided this was a state matter, and just as the NAACP filed an appeal, the state repealed the statute, substituting a requirement that job applicants submit a membership list of organizations and associations. Charleston teacher Septima Clark—who listed her NAACP membership, lost her job, and couldn't persuade other teachers to resist—described a "systematic campaign to wipe out the NAACP."[77]

On February 8, 1957, Timmerman signed into law a prohibition of barratry, making it unlawful to invite or solicit a lawsuit without direct interest in the relief. Southern legislators acknowledged they aimed the rash of barratry laws at the NAACP and its support of parents' school desegregation petitions. A *Columbia Record* editorial blamed "the NAACP's injection of itself" as "the moving spirit and financing agent in the school desegregation cases." The NAACP, not white supremacy, sparked the South's resistance to "the reinterpretation of the Constitution by the Supreme Court," said the newspaper. South Carolina was not original in such measures, termed "massive resistance." Deep South states, determined to eliminate the NAACP, demanded membership and contributor lists, barred teachers' membership, required anticommunism vows, and defined civil rights lawsuits as malpractice.[78]

Both sides understood that equitable teacher pay, equal access to higher education, the legal end of "separate but equal" schools, and a seat on the bus depended on the commitment and funds of local NAACP membership and the drive and initiative of state and national NAACP leadership. The steady targeting of individuals, accomplished by the WCC and KKK, became a statewide bombardment. Conference fundraising letters relinquished expectations that city, county, or state employees would join the NAACP and jeopardize their jobs and, instead, asked for contributions to the LDF, separate from the NAACP since 1957. Hinton, who had pretty much seen it all by now, said the barratry law would have little effect and, if necessary, would be tested in the courts. He added that social and Christian change, always resisted, eventually succeeded. He recommended that "the measuring yardstick should not be one of color but of character and Christian manhood." This was close to a sign-off for Hinton, who had another calling on his mind.[79]

Hinton relinquished his position as president in 1958, announcing his retirement before October's annual meeting. The South's venomous focus on the NAACP had taken its toll. State NAACP membership had fallen to 2,202, its number of branches to thirty-one. Southern membership dropped from 130,000 to fewer than 80,000. "It is time for another person to take over the reins of our state conference," Hinton wrote the remaining branches. That person was Rev. Isaiah DeQuincey Newman, longtime first vice president of the conference. At the annual meeting, Hinton acknowledged that "it is true economic reprisals and some violence have caused a loss of [NAACP] membership, but it is remarkable the conference has lived and been able to pay its way." True to his character, he offered no hosannas: "The fight has just begun and must become of greater proportions." And, typically, he also reminded his audience of 200 that "our cause is not only true but will triumph."[80]

He was sixty-seven. Hinton had been serving as supply preacher at Columbia's Second Calvary Baptist Church. He became pastor in 1959; he also served as chaplain at the segregated state prison and state mental health facility. In 1964 the NAACP named him a vice president on its board of directors. In 1966 Pilgrim named him chairman of its board of directors. Under his leadership Second Calvary built a new church and burned the mortgage before his death in 1970. Hinton was a man who could tell Marshall, immediately after his abduction: "I am more fully determined than ever to carry it thru." Wrote McCray in 1964, "The last 25 years clearly and indelibly place his name among immortals of the race.[81]

"He was dynamite in his day," said Noble Cooper. "He was almost like God."[82]

Two

No Such Thing
as Standing Still

Briggs v. Elliott

In 1946 seventeen Clarendon County parents bought a much-used yellow school bus. It cost seven hundred dollars, a fortune to people who were farmers and sharecroppers, cooks and maids, who still drove mules and wagons. This was their second used bus, purchased to get their children to school. South Carolina provided transportation only to white schoolchildren. The black children of Davis Station walked nine miles, one way, to school in Summerton, a town of 1,500. Earlier, farmer Levi Pearson had provided a ride in the back of a pickup, boards serving as benches. But a school bus was the proper solution. That first bus didn't last a year; the parents couldn't keep it running. The second bus broke down, too, constantly. The children called it "the sunshine bus" because it quit on rainy days. Along the way the parents asked for help: for gas for the truck, for money to buy a bus, for repairs, gas, and a driver. School officials turned down every request.[1]

So Levi and Hammett Pearson, brothers and neighbors who farmed land they owned near Davis Station, and friend Joseph Lemon chipped in for the buses. "They'd have a meeting at least once a week to collect funds to keep the bus running. But that old bus was pretty well all worn out," said Ferdinand Pearson, the fourth of Levi Pearson's children. "It periodically was broken down to and from school, and they had to pay a driver, and money was hard to come by." Levi and Hammett Pearson hadn't attended school, but the brothers wanted a better life for their children. When their wives died two weeks apart in 1930, the two made a deal. Levi Pearson, born in 1892 and the elder by three years, took Hammett Pearson's children to raise. Hammett Pearson went away to work, to Philadelphia and to Newport News, Virginia.

Gone almost ten years, he sent back money that helped the combined families survive. Hammett Pearson had four children by his deceased wife and six more with his second wife. Levi Pearson raised twelve children with his two wives.[2]

Once they were reunited, Levi Pearson's oldest son, Willie, read newspapers aloud to the brothers before the noonday meal. They also listened daily to the radio. Their experience and accrued wisdom functioned collectively. "Poppa and Levi were like one; one would never do anything without getting the opinion of the other," said Phynise "Piney" Pearson, Hammett's daughter. The brothers believed that Jim Crow, and their children's consequent deprivation, could be fought. "They knew what wasn't in the Constitution but just a way to do things," said Ferdinand Pearson.[3]

When it was too cold for the Pearsons to farm, their children faced the cold anyway, trudging miles to school. Ferdinand Pearson walked seven miles, one way, from Davis Station to Mount Zion School, which had two rooms and one stove. "We usually gave ourselves two hours to make it," he said. Siblings Jesse and Piney Pearson walked nine miles, one way, from Davis Station to Scott's Branch school in the town of Summerton. "I'd leave home at dawn of day, and I'd be at school on time," said Jesse. Piney cut cardboard to line their shoes, then wrapped the shoes in plastic. No one had a wool coat. The children wore homemade flannel underwear and layers of cotton hand-me-downs. When it rained they arrived at school wet and stayed that way.[4]

Soon—in for a penny, in for a pound—the Pearsons asked for far more than a ride to school. Far more was needed.

In the 1940s in Clarendon County, white children attended school in brick buildings with paved playgrounds, gyms or auditoriums, lunchrooms, a teacher for every grade, class sizes of no more than thirty students, heat, water fountains, indoor toilets that flushed. Black children studied in abandoned Masonic or hunting lodges, in buildings built by missionaries, or in cabins built by impoverished parents, most often adjacent to a tiny rural church. Among Clarendon County's dozens of one- to four-room schools for black children, Liberty Hill had no running water; children used the neighboring minister's well. Rambay School had not one desk; children sat around two narrow tables. At Scott's Branch, which housed all grades, one first-grade teacher taught sixty-seven students, another taught sixty, and the second-grade teacher taught seventy-nine. None of the schools had indoor toilets for boys or girls. At Scott's Branch more than seven hundred students made do with fourteen outdoor privies. White schools' discarded books—scribbled in, pages missing, out of date—provided their only written texts.

No school libraries meant no reference books or supplementary reading. For warmth children chopped firewood for stoves or oil drums. They dipped water from buckets filled at wells. They toted lunch, often no more than a biscuit, from home. Parents paid tuition and book rent and, because of the distances, sometimes paid others to board their children nearer a school. South Carolina spent $221 annually per white student versus $45 per black student for school facilities. Of the 979 one-room schools in the state, 799 served black children.[5]

"Every day, coming for school, we would pass the white school. I would pass, and they had a big, beautiful gym," said Andrew Lee Ragin. The son of Hazel and Zelia Ragin, he attended Scott's Branch. "I was a little boy, and I could climb a tree and look at them playing ball. I'd get pecans and go on home. I'd get pecans there, even though we had a pecan orchard. Everything was better for them."[6]

All-white school boards governed South Carolina public schools, which were funded mostly by local monies, mostly funneled to the white schools. Clarendon County's white teachers earned $1,800 a year, double black teachers' pay, even though the black teachers taught far more students and more than one grade at a time. Statewide a white teacher earned on average $2,057 compared to a black teacher's $1,414. White citizens, who earned the majority of income, rationalized disparities by insisting they paid the majority of taxes. Black citizens paid for and built schools themselves or shared in the cost of missionary or Rosenwald schools, subsidized by Sears, Roebuck, and Company executive Julius Rosenwald. State statutes required segregated railroads and ferries, recreation centers and parks, carnivals and tent shows, motor carriers and passenger buses, waiting rooms, water coolers, restrooms—and schools. The state constitution of 1895 said, "Separate schools shall be provided for the children of the white and colored races, and no child of either race shall ever be permitted to attend a school provided for children of the other race."[7]

In nearby Summerton black customers could enter stores, but they couldn't try on clothes or shoes and couldn't return what didn't fit. In drugstores they could buy ice cream but had to eat it outside. The local diner was off limits. As evening fell a siren blew, and all black residents had to leave the main streets of downtown. A black person existed—or ceased to exist— on white people's terms. "My grandfather was lynched," said Andrew Lee Ragin. "A white guy came into a field and chopped him down. Nobody said anything about it, and it goes unnoticed, like nothing happened. But it's not really forgotten."[8]

When Robert and Carrie Georgia and their children visited a grandfather in nearby Saint Paul, the children piled into a wagon pulled by a mule, a lantern lighting their way home. "Cars would pass by, and they would shoot in the air and then come back and shoot again, boom, boom," said son Normel Georgia. "They tried to keep the community frightened enough not to try for changes."[9]

The schoolchildren's parents knew a way out: education. During the first Great Migration, 1.6 million black southerners left, escaping Jim Crow laws, deep poverty, and racial violence. But they left behind family ties, family land, and the tight communities they had created with kinship and religion. Many believed saying goodbye to home shouldn't be the antidote. Equal opportunity, particularly in education, could fuel a better life wherever you lived. The National Association for the Advancement of Colored People (NAACP) took that view with its relatively new and newly successful legal campaign. In 1935 Charles Hamilton Houston, the first special counsel of the NAACP, set into play what was termed an "equalization strategy," suing for facilities for black students that were equal to those for white students. Thurgood Marshall became chief legal counsel in 1936 and, in 1940, founded the Legal Defense and Educational Fund (LDF), focused on ending legal segregation. In South Carolina, Marshall found partners: the first black attorneys post-Reconstruction, activist preachers, a strong leader of the NAACP state conference, and, most important, parents ambitious for their children. But at first the dream of Clarendon County's black parents was so basic: a reliable, affordable means of transportation. They had to get those children where they needed to go.

Clarendon County's flat, rural roads wandered from cotton field to tobacco field to pine forest, its people poor and uneducated, 70 percent of them black, almost everyone, white or black, doing what their parents, grandparents, and great-grandparents did, which was farm. At a time when few people owned cars, Clarendon County was isolated and isolating. The county seat of Manning was sixty-four miles from Columbia, the state capital. Summerton was ten miles from Manning and seventy-eight miles from Columbia. People still suffered from pellagra, caused by malnutrition, and died of malaria. Even after the completion of the Santee-Cooper Hydroelectric and Navigation Project in 1942, rural homes and the black children's schools lacked electricity. Statewide just 1 percent of the black population older than twenty-five possessed a bachelor's degree, and just 7 percent of the white population did. Far more common in Clarendon County, for white and black residents, was a few years of elementary school. Summerton was impoverished and insular, its long dirt roads bordered by farm fields worked by people still caught in the rigid economic and social structures of the South's slave-haunted past.[10]

The Reverends Joseph Armstrong "J. A." DeLaine, James Washington Seals, and Edward Eugene "E. E." Richburg called this home. Rare beings, they were college-educated black men pursuing citizenship rights, such as the vote. They joined—and pushed—the Pearsons' quest. Reverend DeLaine documented disparities, petitioned officials, and traveled to far-off Columbia and Charleston to meet with attorneys. Reverends Seals and Richburg served as copilots and, eventually, relief pilots. A sturdy, short man who wore round glasses, Reverend Seals officiated at Saint Mark African Methodist Episcopal Church (AME) in Summerton. Black churches were the only safe communal space for meetings; white people supervised black schools, and town parks were segregated. Saint Mark, where it was natural for many to gather, became the in-town meeting house. Liberty Hill AME, the county's largest black church, became the countryside meeting house. Pastor Richburg had served as chairman of the seventy-five-member Elloree NAACP branch, and he encouraged his parishioners and, later, petitioners with kindness and humor. Heavy-browed and strong-jawed, he wore black-framed glasses and kept a thin moustache.[11]

Reverend DeLaine, elegant and eloquent, may have felt more than most the fire and the fury of loss. He seldom hesitated to voice his outrage. He stood beside the Pearsons, sometimes in front as the spokesperson. The eighth of seven sons and six daughters, Joseph Armstrong DeLaine was born near Manning in 1898, his father a minister. Both his mother's and his father's sides of the family included white ancestors and freed men and women who owned land before slavery's end. At fourteen he ran away from home rather than accept a lashing by cane, the penalty for defending a sister from a white boy's assault. He worked and lived on his own in Atlanta, Georgia, returning to South Carolina in 1917 to train as a teacher at Allen University in Columbia. Employed as a teacher and a carpenter, he saved money to buy land. The AME Church licensed him to preach in 1923, and he built his own first parsonage. He completed his bachelor's at Allen in 1931, the year he married Mattie Belton.[12]

In 1934, upon recovery from a near-fatal spider bite, Reverend DeLaine returned to Clarendon County, accepting an AME appointment to two Spring Hill churches. He also served as principal and head teacher at Bob Johnson Elementary School, where he met the Pearson brothers. Wife Mattie Belton DeLaine taught at Spring Hill Elementary School. The DeLaines accrued status. He was a preacher and teacher; his wife and sisters Carrie

This Masons' lodge served as Spring Hill Elementary School until 1950. Teachers Mattie Belton DeLaine, wife of Rev. Joseph Armstrong DeLaine Sr., and Helen Richburg, wife of Rev. Eugene Edward Richburg, accompany their students. The DeLaines and Richburgs were eventually fired from their jobs and suffered Klan attacks.
Courtesy of South Caroliniana Library, University of South Carolina, Columbia

Martin and Rowena Oliver were teachers too. His properties included a farm with four tenants. He participated in AME church governance, subscribed to black-owned newspapers and magazines, and raised funds for the NAACP, all to support what he described as "a more progressive attitude in the colored people of Clarendon County." He never lost the satisfaction he took in his independence and community standing. His sense of dignity is obvious in photographs throughout his life: the ramrod posture, the direct gaze, the impeccable dress.[13]

By 1940 the DeLaines' duties had grown. The couple had three children: Joseph Armstrong Jr., called "Jay," Ophelia, and Brumit Belton, called "B.B." Reverend DeLaine was named principal of Liberty Hill School, which served eight grades, and the AME bishop appointed him to the Pine Grove–Society Hill preaching circuit. Mattie DeLaine taught at Scott's Branch. They built a home just past Summerton's town limits. As the civil rights activism of the 1940s stirred, Reverend DeLaine added to his responsibilities. Flooding in 1941, caused by dam construction, submerged a bridge and forced schoolchildren and parishioners to paddle boats to Society Hill's church and school.

Reverend DeLaine wrote letters to local, county, state, and federal officials asking for a solution. He accepted the post of secretary to the county's Negro Citizens Committee, with its 105 members, in 1942. Such local committees, secretly affiliated with the NAACP, focused on voting rights. Reverend De-Laine's chronic health problems and a stint in a sanitarium forced a pause, however.[14]

Activism came to Summerton in fits and starts. Briefly Manning served as home to a Clarendon County NAACP branch, organized in 1943 by Rev. Eugene Avery Adams Sr., founder of the S.C. Citizens Committee and president of the Columbia NAACP branch, and James Myles Hinton Sr., president of the South Carolina Conference of Branches of the NAACP. At the time the NAACP had built strong membership only in Columbia. The capital city held 964 members, while the rest of the state had only 600 more. Reverend DeLaine, who served as local branch secretary, wrote the national membership director to request mail in plain envelopes only. "You see I am a preacher in this county and a public-school teacher too. My living largely depends upon the ones that fear and hate the NAACP. My activities have already been under question."[15]

In April 1946 the NAACP gathered key players in Atlanta to discuss legal tactics for education lawsuits in the South. Strategists included attorneys from throughout the South and Washington, D.C. Attendees included Hinton, Marshall, and Robert Carter, LDF assistant special counsel. Among the conference topics was bus transportation for black schoolchildren. In Virginia, NAACP attorney Oliver Hill simply walked black children to the bus stop for white children and insisted all be allowed on the bus. He got a bus. Hinton came home with possibilities awhirl.[16]

In Summerton efforts to sustain the NAACP branch had languished. However, after a long hospitalization, Reverend DeLaine returned to action, sticking up for black World War II veterans. Summerton officials denied them their GI Bill benefits, which included housing and education. Reverend DeLaine petitioned the state Department of Education for agricultural classes for eight black veterans, including Jesse and Ferdinand Pearson. During World War II, Jesse Pearson fought in Italy; Ferdinand Pearson fought in France, Belgium, Germany, and Okinawa. The state limited its yes; the veterans had to find their own teachers. They did, and that gave all a taste of winning, winning what was theirs by right.[17]

In June 1947 Reverend DeLaine attended the Columbia summer school of side-by-side Benedict College and Allen University. At a general assembly, Hinton issued a challenge: find someone and some way to get school buses.

Hinton told the assemblage, "No teacher or preacher in South Carolina has the courage to get a plaintiff to test the School Bus Transportation practices of discrimination against Negro children," a challenge that energized the Clarendon County minister. Hinton wanted more than letters or petitions; he wanted a lawsuit. Afterward, Reverend DeLaine said, a professor in a course on race and culture put him "on the spot" to take up the challenge.[18]

Reverend DeLaine answered the call. He was the best person to do so, believed his sons. "In Clarendon County, there was a certain aura of confidence that when he spoke it was gospel truth, and when he said something was to be done, it was done," said Jay DeLaine. And the local World War II veterans seemed ideal petitioners. "Hinton suggested get somebody with the nerve to protest the system, they would try something legally," said Ferdinand Pearson. The black veterans had risked life and limb, only to return to a state limiting their access to jobs, voting, education, and housing. Given white people's rigid control and their own intractable poverty, they feared nothing would ever change for them, or worse, for their children. "They didn't have anything to lose," said Brumit DeLaine.[19]

When the Pearsons asked for help buying and operating the Davis Station bus, they knew that even a hat-in-hand appeal challenged authority. While their request surprised local officials, the answer was not surprising. Roderick Miles Elliott Sr., chairman of the School District 22 board, replied, "We ain't got no money to buy a bus for your nigger children." But Reverend De-Laine preached, "There is no such thing as standing still. We are either going forward or drifting. We are building or tearing down." Living up to his word, he volunteered as point man. "Whether it be Moses or Joshua or another minister, he must lead the way," he preached. When Reverend DeLaine was later forced to retreat, other stalwarts of the community—the Pearsons, Reverend Richburg and Reverend Seals, and dozens of courageous petitioners—persisted. "They would say, 'Listen, we started it, and we'll finish it,'" Piney Pearson said of her father and uncle.[20]

Registered, Return Receipt Requested

On June 22, 1947, Reverend DeLaine, Jay DeLaine, and Levi and Hammett Pearson met with Hinton and Columbia attorney Harold R. Boulware Sr., local counsel for the NAACP. Eight days later they returned to settle who would sue for a bus and who would pay for the lawsuit. Hinton and Boulware were interesting partners: one fierce, the other jocular, both intrepid. Hinton, born in 1891 in North Carolina and orphaned as a toddler, grew up in New York City. An infantry lieutenant during World War I, he moved to Columbia in 1938, representing the Pilgrim Health and Life Insurance Company. Elected president of the Columbia NAACP branch in 1939, Hinton took over the state conference in 1941. Between 1943 and 1947, the NAACP sued South Carolina for equal pay for black teachers, for an end to the all-white Democratic primary, and for black students' access to a law school. Each time the NAACP won.[21]

Hinton was bold, but in a studied way, methodically assuring himself of all the facts before acting. He was short, stout, intense, and indefatigable. He would go days without sleep as he sold insurance; raised four children; opposed day-to-day racism in letters, speeches, personal encounters, and legal challenges; expanded NAACP branches statewide from thirteen to eighty; and coaxed from NAACP members an annual dollar in dues plus a little more for any current lawsuit.[22]

Boulware grew up at Harbison Agricultural Institute near Columbia. His father was dean at the school, which had relocated after night riders, groups of white men who attacked black people after dark, burned down the original Abbeville school in 1911. When Boulware opened his Columbia practice in 1941, he was Columbia's only black lawyer, one of five in the state. He was ready for this lawsuit. A graduate of Howard University School of Law, for his senior class project he prepared a case for desegregating the University of South Carolina. A big man, over six feet tall and more than two hundred pounds, Boulware told stories and jokes nonstop, played pinochle night into day, and accepted chickens and used cars for legal fees. One payment came by passing the hat: "I took my fee home in a bucket, in nickels, dimes and quarters," he said. He dealt with death threats calmly by taking the family on brief trips out of town or state. Once a law enforcement officer smuggled him out of town in the trunk of a car.[23]

Everyone involved knew that most civil rights lawsuits died quickly at the local level thanks to intimidation and violence. Or they died at the state level since the white power structure invoked states' rights, guarded by an all-white judiciary sustaining a chokehold on black citizens' economic, political, and daily life. Foot-dragging, appeals, and legislative end runs circumvented petitions and lawsuits. So the wish for a bus seemed just a slightly better than hopeless pursuit. The agreed-upon petitioner was Levi Pearson rather than his brother. "My dad being a person who would sacrifice to help out not only his family but people in general, he stood up for the task," said Ferdinand Pearson. "Him and his brother, they were extra close, but his brother had short patience. He would lose control of his temper, so Daddy was the better one. He had patience and determination with Hammett supporting him. He was the head man, saying 'I will.'"[24]

On July 29, 1947, Boulware mailed—registered, return receipt requested—a petition to the district's board chair, the county superintendent, and the state Board of Education's secretary. The petition requested school bus transportation for School District 26. The white officials' goal—to refuse formal acknowledgment and thus legitimacy—meant extended periods of silence followed. Seven weeks later L. B. McCord, a Presbyterian minister and the county superintendent, referred Levi Pearson to the district trustees. Eight weeks after that, the school board's Vander Stukes wrote Boulware that Pearson had dropped the issue. That wasn't true. Local attorney S. Emory Rogers, hired by the board, was stalling. Pearson protested to Boulware. Boulware wrote McCord, copying the state Board of Education again, to ask for a hearing. Pearson signed a December 16, 1947, letter that said, "Mr. Vander Stukes or any other person assume too much when they assume that I am not interested in the Bus Transportation Suit." Rogers designed another stall, delivered by Stukes: "We do not feel that there is anything at present before the board." So Boulware requested a hearing before McCord.[25]

The Summerton NAACP had all of two members at this point and was no help. Gloster B. Current, the national branch director, wrote Hinton that Summerton did not elect officers in 1946, and its previous officers were "incapacitated." That didn't stop Hinton. At the NAACP's annual state conference, he explained the plan to end segregation and pushed his fifty-one branches for approval. He warned, "Converting Negroes as a whole to the anti-segregation concept is going to be a long and hard procedure because the white supremacy pattern has ingrained itself into every one of us." James T. McCain Sr., president of the black Palmetto State Teachers Association (PSTA), and A. T. Butler, its executive secretary, spoke twice—in the keynote address and on a panel—about combining the numerical and financial strength of the PSTA with the legal strength of the NAACP. McCain and Butler listed inequities to be challenged: inadequate facilities, too few high schools, too few well-prepared teachers, subsistence pay, and no transportation. It was time to fight for the children, McCain declared.[26]

Hinton, delivering one of his trademark fiery speeches, said "separate but equal" was a fraud: always separate, never equal. He flung out another dare: "Now that the decision is made, I want to request that anyone who is not willing to take a stand against segregation and its evils to come up NOW and let us return to you that lousy dollar that you paid as your membership fee—or forever after hold your peace." Hinton always made public his plans for battle. The *Columbia Record,* the capital city's afternoon newspaper, reported that the NAACP would press for full integration in all public institutions.[27]

Hinton had convinced NAACP members that they could meet the expectations of the NAACP's national board of directors and the LDF's Marshall. Like Hinton, Marshall was an around-the-clock worker, handling with his staff as many as five hundred cases a year. Six foot one, he was precise and eloquent in court, but with friends and plaintiffs he became a joker, a card player, a drinker, at home in any home. Marshall admired and trusted Hinton. He flung to Walter White, NAACP executive secretary, and Roy Wilkins, editor of the NAACP magazine the *Crisis,* a Hinton-like challenge: "If you want to fight for separate but equal schools for Negroes, which the proponents themselves of this scheme have proven impossible, you don't need me. Get another lawyer!"[28]

On the Summerton front, however, a new year arrived without further action. Reverend DeLaine, ill with pleurisy, wrote despairing letters to the national NAACP and then to Hinton. He complained that other local NAACP officers had done nothing since his 1943 health crisis, and he remained unable to participate. He asked about the bus transportation case, saying others lacked leadership ability, and their inaction had resulted in everything "growing cold and wandering now." But this was just another pause. By February 10, 1948, Boulware had finished the legal papers and mailed them to New York City for review by Marshall and Carter. The school board granted a February 27 hearing with Boulware. The result was backlash, including teacher firings and refusals to allow black teachers to register to vote.[29]

Black plaintiffs were rare; so were black attorneys, such as Boulware. In South Carolina, between 1901 and 1950, only sixteen black attorneys had been admitted to the South Carolina Bar Association. The NAACP played a vital role in supplying attorneys, inspiring and screening plaintiffs, and encouraging fundraising. Boulware played a necessary role as local counsel, assisting the LDF attorneys. And no lawsuit could exist without local support. To keep the effort alive and paid for, Hinton resuscitated the Summerton NAACP. He appointed Levi Pearson as president and Sarah Z. Daniels as vice president. She was a previous president of the Manning NAACP branch, active in voter registration, and, consequently, soon fired from her job teaching. Hinton appointed Reverend Seals as treasurer and Reverend DeLaine as secretary. The NAACP required no fewer than fifty members for an active charter, so Hinton asked Pearson to secure fifty-five one-dollar memberships.[30]

On March 16, 1948, Boulware and Marshall filed Levi Pearson's lawsuit. He sued the local board of education—chairman Elliott and members J. D. Carson and George Kennedy—on behalf of James Pearson, a son from his second marriage. James Pearson was denied free transportation to and from school in buses owned by the County Board of Education, denied this solely because of race, said the civil action. This denial violated the Equal Protection Clause and the Due Process Clause of the Fourteenth Amendment.[31]

At the time South Carolina contained more than a thousand school districts. One school could be a district unto itself with its own board. While elementary schools for black students were scattered about rural areas, high schools were few and far between. Consequently James Pearson attended tenth grade at Scott's Branch in School District 22 even though he lived in School District 26. On April 7, 1948, three officials drove to Levi Pearson's farm: a tax auditor, McCord, and Stukes. They declared that Levi Pearson paid his taxes in still another school district. They said a road a few acres from his home formed a dividing line between two districts, and he paid taxes in School District 5, where a ninth and tenth grade had been added that very school year. The Pearson brothers had every district covered. Levi Pearson owned 25 acres in one district and 170 in the other; he and another son provided tax receipts. Hammett Pearson offered a tax receipt for District 26, and one of his daughters attended Scott's Branch in District 22. He volunteered to step in.[32]

Stalls, blockades, and shady shenanigans were part and parcel of Jim Crow's defense. Often enough this worked. Activists were worn down or frightened away; petitioners gave up or disappeared before anyone reached a court of law. The Pearsons' persistence worried white officials. The school board's next decision—to engage Robert McCormick Figg Jr.—was something special. The board added the well-connected Charleston attorney to its existing team of two local attorneys and a state senator. Whenever there was a challenge to segregation in South Carolina, there stood Figg. He designed ways to block black citizens' registration and voting. He defended the state's white primary. He was behind tiered teaching certificates that continued the inequities in black teachers' employment and pay. He advised J. Strom Thurmond in his successful run for state governor. When Thurmond became the Dixiecrat or States' Rights candidate for president, Figg wrote some of his speeches.

Figg created a new answer: he wrote that James Pearson was not "lawfully enrolled" in his school and thus not entitled to transportation. Busing only white students to white schools in District 26 was "not discrimination but only an incident of classification arising from the state's constitutional mandate of separate schools for the races." In other words James Pearson had no standing, and no plaintiff meant no lawsuit. On June 8, 1948, the day before trial, the NAACP backed off. The confusion about school districts surely doomed success in court. Marshall asked that *Pearson v. Clarendon County Board of Education* be dismissed. This wouldn't be Figg's only surprise maneuver in the months and years to come.[33]

The district officials didn't offer A. M. Anderson, principal of Scott's Branch for eighteen years, a contract for the upcoming school year. But the heat of white people's ire focused on the Pearsons. They assessed exorbitant penalties: no bus, and now no combine, no seed, no fertilizer, no loans. No white farmer or distributor allowed the Pearsons to borrow machinery at harvest time or sold them the supplies required for farming. No one would gin Pearson cotton. Fertilizer dealers refused to sell Levi Pearson fertilizer; oil dealers refused to sell him oil. Black people were afraid to talk to the Pearsons; white people wouldn't. The younger Pearson children worried that any food their parents purchased was poisoned. At night they listened as men fired shots at their homes and their fathers fired back into the air, announcing their readiness. When the gunfire started, their parents pushed them under the beds. When Piney Pearson was too afraid to sleep, her father would tell her, "Don't worry. Say your prayers."[34]

"Most every small family farmer would depend on credit for harvesting time, and he was denied that," said Ferdinand Pearson of his father. After Levi Pearson was denied credit, he cut timber on his land to sell for much-needed cash. No one would buy the timber, which eventually he smuggled to friends and sold under their names. "The price he was offered would be giving them away," said Ferdinand Pearson, who slept in the woods some nights to protect his family, who then could say he wasn't home if night riders called. Each time Ferdinand Pearson went into town, his wife and children worried he wouldn't return alive. Levi Pearson walked twenty miles to buy food, carrying it home on his back because no one would sell him gas and neighbors were afraid to give him a ride. At the Davis Station baseball games, he stood alone because his neighbors feared talking to him.[35]

"I believe God wants me to do it. God wants me to make the sacrifices," Levi Pearson often said. This wasn't the end. "The thing that stopped the case, I guess it was meant to be. It didn't actually kill the suit; it made it better," said Ferdinand Pearson.[36]

Equal Everything

The end of World War II had inevitably brought change. In April 1947 Jackie Robinson played his first game for the Brooklyn Dodgers, desegregating Major League Baseball. In June 1947 at the Lincoln Memorial, President Harry S. Truman became the first president to address a national NAACP conference. After his Commission on Civil Rights recommended anti–poll tax and anti-lynching laws, Truman bolstered the civil rights division of the U.S. Department of Justice and appointed the nation's first black federal judge. In July 1948 he signed executive orders desegregating the armed forces and the federal workforce. South Carolina resisted every iota of change. Thurmond, on the Dixiecrat stump that year, declared, "One of the most astounding theories ever advanced is that the Federal government by passing a law can force the white people of the South to accept into their businesses, their schools, their places of amusement, and in other public places those they do not wish to accept."[37]

Hinton continued to muster his forces. The 1948 state conference of the NAACP ended with another battle cry: "We emphasize our unalterable opposition to any form of segregated education. Equality of citizenship must begin in the school system and our branches are instructed to carry on a campaign both in the Negro communities and in the cities and towns to end segregation in the elementary, high school, college and university levels." The resolution continued, "The SC Conference of the NAACP opposes segregation in all forms. It opposes the distribution of prejudiced textbooks, the denial of higher education in state-operated universities, the unequal distribution of funds to Negroes and whites in the South and the disproportionate salaries paid to Negro and white teachers. The SC Conference of the NAACP is determined to gain for the Negro full education opportunities on every front."[38]

Stubbornness was a necessity. "We met with Attorney Marshall to plead for one more chance to get petitioners," said Jesse Pearson. Marshall hesitated to invest further NAACP energy and funds in an isolated southern community pervaded by illiteracy, poverty, and white supremacy. And the thwarting of Levi Pearson's petition reminded all of the risk inherent in a single petitioner. On March 12, 1949, Marshall, Carter, and Spottswood W. Robinson III, also an NAACP attorney, met with Boulware, state NAACP members, and a liaison committee from the PSTA. A full contingent from Clarendon County also attended: the Reverends DeLaine and Seals, and Levi and Hammett Pearson, as well as young adults Jesse, Willie, Ferdinand, and Charlotte Pearson.[39]

Marshall stunned the Clarendon delegation. He told them that the NAACP no longer held interest in bus lawsuits and, therefore, Levi Pearson's lawsuit. The goal was no longer a bus; the goal was desegregated schools. Varied success challenging segregation by suing for equality in higher education had refined the NAACP argument that segregated schools, separate and unequal, violated the Fourteenth Amendment's promise of equal protection under the law. The Clarendon delegation argued back. They persuaded Marshall of their appetite for the new goal and their ability to find sufficient petitioners, petitioners brave enough to ask for more than a bus. Finally all attending agreed to aspire to legal action on elementary and high school levels and support encouraged through speeches and letters to NAACP branches. Two weeks later the PSTA voted to donate one thousand dollars to a lawsuit. At the end of March, Eugene A. R. Montgomery, executive secretary for the state NAACP, pitched the legal goals twice in Clarendon County to more than four hundred. He secured fifty possible plaintiffs.[40]

Reverend Seals urged Reverend DeLaine and Marshall to persevere. "He wasn't afraid; he was the guy who would hold your back," said James Morris Seals, a grandson raised by the pastor. And Reverend Richburg was undeterred by the slow progress. Clocking three years without an outcome didn't surprise him. He understood that "down here it is one thing after another." Montgomery added steady state NAACP support. He made Clarendon County a weekly stop. Hired by the state conference in 1948, Montgomery was twenty-five but had packed a lot into his youth. He attended Claflin University's private elementary and high schools, then earned a bachelor's there. He served in the Marines during World War II, working in personnel, thanks to his college degree. After three years of service, he headed to Atlanta University, where he earned a master's in social services. Lean, soft-spoken, and serious, Montgomery preferred working in the background. Driving the dirt roads, he encouraged potential petitioners face-to-face and hand-to-hand.[41]

For secrecy and safety, Montgomery tucked his appearances into church gatherings and NAACP meetings, which were focused on introducing parents to the legal plans and seeking signatures pledging an interest. He based the search for petitioners at four churches: Mount Zion AME, Union Cypress AME, Saint Mark AME, and Ebenezer Baptist. The churches filled with the curious, the anxious, and the hopeful. Children attended with their parents, doing schoolwork then sleeping in the back pews. After a May meeting at Saint Mark, Montgomery wrote that he was certain action could begin because he was assured of the people's support.[42]

Attorney Marshall zoomed in and out of the county, appearing at meetings, staying overnight at someone's home then leaving, his schedule always a secret. Next to Levi Pearson's home, "there was a big old tree, and a table under the tree. They would work all day under that tree," said Jesse Pearson. Marshall told the Pearsons, "I'll be prepared to ask a thousand questions." The NAACP lawyers had decided that a minimum of twenty petitioners was necessary and that either Summerton or Manning offered the best illustrations of unequal facilities. Within each of the school districts, both elementary and high schools for each race could be paired and compared, although the woefulness of the Summerton schools made a more dramatic story.[43]

Soon Montgomery reported "the grand work outlined." On May 12 he had visited Saint Mark AME "to receive authorization papers from parents in various districts in the county for legal action to equalize the educational facilities and opportunities for their children." This time the lawsuit asked for buses, books, and buildings, for all that white children had. Reverend De-Laine adopted the NAACP language and called the new focus "asking Equal Everything."[44]

As spring turned to summer, officials in Summerton inadvertently heightened the black community's commitment by ignoring another school issue. Parents believed the newly appointed Scott's Branch principal, S. Isaiah Benson, was a shill for the white community. And they were tired of him. Students and parents accused Benson of charging high school students from other districts twenty-seven dollars, far more than the seven dollars usually required for coal, class materials, and book rent. Students and parents complained that Benson didn't account for eight hundred dollars raised from rallies, didn't distribute textbooks whose rental fees had been paid, discharged popular teachers, inserted derogatory comments in transcripts, and withheld some seniors' diplomas. When eighteen seniors demanded a meeting on June 4, 1949, the district and county superintendents wouldn't respond.[45]

Reverend DeLaine watched as "a great stir rose among the people, already incensed," when white officials also didn't attend. Students mailed the officials notice that a second meeting would be held at Saint Mark AME four days later; again no officials showed up. At the meeting students made their points and left. The parents stayed, and the angered adults elected Reverend DeLaine to lead a Parents Committee on Action, with backup from Robert Georgia and Edward Ragin and Reverend Richburg as secretary. Twenty members of the senior class at Scott's Branch High, including Reverdy Wells, class president, signed a list of complaints against Benson.[46]

From June through September, the committee presented the complaints to district trustees, provided two petitions, sent a registered letter, and asked the state Department of Education to intercede. The committee achieved two hearings but no resolution. District trustees held one hearing on the very day that notice of it was delivered to Robert Georgia, then ruled that nothing could be done since neither witnesses nor exhibits were offered. On June 11 the district officials fired three teachers and Reverend DeLaine from his principalship at Silver. The white officials withheld or altered students' transcripts, and that complicated or, in the case of Wells, ended some seniors' college plans. In July more than fifty parents petitioned the trustees to refrain from dismissing any teachers who hadn't been let go before the charges against Benson. Objecting to the firings, the parents wrote that their dissatisfaction rested with the Benson conflict, not teacher performance.[47]

Parents had asked, in August and again in September, for a rehearing. Finally McCord granted one. About three hundred parents and students attended the October 1, 1949, hearing at the Manning Courthouse. Many had practiced testimony the night before with the Reverends DeLaine, Richburg, and Seals, who handed out copies of the Declaration of Independence and the U.S. Constitution. The county board found Benson guilty of failing to teach the required number of class periods but ruled that no evidence proved he had misappropriated school funds. Benson left town. Neither students nor parents found this a satisfactory resolution. Instead this extended the life of the parents' committee.[48]

Ophelia and Brumit DeLaine attended Scott's Branch at the time. Ophelia DeLaine was impressed with her father's strategic thinking, She believed that "the people had to conclude for themselves that there was no one else who could lead the group successfully." At meetings Reverend DeLaine repeatedly refused nominations to become the formal leader of the group, using the rhetorical questions and exhortations of a preacher. He wrote later that he had refused three times because of his frail health and what he called "the unstability of the parents." He wrote of himself, "He was given almost a dictator's power. The goal was to exhaust every effort until we reached the U.S. Supreme Court. This was a political maneuver. It worked." Reverend DeLaine thought the furor raised was all to the good rather than a sidetrack. The parents had united and made public promises; their energy would get signatures for the NAACP petition. "This was the Psychological Meeting which conditioned the minds of the mass of the parents in District 22," he later wrote for the *AME Church Review,* the official church journal.[49]

Jesse Pearson held dear Reverend DeLaine's warning at the second meeting at Saint Mark AME: "This will be rough. Some will fall on the wayside. Some will lose their jobs; I definitely will lose mine. If you are willing to go ahead regardless, I will go ahead." For Jesse Pearson it was a heroic, even biblical moment: "And the people said, 'We will.' He said, 'Someone may die on the way. Would you go on?' And we pledged we would go on regardless."[50]

Take Your Names Off the List

H. B. Betchman, District 22's superintendent, offered Reverend DeLaine the Scott's Branch post vacated by Benson; the minister declined. Briefly Mattie DeLaine took an acting principal post, each offering intended to co-opt the DeLaines. Impediments and delays had roused adults accustomed to suffering silently. Preaching fed their new courage, filling the churches and strengthening resolve. The work—under oak trees, on hard pews, inside small houses, on long dusty drives, in laboriously written letters—yielded an ample number of pledges to sign the NAACP petition to equalize District 22 schools. On November 11, 1949, the "Equal Everything" petition arrived from New York City. The accompanying letter warned it might be dangerous to sign petitions during a public meeting. So Montgomery and Hinton redirected willing petitioners from the meeting at Saint Mark AME to a house a few blocks from the church. Families walked down a dirt road, past the DeLaine home to the plain brick house of Harry and Eliza Briggs. "Folks the Reverend DeLaine wanted to sign, he sent to us," said Eliza Briggs. The petitioners formed a line winding from the road into her tiny front room, the burden shifting at this point from the Pearsons to the parents and children of Summerton. First to sign was Harry Briggs Sr., followed by Eliza, then children Harry Jr., Thomas Lee, and Katherine Briggs.[51]

Harry and Eliza Briggs belonged to nearby Saint Mark. Although the parents and the three oldest of their five children signed, all the Briggs children could walk down the dirt road and cross the street at the DeLaines' house to Scott's Branch. A bus ride had never been the Briggses' issue, but equal opportunity was. In Summerton, "if you were not a trained teacher, you worked in somebody's field or were somebody's hand in the big house," said youngest son Nathaniel Briggs. The Briggs family hoped for more. Harry Briggs Sr. was an only child; his mother, a maid; his grandmother, a cook for a white family. But Eliza Briggs's parents, the Gambles, owned their own land, with a home on it. The Gambles farmed two hundred acres, growing tobacco, rice, sugar cane, and corn. They drove a surrey, rather than walking or riding a mule to church. They employed farmhands.[52]

Harry Briggs Sr. had attended school through the eighth grade. He fought in Europe during World War II. When he returned, the family benefitted from the postwar investment in U.S. highways. During the late 1940s and early 1950s, construction extended U.S. Route 301, which split Summerton, all the way to Tampa, Florida. Gas stations and motels—renting rooms and selling fuel, meals, souvenirs, and pecan pies—sprang up along this main route south, more than one thousand miles of road from Delaware to Florida. Harry Briggs Sr., compact with a close-lipped smile, got a job in town as a gas station attendant. Eliza Briggs, slender and fine-featured, worked as a maid in the town's motels. They quietly resisted Jim Crow customs. The couple and their children did not patronize white-owned restaurants, where black patrons had to buy food at the back door. They did not pick cotton on white farmers' land for extra cash, only their own and friends' land. Nor did the family sharecrop.[53]

In all 107 parents and children signed, asking for "educational advantages and facilities equal in all respects to that which is provided for whites." The petition described the white children's elementary and high schools as modern, safe, sanitary, well equipped, and uncrowded. The petition described the only schools available to black children—Liberty Hill, Rambay, and Scott's Branch—as aged, dilapidated, unhealthy, overcrowded, and insufficient in terms of the number of teachers and the size of classrooms. The schools lacked central heating systems, running water, and adequate lighting, which the white children had, noted the petition. The petition also cited the lack of bus transportation in the two pages of inadequacies, all drawing to a close with the invocation of the Fourteenth Amendment's guarantee of equal protection. The petitioners asked the trustees and superintendent of District 22 and the county board of education to grant their attorneys a hearing and to stop discriminating against the black schoolchildren.[54]

Montgomery informed Reverend DeLaine—after the signed petition was mailed to Marshall on November 12—that it was time for Reverends DeLaine and Seals to raise money. The plan was to wait thirty days for a local response then file in court. *The State*, the capital city's morning newspaper, announced the petition on November 13, sticking to the basics: "A Clarendon county school district was asked formally yesterday to give white and Negro children public school facilities 'equal in all respects,'" and "the petition charged that Negro children 'are being discriminated against solely because of their race and color.'" Hinton added pressure by disclosing that parents and their children had signed similar petitions in Lee, Fairfield, and Orangeburg counties. Summerton officials held a town meeting to devise ways to discourage petitioners and posted petitioners' names in Manning's courthouse for all to see.[55]

White people hired and fired, rented or sold land, provided loans and mortgages, and sold farming supplies and equipment, fuel, groceries, and dry goods. So punishment came quickly and easily. At the gas station where he worked, Harry Briggs Sr. got his Christmas Eve bonus: a carton of cigarettes and a firing. Soon the bank called the Briggses' mortgage due. When he was refused work even in neighboring counties, he tried farming. No one would loan him money, gin his cotton, or buy his crops. He took odd jobs under an assumed name. "Those were some hard days we were on," said Eliza Briggs, a shy woman who spoke Gullah, a Sea Island creole language. But she trusted Reverend DeLaine. "He do like Moses; we were at the Red Sea, and he opened the way."[56]

Henry Brown, wife Thelma, and children Vera, Willie, Marian, Ethel, and Howard Brown signed. Henry Brown worked in the white Summerton schools as a janitor and had struck up a friendship with a white principal who would drive to the Browns' home and chat. Henry Brown, who had completed the seventh grade, had many talents: he also farmed cotton and corn on inherited land, ran a sugar cane mill and a canning factory, worked as a blacksmith, and played the piano. Refused service at the local gins, he took his cotton elsewhere. Despite his refusal of his boss's demands that he remove his name from the petition, he kept his school job until 1955, when reprisals recurred.[57]

A few more lines down the petition, Annie Gibson signed, as did her husband, William, and their children Maxine, Harold, and William Gibson Jr. The Gibsons were sharecroppers, often a lifetime arrangement. Their landlord kicked them off the land. William Gibson began work in a black-owned funeral home and farmed for others. Outspoken and outgoing Annie Gibson was fired from the Windsor Motel, known for a towering highway sign adorned with a bathing-suited woman arched into a dive. The owner fired Eliza Briggs and Mazie Solomon too. They all found work at the Summerton Motel, known for its pecan pies, but that didn't last. Their white supervisor told them the owner would fire the women if they didn't remove their names. And if he didn't fire them, city officials would cut off the motel's water and sewer and block the trucks delivering pecans for motorists headed to Florida. "We never got back like we were before," said Annie Gibson.[58]

Robert Georgia signed, as did wife Carrie and two of their children, Charlie and Jervine Georgia. Robert Georgia, who farmed land he had inherited from his grandfather, sold beans, peas, and other vegetables from a wagon pulled by a mule. "My father had purchased a wagon, and [the seller] took back the wagon and threatened to take the mules to discourage him being affiliated with the NAACP and meeting with them," said Normel Georgia. But the reedy, big-eyed man had been under pressure before. After U.S. District Court Judge J. Waties Waring had ruled the white primary illegal, Robert registered to vote and called son Normel to come home from Benedict College to do so too. To protect his son, Robert Georgia and two friends escorted Normel to the registrar's office. When they left the registrar, white men followed and even shot at Normel, but the father and son were a citizenship team. "He always encouraged me to be patriotic. I knew we were being treated wrong, and I was encouraging him to do something about it," said Normel Georgia. When threats against the petitioners increased, "He would say he was willing to die for his rights, and that was real."[59]

Senobia Hilton, whose husband, Joseph, signed, was fired from her job as a school cook. Hazel Ragin and wife Zelia followed on the petition's fifth and final page. Hazel Ragin was the area's only house painter, but white residents refused to hire him afterward. The green-eyed Hazel Ragin also farmed his own land and had earned respect as an expert hunting and fishing guide. Son Andrew Lee Ragin carried the game on the hunting excursions. "Little children would be there, and they would make fun of us. They would put their hands in our hair and call us little darkies and give us a nickel," he said. Hazel Ragin trained bird dogs; he knew where the fish were biting. Such skills became his means to a living; visiting sportsmen cared more about the wildlife than politics. And because Hazel Ragin was a known marksman, the family felt safe on their land. "We were fighting all our lives," said Andrew Lee Ragin. "We were stern; we weren't afraid."[60]

Rebecca Richburg's name and that of her daughter and namesake followed a few lines later. She didn't work outside the home, but husband John Hazel Richburg was a blacksmith. He shoed horses, sharpened tools, and sold hog and chicken feed and sodas at Senn's Mill. The mill owner said Rebecca Richburg had to remove her name. According to son John Wesley Richburg, his father answered, "I'm pretty sure she'll keep her name on. She takes her own choices." The blacksmith kept his job, despite later ignoring an order to stop serving black customers.[61]

Mary Oliver signed in the last column of the fifth page, her signature followed by those of son Louis Jr. and daughter Daisy Oliver. Mary and Louis

Oliver owned Oliver's Café on Railroad Avenue as well as a fish camp and a farm. Louis Oliver also managed jukeboxes throughout the county. The Olivers attended Liberty Hill AME, where Reverend Richburg's sermons encouraged their activism. The couple belonged to the NAACP and held voter registration tutorials in the café. Louis Oliver and nine of his twelve siblings had attended college, encouraged by progressive parents who believed each generation should do better than the last. When his vendors quit supplying him, saying they would lose other clients if they continued, he paid friends in the same businesses to purchase the goods he needed as if for themselves. In the dark of the night and armed with a pistol, he picked up the goods in a truck. He still lost money even with this subterfuge, but the café stayed open, with family and friends guarding it, and Mary Oliver continued working there.[62]

The signatures of Henry Scott, a sharecropper, and Mary Scott, who cleaned the white schools, came near the end. "He was told you can't farm this land because you signed the petition, and what you planted, you can forget about it," said Learnease Trammell, who lived with his grandparents. "He had planted, and they took it. No seeds, no nothing. They took everything." The Scotts did own two acres in town. "My grandfather built a little shack on this, and my grandmother and he lived in it until he could build a house. Other farmers would help him after their work hours. Their things were stacked up outside, covered with whatever they had."[63]

The Scotts were followed by the Stukeses: Willie Mood Stukes Sr., a mechanic and U.S. Navy veteran, signed along with his wife, Gardenia, and children Gardenia, called "Denia"; Louis W.; and Willie Stukes Jr. The elder Stukes was fired from his gas station job, where he was a senior mechanic on a salary. He came home furious; his wife wept at the news. An anxious discussion followed in which the couple acknowledged that "all they had to do to get the job back was take their names off the list," said Denia. Their names remained, and Willie Stukes Sr. became a "shade tree mechanic," repairing cars in his yard.[64]

Of the three leading ministers, only Reverend Richburg signed. Boulware had suggested that none of the DeLaines sign, according to Ophelia DeLaine. Reverend Seals, who was raising a grandchild, lacked children in the pertinent schools. That didn't protect him because petitioners met at his church and he was treasurer for the Summerton NAACP. Superintendent Betchman had threatened the minister before about holding meetings at Saint Mark. Reverend Seals would offer his school register, willing to resign. This round, he told *Afro-American Magazine*, Betchman asked, "Are you ready to play ball?" Reverend Seals said he replied, "Mr. Betchman, if what I've played isn't ball, I don't know the game." This time Betchman took Reverend Seals's register, his official tally of students. But that wasn't enough.[65]

Reverend Seals was also fired from his job teaching veterans, as was William Ragin. Seals had twenty-five years of teaching experience; Ragin had ten and a college degree. Rebecca Seals, the minister's wife, was fired from her teaching job. She left for New York City, where she took domestic work to support the family. Bankers called due debts and mortgages for Seals, William Ragin, and Lee Richardson. When a feed and seed dealer ordered Lee Richardson to pay up immediately, he couldn't. When the dealer threatened to take Lee Richardson's two mules, neighbors took up a collection and paid. When Lee Richardson was evicted, John E. McDonald, a farmer and landowner, purchased land and the home on it for the Richardson family.[66]

People were afraid, reasonably so, because even association resulted in reprisals. School officials fired not only Reverend DeLaine and his wife but also his two sisters and a niece. "You're being held hostage," explained Normel Georgia. As consequences continued people just dropped away. "A lot of people say to me, 'You don't sign, you wouldn't be in what you in,'" said Eliza Briggs.[67]

While petitioners accepted that some were just too vulnerable to participate, or even continue friendships, they were far less accommodating of spies among their own. During meetings at churches, windows stayed open to release southern heat. "Certain people, we were told, listened outside the windows," said Daisy Oliver. "We knew about that." Letters were opened and resealed before delivery; everyone discussed that. "You were under surveillance at all times," said Normel Georgia. Reverend DeLaine called those who reported to the white power structure "handkerchief heads," "pimps," and "belly crawlers."[68]

Death Calls

December arrived, another hard month. Three times Reverend DeLaine received warnings that "the KKK was going to take me to ride if I did not shut my mouth." Then a white woman, disgusted by what she overheard at a meeting at her home, warned the minister that certain white men intended an ambush to wound or kill him. She named a possible assailant, a biracial man who attended Liberty Hill AME and declared only white people were his friends. She warned Reverend DeLaine that this man would pick a fight, and witnesses would testify Reverend DeLaine had started it. This would ensure that, if Reverend DeLaine survived, he would face a criminal charge, and if he died, the assailant could claim self-protection. On a December 15 trip to the post office, "just as my feet struck the sidewalk, the named culprit appeared in front of me. He said, 'Me or you got to go to hell today.'" The minister used a pocketknife to feign a gun in his pocket and replied, "What do you want to go to hell for? I'm not going," as five complicit white men watched. At that moment "God sent me James Brown to stop between us and the white witnesses" in his Esso truck. Brown, "like an angel from heaven," wanted to tell Reverend DeLaine that he had resigned rather than be fired from the driving job he had held for nineteen years.[69]

The minister hopped in the truck, escaping the attack. But the flares of anger from the white community continued into the spring of 1950. The De-Laines owned land and a home; as a preacher he possessed the economic protection of his congregation. White officials found another way to punish him: on January 24, 1950, he was charged with slandering Benson, the Scott's Branch principal parents and students had worked to remove. Benson sued for $20,000. Once again warned in advance, Reverend DeLaine had pre-emptively transferred titles to his land, including thirty-three lots in town, to others. Found guilty by an all-white jury several months later, he was fined $4,200, which a judge reduced to $2,700.[70]

In March a crop duster scattered a death threat signed by the Ku Klux Klan. The handbills, strewn about petitioners' land and the Scott's Branch schoolyard, warned that court appearances would be "perilous." The Stukeses' daughter Denia, playing outside that Saturday, grabbed a few sheets for her parents, excited by the surprise from the sky. When she handed the papers to them, she was startled by "the look of just horror on their faces, and my dad jumped up and ran to the door and closed it." Willie Stukes Sr. loaded two shotguns and placed one at the front door and one at the back.[71]

Notwithstanding the crop duster and KKK signature, law enforcement initially suspected Reverend DeLaine. The note was addressed "Warning Benson." The half-sheets of mimeographed text said, in part, "TELL YOUR 'DARKY' SUPPORTERS THAT IF THEY WANT TO DIE WITH YOU COME AND WITNESS FOR YOU." Reverend DeLaine, ill again, had been in Columbia for two weeks, so his wife took copies to him and then to the NAACP, which alerted law enforcement and the Justice Department. Investigators from the South Carolina Law Enforcement Division found the original stencil in the white students' high school but didn't look further for a culprit.[72]

In April a white man killed James McKnight, a resident of nearby Rimini. Black travelers couldn't use the restrooms of gas stations operated by white owners, so while driving between Summerton and Manning, Mc-Knight stopped to relieve himself. A white man passed by, circled back, and attacked, beating McKnight to death. Relatives in McKnight's car, including his sister, uncle, and children, watched in horror. Reverend DeLaine asked the FBI to investigate, linking the killing to a "Reign of Terror" connected to the November petition. He believed the assailant mistook McKnight for a petitioner. The FBI report, the assailant's name deleted, said a local coroner inquest did not summon eyewitnesses, even though McKnight's relatives had reported that the assailant "hit McKnight with a stick and then kicked him in the groin and then hit him with a stick several times, and that McKnight suffered a crushed skull." The assailant testified at the inquest that he "hit McKnight with his fist" and broke his neck. The FBI found no civil rights violation. Neither local nor state law enforcement investigated or filed charges.[73]

In the midst of this, Reverend DeLaine's bishop transferred him. Eight years was the AME limit to be posted in one place. To stay close by, Reverend DeLaine had ministered to Antioch AME in tiny Rimini from 1948 to 1950. The new assignment sent him fifty miles away to Saint James AME in larger Lake City, although the bishop's plan had been to send him farther— to Bermuda. The transfer felt like a penalty to the DeLaine family. His sons believed the move a deliberate effort to cool down Summerton. Reverend DeLaine kept the Summerton home and spent at least two days a week in Clarendon County, but the petition burden shifted to the Reverends Seals and Richburg, with Richburg named the local leader.[74]

While the Reverends Seals and Richburg continued to preach and work for civil rights, other ministers feared the destruction of their pastoral communities and churches if they allowed meetings. Reverend Seals warned grandson James Morris Seals not to visit certain stores or speak to certain white people. The Seals family endured periodic visits by the KKK, whose members would circle the house several times then drive away. After the first harassment, Reverend Seals brought home a shotgun and a rifle. Until the DeLaines moved, armed neighbors guarded their Summerton house, where the family kept guns over every door, guns the sons knew how to shoot. Now protection of Reverend Richburg intensified, with parishioners double-checking on the family and remote Liberty Hill AME during the day and guarding the parsonage and church at night.[75]

On May 16, 1950, the NAACP filed *Briggs v. Elliott* in federal court in Charleston. The school district trustees answered that the state constitution and state law required separate schools and that the District 22 schools,

Briggs v. Elliott petitioners and supporters frequently met at
rural Liberty Hill African Methodist Episcopal Church. Harry Briggs Sr.
stands in the center of the first row of men. In the top row, left to right,
stand Rev. James Washington Seals, Rev. Joseph Armstrong DeLaine,
and Rev. Edward Eugene Richburg, pastor of Liberty Hill.
Photo by E. C. Jones and Cecil J. Williams. Courtesy of Cecil J. Williams

"though separate, are substantially equal," courtesy of a time- and court-
honored interpretation of *Plessy v. Ferguson*. That 1896 Supreme Court ruling on segregated railway carriages in intrastate transportation said that the
Fourteenth Amendment "could not have been intended to abolish distinctions based upon color." A short article in *The State* noted, "The complaint
charges that Negro children are discriminated against solely because of their
race and color" and that discrimination resulted in "Negro children using
inferior school buildings and facilities and in their being denied free bus
service offered whites."[76]

The article adjoined another on a KKK parade in Denmark, South Carolina, set for May 20, "with fiery cross burning," the public invited. The notice
reminded readers of a previous parade "with hundreds of hooded members
participating in a steady downpour of rain." Reverend DeLaine worried about

the strength of the KKK in Lake City. His daughter said he thought of the transfer as a choice between the devil and the deep blue sea. The NAACP's Adams told Reverend DeLaine, "Just go on to Hell, and God will bring you out all right."[77]

This was still just the beginning. Not until *Briggs v. Elliott* made its way into the courtroom of Judge J. Waties Waring did it become a lawsuit to change a nation.

The Man They Love to Hate

The Clarendon County petitioners found themselves before a unique southern judge. Waring was white, educated, an eighth-generation Charlestonian born into two prominent families, yet amazingly inclined to the petitioners' view. With his long nose, thin lips, bow ties, and house on Charleston's Battery, he seemed the quintessential Deep South patrician. However, within a few years on the bench, he transformed from an insider who assisted in the congressional campaign of white supremacist Ellison DuRant "Cotton Ed" Smith to an outcast who opposed what he labeled the "slavocracy." Waring came to district court late in life; he was sixty-one when appointed in 1942. He came to his radical-for-the time views on race late in life, too, losing his position in Charleston politics once his rulings challenged white supremacy and his place in society once he divorced his Charlestonian wife and married a twice-divorced native of Detroit, Michigan. Waring ruled in favor of black teachers who sued for salaries equal to those of white teachers. He set a deadline to open a law school in Orangeburg at the state's only public black college. He ordered an end—twice—to South Carolina's whites-only primary. In speeches and interviews, Waring attacked "the false doctrine of white supremacy" and championed "the abolition of legal segregation."[78]

By the time *Briggs v. Elliott* reached Waring, *Time* magazine had dubbed him "the Man They Love to Hate." White Charlestonians ostracized the Warings. Concrete blocks and bricks crashed through their living room window; a KKK-signed cross burned in their yard. The South Carolina legislature passed a joint resolution to provide funds to purchase the couple two one-way tickets out of the state, provided they "never return," and to erect a plaque to the Warings in the mule barn at Clemson College. In the 1950 congressional race, Senator Olin D. Johnston and former governor J. Strom Thurmond vied in attacks on the "Trumanistic" Waring.[79]

Figg and Marshall had appeared in Waring's courtroom before. In the 1930s Figg and Waring helped shape the city and county of Charleston.

Waring worked in the mayoral campaign of Burnet Rhett Maybank and accepted appointment as the city's attorney and Maybank's chief adviser. Figg, elected solicitor of the Ninth Judicial District, served as attorney for Charleston County Council and County Board of Education. In 1942 Maybank helped secure district court nominations for Waring and George Bell Timmerman Sr., although the Charleston bar promoted Figg. That was Waring's past. NAACP attorneys Marshall, Carter, and Boulware represented a new story. As Waring remade himself into a renegade, he associated with Eleanor Roosevelt and black dignitaries such as diplomat Ralph Bunche, awarded the 1950 Nobel Peace Prize, and Benjamin Mays, a South Carolina native and president of Atlanta's Morehouse College. When Waring visited New York, his social life included Marshall and Walter White, the NAACP executive secretary.[80]

When the National Lawyers Guild honored Waring, he addressed Marshall during his speech, saying, "Well, no Negro would have voted in South Carolina if you hadn't brought a case," referring to *Elmore v. Rice*, the voting rights lawsuit that the NAACP won in his court. When the American Council on Human Rights honored Waring, he said, "Gradualism might accomplish something in 500 or 600 years, but unfortunately none of you will be here then, and we want to see something done in the meantime." When he told a Virginia audience that "every court decree is force," and "force, not gradualism is the only way to gain rights for the Negroes in the South," Rep. L. Mendel Rivers unsuccessfully called in the U.S. House for Waring's impeachment.[81]

All the players were aware of a dramatic possibility with this case: ratcheting up to what some documents called "nonsegregation." So far no lawsuit had succeeded at defining segregation as establishing inequality by its nature. Success was possible with Waring, but a constitutional challenge required a three-judge panel, which would include Judge John J. Parker, chief judge for the U.S. Court of Appeals for the Fourth Circuit, and George Bell Timmerman Sr., an avowed segregationist and U.S. district court judge. South Carolina's white politicos knew exactly that, counting on Timmerman, not quite sure about Parker, worried about Waring.[82]

They had another worry: the highest court had signaled a shift. On June 5, 1950, the Supreme Court decided *Sweatt v. Painter et al.* and *McLaurin v. Oklahoma State Regents*, two NAACP challenges of "separate but equal" in higher education. Chief Justice Frederick M. Vinson delivered both opinions, saying each case posed different aspects of a general question: "To what extent does the Equal Protection Clause of the Fourteenth Amendment limit the power of a state to distinguish between students of different races in professional and graduate education in a state university?" In unanimous decisions the court said that a separate and inferior school for plaintiff Heman Sweatt and education restrictions imposed on plaintiff George McLaurin violated the Equal Protection Clause. The Court's decisions admitted Sweatt to the University of Texas Law School and removed restrictions, such as exile to a desk in the hall, that had set apart McLaurin at the University of Oklahoma.[83]

In July a New York NAACP conference brought together attorneys, southern NAACP branch leaders, and state conference presidents, including Hinton. The NAACP determined that all education lawsuits should seek the "final relief" of "nonsegregation." In October the national board agreed. Waring and the NAACP's White had privately discussed exactly this. On November 17, 1950, at a pretrial hearing, Waring dismissed the Clarendon County lawsuit without prejudice so Marshall could file for the whole shebang. And so *Briggs v. Elliott* became the first lawsuit in the nation challenging segregation in the public schools.[84]

Reverend Seals informed Reverend DeLaine that families needed to sign a new petition. The Reverends Seals and Richburg took the lead days before Christmas, rounding up likely signers. Reverend DeLaine traveled from Lake City to help, venturing into nearby Manchester Forest to find the Ragins, who were on a deer drive. At this point no one in Summerton held illusions as to the high cost of signing. Consequences already ranged from jobs lost to a life taken, every penalty aimed at forcing not only renunciation but also lasting suffering. "We were asked for a bitter job again," Reverend DeLaine wrote. "To sacrifice our happiness, our economic opportunities and generally ourselves and friends. This we did."[85]

Twenty adults and their forty-six children, a deliberately limited total, signed the new petition at Saint Mark; it was filed December 22, 1950. For seventeen of the twenty adults, this was their second round, despite NAACP attorney Robert Carter's appearance at Saint Mark to emphasize the dangers to come. One adult from each home, handpicked for staying power, was the agreed-upon formula to reduce further impact of white opponents' responses. The petitioners included adults Harry Briggs, Annie Gibson, Mose Oliver, Bennie Parson, Edward Ragin, William Ragin, Lucrisher Richardson, Lee Richardson, James H. Bennett, Mary Oliver, Willie M. Stukes, G. H. Henry, Robert Georgia, Rebecca Richburg, Gabrial Tindal, Susan Lawson, Frederick Oliver, Onetha Bennett, Hazel Ragin, and Henry Scott. The complaint challenged the state's segregation laws, saying, "In short, plaintiffs and other Negro children of public-school age in Clarendon County, South Carolina are being denied equal educational advantages in violation of the Constitution of the United States."[86]

Briggs v. Elliott was not just another in a line of NAACP cases. At this moment it was one of a kind. No longer was it of moderate concern, either, to the state's white power structure. In 1936, when *Murray v. Pearson* forced Maryland to admit a black student to its only law school, S.C. Speaker of the House Sol Blatt was indifferent: "We'll just hire a nigra lawyer for a faculty and give them a Sears Roebuck catalogue for a library." But *Briggs v. Elliott* fulfilled exactly what the NAACP had envisioned in the 1930s when Houston decided Jim Crow should be attacked through the South's remarkably unequal schools. "The opening gun in what could be a long, drawn out court fight aimed at breaking down the traditional policy of segregation in the South Carolina public school system was fired here today," reported the Associated Press on December 22, 1950.[87]

District 22 answered in January that discrimination did not exist in Clarendon County schools because the schools were "substantially equal." And segregation existed as a proper application of states' police powers, granted under the Tenth Amendment to the U.S. Constitution. James Francis Byrnes, South Carolina's newly elected governor, revealed deep concern. Byrnes had served in Congress from 1911 to 1925 and in the Senate from 1931 to 1941, where he blocked anti-lynching bills but supported President Franklin D. Roosevelt's New Deal. He had served as a justice of the Supreme Court in 1941–42 and as secretary of state in 1945–47 under Truman. Rumor said he ended retirement to secure segregation. He announced that he would safeguard segregation by actually acknowledging the "equal" side of the equation, building new schools for black children and funding the project through a state sales tax. In his January 1951 inaugural address, he said, "It is our duty to provide for the races substantial equality in school facilities. We should do it because it is right." He invoked the sacrosanct notion of states' rights: "If we demand respect for states' rights, we must discharge state responsibility. A primary responsibility of the state is the education of its children." Weeks later, in his first address to the legislature, Byrnes promised, "We need have no fear. Our school buildings will not be wasted. We will find a lawful way of educating all of South Carolina's children and at the same time providing separate schools for the races."[88]

In Summerton another man died: Willie Stukes Sr.. On January 13, 1951, daughter Denia was standing at a back window and saw a jack flip from under a car her father was repairing. The car crashed down on the veteran.

Stukes's wife and daughter rushed to the rescue, trying and failing to lift the car. With the help of neighbors, they pulled his body free. Stukes was dead. He was just thirty-one. Denia Stukes said her father's death was labeled "as one of the tragedies" resulting from white Summerton's retaliations. At the end of the school year, the family moved to Philadelphia, Pennsylvania, to live with relatives.[89]

In February, Byrnes asked state attorney general T. C. Callison to take over the state's defense since a ruling could affect not only Clarendon County but all state schools. In March, when Byrnes addressed the South Carolina Education Association at Columbia's Township Auditorium, his tone had hardened. Describing the Clarendon County lawsuit to almost eight thousand white teachers, he blamed the NAACP and Truman. Thin, balding, with downward-sloping eyebrows and narrow eyes, Byrnes consistently argued that "this is a white man's country and will always remain a white man's country." He promised the teachers, "Of only one thing can we be certain. South Carolina will not now, nor for some years to come mix white and colored children in our schools." Moreover if segregation could not be preserved legally, "reluctantly we will abandon the public-school system." He had reason to be concerned: in Kansas and Washington, D.C., black parents had filed similar lawsuits, while a memo from the NAACP's New York office pointed to *Briggs v. Elliott* as the case garnering the most interest.[90]

Hinton answered Byrnes: "Negroes will not turn back. Whites and Negroes will have public schools in South Carolina after all of us have died and present officials either are dead or retired from public life." The petitioners stood as proof to Hinton's rebuttal. Their willingness to sign and then sign again signaled once again that withheld goods and services, firings, canceled loans, and violence did not deter them. As Reverend DeLaine later observed, "The bitterness and economic pressure was a great stimulant for the Negro people to stand firm in the fight which they felt was right." In a pretrial press release, the NAACP announced that the nominal defendants might be Clarendon's school officials, but "the real defendant is the segregated school system."[91]

In May, Montgomery drove psychologist Kenneth Clark from Charleston to Summerton. Clark had traveled by train, with attorneys Marshall and Carter, from New York City for the trial. In his suitcase he carried four diapered dolls, two ivory and two brown, to show the children of Scott's Branch. Carter had searched for another way to persuade the Supreme Court that black children in segregated schools were denied an equal education, that segregation itself hampered their development. A study by Otto

Klineberg, a Columbia University professor, seemed to fit. Klineberg found that the longer southern black children attended integrated urban schools after their parents' migration North, the higher they scored on standardized tests. Klineberg sent Carter to Kenneth and Mamie Phipps Clark, who had founded the Northside Center for Child Development in Harlem. They, too, were interested in ways to measure the damage that segregation inflicted.[92]

In a classroom in a barracks addition to Scott's Branch, Kenneth Clark allowed Celestine Parson to consider two plain dolls molded from plastic. She suspected she was talking to the "doll man" because she and her parents, Bennie and Plummie Parson, were among the people that white residents called troublemakers. The three had signed the first petition, and then her father had signed, for her, the petition for desegregation. Clark offered the dolls and asked a few questions. "He asked which doll was the better doll. He asked which doll was prettier, what was my feeling." Celestine Parson had never owned a black doll; they didn't exist in Clarendon County. "The only doll we could buy was a white doll; it must be superior," the thirteen-year-old reasoned. "Since white children had all the privileges, the better schools, the buses, there had to be something that made us different, and the white doll had to be the better doll." That's what she told Clark, as did most of the other black children interviewed.[93]

All the while state attorney general Callison, Figg, and Rogers traded information: a delay in renovations at Scott's Branch, no social scientists willing to vouch for segregation, a wish list of black leaders Byrnes hoped would testify for South Carolina, a legislative committee looking for an "advisable course." The NAACP issued a special bulletin to all state branches, predicting, "What happens in Clarendon County will affect the future of every colored citizen for generations to come." Thurmond had the same thought, cast as a worry. He wrote Figg suggesting the state default: "Then only this district would be affected, while a decision of the court, of course, would affect the entire circuit."[94]

Figg had a plan of his own.

Caravan to Charleston

The families' day in court finally arrived. The morning of May 28, 1951, Clarendon County's black residents rose early for the trek to Charleston. Hammett Pearson made the trip, predicting that "this may one day be history" to son Jesse Pearson, who brought his camera. "Many people who were aware of what was going on stood out to watch. Others joined the caravan," Reverend

DeLaine wrote. Harry and Eliza Briggs collected enough relatives to fill eight cars. The adults left the children with Charleston relatives and attempted to enter the Broad Street courthouse. Hundreds of black citizens filled the cobblestone streets, coming from as far away as Georgia and Alabama.[95]

"They didn't let us in," said Annie Gibson. "They put a rope around, and we couldn't cross the rope. After they found out we were petitioners, they took the rope down and invited us in." More than five hundred jammed the courthouse corridors, hoping to catch a word or two or squeeze into the courtroom. Two women fainted in the ninety-plus-degree heat. "A very few got good seats; a few more stood shoulder to shoulder for hours in the courtroom, which was so crowded that they could not even move. The others stood in the doorway and in the hallway," reported John H. McCray, editor of the *Lighthouse and Informer* and a blunt and impatient commentator on Deep South segregation. Tall, with a high forehead, full cheeks, and a short mustache under a short nose, McCray published the black-owned newspaper in Columbia from 1941 until 1954.[96]

Figg stunned all, trying to end the trial the minute it began. The Clarendon County trustees' answer implausibly argued wooden buildings missing electricity and running water were equivalent to brick buildings with lights, water fountains, and restrooms. When court opened, the expert on segregation's defense stood before plaintiff's counsel could deliver the traditional opening statement. Figg announced the state "conceded that inequalities in the facilities, opportunities and curricula in the schools of this district do exist." He said this concession should "eliminate the necessity of taking a great deal of testimony." He said the legislature had created a building program, funded by the sales tax, to "insure educational opportunity for all children throughout the state." Thus he didn't oppose an order finding inequalities.[97]

Figg wanted to prevent the NAACP attorneys from building their full record of horrors, which they could tie to the inequality imposed by segregation as a violation of the Fourteenth Amendment. Figg wrote afterward to a Charleston friend, "We conceded inequality of facilities at the outset of the case because we knew we could not prove equality and that the other side could put in about two days testimony as to inequality. We hoped by doing this to upset the plans of the plaintiffs to make the kind of record which they wished to make for the court in Washington, and I am inclined to believe we succeeded to a substantial extent." The ploy did cut short the NAACP's array of witnesses, but Carter and Marshall got their job done. Marshall's opening statement set forth the two-prong argument the NAACP would follow: the schools were "unequal physically," and "segregation of pupils in and of itself is a form of inequality." The testimony of Matthew Whitehead, Ellis Knox, Kenneth Clark, and Helen Trager provided ample illustrations.[98]

Whitehead, a Howard University education professor, visited Rambay, Liberty Hill, and Scott's Branch schools for black students and Summerton Elementary and Summerton High schools for white students in November 1950 and April 1951. He described what he saw to Carter with meticulous attention to detail and some outrage. "In the Summerton Elementary School each pupil had a desk. In the Summerton High School each pupil had a desk. At the Rambay School for Negroes, there was not a single desk in the entire school," he testified. Whitehead spoke of indoor flush toilets for white students, outdoor earth toilets without running water for black students. At Scott's Branch two toilets served 694 students. He listed "blackboards, music rooms, charts, maps, globes, slides, stereoopticans" for white children but an absence of any visual aid but blackboards, "inadequate by all standards," for black children. The white children had an auditorium and a gymnasium; the black children had neither. White children were provided school lunches; black children were not. White children drank indoors from "running fountains," black children from uncovered galvanized buckets filled by a pump at Rambay and filled by a nearby well at Liberty Hill. Summerton Elementary school offered seven grades and seven teachers; Rambay had seven grades and two teachers. At Summerton Elementary no more than thirty-one students were in a class; at Scott's Branch class size ranged from thirty-eight to seventy-nine students.[99]

Ellis Knox, also a Howard education professor, cited twenty years of experience in educational surveys, then got down to business: it was impossible to provide equal educational opportunities and instruction for segregated black children. Segregation itself created inferiority. Knox explained, "The reason is that when children are segregated, that segregation cannot exist without discrimination, disadvantageous to the minority group, and that the children in the Negro schools very definitely are not prepared for the same type of American citizenship as the children in the white schools."[100]

Clark, a professor of psychology at New York City College, explained that he offered each child tested two dolls, exactly alike except for color. Clark tested sixteen Scott's Branch students between the ages of six and nine years old and ten children between the ages of twelve and seventeen. Among the younger children, ten liked the white doll better. Ten considered the white doll the "nice" doll. Eleven thought the brown doll looked "bad." All sixteen knew the white doll looked like a white child and the brown doll like a "colored" child, Clark was careful to note. Yet seven picked the white doll as looking like themselves. The Clarendon County children were "definitely harmed," and the injury to them was "enduring," said Clark.[101]

On the second day, Helen Trager reinforced the point that segregation harmed black and white children. Trager, a psychologist and Vassar College lecturer, and Marian J. Radke, of the Philadelphia Early Childhood Project, had conducted similar tests with 250 white and black children. The two used cardboard dolls with nice or shabby clothing and nice or shabby houses. The white children who gave the worst clothes, houses, and work assignments to the black doll were also the most hostile toward black people. The researchers interviewed the children about race and found that both white and black children "perceived Negro as meaning that you are not liked by people, that you won't be asked to play, that you won't be allowed to do the things that other children do." Figg wanted to pin blame on children's homes rather than their schools, but Trager added this: "It was the playground. It was what they saw on the bus. It was what they knew about where their father worked—or couldn't work." It was all of their learning, she said.[102]

Figg presented E. R. Crow, director of the new Educational Finance Commission (EFC). Figg asked about "mixed schools," and Crow said, "The existence of the feeling of separateness between the races of this State would make it such that it would be impossible to have peaceable association with each other in the public schools." Asked again about mixing of the races, Crow said, "In my opinion it would eliminate public schools in most, if not all of the communities in the State." When Marshall examined Crow, he asked, "Do I understand you to say that the people of South Carolina would deprive their own children of an education rather than open their schools to all races equally?" Referring to white South Carolinians, Crow replied that he believed local voters wouldn't support taxes for schools and the state legislature wouldn't appropriate money for schools. He wasn't guessing. In March, Byrnes had told South Carolina Education Association members that abandoning the public-school system was "the lesser of two evils." The South Carolina House endorsed this; a special legislative committee favored, on record, closing public schools if the state lost in court.[103]

In his closing argument, Marshall referred to testimony in the NAACP's higher education lawsuits—*Gaines v. Canada* in Missouri, *Sipuel v. Board of Regents* in Oklahoma, *Sweatt v. Painter* in Texas—linking segregation and inequality. Even when facilities were equal, segregation itself deprived people of an opportunity to study, he said. With only white officials in the public-school system, "there is not just segregation involved; there is exclusion, if you please." And "in the segregated school systems in this country, without any exception in any place in the United States, segregation means inferior." An equal education could only be provided the plaintiffs, said Marshall, if they were admitted to the schools set aside for white children.[104]

Figg noted that the same Congress that accepted the Fourteenth Amendment also retained segregation in District of Columbia schools. He said that the Supreme Court had not overruled *Plessy v. Ferguson,* even though *Sweatt v. Painter* presented an opportunity. He asserted that the High Court, up to this point, still accepted that segregation did not violate the Equal Protection Clause. The power of the states to separate the races in public schools was "normal." Separate schools were "the normal thing," he said repeatedly. Figg proposed that the court provide South Carolina time to design an end to inequalities while monitoring its own progress. Judge Parker responded, "Well, I'm not much impressed with that." Parker had no intention of being the first judge to relinquish *Plessy v. Ferguson,* but he wasn't willing to ignore the pitiful state of Clarendon County schools. "You have come into court here and admitted that facilities are not equal, and the evidence shows it beyond all peradventure," he said. "Now, it seems to me it's not for the court to wet nurse the schools."[105]

Waring interrupted: "As I understand it, this Court has got to face the issue of whether segregation is inequality *per se* or not." But Parker said Figg argued that segregation should not be abolished. Parker wanted to know what decree Figg suggested. Now was not the time for "mixed schools," because "utter confusion would exist," said Figg. He hit on a worry of the LDF attorneys when he said that desegregation of public schools shouldn't be compared to desegregation of graduate and professional schools. All the state wanted was a reasonable amount of time to raise money and build and furnish equal but still separate schools, said Figg. Besides, inequities had more to do with Clarendon being rural than racist, said Figg, a claim that required ignoring the entire history of the state.[106]

Marshall, in his final rebuttal, said that all the lawsuits mentioned ended with a court acknowledgment that the Fourteenth Amendment, at the least, required equality. "Yet in their own argument they admit that they have operated these Negro schools in South Carolina over a period of eighty years, and after a period of eighty years the best that they can possibly show to the Court in good faith, or to demonstrate the good faith of South Carolina, is that as of today the Negro schools are forty million dollars behind the white schools. . . . The only dispute," therefore, "is as to what we mean by 'equal.'"[107]

Parker wanted briefs before the judges ruled. The NAACP brief noted that race was the only difference between the children excluded from and

the children attending the segregated Summerton Elementary and Summerton High schools. Requiring black children to attend segregated schools
"gravely endangered their ability to grow into and function as well-adjusted
human beings." Their injuries were "likely enduring," unconstitutional, and
similar to those inflicted in *McLaurin v. Oklahoma*. The state's brief sounded
a hopeful note—the 1951 construction program promising a "striking improvement" in black children's schools—and the dire prediction of "a violent
emotional reaction" to "mixed schools." The brief asked for time to make a
plan that would end the inequality.[108]

On June 17, 1951, at Liberty Hill AME, a statewide testimonial honored
the plaintiffs and their children. "He that would be FREE must be FIRST to
STRIKE the BLOW!" proclaimed the program, which praised Marshall, Carter, and the petitioners. "Many of us who sit in comfortable and safe homes
in other sections of the country will never understand the courage of these
people in Clarendon County, a rural prejudiced southern community, who
dared the risks involved in their bold challenge to white supremacy." The
plaintiffs received merit awards. Hinton and Montgomery spoke, as did Reverend DeLaine, to about 1,500 people. Four days later a majority decision
granted an injunction to equalize educational facilities, requiring the state
to report progress in six months. The opinion denied an injunction to abolish segregation: "Segregation of the races in the public schools, as long as
equality of rights is preserved, is a matter of legislative policy for the several
states, with which the federal courts are powerless to interfere." The Supreme
Court ruling in *Plessy v. Ferguson* remained, that separate schools were "a
valid exercise of legislative power."[109]

The June 23, 1951, majority opinion warned courts would be stepping "far
outside their constitutional function were they to attempt to prescribe educational policies for the states in such matters [as segregation], however desirable such policies might be in the eyes of some sociologists or educators."
The opinion cited *Gong Lum v. Rice*, in which a Chinese child was excluded
from a school for white children in the 1920s: "The decision is within the dis-
cretion of the state in regulating its public schools and does not conflict with
the Fourteenth Amendment." The opinion said that segregation in public
schools was different from segregation in graduate and professional schools
and that removing inequities in District 22 was all the relief that could be
reasonably requested and granted.[110]

Waring wrote a furious twenty-page dissent, laying out his view of southern hypocrisies. He called the state's admission of inequities a maneuver to
avoid the lawsuit's primary purpose. He debunked "talk of blood and taint

of blood," asserting, "The whole discussion of race and ancestry has been in-termingled with sophistry and prejudice." He dismissed references to *Plessy v. Ferguson,* noting the Supreme Court was not considering railroad accom-modations in the recent higher education rulings. Instead he invoked *Sweatt v. Painter* and *McLaurin v. Oklahoma,* decisions "considering education just as we are considering it here." He called doubt on the state's promises: "The estimates as to the cost merely of equalization of physical facilities run any-where from forty to eighty million dollars."[111]

Finally, Waring wrote, it was clear "that segregation in education can never produce equality and that it is an evil that must be eradicated. . . . This case presents the matter clearly for adjudication and I am of the opinion that all of the legal guideposts, expert testimony, common sense and reason point unerringly to the conclusion that the system of segregation in education ad-opted and practiced in the State of South Carolina must go and must go now. *Segregation is per se inequality.*"[112]

Decisions by three-judge panels may be immediately appealed to the Su-preme Court, and this was. Better yet, *Briggs v. Elliott* would not be alone in challenging school desegregation. In all, seventeen states and the District of Columbia required segregated school systems; four more didn't require but did allow segregation. Underway were more challenges, from Virginia, Kansas, Washington, D.C., and Delaware.[113]

To the Supreme Court—and Back

Byrnes and the state legislature opened South Carolina's wallet: a three-cent sales tax, South Carolina's first, to pay for expanded school programs; a $75 million bond issue for school building construction; a statewide busing pro-gram; and higher teacher pay. Byrnes lauded the "unselfish interest" the leg-islature had shown the state's children. An attorney friend of Figg's noted of white voters, "The fact that South Carolina almost without a murmur has imposed a seventy-five million bond issue and a sales tax largely in order to maintain segregation shows the almost unanimous sentiment in favor of segregation." Byrnes also got escape clauses: district superintendents autho-rized to permit student transfers from one school or district so that all-white attendance at all-white schools could be preserved and district trustees au-thorized to lease or sell school property to private individuals or groups if segregation ended. Byrnes tried to talk Bishop Frank Madison Reid Sr. into accepting all responsibility for black children's education, reportedly offer-ing to sell the AME Church all the black public schools for a bargain price, a dollar a school. The EFC warned that the equalization program would be expensive and difficult. W. B. Southerlin, reporting on just Clarendon's twenty-three elementary schools for black children, said each needed much work to be "useable for the most meager purposes."[114]

The NAACP attorneys proclaimed a national impetus in their jurisdictional statement, quoting Truman's Higher Education Commission report: "The time has come to make public education at all levels equally accessible to all, without regard to race, creed, sex or national origin." They emphasized the result of the South's remaining segregation: institutionalized poverty. In contrast the state sounded in perfect accord with Parker's courtroom commentary. Figg wrote that the meaning of the Equal Protection Clause had long been settled. Given seventy-five years of segregation and its acceptance by the courts, it was a "late day" to say that children's constitutional rights were violated. The only question pending: equalization of educational facilities.[115]

Byrnes found a much-celebrated attorney to say this before the Supreme Court. He engaged John W. Davis, a friend, a regular visitor to South Carolina, and a veteran of 250 Supreme Court cases, more than any other lawyer alive. The West Virginia native had served as U.S. solicitor general and as ambassador to Great Britain. In 1924 Davis won the Democratic nomination for president but lost to Calvin Coolidge. When he accepted the defense of segregation, he was seventy-nine and proof of South Carolina's determination to preserve white supremacy. A representative of the old guard with his white hair and waistcoats, he seemed an inevitable choice to defend the past. He engaged with relish, sure of himself, unimpressed with his opposition, contemptuous of legal arguments that invoked schoolchildren's perceptions. In October he wrote Figg that Trager's testimony discredited "high-flying psychologists" via her "astounding conclusion" that by age five white children knew they were white and black children knew they were black.[116]

In Clarendon County NAACP membership climbed from 168 to 453. At the state conference's annual meeting, Hinton said, "There is much room for joy in having been the first state to attack segregation in public school education on the elementary and high school levels, and the case now before the United States Supreme Court has made and left a lasting impression upon the minds of the whites who are [loath] to let segregation go." The financial cost was high. The state conference reported more than ten thousand dollars in bills paid off, a point of pride for Hinton.[117]

The personal cost was higher. In October the DeLaines' former residence in Summerton burned to the ground. Only chimneys and the foundation remained in the morning's smoky light. Neighbors told the family that the fire department refused to put out the fire. The home was one-tenth of a mile outside the city limits, three-tenths of a mile from a fire hydrant. An FBI report dismissed the refusal, saying the town owned no hose long enough to bridge the distance from house to hydrant and no Summerton law compelled a firefighter to put out a fire. Orphelia DeLaine wrote later of rumors that a local alcoholic was paid to set the fire. The 1950 slander judgment against Reverend DeLaine, thanks to his preemptive actions, had failed to collect the titles to his properties, but after the fire the court collected in full his house insurance of eighteen thousand dollars, almost seven times more than the judgment.[118]

While pressure applied to the petitioners kept increasing, pressure on the state eased. The required six-month report to the District Court announced Clarendon's thirty-four school districts consolidated into three, nine buses provided for school transportation, and a bid accepted on a $261,000 high school for black students in Summerton. The state sales tax survived a court challenge. The sale of school bonds, the equalization of teacher salaries, the establishment of the EFC had occurred. But no one could pretend the schools suddenly were equal. The NAACP attorneys pointed that out. Besides, even if facilities were made comparable, equal educational opportunities couldn't be obtained in a segregated school system, they argued. Figg held that a "final determination" on equal facilities was needed; any appeal was premature.[119]

The District Court sent the six-month report forward, and the Supreme Court sent *Briggs v. Elliott* back. This move, and the docket order created by the departure and return of *Briggs*, resulted in the five segregation cases being collected under the name *Brown v. Board of Education*. Justices Hugo Black and William O. Douglas dissented on the *Briggs* remand to District Court, taking a Waring-like stance that additional facts were "wholly irrelevant" to the constitutional questions. Waring himself declined to sit on the upcoming hearing; he had said his piece. "In my opinion, the report and this decree have no place in this case," he wrote of the local 1951–52 shuffles. Waring retired from the bench, effective January 28, 1952, and packed his bags for New York City, "outside the curtain of White Supremacy."[120]

Supplementary report in hand and following a second hearing, the District Court met again on *Briggs v. Elliott*. Judges Parker, Timmerman, and Armistead M. Dobie said they were satisfied. Their March 1952 decree accepted the state's prediction that all would be equal by fall, noting $5.5 million was being spent on school construction for black children, compared to $1.9 million for white children. The problem was not with laws requiring segregation but the way they had been administered, the judges declared. In May, on appeal, *Briggs v. Elliott* again made its way to the Supreme Court. Headed there were other lawsuits challenging segregation in public schools.[121]

A Kansas three-judge panel had accepted testimony that black students were psychologically harmed: "Segregation of white and colored children in public schools has a detrimental effect upon the colored children. The impact is greater when it has the sanction of the law; for the policy of separating the races is usually interpreted as denoting the inferiority of the Negro group." A Delaware decision did not rule segregation itself unconstitutional but did offer a one-two punch that Marshall had requested in *Briggs v. Elliott*: segregation as practiced was illegal, and the appropriate remedy was immediate admission to the white schools.[122]

Davis clung to his disdain. He wrote Figg of the social science testimony, "I seriously say that if that sort of 'guff' can move any court, 'God save the state!'" His briefs stuck to well-developed themes: South Carolina was building schools. Even taking at face value claims of children's psychological damage didn't invalidate the power of the state to proscribe regulations, such as separate schools. Besides, a Summerton classroom would "average three white pupils and 27 colored." This was white residents' great fear, a fear the all-white southern judiciary took seriously and shared, that white public schools would become majority-black schools.[123]

October passed as the Supreme Court gathered cases to hear together. Justice Douglas objected to this delay, saying additional facts were irrelevant to the constitutional question. When December arrived, the Supreme Court had collected five: *Dorothy Davis v. County School Board of Prince Edward County* in Virginia; *Oliver Brown et al. v. the Board of Education of Topeka, Kansas; Bolling v. Sharpe* in Washington, D.C.; and *Belton v. Gebhart* and *Bulah v. Gebhart* in Delaware's court of chancery, which heard issues of equity. Only in Delaware did the decisions order the child plaintiffs admitted to their nearby white schools. Delaware chancellor Collins J. Seitz wrote that a plaintiff satisfactorily showing an existing and continuing violation of "separate but equal" was "entitled to relief immediately, in the only way it is available, mainly, by admission to the school with superior facilities."[124]

Of the consolidation of cases, Davis wrote Figg, "Now I ask myself what does this mean? Does the Court want to dispose of the question once and for all in every conceivable phase? If so, does it want to put the question finally to rest in favor of the existing situation or wipe out segregation entirely? I cannot think that the latter is its purpose, but I confess some uneasiness." Byrnes dealt with his own discomfort with a preemptive strike: make it possible to eliminate public schools. On November 3, with a high turn-out expected on Election Day, he urged white South Carolinians to approve an amendment removing the state's constitutional responsibility to provide public schools. Voting against the amendment would "force the mixing of races in the schools," he said. Voters, overwhelmingly white in number, an-swered two-to-one that they were comfortable living in a state without public education. Jonathan Daniels, a North Carolina editor, commented that vot-ers' willingness to abandon the schools proposed "something beyond seces-sion from the Union. They urge secession from civilization."[125]

In the legal briefs that followed, the NAACP promoted the role of the judiciary and attacked the states' rights posture. On South Carolina's con-tention that segregation of schools should remain legislative policy, LDF attorneys wrote: "This proposition is amazing in its bald assertion that, if a state decides that its continuing imposition of segregation is desirable, there is no issue for the independent decision of this Court as to whether segregation can be squared with equal protection of the laws." The NAACP argued that South Carolina's intentions in the past and present were clear: minimize the civic life of black citizens. The NAACP cited machinations to restrict black citizens' voting rights as a recent effort at ignoring equal pro-tection.[126]

South Carolina said new schools for black students would be ready for the 1952–53 school year. The state said that doing as the appellants asked, immediately admitting black children to the white schools, was impractica-ble: 2,799 black children and 295 white children attended Clarendon County schools. As had been asserted in court and threatened outside court, white students would not attend majority-black schools. Davis and Figg reached back to Reconstruction-era governor Robert Scott and his opposition to "mixed" schools. Scott, who had appeared in earlier briefs, reappeared, his argument reapplied in capital letters: relinquishing separate schools would repel white people from the education they need, "AND VIRTUALLY TO GIVE OUR COLORED POPULATION THE EXCLUSIVE BENEFIT OF OUR PUB-LIC SCHOOLS." Invoking the police powers of the state, the brief argued that states' rights trumped black people's constitutional citizenship rights.[127]

By necessity the state arguments ignored changes occurring in the sec-ond half of the twentieth century. More than two hundred black students had enrolled in formerly all-white southern colleges. The Congress of In-dustrial Organizations (CIO) had banned segregation on all properties owned or leased by the union in the South or elsewhere. Truman's executive orders had desegregated the federal workforce and the armed services. In

Columbia, for example, black and white troops trained together at Fort Jackson, a U.S. Army post. Near Aiken, South Carolina, black and white workers built together the Savannah River Plant, better known as the "bomb plant," and ate together in the cafeteria.[128]

The U.S. government filed an amicus curiae brief with the Supreme Court supporting the appellants and casting into relief the international penalty for defending segregation. "The United States is trying to prove to the people of the world, of every nationality, race and color, that a free democracy is the most civilized and most secure form of government yet devised by man. We must set an example for others by showing firm determination to remove existing flaws in our democracy." Obviously, then, a society where only certain people possess voting rights or only certain people fully benefit from public education was problematic nationally and internationally. "'Separate' but equal is a contradiction in terms," the brief said. "The Government submits that compulsory racial segregation is itself, without more, an unconstitutional discrimination."[129]

In Summerton, 1952 brought a new, brick Scott's Branch, the state's first "equalization school," long and low-slung with many windows. More school construction underway altered what the EFC's Crow acknowledged as "one of the Nation's most antique school systems." Black and white teachers' salaries were equal, and black schoolchildren finally rode school buses. But the vindictiveness in Clarendon County continued. Harry Briggs Jr., hired as an assistant bus driver, was fired within a few weeks when white supervisors recognized his name. He tried a paper route, but death threats led his mother to insist that he quit. And then the Briggs cow was arrested. The older Briggs brothers milked the cow, but Nathaniel Briggs was entrusted with walking the cow to and from pasture. Discovered free of its tether and eating grass in a nearby segregated cemetery, the cow was taken to jail. "They hated Harry Briggs so much, they locked up the cow," said Nathaniel Briggs. The rural expectation of neighbors returning animals was gone; a wandering cow now cost its owner a fifty-cent fine.[130]

Different from Everybody

Finally, on December 9, 1952, nine white U.S. Supreme Court justices heard the Clarendon petitioners. Reverend DeLaine gained admission despite fewer than fifty seats available to the public. Marshall began his argument at 3:15 P.M., following colleague Carter on Kansas. He told the justices that South Carolina statutes were unconstitutional not only because they produced inevitable inequality in school buildings but also because government-imposed segregation itself denied equality. Even though the *Sweatt* and *Mc-Laurin* decisions concerned graduate and professional school, they applied "down the line" if evidence showed injury. And the humiliation children underwent as long as they attended segregated schools was "actual injury."[131]

Justice Felix Frankfurter raised a favorite point of white southerners, the ratio of black to white, asking about states with a "vast congregation of the Negro population." In 1950, in South Carolina, black people made up 39 percent of the population, 70 percent in Clarendon County. Marshall replied that you couldn't "throw aside" the rights of the individuals within a group. Frankfurter then said, "It does not follow because you cannot make certain classifications, you cannot make some classifications." Marshall demurred, pointing out South Carolina's poor record in voting rights. Frankfurter came right back, saying South Carolina had argued the Fourteenth Amendment didn't prohibit classifications. Marshall answered that competent testimony said segregating schools was an unreasonable classification, and "the least that the state has to do is produce something to defend its statutes." Said Frankfurter, "I follow you when you talk that way." Marshall then ticked off three points: He cited the Supreme Court's *Sweatt* and *McLaurin* decisions. Of South Carolina's legally segregated schools, on a classification basis, "these statutes were bad." He made the broader point that "racial distinctions in and of themselves are invidious." He concluded, "Any of these three would be sufficient for reversal."[132]

When Davis took the floor, he celebrated South Carolina's "surge of education reform and improvement." He said there could be no doubt that schools in Clarendon County would be equal. Besides, Davis said, once lawyers and judges ascertained the scope of the Fourteenth Amendment, their work was done, because "the rest must be left to those who dictate public policy, and not to courts." To win Davis needed to limit the Supreme Court's power and the justices' perception of the Constitution's power. Justice Harold Burton said, "But the Constitution is a living document that must be interpreted in relation to the facts of the time in which it is interpreted. Did we not go through with that in connection with child labor cases and so forth?"[133]

Davis's reputation loomed so large that the *Washington Afro-American* called his encounter with Marshall a "David and Goliath struggle." Davis understood the white South and its laws, but perhaps he no longer understood the changing times. He mocked the testimony of Clark and Trager, saying social scientists found what they wanted to find. He invoked Reconstruction, saying South Carolina had "mixed schools" briefly after the Civil War, until 1878, and operated segregated schools afterward in the light of that experience. He said its legislature had created a public-school system "in accordance with the wishes of its people." NAACP attorney Carter wrote of Davis, "His was a mean-spirited approach, intended to demean and humiliate."[134]

Marshall did not let this pass. When Davis referenced South Carolinians, he erased the existence of black South Carolinians. Not one of the legislatures in the segregated states had black representatives or senators to speak for them. At the start of his rebuttal, Marshall said, "It seems to me that the significant factor running through all these arguments up to this point is that for some reason, which is still unexplained, Negroes are taken out of the mainstream of American life in these states." The only way South Carolina could sustain segregated schools was to show that "the Negro as Negro—all Negroes—are different from everybody else," Marshall insisted. That had not, and could not, be claimed. The Court must consider not what was reasonable to the South Carolina legislature, he said, but what was reasonable given the Fourteenth Amendment.[135]

The justices were divided. They did not decide *Brown v. Board of Education* that term. Instead the court restored the cases to its docket for reargument, asking for further briefs addressing the Fourteenth Amendment and its creators' intentions. The justices also asked for proposals regarding decrees if the court did decide segregated schools were unconstitutional. In the months that followed, states' district attorneys rummaged through historical records; thirty-seven states existed at the time of the Fourteenth Amendment's approval. Figg wrote Davis that no one had believed ratifying the Fourteenth Amendment would do anything "except get the State back into the Union." A state researcher informed Figg that even though the South Carolina Constitution of 1868 authorized integrated public schools, "Even the scalawags, carpetbaggers and negroes obviously realized that such a system would not work." The state's ensuing brief argued that the Fourteenth Amendment, ratified on July 9, 1868, was not intended to outlaw school segregation.[136]

Marshall attended a mass meeting at Allen University, where Hinton handed him a check for $5,060 raised by the branches. The national NAACP called for additional help, sending out emergency telegrams seeking fifteen thousand dollars to fund the required research. Teams of lawyers and historians cast about for the most powerful and useful arguments. Establishing intentional inequality, which implied the Supreme Court's duty to employ the Equal Protection Clause, was among the tactics chosen. The team chose a speech by U.S. Congressman Thaddeus Stevens, a Radical Republican known as "the Great Commoner." Stevens said that when states made distinctions in the same law between different classes of individuals, Congress had the power to correct the inequality. The NAACP brief concluded the Fourteenth Amendment was intended to prohibit state-imposed racial discrimination.[137]

On September 8, 1953, Chief Justice Vinson died. President Dwight D. Eisenhower selected Earl Warren, California's governor, as the new chief justice. An interim appointment allowed Warren to start in October, his confirmation following months later. A son of Norwegian immigrants and a native of Los Angeles, Warren had served as a district attorney for fourteen years and attorney general for four, making a name for himself fighting organized crime. In 1942 he supported removing citizens of Japanese heritage from the West Coast and confining them in internment camps throughout World War II. After the war Warren integrated the state's National Guard, appointed black judges, and expressed regret about the internments. Californians elected him governor for three terms; he ran with Thomas Dewey in the 1948 presidential election; he vied for the Republican nomination in 1952. After Eisenhower won, the president promised Warren a Supreme Court post, even though Warren lacked bench experience.[138]

Vinson had influenced the court's stall on *Brown v. Board of Education,* and his death before reargument led tart-tongued Justice Frankfurter to say, "This is the first indication I have ever had that there is a God."[139] Frankfurter might well have reiterated his sentiment when Warren was appointed. Warren would seek and get unanimity.

All parties returned to the court for three days, beginning December 7, 1953. South Carolina and Virginia argued together and first. Reverend DeLaine attended again. As he waited in line, the Clarendon County minister told a *Baltimore Afro-American* reporter, "There were times when I thought I would go out of my mind because of this case." He predicted South Carolina's petitioners would win.[140]

Marshall predicted the court would end segregation in public schools, although he warned full integration in some southern states might take thirty years or more. In fundraising speeches Marshall told audiences, "The soul of the white man is in the hands of the Negro." He issued a promise: "Come Hell or high water, we are going to be free by '63," a reference to the Emancipation Proclamation of 1863.[141]

Figg and Davis predicted the preservation of segregated schools everywhere but the District of Columbia. They singled out Washington, D.C., as a bone to toss since the 1952 Republican Party platform promised segregation's end in the district. "All in all, it has been a right good fight, and I believe that we have won everything except the decision (if we do not get that)," Figg wrote after the 1953 arguments.[142]

Meanwhile Chief Justice Warren worked to build consensus. The justices met at each conference to discuss the briefs and arguments and their own research, testing approaches but holding back their own opinions until the discussions ended in February 1954. This worked. "On the first vote, we unanimously agreed that the 'separate but equal' doctrine had no place in public education," Warren wrote. All maintained secrecy while Warren wrote the opinion himself, vetting it with the other justices, including the hospitalized Robert Henry Jackson. During this period Eisenhower invited Warren to a White House dinner also attended by Davis. Throughout the dinner the president praised Davis at length, telling Warren what "a great man" Davis was, Warren recalled. On the way to after-dinner drinks, the president took the inappropriate step of speaking up for the southern segregationists, advising Warren, "These are not bad people. All they are concerned about is to see that their sweet little girls are not required to sit in school alongside big overgrown Negroes."[143]

For weeks observers and journalists packed the Supreme Court Building, awaiting the *Brown v. Board of Education* decision. On May 17, 1954, a Monday, at 1 P.M., Warren ended the suspense. "As we Justices marched into the courtroom on that day, there was a tenseness that I have not seen equaled before or since," he recalled. As he spoke, it wasn't obvious where the opinion was going. Several paragraphs in, Warren read that, unlike *Sweatt v. Painter*, "the Negro and white schools involved have been equalized, or are being equalized." But the decision could not turn on comparisons, he said. "We must look instead to the effect of segregation itself on public education." He reached the decision's core with a rhetorical flourish: "We come then to the question presented: Does segregation of children in public schools solely on the basis of race, even though the physical facilities and other 'tangible' factors may be equal, deprive the children of the minority group of equal educational opportunities? We believe that it does."[144]

The *Sweatt* and *McLaurin* decisions received their due; similar considerations should be provided "with added force" to children in elementary and high schools. In what was said next, the decision also gave social scientists their due as modern authorities and recognized generations of black people's pain: "To separate them from others of similar age and qualifications solely because of their race generates a feeling of inferiority as to their status in the community that may affect their hearts and minds in a way unlikely ever to be undone." Then, in an echo of Waring's dissent, Warren read, "Separate educational facilities are inherently unequal. Segregation deprived the plaintiffs of equal protection of the laws, guaranteed in the Fourteenth Amendment." Segregation in public schools had been declared unconstitutional. *Brown v. Board of Education* was unanimous, a powerful reinforcement of the decision. Warren had written an opinion that was plain and short, "so it could be published in the daily press throughout the nation without taking too much space," he explained. And it was, word for word.[145]

At a New York City press conference, NAACP leaders described the decision as the "vindication of a 45-year fight." Marshall said, "There is no possibility of getting around this clear-cut interpretation of the Constitution." Nevertheless the South's attorneys general and governors immediately set emergency meetings to orchestrate resistance. A complication existed that gave segregationists hope: enforcement of the ruling awaited arguments by attorneys general in the *Brown v. Board of Education* states. Only then would the Supreme Court rule on next steps. Warren wanted further arguments in April 1955 with the implementation order to follow. In Columbia, Hinton spoke cautiously in public. He said, "Negroes, though happy, are most mindful of the seriousness of the decision and will welcome the appointment of a committee composed of leaders of both races to sit down and work out plans for the best interests of all citizens of South Carolina." That was not going to happen.[146]

Eisenhower asked for calm. Privately he said that he didn't believe that black students were injured by being educated separately from white students. Publicly he said obliquely that he stood for honesty, decency, justice, and fairness in public policy. Byrnes said he was shocked and urged restraint. The *Columbia Record*'s May 17 headline, "South Loses in Court; Segregation Must Go; Time to 'Mix' Put Off," took up a quarter of the paper's front page, as if a world war had been declared. All but one front-page article focused on the ruling. The newspaper assured its white readers that the governor and legislature had ensured segregation remained. In March the legislature had ratified the constitutional amendment permitting public school closings. Decide to close the schools or "mix": that was the immediate problem, according to the *Columbia Record,* describing only the latter as "abhorrent" to white southerners and predicting "strong sentiment for giving up the school system" to evade the court decision. In Clarendon County, McCord said, "There is one set and determined purpose that they will not go to school together."[147]

In Summerton black residents' reaction was subdued, cautious, and private. Hinton warned, "Think much and talk little." The ruling came on a Monday, and word passed slowly, person to person, since few had phones. William Hilton, stringing wire in a pasture, came home soon after his wife heard the news on the radio. They sank to their knees to pray, Hilton offering thanks to the justices, calling them the "nine fathers of the country." Perhaps the battle-weary plaintiffs suspected what was to come: one of the Supreme Court's most crucial decisions would be, in the South, one of its most reviled by those in power. And the decision would not help the petitioners' children.[148]

Brown I, as it came to be known, didn't answer key questions: How would segregation end? When? Attorneys for the black schoolchildren had asked that segregation end by September 1956. Attorneys for South Carolina had claimed that immediate compliance would destroy the public-school system. Byrnes said Clarendon County should deny admission to black schoolchildren until ordered to admit them. Other districts, he said, were not parties to the lawsuit and thus should "ignore the threats of the NAACP, refuse to admit Negro students," and employ black teachers only for black schoolchildren in the next year. Hinton said parents would file petitions in nine school districts but not in Summerton, which was directly affected by the court's order.[149]

Davis died of pneumonia in March 1955, so Figg and Rogers represented South Carolina in the next round before the Supreme Court. Short, heavyset, and bejowled, Rogers perfectly represented the attitude that segregationists held and would perpetuate. He asked that the case be sent back to the District Court without instructions as to how and when the schools would desegregate. Rogers said, "Mr. Chief Justice, to say we will conform depends on the decree handed down," which sounded as if Rogers believed the state was free to ignore a Supreme Court ruling. When Warren asked if Rogers was not willing to say an honest attempt would be made to comply, Rogers said, "No, I am not. Let's get the word 'honest' out of there." When Warren demurred, Rogers said, "No, because I would have to tell you that right now we would not conform—we would not send our white children to the Negro schools." Marshall argued that the government should enforce the U.S. Constitution in South Carolina as well as any place else in the nation and that the order must be immediate, not "geared down" for community customs or attitudes. Rogers said, "I don't even want to be pinned down to five years."[150]

The Supreme Court set no deadline. On May 31, 1955, in *Brown II*, the court gave local school authorities the primary responsibility to solve whatever problems blocked desegregation. The lower courts were given the power to judge the good faith of local actions. At stake was admitting the plaintiffs to public schools as soon as practical, wrote Warren in the seven-paragraph ruling. How soon was that? The cases were remanded to district courts to issue orders as necessary to admit children to public schools "on a racially nondiscriminatory basis with all deliberate speed." That key phrase, "all deliberate speed"? Six southern states—Alabama, Florida, Georgia, Louisiana, Mississippi, and South Carolina—interpreted that as slower than molasses.[151]

Summerton, as the district directly affected by the Supreme Court's order, had spent fourteen months not developing a plan and now had no deadline to do so. In anticipation the state legislature decreed that state aid would end to any schools ordered to accept student transfers and that Clarendon County could cut off county school funds. At a June meeting called by District 22's school board, white parents argued about closing schools immediately or operating in the fall on a segregated basis. Also in June, after an Atlanta emergency meeting of southern NAACP branches, the NAACP encouraged immediate petitions throughout the state to desegregate school and provided a sample petition. Saying state laws and practices must yield to the decision, the Atlanta declaration said, "This is the law of the land which applies to every state, county, city, and hamlet. There will be no local option on this." A stalemate loomed: if schools didn't desegregate, a constitutional violation and loss of federal funds; if schools did desegregate, white parents' wrath, abandonment of public schools, and loss of county and state funds.[152]

Hinton said, of *Brown II*, "It was all we could have hoped for." J. D. Carson, chairman of the Summerton school board, said, "We will keep the races separate, and if we have to close the schools, we'll close. If we close one school, we will close them all." At this point the state had spent $52 million on improved or new school buildings, 65 percent of the total on buildings serving black schoolchildren.[153]

On July 11 Marshall attended a mass meeting at Liberty Hill AME. There Hinton announced that the NAACP had informed state attorney general Callison that five hundred names would be added as plaintiffs. The more plaintiffs, the more support, Hinton told the several hundred attending. Behind this was the fact that many of the original parents and child plaintiffs had moved out of state or the child plaintiffs had graduated from the segregated schools. After all, nine years had passed since the "sunshine bus." Gone were members of the Stukes, Briggs, Richburg, Ragin, Brown, Oliver,

Seals, and Georgia families, to name a few, the children to boarding schools, work, or college, the adults to Baltimore, Detroit, Philadelphia, and New York City.[154]

On July 15 attorneys Marshall and Boulware returned to court in Columbia, as did Rogers and Figg. They appeared again before Parker, Dobie, and Timmerman. Attending were pastors DeLaine, Richburg, and Seals. Marshall provided the court a list of 187 more plaintiffs. Figg said that South Carolina wanted continued segregation and an indefinite amount of time to work on a desegregation plan. Otherwise "it cannot be reasonably expected that public education will survive." Marshall, who wanted desegregation that school year, or 1956 at the latest, pointed out that Baltimore, the District of Columbia, and St. Louis, Missouri, had all desegregated within months. He argued that the Supreme Court had clearly stated that maintaining segregated public education was unconstitutional. Thus Clarendon County didn't have the right to say, as Marshall put it, "At least for one more year, we are going to violate the law."[155]

The District Court's July 15, 1955, decree said, "Nothing in the Constitution or in the decision of the Supreme Court takes away from the people's freedom to choose the schools they attend. The Constitution, in other words, does not require integration. It merely forbids discrimination. It does not forbid such segregation as occurs as the result of voluntary action. It merely forbids the use of governmental power to enforce segregation." Marshall said the NAACP attorneys would not present black children to the white Summerton schools that fall; such action was not necessary and wouldn't have legal significance.[156]

The Squeeze

In August, South Carolina parents petitioned for desegregated schools. They petitioned in Elloree, Sumter, Orangeburg, Florence, Hopkins, Charleston, and Mount Pleasant.

In Elloree, about eighteen miles from Summerton, thirty-nine parents asked for school desegregation. Within days of their August 5 petition, Mayor W. J. Deer started a White Citizens' Council (WCC). Petitioners were given thirty days to move out of homes and off land. An NAACP leader was warned to leave town. In Sumter, about twenty-three miles away, eighty-one parents in town and forty-two more outside of town petitioned. A meeting to form a Sumter WCC brought in five hundred. In Orangeburg, about thirty-five miles from Summerton, fifty-seven parents petitioned. In response

WCCs popped up within Orangeburg, Edisto community, and neighboring Bowman, North, and Eutawville.[157]

In Summerton, Reverend Richburg signed up sixty-five potential new petitioners at Liberty Hill AME. Attorney Rogers had already made sure that Summerton had a WCC. Neighboring Manning formed a WCC, with 267 joining during the initial meeting. Eight more WCCs, all in towns within fifty miles of Summerton, added hundreds more members. On August 27 a newly organized Klan met midway between Summerton and Manning on U.S. 301, where the rally couldn't be missed. Speaker Bryant Bowles, of the National Association for the Advancement of White People, drew 1,000 in robes.[158]

This was life under siege. A plantation manager in Sunflower County, Mississippi, had founded the first WCC in July 1954, determined to maintain segregation after *Brown I*. The councils—sometimes described as the "new Ku Klux Klan" or "manicured Kluxism"—spread quickly throughout South Carolina, in part due to Rogers' efforts. Rogers spoke at most initial meetings, stirring up white resistance not only to segregation but also to the NAACP. As one South Carolina journalist explained it, WCC members intended to "expose left-wing tendencies of the NAACP which would come among our innocent colored citizenry and foment race hatred" and try "to destroy our way of life." Often mayors led the councils. Every one of Kingstree's lawyers joined its council. As Rogers traveled the state, he also promoted the power of economic retaliation, refined from Clarendon County use into what was now called "the squeeze" or sometimes "the freeze."[159]

Local school boards had no intention of responding to the NAACP petitions by school's start; everyone knew this. But black parents asked in August for desegregated schools in Alabama, Arkansas, Florida, Georgia, Louisiana, North Carolina, Mississippi, South Carolina, and Virginia. At the NAACP's 1955 national conference, Marshall said, "I do not know how many years it will take to desegregate public schools in the Southern states. I don't believe anybody knows how long it will take. Two things are certain. One is that it won't take as long as any diehard Southern official wishes, and secondly, regardless of how long it takes, the period of time will be a much shorter time than it would have been without these Supreme Court decisions."[160]

Childhood had ended for many of District 22's young petitioners. Only nine children, of the original child petitioners, remained to benefit by the 1955 decision that schools would desegregate with "all deliberate speed." When the 1955–56 school year started, white men guarded Summerton's white schools with rifles, just in case any black students showed up. Eight southern states—Alabama, Florida, Georgia, Louisiana, Mississippi, North Carolina, South Carolina, and Virginia—chose "outright defiance" and "deliberate stalling," as the *Baltimore Afro-American* put it. In WCC speeches Rogers pushed for collaboration among the southern states, saying a united front could buy at least twenty-five more years of segregation.[161]

Livelihoods and lives were in jeopardy again. School officials fired Carrie Richburg Nelson at Spring Hill and Eddie Richburg and Gracie Palmer Richburg at Saint Paul schools. Joseph Richburg, brother of Carrie and Eddie and husband of Gracie, was fired from his job teaching veterans. J. Haskell Richburg, the father of the Richburg sisters and the brother of Reverend Richburg, was fired from his job at a gin. Sisters Eddie Richburg and Carrie Richburg Nelson and sister-in-law Gracie Palmer Richburg told the *Washington Afro-American* that Superintendent H. B. Betchman promised their jobs back once Haskell and Joseph Richburg, who also worked as a barber, removed their names from the local list of 187 petitioners. Boulware and Marshall did remove the names. No one got a job back.[162]

So Carrie Richburg Nelson moved to Columbia, where her husband continued his studies at Allen University. Eddie Richburg left for New York City and the support of an uncle. She swore she would never return and didn't, leaving a new car to rust on her father's land as a deliberate symbol of destruction. Gracie and Joseph Richburg moved to Baltimore. She took domestic and then laundry work; he tried construction, then meatpacking. Haskell Richburg, who owned local land, stayed and continued to farm.[163]

Next vendors stopped supplying Oliver's Café, run by Mary Oliver since her husband's 1951 death; a shop owned by Rebecca Brown; and a grill and service station owned by Robert Smith, who was not a petitioner but a successful businessman in town. "Several bread salesmen pleaded with me to take my name down. I told them I'd never do it," said Mary Oliver, who had signed all the petitions and promised her husband she would persist. "I promised him that I'd be a woman," she told journalist McCray, now reporting on the South for *Afro-American* newspapers.[164]

Reverend Richburg, who was also principal at Dantzler Elementary in Orangeburg County, was fired from that post when he refused to end his continued support of petitioners and the NAACP. Henry Brown, the janitor who had survived earlier penalties, told McCray that when he was fired he confronted Betchman. "I asked him why, and he told me they weren't going to let any of them who signed the list work." His son was fired from the George Smith grocery store, as was coworker Thomas Lee Briggs. The family income shrank. Wife Thelma Brown, mother of their twelve children, didn't work outside the home. Henry Brown didn't allow his daughters to babysit or clean for white Summerton. "He was afraid of what could happen in white people's homes," said daughter Beatrice Brown.[165]

Some white residents seemed to expect the petitioners to understand, even excuse their actions. And some did. "The thing is, these white people had to live in this town too. They couldn't step out too much," said Beatrice Brown. When teen Daisy Oliver discovered a WCC sticker on her doctor's office door, she entered, waited until all patients were seen, and then asked him why. "Sometimes you have to get along to keep doing the things you do, he said, the good things." She discussed this with her grandmother, who was dismayed, too, but explained further, "If he didn't do it, they might do something to his office, and he wouldn't be there to serve the people." The teen lived in the country with her grandparents and started having nightmares that her parents' house, between the Briggs and DeLaine homes, was burning. "It was just sad, so much time wasted trying to protect yourself, trying not to say the wrong thing or do the wrong thing."[166]

Reverend DeLaine remained in Lake City. In June, in what Lake City segregationists called Operation Shoot 'Em Up, someone fired shots into the home of Walter Scott, the branch NAACP president, more than once. But Reverend DeLaine was the red-hot focus. Employees at an Esso Shell Oil station near the DeLaines' home began harassing Mattie and Ophelia De-Laine, deliberately frightening Mattie DeLaine by slowly driving their cars behind her as she walked, once ordering her to get in. The pastor wrote the company's Columbia office to complain. On an evening when Rogers held a WCC rally in Lake City, someone threw garbage at the DeLaines' home. Four nights later vandals throwing bottles hit and broke a window. A few nights later, after honking cars passed the house, a driver returned to throw rocks. On several nights, as car caravans passed, drivers shot guns into the air. Reverend DeLaine, with his children's assistance, recorded and reported a license number but got no police response. A September WCC meeting drew seven hundred. On the first day of October, two dozen men burned a cross across the street. The night of October 5, Saint James AME burned down while Reverend DeLaine attended an AME conference in Charleston. The Reconstruction-era church, with brand new pulpit and pews, was destroyed within and its steeple and roof charred before firefighters stopped the blaze. Investigators determined arson was at fault.[167]

On October 7 the DeLaines received an anonymous letter, postmarked Lake City. "Several hundred of us have had a meeting and pleged our selves to put you where you belong, if there is such a place." The writer added, "I wonder if ever heard about the Negro Postmaster that was send to Lake City and was notified to leve. He refused. However he left, but in a coffin." This was a death threat, a reference to the 1898 murder of Frazier Baker, Lake City's first black postmaster. Eleven white men set fire to the Bakers' combined post office and home, then shot to death Baker and two-year-old Julia, held in mother Lavinia Baker's arms. Lavinia Baker was wounded, as were two daughters and a son; two other children escaped without wounds. The survivors fled to a neighbor's. The letter to Reverend DeLaine continued, "So we have decided to give you 10 days to leave Lake City and if you are not away by then rather than let you spread your filthy dirty poison here any longer. We have made plans to move you if it takes dynimite to do it. This is final."[168]

Death-Defying Escape

The minister didn't get ten days. On the night of October 10, 1955, white men gathered across the street from the DeLaine home while others in car caravans shot at the house. Mattie DeLaine peered from behind a window shade to see gunfire light the night and kick up the dirt. She fled from the back door to a neighbor's while her husband, armed, waited for the next barrage. This time, he shot back, to mark the car, a tactic he had informed the sheriff that he would use. "He was not one to mess around. When he was angry, he was cold and calculating and very calm," said Jay DeLaine. With neither wife nor belongings, Reverend DeLaine zoomed away, choosing what he thought was the safest route to Florence, twenty-four miles away. At a crossroads three men spotted him in his 1953 Mercury and dashed to their car. In the chase that followed, the pursuers and pursued flew down unlit roads, the pursuers eventually giving up.[169]

Jet magazine described the escape: "During a hectic and sleepless week-long flight from South Carolina's rabidly anti-Negro 'lowlands,' where he is a 'marked man' for his civil rights efforts, the father of three children outdistanced a revenge-bent mob of whites in a 90-mile-an-hour auto chase, hid in the cab of a huge trailer truck—whose sympathetic white driver carried him 100 miles—and flew brazenly as a 'Mr. Brown' on an airplane to reach his final destination." In fundraising speeches DeLaine described traveling at night, hiding during the day in homes, garages, and bus stations. He told a New York audience, "The cowards now operating in the name of white supremacy would lynch Christ if it would serve their ungodly purpose."

National media found the story irresistible, particularly since DeLaine's long-term safety remained in question.[170]

The stories of how he escaped multiplied. In one report attorney William Bennett, a friend and NAACP activist, spirited DeLaine from Florence to Charlotte, North Carolina. Another version had Bennett smuggling both DeLaines out of Florence, the pastor on the floor of Bennett's car, covered by a blanket and household goods, while wife Mattie DeLaine and Bennett posed as a couple on the move. In another version Reverend DeLaine flew from Charlotte to Washington, D.C., where cousin Levi DeLaine drove him to Trenton, New Jersey. Mattie DeLaine said her husband almost ran out of gas on his mad drive to Florence; his pursuers gone, he stopped at a gas station, where a sympathetic trucker told Delaine of a search underway and offered a ride to New York City. At any rate, on October 13 DeLaine wrote J. Edgar Hoover, director of the FBI, of the events and his New York whereabouts. It's possible he and friends crafted the various stories to protect those who helped him flee.[171]

Metal shards injured two of the three white men in the Lake City car that Reverend DeLaine dinged. On October 11 the car's driver, James Leroy Moore, swore out a warrant against the minister for assault and battery with a deadly weapon. Moore operated the Esso Shell Oil station near Saint James AME. Newspapers identified the injured passengers: Harry Gause, an Esso employee, and Donald Graham. Reverend DeLaine wrote the FBI: "I am not trying to dodge the FBI and I do not seek to dodge JUSTICE but I am here trying to dodge INJUSTICE." He also wrote newspapers in Charleston, Columbia, Florence, and Charlotte to say that Lake City police had failed to provide requested protection and arrived forty-five minutes after he reported gunfire. "I would have my friends and enemies know that 'Having obtained help from God I continue untill this day.'" Of his choice to return gunfire, Brumit DeLaine said his father reasoned that "God helps those who help themselves, and God gives you the resources to do what you need to do, and this was a situation where he had to act for his own protection." From his New York haven, Reverend DeLaine told supporters, "I shot in Jesus' name. I wasn't trying to kill anyone. I shot to mark the car."[172]

On the same day Reverend DeLaine was hunted, representatives of thirty-eight WCCs met in Columbia and formed the South Carolina Association of Citizens' Councils to preserve "state's sovereignty and the bi-racial society," choosing Rogers as the first executive secretary. At a Lion's Club meeting, Lt. Gov. Ernest F. Hollings praised the Elloree WCC for its efforts to preserve school segregation, calling May 17, 1954, "a day that will live in legal infamy." He reassured his audience that state laws allowed school boards to close schools as well as open them. On November 3 the Florence County grand jury returned an indictment against Reverend DeLaine for assault with a deadly weapon. The national press depicted a heroic escape from white thugs; South Carolina's white press and politicians described a fugitive fleeing justice.[173]

Bishop Reid, of Columbia, said DeLaine had to run for his life. Mattie DeLaine retreated to the Columbia home of brother Willie C. Belton, where she rested under a doctor's care for more than a week. Bennett, with the protection of police, moved the DeLaines' furniture from the Lake City home to the capital city. Another AME bishop, D. Ward Nichols, appealed to New York governor Averill Harriman "to refuse to send this man of God to an almost certain chain gang conviction and death at the hands of his enemies, the White Citizens' Council, which is nothing more or less than the Ku Klux Klan reborn." Nichols was influential, thanks to Harlem's political clout and his membership on the boards of the National Council of Churches and the World Council of Churches. He and thirty-five other AME clergymen accompanied Reverend DeLaine on December 2, when he surrendered to New York authorities. Released under bond, he resided under Nichols's supervision, so his location was public knowledge. The bishop predicted, "Rev. DeLaine will never return to the South—either as a fugitive from justice or a preacher."[174]

He was right. The South Carolina minister became a cause célèbre. The National Council of Churches, the American Jewish Congress, and baseball great Jackie Robinson made appeals for Reverend DeLaine's safety. Nichols said, "I gave him asylum in the same way we give refugees from Europe asylum. Reverend DeLaine was a refugee from a foreign country within the confines of the U.S." The Justice Department dodged involvement, saying the situation didn't fit the federal fugitive law. South Carolina sent arrest papers, but when New York didn't honor the warrant, the governor decided not to pursue an extradition request. "In my opinion, South Carolina is well rid of this professional agitator," said Gov. George Bell Timmerman Jr. in the new year. The governor said he wanted to prevent the NAACP from using Reverend DeLaine for fundraising or, in a trial, for propaganda. A week later the state WCC named Moore man of the year because he "rid this state of a professional agitator."[175]

White officials at all levels kept declaiming defense of segregation. The governor promised "no compulsory racial mixing in our state." State senator L. Marion Gressette, who headed the aptly nicknamed Segregation

Committee, vowed, "There will be no integration of any kind in South Carolina." White residents of Summerton agreed in a meeting that court-ordered admissions of black children would result in schools being closed. The Manning WCC, which counted McCord among its founding members, sent a warning letter to black Summerton leaders. The Presbyterian minister wrote a sixteen-paragraph letter, published on the *Columbia Record*'s front page, that linked the NAACP and integration to Satan. He defended the WCC's stance as godly, writing, "We stand definitely and firmly against the mixing of races in schools and churches."[176]

Reverend Richburg received threats from the Klan, which promised him a kidnapping and horsewhipping. Following a Klan rally, a five-foot cross burned in front of the Manning Training School. Four shotgun blasts, fired from a moving vehicle into the Fleming-DeLaine Funeral Home in Manning, left more than 270 pellet holes but didn't harm the sleeping Billie Fleming, a cousin of Reverend DeLaine's. White bosses ordered black workers on area plantations not to use Fleming's hearse or funeral home. As was common in rural areas, Fleming's hearse also served as an ambulance, but hospitals refused the sick their medical care if they arrived in his vehicle.[177]

This was just the start of another wave of misery. In Elloree, Sumter, and Orangeburg, the WCC's unrelenting pressure on black petitioners led many to withdraw their names—fourteen of seventeen succumbed in the Santee area of Elloree School District. In Sumter the school district's attorney sued local NAACP leaders who publicly challenged signature retractions obtained by the attorney. "The membership of the NAACP has been so secret in the past that the petitions will now serve to identify a Negro as a probable member of the organization," crowed Rogers.[178]

Roy Wilkins, named executive secretary of the NAACP in 1955, granted the *Columbia Record* an interview in September. Asked why people wanted their names removed from desegregation petitions, Wilkins said petitions most often were signed during public meetings "at which the whole purpose was explained." Citing "economic pressures" on petitioners, such as job loss, he explained that "some of them claim misunderstanding as an out." Wilkins asserted, "It is difficult to believe that any literate Negro did not understand what the situation was." He added, recalling Judge Parker's phrase, "The NAACP will not be satisfied with voluntary segregation. Asking Negroes to accept voluntary segregation is asking them to accept less than the courts have said they are entitled to." Wilkins and Marshall repeatedly pointed out that a constitutional right had been established, and South Carolina continued to ignore it. In December in the *Crisis,* the official publication of the

NAACP, Wilkins wrote about violent responses to *Brown I* and *II.* "Negroes have been the immediate victims," but the real target was the nation and its Constitution, he believed. "It is a war against the right of petition, against legal redress of grievances, against the exercise of the franchise, and against equality under the law."[179]

According to Clarendon County attorneys and school officials, desegregation of the student population—2,799 black students and 295 white students—would require admitting a few white students to all-black schools, and officials would close public schools before that would happen. "There is nothing the white South can do to turn the Negro back," Hinton warned in rebuttal. But white supremacists in the area were doing quite a lot.[180]

"Fire those employed by whites, run sharecroppers and tenants off farms, and terrorize the Negroes who can't be reached otherwise," observed the *Pittsburgh Courier,* which investigated WCC tactics. In Elloree white landlords told petitioners to relocate. The Orangeburg mayor, who distributed Coca-Cola, stopped deliveries to black businesses. Credit ended for the local Standard Oil Esso, whose black owners were petitioners. Gasoline delivery stopped for a Shell Station operated by a petitioner. The local Coble Dairy ended home milk delivery to petitioners. Local Sunbeam bread ended delivery to petitioners. Stores canceled accounts. "The firings have taught Negroes some valuable lessons: (1) No one should be permitted to sign petitions who can be pressurized; (2) Quality, not quantity, of petitioners is most valuable, and (3) You can't do business with Citizens' Councils," the report concluded.[181]

No Candy from Santa Claus

At year's end the Associated Press named the *Brown* decisions the top story of the year in South Carolina. Five of the top ten South Carolina news stories concerned segregation, including Reverend DeLaine's escape from the state as well as legislative action to end compulsory school attendance and delegate to local school boards pupil enrollment and assignment. Segregation remained the focus in 1956, too, a year in which resistance, repercussions, and reprisals escalated.[182]

In February 1956 Governor Timmerman signed an interposition resolution. In theory this placed the sovereignty of the state's constitution between public school officials and federal courts. The state appropriations bill contained provisions to close state parks if desegregation litigation began and to close state-supported colleges if a court ordered desegregation. In a concurrent resolution, the South Carolina legislature also asked the Justice Department to place the NAACP on a subversives list. On the same day, the legislature passed a resolution approving the founding of citizens' councils in the state to "make every legal and moral effort to maintain the segregated public schools of our State" and "continue the present American way of life."[183]

In March, Timmerman signed into law legislation prohibiting the hiring and requiring the firing of any city, county, or state employee who belonged to the NAACP. He also signed a joint resolution creating a committee to investigate NAACP activity at South Carolina State College, the only state-supported college for black students. The governor and senators Thurmond and Johnston attended a statewide WCC rally in Columbia. Thurmond and Johnston often attended WCC meetings, and Thurmond spoke at them. The unrelenting pressure on black activists escalated with the rise of the WCC and politicians' hostile focus on NAACP members, variously described as outside agitators and communist or Jewish conspirators.[184]

Someone fired shots again into Fleming's Manning home and into Walter Scott's Lake City home. On October 2 Reverend Seals's home was destroyed by fire while he was visiting his wife in Brooklyn. "They got my teaching job, and they fired my wife, too, but we ain't quivering," he had told an *Afro-American* reporter in 1954. Despite being denied credit or work to supplement his church income, despite the end of his pig farm, despite Reverend DeLaine's departure, Reverend Seals hadn't paused. But the loss of his home, which was underinsured, and its furnishings, which were not insured, devastated him. Gloster Current wrote Wilkins that antagonism and pressure had concentrated on the Summerton minister in recent years, resulting in Reverend Seals's sending his thirteen-year-old grandson to New York to escape the constant threats. The pastor had little left. But he told his grandson that God had called him, so he had to stay.[185]

Evidently no punishment felt too petty, including Santa Claus's surprise refusal to distribute candy and fruit to black children along Christmas parade routes or the fence Lee Richardson's white neighbor built to block Richardson's only access to his home and farm. "Here what the White Peoples saying You Negroes are making it hard for us and we going to make it hard for you," wrote L. A. Blackman, NAACP branch president in Elloree. But the councils' "squeeze" eventually boomeranged. After all, Clarendon and Orangeburg Counties were majority black. Businesses participating in the WCC members' refusals of jobs, goods, or credit said goodbye to the majority of their workers, customers, and debtors.[186]

The WCC had distributed lists of petitioners and NAACP members, asking white business owners to deny service or credit. So in Orangeburg, Elloree, and Summerton, black activists distributed lists of WCC members or sympathizers, asking neighbors and friends to boycott their products or stores and to refuse to work in their fields. The *South Carolina Independent*, a four-page publication, exhorted, "The economic squeeze can be operated from both ends," and suggested techniques, such as buying only from black-owned businesses and starting cooperatives. At South Carolina State, students staged a walkout, hanged a legislator and the governor in effigy, and boycotted food and drink products distributed by WCC members on or off campus.[187]

The state NAACP temporarily held a fifty-thousand-dollar reserve fund at Victory Savings Bank in Columbia, available for loans to those who lost their jobs or were threatened with the loss of homes or land. Modjeska Monteith Simkins, state NAACP corresponding secretary, had worked with and housed Marshall during his *Briggs v. Elliott* work. She used the family-owned bank to provide financial support and coordinated relief efforts. She even hauled goods in a trailer. Sympathy outside the state led to "mercy caravans," care packages, and truckloads of food and clothing, distributed by Reverend Richburg. Three truckloads of food and clothing for Orangeburg and Clarendon county residents arrived on the same day the general assembly barred NAACP members from holding municipal, county, or state jobs.[188]

Henry McDonald drove back and forth to Washington and New York City to pick up loads of food and clothing. "He stayed with it through the suffering," said daughter Shirley McDonald Patterson. "He was going to take a stand; that was his word. He said it was time, and it was right." In Elloree so many donations arrived that Blackman, the NAACP branch president, built a warehouse. Relief there went first to NAACP members, and thus membership increased rather than dwindled. At year's end Blackman described the economic pressure as "the best thing for unifying us."[189]

The financial assistance saved a few. In 1957 white farmers refused to rent harvesting equipment to Clarendon farmers identified as petitioners or NAACP members. Crops rotted in the fields. Hammett Pearson and Fleming made personal appeals locally to no avail. Subsequently about eighty black farmers formed the Clarendon County Improvement Association (CCIA), supported by the NAACP, the National Committee for Rural Schools, retired Judge Waring, and others, and administered by Fleming. With more than one hundred thousand dollars in assets, the CCIA made loans for seed, fertilizer, insecticide, and farm implements to more than 150 families. McCray wrote, "The victims failed to starve to death, failed to change their minds on integration and, instead of getting down in spirit and beaten and begging, learned they could display more independence than ever before, another thing the WCC leaders hadn't counted on." The CCIA's thirteen local directors included the tenacious Jesse and Hammett Pearson and Reverend Seals. This made others bolder. One man told McCray, "To hell with them. The NAACP takes care of us."[190]

South Carolina's schools remained segregated. In July 1958 eight Clarendon County parents signed petitions to desegregate schools in Manning and east Clarendon. The petitions asked school officials to take "immediate steps to reorganize the public schools in your jurisdiction on a nondiscriminatory basis." Lincoln C. Jenkins Jr., the Columbia attorney who filed the paperwork, said these were not NAACP petitions. "The time for procrastination has passed," said Jenkins's letter. School officials answered that the schools operated in accordance with existing South Carolina laws, and they expected no changes in law. That was where the matter stopped.[191]

An editorial in The State summarized white officials' reasoning: "It would be a great tragedy to do anything that would cause schools to close." State law decreed that an integrated school lost its public funds, as did the school from which the student transferred. The State argued that anyone pushing desegregation was not asserting rights as a citizen nor complying with a Supreme Court order but, instead, was hurting "the innocent children." An Associated Press review at the start of the 1958–9 school year found 777 of approximately 3,000 southern school districts had desegregated. However, "a solid wall of school segregation has been maintained in Alabama, Florida, Georgia, Louisiana, South Carolina, Mississippi, and Virginia." Deep South legislatures had passed more than two hundred laws to preserve segregation.[192]

In July 1959 Jenkins and parents tried a different tactic. In Summerton eighteen parents asked for their children's reassignment to white schools. The district now had one all-white and one all-black high school and one all-white and three all-black elementary schools. In Manning ten parents asked for their children's reassignment. Some of the 1947–51 petitioners, still with schoolchildren at home, dared sign again: Annie Gibson, Joseph Hilton, Mary Oliver, Levi Pearson, William Ragin, Lee Richardson, and Lucrisher Richardson. The school boards blocked the requests by not meeting before school started.[193]

On September 7, 1959, Jenkins simultaneously filed parents' reassignment requests with the board chairmen of all three Clarendon districts. Fifty-one students wanted reassignment to white schools. Thirteen years had passed since parents asked for a bus. Five years had passed since the Supreme Court ruled public school desegregation unconstitutional in *Brown I*. Clarendon County had not produced a plan to desegregate. Governor Hollings was the third South Carolina governor to resist the *Brown* decisions. Evidently equating black parents with World War II's Axis powers and channeling British prime minister Winston Churchill, he vowed, "We'll fight the enemy at the crossroads and the hedgepaths."[194]

In November 1961 Reverend DeLaine asked the NAACP to assist Harry Briggs, who was living in New York City. Reverend DeLaine, who preferred going straight to the top, wrote to Wilkins. At this point he had soured on the NAACP. He began his letter, "I regret that I now am beginning to doubt and get bitter because of your neglect of the extreme CASUALTIES from the legal battles which have made the NAACP great." He listed what he had done between 1943 and 1950, then scolded the NAACP for not seeing Harry Briggs Sr. as "a symbol of victory which is not yet fully realized" and a "reminder to the hate mongers." He listed Briggs's achievements: opening his home to the 1949 petition signing, allowing the family's names to be first on the petition, refusing to retract his signature, and accepting the consequences. "Harry Briggs name is widely known in South Carolina and he doesn't have a dog's chance to make a living there," wrote Reverend DeLaine. Now the pastor of Calvary AME in Brooklyn, he wanted the NAACP to underwrite purchasing a New York home for the family.[195]

Since 1957 Harry Briggs Sr. had lived apart from his family off and on, sending money home. For a time Eliza Briggs and younger children Katherine, Willie Moses, and Nathaniel joined him in Florida. "We were poor," said Nathaniel Briggs. "There'd been no steady job for a long time. We moved to Florida on a Greyhound bus, with a rope tied around a suitcase, a rope tied around a box, and that was our luggage. That was our stuff." The five lasted there a year. Just Harry Briggs Sr. and Eliza Briggs stayed in Miami, while grandmother Hester Gamble cared in Summerton for Harry Jr., Thomas Lee, Katherine, Willie Moses, and Nathaniel. When Harry Jr. and Thomas Lee finished high school, the two moved to New York City to live with an uncle. Then an unpleasant return to Summerton propelled all the family to New York in 1961.[196]

Current visited the four-room apartment in the Bronx, where he met the family, including Harry Jr., twenty-one and suffering from epilepsy; Katherine, eighteen; Willie Moses, fifteen; and Nathaniel, fourteen. Current reported them a "dispirited family" in "dire need of clothing and some household goods," as well as a job for Katherine and a better job for Harry Briggs Sr., who earned $65 a week at a gas station and paid $110 a month in rent. Current provided a $200 gift for immediate needs, requested permission to send Eliza Briggs to Macy's for winter clothing, and recommended fundraising to help the family with housing. He then obtained hospital interviews for Katherine, a high school graduate who wanted to be a nurse, and a doctor to treat Harry Jr. Dealings with Reverend DeLaine unnerved Current and unsettled Wilkins, who called the minister "difficult to understand" and "caustic." Wilkins thought providing funds or assisting with mortgages "the worst possible precedent in our future relationships with families," but he did accept Current's modest recommendations and did apologize to the Briggses.[197]

In October 1962 Reverend DeLaine addressed Wilkins again, this time for Levi Pearson. Pearson, who had been hospitalized, wrote of the lasting bitterness of white people in Clarendon County, who continued to refuse him credit. "Hope you cuod Help me; send me some money. I wood send it Back to you." His request for help was no indication of regret. After his death widow Viola Pearson told Sumter's *Daily Item*, "'I'd say, 'Levi, you going out there to do that? You know how these people is, you not going to get nothing.' He'd say, 'Viola, you can say what you want, but I'm going out to sue if it leads to my grave.'" His reason: "These poor little children." Reverend DeLaine enclosed Levi Pearson's letter and praised him: "There was a time when Levi Pearson was only person with the Courage to Challenge all Clarendon County, South Carolina with the backing of the NAACP." Reverend DeLaine may have felt personally aggrieved, and he was not always diplomatic, but his main point was true: "And the ones who endured the hardness until the May 17, 1954 Decision were severely persecuted by the opposition and forgotten by the ones who appreciated the pioneering courage."[198]

As a Wilkins assistant wrote to Henry Lee Moon, public relations director of the NAACP, "The full story of the persistent and relentless prosecution of militant Negroes in South Carolina has never been told." And as Wilkins wrote to Harry Briggs Sr., perhaps in consolation, "Our association, of course, is primarily concerned with combating segregation and discrimination yet we know in situations such as yours, those who have been willing to carry on the fight have become the innocent victims of the crusade."[199]

Despite continuing lawsuits, South Carolina public schools remained segregated through a dual school system that was supported by the 1963–75 openings of more than two hundred private schools that were dubbed segregation academies. Pressure to desegregate did increase when the 1964 Civil Rights Act authorized the Department of Justice to file desegregation lawsuits and the Department of Health, Education, and Welfare to with-hold funds from segregated schools. In 1965 five black students enrolled in all-white Summerton High School under court order rather than what was called "freedom of choice," which supposedly gave all students the right to attend any school in a district. The family names of the first black students at Summerton High School were familiar: Charles Hilton, Rita Mae McDonald, Mary Oliver, Lucretia Ragin, and Leola Ragin.[200]

In 1966 Rita Mae McDonald graduated from Summerton High School, the first black student to do so. Her father, John E. McDonald, had registered her for a white school when she was in second grade, but not until her senior year could she enroll in one. McDonald drove her to school every day in his truck, a shotgun by his side. He refused a bribe to end her attendance. White classmates threw her books in trash cans, stole her class notes before exams, and excluded her from senior class functions. After McDonald and the NAACP called in the Justice Department, Rita Mae's English teacher revealed instructions to fail the senior so she couldn't graduate with her class.[201]

Not until 1970 did South Carolina's public schools desegregate. When the U.S. Fourth Circuit Court of Appeals ordered the implementation of a Department of Health, Education, and Welfare plan for the 1970–71 school year, only 24 of 2,261 black Summerton students had attended a formerly all-white school, and no white students had attended any all-black school. Before the start of the school year, the white school board closed the Summerton High School building rather than accept black students. A scholarship fund insured that impoverished white students could attend private Clarendon Hall, founded in 1965 as Summerton Baptist Church School. By 1972 one white student remained in the public schools. And that didn't change. In 1994 the brick Scott's Branch High School, the state's first "equalization school," graduated its last seniors, fifty-two black students. The student body at the new Scott's Branch High School remained black, with an occasional Hispanic student. Clarendon Hall accepted its first two black students in the 2001–2 school year and continued to be around 98 percent white.[202]

For this reason, sometimes in his later years, when anyone asked Harry Briggs Sr. what had been accomplished, he ignored the big picture. He thought of his children and the children of his friends and answered, "Nothing." The family didn't talk about the court case, but when pushed, Briggs did tell his children he would do it again. He said he would do it again because, in the long term, it was what was best for all the children.[203]

Three

Forward Motion

Cecil Augustus Ivory

Climbing high into a pecan tree, Cecil Augustus Ivory lost his grip,
fell, and fell far. A doctor told his mother he had suffered a serious spinal
injury and would not walk again. The family accepted the diagnosis; they
had no money for medical treatment. For six months Ivory lay in bed,
forever for a fourteen-year-old. Then, using two cane-bottom chairs as
crutches, Ivory dragged himself until he could step and stepped until he
could walk. He persisted until he ran—and ran a football to score.

Cecil Augustus Ivory grew up in Arkadelphia, Arkansas, a farming and lumber community of three thousand or so, referred to as the "Athens of Arkansas" for its four small colleges. Born in 1921, the third of four children, he grew up in a home without running water or electricity. He lost his father to a fever when he was a toddler. He overcame injuries from a crippling accident. A striver from the start, Ivory dreamed bigger than those around him. He feared his education would end in the tenth grade, but he wrangled a seat at Cotton Plant Academy. He finished secondary school while supporting himself through odd jobs for a local white woman. He had honed himself from bedridden child to star of the football and basketball teams, and reports of the six-foot-six athlete traveled to Rev. Byrd Randall Smith, the president of Mary Allen Junior College in Crockett, Texas. Smith offered Ivory a football-and-work scholarship. Ivory owned nothing; for his 270-mile journey his employer provided her husband's discarded clothes and a suitcase to hold them.[1]

Ivory graduated from Mary Allen in 1939. The junior college closed due to financial problems, but Smith took Ivory with him to Harbison Agricultural and Industrial Institute in Irmo, South Carolina. There Ivory did odd jobs. A professor at Johnson C. Smith University in Charlotte, North Carolina, heard of the bright Mary Allen graduate who wanted to study religion. He secured a work scholarship for Ivory, who completed his bachelor's in 1944. Ivory entered the university's seminary, graduating with a divinity degree in 1946, tops in his class and with a first prize in homiletics. In 1945 he married that professor's granddaughter, Emily Richardson, and while she finished a bachelor's in elementary education, he worked at a Merita bakery to support them. Ivory returned to Harbison, fulfilling a promise made to President T. B. Jones, another Ivory booster. For two years he served as chaplain and coached the softball and basketball teams. In October 1948 he was installed as pastor of Rock Hill's Hermon United Presbyterian Church, its Late Gothic Revival building completed in 1903 by its own members.[2]

Most residents of Rock Hill, a town of twenty-four thousand on the South Carolina–North Carolina border, held low-paying jobs, white workers in textile plants, black workers in service jobs or as sharecroppers and farmers outside town. Rock Hill did have two black dentists, several educated black ministers, and the black presidents and professors of Clinton Normal and Industrial Institute and Friendship Junior College. But race trumped any education or profession. White citizens, two-thirds of the population, ran everything. Ivory, a big man gearing up to make an outsized impact, soon rattled those in charge because he was both confrontational and likeable. To his core he believed in equality and, accompanying equality, equal opportunity. It helped that he was fearless.[3]

On May 17, 1954, the Supreme Court ended legal segregation of public schools in *Brown v. Board of Education of Topeka, Kansas,* a decision incendiary to the state's white supremacists not only for its consequences but its roots: *Briggs v. Elliott* in Summerton, South Carolina, the first of the five lawsuits comprising *Brown.* In Columbia weeks later, Sarah Mae Flemming sued South Carolina Electric and Gas Company, which operated the capital city's segregated bus system. Weeks after that, St. Anne's Parochial School in Rock Hill accepted five black children from St. Mary Catholic Church, becoming the state's first and only desegregated school, public or private. Ivory paid attention.[4]

On June 22, 1954, bus driver Warren Christmus ordered Flemming off a crowded Columbia bus when she took a second-row seat vacated by a white woman. South Carolina law and custom confined black passengers to the back of the bus, but every seat was taken. Embarrassed, Flemming stood to leave. Christmus said he stretched his arm across the aisle to prevent her departure from the front door, exclusively used by white riders. Flemming said Christmus struck her in the belly, knocking her off her feet. Friend Julia

Elizabeth King said so too; she caught Flemming as she fell. Ordered by the bus driver, "Get out, and get out through the back," Flemming and King pushed their way through passengers to the rear door. Pain afterward forced Flemming to the hospital. Bus drivers, granted special police powers to enforce segregation, freely behaved aggressively, ordering out of their seats, ejecting, or holding for arrest black customers. Daily humiliations were rife.[5]

Flemming grew up on a farm in Eastover and left secondary school to help support her six younger siblings. She rode the Columbia bus to two house-cleaning jobs. Modjeska Monteith Simkins, secretary of the state NAACP conference, connected the twenty-one-year-old to a local white attorney, who bowed out after death threats and a cross burning, and to NAACP counsel. Flemming sued, saying segregated intrastate transportation violated her Fourteenth Amendment rights to equal protection. She asked for twenty-five thousand dollars in damages. Despite the Supreme Court ruling in *Brown v. Board* that segregation was a denial of equal protection of the law, *Flemming v. South Carolina Electric and Gas Company* traveled through District Court three times, the Fourth Circuit Court of Appeals twice, and the U.S. Supreme Court once. District Judge George Bell Timmerman Sr., who dismissed the case twice, said the doctrine of "separate but equal," established in 1896 in *Plessy v. Ferguson,* held sway. He wrote that *Brown v. Board* affected public education, not public transportation, and, besides, the court had accepted "sociological and psychological factors" as grounds for desegregation. Timmerman averred, "One's education and personality is not developed on a city bus."[6]

The Fourth Circuit Court of Appeals said otherwise, that *Brown v. Board* and *Henderson v. United States,* a 1950 decision ending segregated dining cars in trains "leave no doubt that the separate but equal doctrine approved in *Plessy v. Ferguson* has been repudiated." The bus company appealed. The U.S. Supreme Court responded by sending *Flemming* back to District Court. In June 1957 an all-white, all-male jury demonstrated even less interest in Flemming's Fourteenth Amendment rights than Timmerman, who told the jury he didn't agree with the Fourth Circuit or the Supreme Court. Within thirty minutes the jury rejected NAACP counsel Matthew J. Perry's argument that Flemming "is not asking more rights than anybody else. But she does say she had the right to sit anywhere." The buses stayed segregated. The NAACP did not appeal again.[7]

Flemming and South Carolina did not capture the public's attention. Montgomery, Alabama's bus boycott, with Rosa Parks and spokesman Rev.

Dr. Martin Luther King Jr., did. Parks was arrested on December 1, 1955, for refusing to give up a bus seat. The ensuing boycott ended on December 20, 1956, following the Supreme Court's affirmation of a district court ruling that Alabama's bus segregation laws were unconstitutional. The ruling cited *Flemming*, saying "separate but equal" was "no longer a correct statement of the law." Ivory was inspired. "After the bus boycott in Montgomery, he began having ideas," said Emily Ivory.[8]

In 1957 opportunity arrived on a Rock Hill bus for Ivory, president of the NAACP's local branch since 1953. On a July evening, Addelene Austin White was riding home on the Star Bus Line. The bus filled in the back, where black riders sat and stood. "A white lady with a seat asked me to sit beside her," said White. The twenty-three-year-old accepted the invitation. Bus driver B. T. Funderburk overheard and objected. "He said, 'Get up. You can't sit there,'" said White. "I got up and said, 'Stop the bus. If I can't sit there, I'll walk.'" Incensed, White walked three miles home.[9]

Other black bus riders were upset, too, and met with Ivory that evening to ask what could be done. The next morning black workers who rode the buses showed up at the stops. But they turned their backs as buses approached. Ivory called a July 15 NAACP meeting. The possibility of a boycott percolated. Ivory met with White, who said of the driver, "He made me mad. He made me feel mistreated, so I left. I didn't mean to start a movement." Ivory told her, "When one is treated bad, it's bad for all." On July 28 pastors announced from their Sunday pulpits a mass meeting the next evening at Ivory's church.[10]

Those attending elected Ivory chairman of the Local Committee for the Promotion of Human Rights, modeled after the Montgomery Improvement Association. Big-boned, with a long face and an electric smile, delivering public talks and sermons with a compelling bass and an emphasis on a meaningful life, Ivory had earned the black community's trust and admiration. He decided a carpool was the first step: nine cars full-time, six part-time, mostly driven by black women who provided rides to work, shopping, and home. "The refusal to ride is 100 percent, where we can provide alternative transportation," Ivory told journalists. "We are law-abiding citizens. All we want is justice and the elimination of discrimination. We'd rather walk than be insulted."[11]

A formal boycott began. On the second day, a caller promised Ivory a house bombing. The man asked, "Are you the nigger preacher?" When Ivory replied, the caller said, "I just wanted to know. That's all right. You'll hear from us." The caller hung up, then called back to say, "I just wanted to know if you were still there before it goes off." Ivory said he would call the police and warned, "In case I have to shoot anybody, my arms are still good." He made that point because his past injury had reasserted itself after a tumble from a truck bed. At Duke University Hospital, in Durham, North Carolina, physicians told him a blood clot, likely from the childhood fall, had permanently disabled him. Ivory, dedicated to forward motion, found himself a sturdy wooden cane.[12]

The Star Bus Line, owned by Paul Knight, had served Rock Hill for about three years under a city franchise. Its three small buses made money, with as many as 350 riders a day, each paying thirty-five cents a ride. Knight quoted state law requiring white passengers to be seated in the front, black riders in the back, and forbidding white and black passengers from sitting side by side. "As long as I live in South Carolina, I intend to obey the laws of the state," Knight said. In an editorial Rock Hill's *Evening Herald* noted black workers were more dependent on bus service than white workers, saying the boycott showed "poor judgment."[13]

Ivory believed the strategies of the civil rights movement required the peace and love of a good Christian combined with the pragmatism of the Lord's helping those who helped themselves. He jotted notes on the backs of bank deposit slips, parsing his philosophy. On one he wrote, "We do not protest against you. We protest your evil and unjust system of segregation and discrimination. We will return your hate with love. We will endure your oppression with patience, but we will protest until death, if need be, your unjust policies."[14]

Armed with a list of grievances, Ivory asked the city council to desegregate the bus service. The council replied that only the state could do so. Knight cut off all black neighborhoods. That was pointless; Ivory estimated 90 percent of black customers had quit the Star Line. On August 3 he called for an extension of the boycott to Knight's taxi company, the Star Cab Company, saying black-owned taxis could "adequately furnish Negroes with more transportation." The ever-succinct Ivory explained, "We just got tired of being pushed around. We decided to ask for what is ours." At the second mass meeting on August 5, 178 donations totaled $160. As White pointed out, support came from folk who had experienced just what she had: disrespect and public humiliation. "The NAACP didn't call a bus boycott. The people did it."[15]

In mid-August the city council refused to order service restored or allow an integrated bus franchise, so the local black churches pooled funds and bought a used thirty-two-passenger bus. The bus, supplemented by three cars, provided rides on a half-hour schedule throughout the day. In late August Ivory estimated the transportation system averaged at least two hundred daily passengers. Drivers kept a tally by issuing tickets to passengers, who returned them with a signature and a donation at issue or during weekly Monday night meetings. Ivory didn't seek NAACP funds or attorneys. Churches around the state loaned buses and donated money, as did the national Presbyterian Church USA. The city couldn't block a free bus service. "He did the paperwork and made out a system," said Emily Ivory. "He had it organized to a tee."[16]

A second bus soon rolled through the city every day with the support of the local junior colleges and churches. "Reverend Ivory was a forerunner, a crusader. Some people are just gifted, and he could get along with all the denominations," said Horace Goggins. A Howard University graduate and U.S. Army veteran, Goggins took over a dental practice in Rock Hill in 1956 and served as NAACP branch secretary from 1959 to 1963. Every Monday at noon, Ivory, Goggins, and other committee members met to map out the week. Edward Billings and the Reverend J. C. Pate served as dispatchers; Clarence Toatley and John Robinson drove. Toatley had driven trucks in the European theater of World War II.[17]

The buses, sponsors' names painted on the side, made an important point: the black community could take care of its own. During one bus meeting, dentist Dewy M. Duckett Sr. urged participants to reduce their dependence on white people in other ways too. He observed of white businessmen, "Segregation is apparently an easy life—no competition." White was pleased to inspire people she admired, particularly Ivory. She believed he had a big heart—"If a child passed by and needed a haircut, he would buy them a haircut"—and now he was sticking up for her. White herself became a local hero: "People would scare me to death, a lady rushing out of her house, yelling, 'Wait, wait, are you the one?'"[18]

Ivory was running a church, the local NAACP, and a bus company—and fundraising for all. A popular public speaker, he traveled to other states to preach or teach to congregations, civic groups, and NAACP branches. He strategized, exhorted, and organized under the constant stress of deteriorating health. His limp gradually worsened until one morning, said Emily Ivory, "He called me into a back room and was sitting in a chair, and I said, 'What's the matter?' and he said, 'I don't know. I can't walk,' and he started crying." He barely paused. He still carried a cane but also used a wheelchair. He saved money so he could seek medical advice at research hospitals, including Johns Hopkins in Baltimore, where the blood clot was removed, and the Mayo

Rev. Cecil Augustus Ivory, who led the Rock Hill NAACP and
the Local Committee for the Promotion of Human Rights, joined the
1960 Emancipation Day Prayer Pilgrimage at the Greenville Municipal
Airport. Participants protested threats to arrest baseball star Jackie
Robinson and others for using the whites-only waiting area.
Courtesy of MIRC, University of South Carolina, Columbia

Clinic in Rochester, Minnesota, where he was fitted for braces. He continued
to drive, using his cane to accelerate and brake, until he could afford to add
hand controls. He assigned each of his three young children—daughter Darnell and sons Cecil Junior and Titus—a place behind his wheelchair to push.
He asked friends, particularly right-hand man Thomas Murdock, a former
Detroit union organizer as big as Ivory, to get him in and out of cars and
buildings.[19]

Ivory's dedication and perseverance earned goodwill. Black leaders knew
him as a minister, president of a literary society, and a member of Kappa
Alpha Psi fraternity and the Utopia Club, as well as NAACP branch president. White leaders knew him as a member of the biracial Rock Hill Council on Human Relations and a frequent correspondent with the mayor and
city council, although his appeals for a biracial committee to consider the

morality and ethics of segregation repeatedly failed. Once Goggins bought tickets to a match with local boxer Joe Louis Adams and discovered they were for the white section. "I called Rev. Ivory and said, 'They need to change our tickets.' He said, 'We ain't changing a damn thing. We ain't changing nothing.' He was a rev who could use all the words," said Goggins. "A whole lot of people were there, and we rolled in and right by, and the blacks were looking at us, and the whites were looking at us, and believe it or not, no one said anything to us."[20]

"Freedom Is Our Total Goal"

Ivory's activism also prompted hostility. Willie T. Buckingham wrote Ivory to warn that his name had been "placed on our list," because "our organization is for the purpose of dealing with and singleing out just such characters as you." Buckingham added, "Do not forget the white men in this nation can make any president they choose, they can elect Congress to vote to their dictates, and abolish the Supreme Court if it becomes necessary." Anonymous writers didn't hesitate to employ every pejorative possible: "We white people don't want to eat next to you coons, nor do we want our children going to the same school with you shines, nor do we in any way wish to socialize with you jigs!" Another anonymous writer, citing Ivory's Local Committee for the Promotion of Human Rights, asked the York County delegation to investigate these "self-appointed professional Negro agitators," who practiced "rabblerousing, Racebaiting, undermining tactics."[21]

Rock Hill's Ku Klux Klan, with a membership of 500, began recruiting teens. The Klan had faded in the area between 1952 and 1954, with 101 members convicted for flogging or kidnapping people. They were back. The local klavern held rallies outside town, attended by up to 1,000; marched downtown; and, after a November 1956 preelection extravaganza of nine crosses burning throughout York County, continued cross burnings in black neighborhoods. Emily Ivory said of her husband, "Some of his followers were fearful, but he never showed any fear at all. He got a pistol, and he would carry it around, and every night he put the pistol on the night table. Some whites would give him calls and say they were coming, and he always said, 'Let them come.'"[22]

By year's end the Star Bus Line was broke and closed. Owner Knight left town. Black workers continued to ride for free or a self-determined donation. A *Pittsburgh Courier* reporter described two children watching a bus pass and announcing proudly, "There goes *our* bus." This flipped the conventions of the day. Black workers had transportation; white workers didn't. "We're waiting for the other people to agree to obey the law of the land," said Ivory.[23]

The daily injuries of racism continued. In May 1959 a Rock Hill officer arrested a young black man for public drunkenness. He had little sight in one eye, and the officer stuck him so violently in his functioning eye that it had to be removed. In a letter to the newspaper, Ivory cited another incident in which police severely beat a young woman confined in their car. Ivory asked that officers "use handcuffs more and billets and/or blackjacks less" and that the city buy a patrol wagon. Following the 1959 Christmas parade, Ivory commended parade officials but added, "It is regrettable, however, that some misinformed innocent (I trust) young white boys had to cast a blot upon this sacred event, in their attempt to mimic the Negro with faces blackned, mop in hands and utterances such as 'Liza I have told you.' I want to believe that the parents of these children did not know of their actions."[24]

In 1960 Ivory seized another opportunity. On Monday, February 1, 1960, four students from the Agricultural and Technical College of North Carolina sat at a segregated lunch counter in Greensboro's F. W. Woolworth, waiting to be served. On Tuesday twenty waited. By Thursday, at sixty-three of the sixty-six stools, black students waited for service. The next week sit-ins spread throughout North Carolina. Ivory immediately met with students of Friendship, the black Baptist junior college. He arranged training in nonviolent direction action from James Thomas McCain Sr., a field secretary for the Congress of Racial Equality (CORE). With a visit and a nod from Rev. Isaiah DeQuincey Newman, field director for the state NAACP, Ivory helped students plan the state's first organized sit-in. On February 12, as many as 150 young black men and women, most Friendship students, entered Woolworth and McCrory's variety stores and Phillip's and Good's drugstores before noon.[25]

At Woolworth white waitresses wiped the counter with ammonia-soaked rags. At Phillip's a white man knocked to the floor the young black man who tried to sit by him. At Good's someone in the white crowd outside threw an ammonia bomb into the store. A hostile crowd kept growing. White bystanders cursed and kicked a female student. Bomb threats forced evacuation. The stores closed at 1:45 P.M. Police escorted the students back to Friendship. That didn't deter Ivory or Abe Plummer, president of the new Friendly Student Civic Committee, founded to run the sit-ins.[26]

Ivory approached the students and their movement the way he approached getting off his sickbed and onto the football field: keep moving toward the goal. In mid-February he and three students attended a student coordinating meeting in Durham, where Reverend King spoke. On February 23 the Rock Hill stores reopened their lunch counters. Students returned at noon, more of them than the stores could hold, thanks to reinforcement from Clinton and Emmett Scott High School. This time the counters were roped off; only white patrons were allowed to pass. Several black students went under the ropes anyway, and white men wrestled one student to the floor while a police officer stood by. On the streets angry white demonstrators threatened the students with weapons such as baseball bats. Afterward Ivory met with the city's police chief, who warned that he would arrest sit-in leaders "if the demonstrations got out of hand." The lunch counters closed again. On February 29 Ivory held a mass meeting attended by seven hundred to nine hundred. The community supported the student demonstrations, he said, and if necessary would end support of any institutions fostering segregation and discrimination.[27]

Students continued to march downtown and picket—with Ivory. "He would come down the streets with the students," his big hands moving his wheelchair quickly, said Fred Roukos Sheheen, a reporter for the *Charlotte Observer*. But underneath Ivory's fervor lurked suffering from pressure sores and swelling. An observer told Emily Ivory, "Your husband really is determined to eliminate segregation from the face of the world." This was so. "'Rev.' Ivory was always out front. He was willing to sacrifice his life, but he kept us nonviolent," said Willie McCleod, a Friendship protestor. "He would always remind us that we don't fight, and he had a way of organizing. He would put an idea out there, and you felt in your heart it would be the right thing to do."[28]

Each Sunday, Ivory held rallies for the students. "They would raise money, honor the students, Cecil would preach, there were lots of songs, and they would go back out and get arrested again," said Sheheen. Rock Hill set the pace for other communities: students protested almost daily and remained nonviolent, in no small part because of Ivory's guidance and— unlike unnerved or disapproving adults elsewhere—his participation. At month's end frequent bomb threats interrupted Friendship students' sleep and studies. Undeterred, on March 15 Ivory and Plummer intensified the protests. Seventy-one Friendship students sang and picketed at city hall or occupied bus waiting rooms, half of the protesters women, everyone arrested as intended. The five at the bus terminals were charged with trespass, the rest with breach of peace. Ivory posted their bonds, $1,455 worth. Afterward 1,100 supporters attended a countywide mass meeting at Ralph W. McGirt

Auditorium to honor Ivory, Plummer, and the seventy other students. The theme: "Freedom Is Our Total Goal."[29]

Somehow Ivory also squeezed in a master's from International Theological Seminary in Atlanta. In May 1960 Johnson C. Smith University awarded him an honorary doctor of divinity with this praise: "He is a minister with the courage of a lion, the tenacity of a bull, the endurance of a camel, the sagacity of an elephant and as many lives as a cat." In service to others, "he has taken the wrinkles of the soul of his people, put marrow in their bones, iron in their spinal column and urged them to walk with head erect with the dignity and prestige of first-class citizens."[30]

On June 7, 1960, Ivory took a turn getting arrested, accompanied by Arthur Hamm Jr., a Friendship student and burly U.S. Army veteran. The two visited McCrory's shortly before noon. Ivory bought a trash can and notebook paper; he invited Hamm for coffee and a sandwich. At the lunch counter, Ivory parked his wheelchair, and Hamm took a counter seat. The waitress didn't serve them, but the manager came over to chat until the police arrived. Officer John Hunsucker Jr. told the manager to ask Ivory and Hamm to leave while he listened. Ivory refused to leave; he pointed out that he had made store purchases. Hunsucker said there would be no discussion, just an arrest if the two men didn't depart. Ivory objected to the threatened arrest. After all, he wasn't occupying a counter seat and had been served twice before coming to the counter. Ivory even offered to depart if the store would provide a purchase refund.[31]

Hunsucker announced the two were under arrest and grimly pushed Ivory in his wheelchair to the police station. Hamm "submitted peacefully to arrest" by a second officer, Ivory wrote Lawrence Still at *Jet* magazine. But Hamm was treated like "a desperate criminal," the officer "catching him in the belt and pushing sometimes lifting his two hundred pounds off the ground" as he ushered Hamm out of the store. The two were charged with trespass, their bonds set at one hundred dollars each.[32]

Days later Ivory accompanied Revs. W. R. Jones and Ida Watson as they made purchases at McCrory's and Woolworth and were refused food service. Ivory said he would continue "until we get what we want." Impressed, the national NAACP presented Ivory a special citation honoring "outstandingly courageous and inspiring leadership of his people" as "Leader of Bus Boycott" and "Counselor to Student Sit-Ins." The state conference awarded Ivory a certificate of merit for the Rock Hill branch's "courageous and unselfish service." At the annual meeting, NAACP stalwart Simkins told the crowd, "'Here's a man in a wheelchair, can't use either one of his legs, and he did more than any of you with all those legs,' and the crowd went wild," said Goggins.[33]

The hurly-burly dominated home too. "The *Huntley-Brinkley Report* team would call to the house to get news. The national president of the NAACP would come by. I never knew how many people I would have for dinner," said Emily Ivory, who cooked in the morning before teaching school then fed whoever arrived that evening. "Or my mother would call to the house and ask for me, and my husband was at the jail, and we'd laugh about it. People would ask the children, 'Where's your daddy?' and one would say, 'He's in jail.' It was serious, and yet it was funny."[34]

On January 31, 1961, ten young men sat at the McCrory's counter while five young women picketed outside. Police arrested all and later released the women. But the young men did not post bail and, after a night in jail, were convicted of trespass and sentenced to thirty days on a road gang or one hundred dollars each. The nine Friendship students and Thomas Walter Gaither, a recent Claflin University graduate and new CORE field secretary, rewrote the script. This new twist was tagged "jail, no bail." They were packed off to York County Prison Camp—without Ivory, who supported them all the way.

"I remember the day we were arrested, he cried because they wouldn't arrest him," said Clarence Graham, one of the group. "He tried his best to get out of the chair. He said, 'Hold on; hold on.'" Ivory dashed off a note to Gaither at the prison camp: "I mean it when I say I will come in and stay with you running a red light or speeding will accomplish this—keep the faith my fellow comrades." Gaither and eight of the Friendship students completed their work sentences, hacking weeds, digging ditches, loading dump trucks with sand. They inspired support from the Student Nonviolent Coordinating Committee (SNCC), formed in 1960 to coordinate nonviolent direct action. Four SNCC volunteers traveled from Atlanta to Rock Hill to sit in and also refuse bail and accept jail. Briefly national stars of the sit-in movement, the Friendship Nine's "jail, no bail" tactic spread to other cities. It cost the system not only monetarily but also morally when officials locked up well-dressed, textbook-reading, nonviolent students for requesting a cup of coffee at a lunch counter. James Farmer, national director of CORE, wrote Ivory that he represented essential "organizational cooperation," referring to competitive tensions between the NAACP and CORE that Ivory miraculously erased. Farmer added, "We have been greatly inspired by your own willingness to face arrest in this fight. With such dedication, victory is bound to be ours."[35]

That same month Rock Hill's White Citizens' Council (WCC) attracted five hundred white supporters to the local high school. A southern movement of white segregationists intent on using their control of the economy—through firings, evictions, denying sales, and denying or calling in loans—to punish activists, the WCC spread throughout South Carolina after its 1954 post-*Brown* founding in Mississippi. Rev. L. B. McCord told the crowd, "We are at war." McCord, a Presbyterian minister, had played a role in attempts to block *Briggs v. Elliott* while education superintendent in Clarendon County. Speaking as the WCC's newly elected state executive secretary, he cited a warning by J. Edgar Hoover, director of the FBI, that communists had picked the pulpit to accomplish their ends, hence activists such as Ivory. Farley Smith, the former state executive secretary, spoke after McCord. Criticizing Ivory and others, Smith said, "Any minister who leads a sit-in, kneel-in, wade-in or any other kind of an 'in' is a sinner before God. How can a minister lead people to break the last commandment I do not understand. That last commandment is 'Thou shalt not covet,' and when they are leading these people in these kinds of acts, they are teaching them to covet."[36]

Neither a communist nor covetous—his suit sleeves and pants always too short, his wheelchair basic—Ivory operated on a few evenhanded, common-sense tenets: If we do not qualify, do not accept us. If we do qualify, do not reject us because of the color of our skin. We do not protest against you. We protest your evil and unjust system of segregation and discrimination. How can you claim to love God, whom you have not seen, when you mistreat me, your brother, whom you see every day? "He was a born leader, and whatever he said, people did," said Emily Ivory. "They had so much faith in him."[37]

Ivory's nonstop activism, which kept him in his wheelchair night and day, imperiled his health. He wasn't just out front; he was the engine. A group of black teachers who donated to the NAACP said they were behind him—but way behind. Fellow ministers provided back up, but as one acknowledged, they lacked his "guts." Ivory knew the physical cost of unceasing devotion, but he didn't slow down. In March he wrote Levi G. Byrd, who led the Chesterfield County NAACP and had pushed founding a state conference, "We will win in due season if we do not give up."[38]

Any time Ivory managed to save a thousand dollars and a few days, he sought another medical expert's advice. He found no cure. In March 1961 the State Highway Department revoked his driver's license. In April and May, volunteers got him to city council meetings, where he pushed again for a biracial group to discuss issues such as "protection of the nonviolent Negro against the lawless white" and the establishment of an integrated bus line.[39]

On May 9, into Rock Hill rode the Freedom Riders. Organized by CORE, Freedom Riders rode Trailways and Greyhound buses through the Deep South, desegregating bus seating and terminal lobbies, restrooms, and restaurants. CORE designed the ride after the 1960 Supreme Court ruling in *Boynton v. Virginia* that the Interstate Commerce Act of 1887 banned all segregation on all public transportation. Gaither, CORE's scout for the bus routes, warned of Rock Hill's violent reactions to the sit-ins and its active KKK.[40]

The 1961 Freedom Ride—beginning on May 4 in Washington, D.C., and uneventful until the arrest of one participant in Charlotte—found violent opposition in Rock Hill. Entering Greyhound's bus depot that morning were John Lewis, twenty-one, a recent graduate of American Baptist Theological Seminary in Nashville and among the leaders of its sit-in movement, and Albert Bigelow, sixty-one, white, a U.S. Navy veteran, and a school administrator. As they walked toward the whites-only waiting room, hostile young men quit the lobby's pinball machines to confront them. One pointed Lewis toward the "colored" waiting room, and when Lewis cited his constitutional rights, two clobbered him, pounding him to the floor. Bigelow stepped between Lewis and the assailants. They beat him to his knees. Then Genevieve Hughes, twenty-seven—white, the first woman on CORE's staff, and one of three female riders—stepped up. They knocked her to the floor. At that point a police officer intervened.[41]

When other officers arrived, the three—Lewis cut and bleeding around his eyes and mouth, Bigelow and Hughes bruised—declined to press charges. Instead they joined fellow riders in desegregating the restaurant before heading to Friendship. That afternoon Ivory awaited the Trailways riders. His cadre rushed to them as, across the street, carloads of white men shouted threats. Ivory just glared. The white men followed the Freedom Riders and their protectors a few blocks, but the riders arrived safely at Friendship, where they spoke at a rally. They ate dinner at Ivory's home. The next morning they desegregated the whites-only waiting rooms of both terminals before their departure.[42]

A week later Ivory announced something he had promised: two black applicants to Winthrop University, a Rock Hill public college for white women. From June through October 1961, Ivory was hospitalized with pressure ulcers so severe they extended into muscle and bone. He returned home to die, killed by an infection on November 10, 1961. He was forty years old. The *Evening Herald* conceded the loss: "C.A. Ivory was a Negro. He was dedicated to the improvement of the lot of the Negro. He went about his work with quiet dignity and deep conviction. He believed passionately that the cause was decent and just and right. There are those who would disagree with him. But he stood for the advancement of his race and he provided courageous leadership for his people."[43]

The sit-ins continued, but his bus line ended. "His death was like a fire that went out," said Emily Ivory, describing the family's and the movement's loss. "He felt it was not the work of God that we should be humiliated, that we should be segregated. There was a certain amount God could do, but we had to do the rest for ourselves."[44]

Four

"Whatever They Call You, That's Not Your Name"

Student Sit-Ins

On Monday, Feb. 1, 1960, at 4:30 P.M., four students from the North Carolina Agricultural and Technical College in Greensboro sat down at a lunch counter after making purchases at the F. W. Woolworth Co. on South Elm Street. The downtown five-and-dime served breakfast and lunch at a counter where white customers sat and black customers stood. The L-shaped counter with its padded swiveling stools seated sixty-six and was the store's moneymaker. Freshmen Ezell Blair Jr., Franklin McCain, Joseph McNeil, and David Richmond stayed seated just past the store's 5:30 P.M. closing, then left by the side entrance. A few white customers muttered racial slurs; one white man asked them to pass the salt; two white women approached to offer encouragement.[1]

They were not the first black people to sit in protest where only white people were seated and served. The Congress of Racial Equality (CORE), founded by an interracial group of students in Chicago, used the sit-in tactic from May 1942 forward, in the South as well as the North. They used the label "tests" for the dining efforts of their small groups of white and black members, who regularly attempted to eat together at dime-store, drugstore, and department-store counters. CORE achieved some success in the early 1950s in St. Louis, Baltimore, and Pittsburgh. CORE also tried to desegregate swimming pools, theaters, and barber shops. In 1950 sit-ins led by Mary Church Terrell in Washington, D.C., resulted in the Supreme Court ruling in 1953 that segregated eating establishments there were unconstitutional. In 1955–58, college students in Orangeburg, South Carolina, occasionally marched downtown to Orange Cut Rate Drugs and dime stores, where they would try to take a seat at a soda fountain or lunch counter.[2]

In 1958–59, members of youth councils with the National Association for the Advancement of Colored People (NAACP) held sit-ins at lunch counters and attempted attendance at white churches in Kansas and Oklahoma cities. They succeeded in negotiating service at three dozen stores. From March through September 1959, CORE staged sit-ins at downtown Miami's five-and-dime stores, beginning with W. T. Grant Company, followed by J. G. McCrory's. The CORE sit-ins expanded to include lunch counters at Woolworth, S. H. Kress and Company, Walgreen Company, three department stores, and the Royal Castle, where a two-bite hamburger sold for fifteen cents. Some of these sit-ins involved as many as eighty participants. Two CORE field secretaries coordinated the Miami efforts: Gordon R. Carey, who was white, and James Thomas "Nooker" McCain Sr., who was black and a native of Sumter, South Carolina. White Miamians beat up Carey and two others, but Carey found hope in the white customers who continued eating while seated next to CORE members.[3]

This round, the tactic caught fire. In 1960 in Greensboro, national interest was piqued by who the demonstrators were: mannerly, well-dressed college students. And interest was piqued by what they did: quietly and peacefully attempt to occupy a counter seat. How they did so also caught interest: a persistent approach that included first buying inexpensive toiletries in the store followed by asking for coffee at the counter, purchases in hand. Upon refusal of dining service, they pointed out that they had already received store service and then sat quietly in their overcoats, waiting for the food that never came. Over a few weeks, the next generation of civil rights activists—teens and young adults unsatisfied with the legal focus of their parents' generation and unsettled by their limited future—decided to take matters into their own hands.

The first Greensboro sit-in occurred after a refusal of service. McNeil had been turned away from the counter of the local Greyhound Bus Depot. He didn't shrug it off, instead debating with Blair about next steps. McNeil proposed asking for food at the Woolworth's counter and, if refused, continuing to sit. The students informed two NAACP advisers. The adults contacted CORE because of its reputation for nonviolent direct action, and Carey packed his bags. On Tuesday twenty-seven men and four women from North Carolina AT&T returned to Woolworth. Dressed in their Sunday best, they sat and read their textbooks from 10 A.M. to 12:30 P.M. The students again occupied seats without being served. Blair said that black adults had been "complacent and fearful," so "it [was] time for someone to wake up and change the situation."[4]

On February 3 students occupied all but three of the seats; participants included black and white women from Bennett College and Woman's College of North Carolina. Waitresses occupied the remaining seats. "Business at the luncheon counter came to a virtual standstill as waitresses ignored the Negro students," reported the *Greensboro Daily News*. At the time twenty-six states, none in the South, had local or state laws forbidding discrimination on a racial basis. A Woolworth spokesperson said the company's policy was to abide by local custom. Malcolm Seawell, the state attorney general, said that he knew of no North Carolina law that prohibited serving members of both races at a lunch counter; neither did he know of any state law that would force a private business to serve anybody the owner did not choose to serve.[5]

On February 4 black high school students joined the effort, but young white men came, too, and blocked the aisles, taking seats and taunting the students. One poured a cola over a demonstrator's head. As the week drew to a close, more students participated in the sit-ins, including white students from Guilford College. But more antagonists appeared, too, including members of a Ku Klux Klan splinter group. On Friday white men sat in all the seats. Dozens of police stood by. They arrested one white man for setting fire to a black student's coat, one for drunkenness, and one for disorderly conduct and escorted out others because of abusive language.[6]

On Saturday, February 6, about 1,400 students showed up at an auditorium rally, and about 1,000 headed downtown. As many as 600 crowded into Woolworth. People stood three-deep at the counter, vying for seats. At lunchtime the North Carolina AT&T football team arrived, wearing letter jackets and carrying small American flags. A little after 1 P.M., a false bomb threat led to Woolworth's closing. When the crowd shifted to Kress, it, too, was closed. Police arrested twenty-one protesters, charging them with trespassing. That evening Woolworth and Kress announced a temporary shutdown of their lunch counters, and the students announced a two-week halt to permit negotiations with city officials.[7]

The hiatus in Greensboro was filled by a flurry of demonstrations in cities throughout North Carolina: Durham, Winston-Salem, Fayetteville, Charlotte, Raleigh, High Point, and Elizabeth City. In High Point about fifty high school students participated, and a fight ended in the arrest of one white and two black youths. Durham's first sit-in, on February 8 at Woolworth, ended midday with a bomb threat and one of four white sit-in participants being taken into protective custody.[8]

On February 9 Joseph Charles Jones, a theology graduate student at Johnson C. Smith University, spoke for 150 students in Charlotte's first sit-ins at eight downtown stores. Jones, who soon joined demonstrations in Rock Hill, South Carolina, twenty-five miles away, told reporters, "Of course this movement here and those in Greensboro, Winston-Salem and Durham are interrelated in that they are a part of my race's efforts to secure God-given rights. But they are not part of a plan and were undertaken independently. We did not consult with groups or individuals at the other schools. There is no organization behind us."[9]

CORE's Carey traveled by bus to Durham because Greensboro lunch counters had closed and the students said they didn't want what they considered outside advice. On February 9 Carey was arrested but not charged during sit-ins at Woolworth and Kress. McCain, who had been on jury duty in Sumter, reached Rock Hill, where sit-in plans were underway despite furor in some North Carolina cities. On February 10 students held sit-ins in Raleigh, the state capital. There whites threw raw eggs at sit-in participants, a false alarm summoned fire trucks, and one store closed when whites outside made their way inside, shoving the store manager and assistants. Within two hours at least seven stores closed their lunch counters, but not before a white man ground his burning cigar on a female protester's back.[10]

Two days later Raleigh police arrested forty-one students from Shaw University and St. Augustine College for a sit-in at a shopping center and for merely setting foot there. Carey made the point that students were willing to be arrested and would continue their protests. He predicted the sit-ins would spread north to Virginia and south to South Carolina. And so they did, faster and farther than anyone might have dreamed, speeding by month's end north into Tennessee, where Nashville's students had been planning sit-ins for months, and Virginia and Maryland, and south into South Carolina, Florida, and Alabama.[11]

On February 12, thanks to students at Friendship Junior College and the assistance of McCain, Rock Hill became the first town in South Carolina to experience an organized sit-in. The Associated Press reported that "a passive resistance movement by Negroes against segregated lunch counters jumped the North Carolina state line today to Rock Hill." White youths gathered, carrying raw eggs to throw, and an anonymous bomb threat closed the stores. The black students needed a police escort to return safely to their campus. Sit-ins spread throughout the state, despite threats from lawmakers. In Manning on February 20, two black travelers sat at a lunch counter, then left. At another store three black women asked if they could be served, then left upon a refusal. A week later Billie Fleming, president of Manning's NAACP, returned home to find bullet holes in his front door.[12]

In Orangeburg on February 25, a march downtown was followed by about two dozen students from Claflin University and South Carolina State College holding brief, organized sit-ins at local stores. The next day students returned to picket the stores that had denied service. In Charleston, also on February 25, black high school students held a mass march downtown. On February 29 in Denmark, fourteen students from Voorhees School and Junior College held sit-ins. On March 1 about twenty-five of Greenville's black high school students held a library sit-in, leaving when trustees closed the building rather than accept them as patrons. As many as two hundred students from Columbia's Allen and Benedict colleges marched downtown on March 2 and 3, attempting sit-ins at Kress, McCrory's, and Woolworth. Simultaneously students also held demonstrations in Rock Hill, Orangeburg, and Denmark. In Florence on March 3, about twenty-five high school students sat at the Kress lunch counter until the police chief and city manager asked them to leave.[13]

On March 4 in Sumter, Morris College students attempted sit-ins at three drugstores. Twenty-six were arrested, "almost before they were able to sit down," the *Daily Item* reported. That same day in Florence, forty-eight youths were arrested when they returned within a half hour for a second try at a Kress sit-in. The Sumter sit-ins were followed by a cross burning on the edge of the campus and the drive-by shooting of a twenty-five-year-old black man. On March 5 students from historically black colleges throughout the state met in Columbia to form the South Carolina Student Movement Association. McCain, who would continue to play an important role, attended as an observer. By March 6 the sit-ins had spread to thirty-eight cities in six southern states, and support rallies had been held in Newark, Washington, Boston, Los Angeles, and Seattle.[14]

Harold C. Fleming, director of the Southern Regional Council (SRC), said the sweep through the South heralded "a shift in leadership and technique to the younger, more militant Negro and to new and flexible uses of the non-violent protest." As the sit-ins multiplied, the *New York Times* concluded students were forcing a "reassessment of Southern race relations." Claude Sitton, a *New York Times* reporter who assiduously tracked the sit-in movement, wrote, "The Negro's struggle against segregation has shifted from the narrow confines of the legal arena to the marketplace." In a February 25 report, the SRC noted, "The deeper meaning of the 'sit-in' demonstrations is to show that segregation cannot be maintained in the South, short of continuous coercion and the intolerable social order which would result." However, southern legislatures responded not by reconsidering segregation in custom and law but by digging in, passing legislation to strengthen trespass laws, such as making "whites only" signs a legal notice or making it illegal to refuse to leave an establishment when asked.[15]

Sit-ins were relatively simple to organize and manage. Participation, once or frequently, fit into a student's schedule. And many black students had lost patience with their elders. For them it was time for something more than petitions, constitutional arguments, and years of appeals. Participants understood that sit-ins—field-tested by CORE and refined to a pragmatic choreography—possessed visual, economic, and moral power. Carey believed CORE's approach was particularly appropriate for the South because "you were facing a potentially violent opponent who was very stubborn." For him nonviolent direct action was a proven means of disarming the opponent, what he called a "flanking operation" he believed could remove the weapon of violence.[16]

CORE had boiled down nonviolent direct action to seven steps: (1) investigation; (2) discussion or negotiation with those responsible; (3) appeals to the general public, through leaflets, for example; (4) raising cause consciousness, for example, through rallies and church meetings (5) training supporters and potential participants; (6) issuing an ultimatum if no desired change occurred; and finally, (7) taking direct action, such as a sit-in, picketing, or a boycott. Frequently, though, students jumped into training, then leaped to direct action. They had no patience or faith in prep work.[17]

For McCain, who did not think of himself as a pacifist, "it was just what worked." Since fall 1957 he had traveled as CORE's first field secretary in the South—to Alabama, Mississippi, Louisiana, Florida, Georgia, South Carolina, North Carolina, and Kentucky—fifty weeks a year for thirty-five dollars a week. He preferred to focus on voter registration. But in spring 1959, he and Carey had helped start the Miami sit-ins. Throughout the South, McCain knew the people and the problems. "People who had heard of CORE would write," he explained. "Any time they wanted someone, CORE would send me down. I would talk to them and find out what they wanted, what they were interested in. I would ask them do they have any problems in the community, and they would tell me. It was just talking and planning."[18]

By the end of March—in a brushfire spread, with no hierarchy of leaders, no conventional central organization—black students in the South had unsettled governors and legislators, endured thousands of arrests, and confidently promised that sit-ins, picketing, and marches would continue. South Carolina's Klan answered with a weekend of cross burnings—four in the city of Charleston, two near Columbia, two near Orangeburg, one near Anderson, one in Seneca, one in Honea Path—as well as unverified burnings in at least eleven counties, most in the Upstate. In Calhoun County alone, one hundred crosses burned; there a Klansman said,"We just wanted to show the public we are organized and ready for business."[19]

White and black shoppers, fearing violence at downtown stores, stayed away. Boycotts, which often followed sit-ins, further reduced sales at stores practicing segregation. In the first few weeks, sales dropped 15 to 18 percent in some Kress stores in the South, according to *Jet* magazine. Woolworth acknowledged black customers had accounted for a quarter of all sales in its three hundred southern stores. The NAACP estimated just a 5 percent loss in sales in 1960 could cost Woolworth alone around $40 million.[20]

Thurgood Marshall, chief counsel for the NAACP, said the sit-ins, picketing, and marches demonstrated youths' impatience with what *Jet* magazine called "the snail's pace of desegregation." The 1954 and 1955 decisions of *Brown v. Board of Education,* which ruled public school segregation unconstitutional, had produced negligible desegregation of the South's public schools. Six states—Alabama, Georgia, Florida, Louisiana, Mississippi, and South Carolina—still practiced complete segregation. *Ebony* magazine added up driving forces for the sit-ins: the *Brown I* and *II* combination of legal affirmation and disappointing follow-through; the inspirations of the 1955–56 Montgomery bus boycott and African nationalism; the tumult surrounding the 1957 desegregation of Central High School in Little Rock, Arkansas; and the momentum of black citizens' rising incomes. News photos of the sit-ins, with seated, stoic black youths hemmed in by howling white youths, made an irrefutable point about equality that discomfited some white leaders, who felt uncomfortable promoting American democracy while presenting this contradictory image to the world.[21]

A small and impoverished state, South Carolina's population of 2.38 million was a third black, a third of its counties half to two-thirds black. Seven historically black colleges and universities dotted the state: Friendship Junior College and Clinton Normal and Industrial Institute in Rock Hill, Allen University and Benedict College in Columbia, Claflin University in Orangeburg, Morris College in Sumter, and Voorhees School and Junior College in Denmark. All were private and backed by black denominations. An eighth school, South Carolina State College, also in Orangeburg, was the only state-supported college for minorities.

These schools functioned as greenhouses, nurturing idealistic, race-conscious, and upwardly mobile students. The students' presidents and professors offered cautious support. They received open support from their churches, which often were home base for planning marches, making picket signs, and holding rallies. They gained the support of CORE and its Sumter-native field director, receiving invaluable training but not much legal and financial support. They gained the support of the South Carolina Conference of Branches of the NAACP, benefiting from its funds and deep experience with legal challenges to Jim Crow. They received coaching from elders, who had overseen school petitions and bus and store boycotts. Plus these students knew each other, often were related to each other, and didn't have far to travel to coordinate or engage in each other's protests. Their networks existed not just through colleges, churches, and relatives but through each other.

On the other side of the equation, these high school and college students lived in a state possessing a history of armed raids and lynchings, of terrorizing black petitioners, and, after the *Brown* decisions, of local and state government using what was termed "massive resistance" to thwart desegregation. Violent opposition—including murder—was carried out with impunity. Law enforcement often refused to investigate reports by individuals, CORE, the NAACP, or media of assaults and cross burnings. Further, when law enforcement made arrests during protests, its target most often was the nonviolent demonstrators, not the whites hurling invective and punches.

Protests flared throughout February and March 1960, when each college's efforts ignited another's, continued in a quieter mode through pickets and smaller, less frequent sit-ins in the spring and summer, then heated up again. Participation depended on many factors: Those who preferred the measured progress of NAACP court cases stuck to their studies. Those who were first in their families to attend college, who were pressured to attend to family dreams, declined or limited participation. Those who doubted their ability to endure nonviolently slurs, spit, a blow, or a beating were encouraged by their peers not to sit-in or march. But hundreds who knew the dangers acted. And in that first year, student leaders such as Thomas Walter Gaither and Charles Frederick McDew and mentors such as the NAACP's Rev. Cecil Augustus Ivory and Rev. Isaiah DeQuincey Newman and CORE's McCain shaped the sit-in movement into a peaceful powerhouse for change not only locally but also nationally. Here are some of the stories, college by college.

Friendship College, Rock Hill: First Sit-In
held Friday, February 12, 1960

As soon as word of the Greensboro sit-ins reached Rock Hill's black community, planning began at Friendship Junior College, founded in 1891 as

Friendship Normal and Industrial Institute. The black Baptist school, comprised a farm and fewer than a dozen buildings, supplied the willing students. Ivory, president of Rock Hill's NAACP branch since 1953 and founder and president of the Local Committee for the Promotion of Human Rights, supplied the tactical and community support. The press took note when sit-ins moved to Rock Hill and thus deeper into the South. Surprise relied on segregationists' assumption that what was termed the Solid South remained unchangeable despite *Brown I* and *II* or the Montgomery bus boycott. When Rock Hill's students sat at local lunch counters, the Associated Press described the textile town on the North Carolina–South Carolina border as occupying "the heartland of the Deep South's total segregation" and as "one of the Deep South's bastions of total segregation." The *New York Times* announced on its front page that the sit-ins had reached "this strongly segregationist state," which was "one of five states that made no effort to comply with the Supreme Court's 1954 decision against school segregation."[22]

Ivory wanted Rock Hill to be the first city in South Carolina to organize student protests. He described interested students who contacted him as being inspired by Greensboro. A big-boned, six-foot-six preacher with an appealing sincerity, Ivory used a wheelchair after a childhood spinal injury worsened in his thirties. His enthusiasm and conviction made it possible for him to work simultaneously with CORE and the NAACP despite a competitive tension between the two organizations. He called in McCain and Newman, field director for the NAACP state conference. Newman met with students on February 9. Ivory named McCain an advisory consultant, and McCain trained the students, using *CORE Rules for Action,* with its smiling Mohandas Gandhi on the red and white cover. The booklet said that nonviolence as a social force used the power of active goodwill, which resisted retaliation; the power of public opinion; and the power of refusing to be a party to injustice.[23]

To prepare potential demonstrators throughout the South, Carey and McCain staged what they called socio-dramas. Portraying sit-in participants and hecklers, volunteers enacted harassment and assaults likely to occur during a sit-in, followed by question-and-answer and evaluation sessions. Carey had predicted that Rock Hill would see sit-ins by mid-February. While he felt confident that conditions were ripe in the South for just such action, Carey also understood something was happening that was "different and much greater" than CORE could have thought up. Rock Hill would illustrate that.[24]

McCain, a quiet man with an intense gaze and a beatific smile, employed nonviolence as a tactic rather than a life philosophy. Born in 1905, he had been raised by his mother and his grandmother, who owned a restaurant in Sumter, while his father worked as a custodian in Washington, D.C. An educator with a bachelor's from Morris College in Sumter and a master's from Temple University in Philadelphia, he returned to Morris to teach, coach, and serve as registrar, academic dean, and chair of the education department in the 1940s. A founding member of Sumter's NAACP branch and its initial president in 1938, he also served as president and treasurer of the Palmetto State Teachers Association while the organization was supporting lawsuits to equalize pay for black teachers and gain black voters' access to the Democratic primary. In 1949, while principal of Palmetto High School in Mullins, South Carolina, he refused to disavow the Summerton-based *Briggs v. Elliott*, the first of five lawsuits comprising *Brown*. School officials fired him. In 1955 McCain served as principal of Scott's Branch High School in Summerton. He lost that job, too, due to his NAACP affiliation, declared by the South Carolina legislature in 1956 as an illegal membership for local, county, or state government employees.[25]

After two years working part-time for the biracial South Carolina Council on Human Relations (SCCHR), McCain became CORE's southern field director in 1957, while wife Ida M. Chennault McCain taught school and raised their three children. He traveled widely, mostly by bus, forming CORE chapters and coaching aspiring voters, particularly in South Carolina, Louisiana, and Florida. His experience was deep, as was his commitment.[26]

McCain was practical in this labor. Always a teacher, he jotted prompts in his crammed-full pocket calendars: Facts mean truth, he wrote. Be cheerful and friendly, he noted. Segregation is America's shame. As the civil rights struggle increases, so do the frustrations of the Negro people, he wrote. He understood how complicated the task was but made his role sound simple. When training demonstrators for picketing and sit-ins, "I would teach them how to react, how to be nonviolent. I would tell them, 'If they come to arrest you, don't resist. You might get hurt,'" said McCain. He required students to anticipate what would happen in these tense moments—name calling, spitting, food thrown, threats, blows—and to practice their stoic response. In discussions before and after, students found in McCain someone who didn't contradict them but listened and explained, who trusted them to choose the roles suitable for themselves and then taught them what to expect and how to survive. A friend called him "a mighty oak" in the movement.[27]

The Rock Hill students elected Abe Plummer as president of the Friendly Student Civic Committee, organized to run the sit-ins. A native of Elberton, Georgia, Plummer was the third of four boys, an early reader, an eighth-grade baseball star, and a high school football star. He stood six feet four inches and saw himself as someone who stood up for what was right. His brothers saw him as someone who wasn't intimidated by circumstances or by others. They fought their way past the white kids on walks to school, then won marbles from them in summer games. Plummer and his Friendship classmates felt a strong allegiance to Ivory. "People were ready to go through a wall for 'Rev.' Ivory. He was that type of person," said Plummer. "He spoke, and he balled his fists up, and because of his physical condition, you felt, 'If this man is going to go out there the way he is, then why shouldn't we?'"[28]

Ivory and Plummer decided that only the coolheaded would participate in demonstrations, students sure to act with "dignity and nonviolence," said Plummer. They named Martin Leroy Johnson, John Wesley Moore, and Arthur Hamm Jr. as second, third, and fourth in command. "We chose those who could go, and we felt would be able to absorb all that mental abuse, all those words that would be thrown. We chose those who would be able to take it and sit there as Reverend Ivory and I wanted us to do," said Plummer.[29]

On Friday, February 12, about 150 male and female students headed downtown, far more volunteers than Plummer expected, many carrying textbooks or Bibles. The word had traveled the night before: we're going to march. Those who collected on campus after morning classes became the demonstrators. It was President Abraham Lincoln's birthday, and Plummer and Ivory selected as targets Woolworth and McCrory's variety stores and Good and J. L. Phillips drugstores. The town was waiting: on February 11 the *Evening Herald* quoted Carey predicting sit-ins by Saturday. Although Ivory and Friendship's president, James H. Goudlock, denied any knowledge when interviewed, white residents were restive. Plummer assigned groups of students to different sites, and some made it into Woolworth and McCrory's around 11 A.M., but so did waiting white opponents.[30]

Plummer and his classmates took all twenty-three stools at Woolworth, and "It wasn't long before everything broke loose." His greatest concern was not himself but Hamm, whose motto was "Hell on wheels." Hamm's size—six feet two inches and more than two hundred pounds—singled him out. Plummer stayed worried. "They got one on each side and one behind, and they called him every name you could call a person. He walked slowly toward the front of the store, and they heckled him, and he walked slowly toward the back of the store, and they heckled him." Hamm rose to the occasion. "He kept his composure," said Plummer, filled with admiration. "They selected him, but they didn't break him."[31]

At the Woolworth lunch counter, the students put up with regular swipes of the surface with an ammonia-coated rag that made their eyes water and their noses run. As Plummer watched, hecklers focused on a female student who appeared white. "They asked her, 'What are you doing here with these niggers?' She didn't respond, and they said it again, and after she refused to say anything, they said, 'Why, she's a nigger, too.'" At Philip's white adversaries punched a student, knocking him off a stool when he sat next to a white man, and kicked a female student. At McCrory's, Friendship students managed to occupy all thirty stools. Occasionally a student would get up and leave, allowing another student, standing protectively at the partner's back, to sit. A white teen threw an ammonia bomb through the front door of Good's. "The Negro youths, male and female, seated at the lunch counter did not move," the *Evening Herald* reported. The news report described the demonstrators as college age or younger, "orderly, polite, well-dressed and quiet," people who used "excuse me" or "pardon me" to move through the crowds. At 1 P.M. bomb threats were called into Woolworth and McCrory's, the same tactic that cut short sit-ins in North Carolina. The local fire department evacuated those stores. By 1:45 P.M. all the stores had closed. Police gathered to protect the departing students from a large group of white opponents yelling threats and curses.[32]

As the demonstrators filed down Main Street, Elwin Wilson threw an egg at a black passerby, Bunt Gill. Gill wiped away the mess as the crowd laughed and jeered. Law enforcement officers formed a line between the angry white men and the students and escorted the students back to Friendship. Ivory found the police protection adequate as the students returned to campus "through a mob of white teenagers and a few white adults." To keep danger out and the students in, "a close police surveillance was placed over the school for several days following this demonstration."[33]

Far worse might have been brewing. In both Rock Hill and York County, white adults "disturbed by a recent Negro sit-down strike" founded White Citizens' Councils, reported the *Evening Herald*. Morrison Shaw, president of York County's WCC, later claimed that WCC members had "pistols on our hips and blood in our eyes." Following *Brown I* in 1954, Mississippi segregationists had started citizens' councils to oppose the NAACP and stop desegregation. In South Carolina, following *Brown II*, citizens' councils sprang up

Elwin Wilson, holding a Confederate flag, and other Rock Hill
youth daily harassed black demonstrators and passersby,
shouting racial epithets and throwing raw eggs.
Courtesy of MIRC, University of South Carolina, Columbia

each time local NAACP branches filed desegregation petitions. WCC members fired, evicted, and otherwise harassed petitioners and members of local NAACP branches, canceled their credit, and called in loans. In April 1956 representatives from South Carolina and ten other southern states formed the Citizens' Councils of America. By December 1958 fifty-nine local councils with a total membership of forty thousand existed in South Carolina, most of the councils led by what the FBI called "leading citizens of the communities."[34]

Overnight, employees at McCrory's and Woolworth removed the counter seats and posted "no trespassing" signs. On the morning of February 13, white men gathered outside both chain stores, handing out cards that read, "Please do not make a purchase in this store until further notice." The cards were signed "The White Citizens," their boycott intended to force reopening the counters to whites only, according to a participant. The *New York Times* reported that "the spread of the protest to this strongly segregationist state raised fears of serious trouble."[35]

South Carolina governor Ernest F. Hollings condemned the sit-ins as "purely to create violence and not to promote anyone's rights." State representative Rex Carter proposed a fine of up to one hundred dollars and a jail term of up to thirty days for anyone refusing to leave a lunch counter once asked to do so by management. On February 16, 125 white men and women gathered at Rock Hill's Celanese union hall to hear Farley Smith, the executive secretary of the Association of Citizens' Councils, Inc., of South Carolina. The *Evening Herald* reported that Smith endorsed "a good Christian, intelligently planned course of action" to oppose what he called the "invasion of eating facilities."[36]

These early sit-ins evoked in white South Carolinians a fervent defense of segregation that included outraged dismissals of the students as dupes and affirmations of white control, use of local and state police power, economic reprisals, and violence. Hollings compared the sit-ins to hula hoops, a fad of the late 1950s. Sitton of the *New York Times* described "dissatisfaction over the slow pace of desegregation" resulting in black students determined "to wipe out the last vestiges of segregation." He warned against early dismissals of the sit-ins as a college fad (his example was panty raids) or as the work of outside agitators. He also noted that older, more traditional black leaders supported the students' use of the nonviolence principles of India's Mohandas Gandhi and Rev. Dr. Martin Luther King Jr., a leader of the Montgomery bus boycott and, since 1957, president of the Southern Christian Leadership Conference (SCLC).[37]

Also on February 16, Ivory took Plummer, Hamm, and McDew, a freshman at South Carolina State, to Durham. They attended a student coordinating meeting set up by the SCLC and CORE. Leaders from NAACP youth and college chapters also attended. "We, at this time, were the lone South Carolina group and felt very lonesome," reported Ivory. King congratulated and encouraged the youth, saying, "Let us not fear going to jail. If the officials threaten to arrest us for standing up for our rights, we must answer by saying that we are willing and prepared to fill up the jails of the South." This stayed with Ivory, who played an important part in the students' shift from bail to jail in 1961. King also reminded the students of "the tremendous force of nonviolence," wrote CORE's Carey with approval. "The students involved have, for the most part, grasped the vital importance of remaining peaceful no matter what happens." Jones, of Charlotte, told the press afterward that attending students had decided to continue picketing and sit-ins, "notwithstanding the arrests, imprisonment or other harassment or punishment."[38]

On February 23 McCrory's and Woolworth reopened their lunch counters. The Friendship students resumed their sit-in efforts that very afternoon, joined by the students of neighboring Clinton Normal and Industrial Institute and Emmett Scott High School. Participation was high, because "everybody saw things needed to change, and it was going to take a major effort to make that change," said Martin Leroy Johnson, who was Friendship's student council president. The students arrived in groups larger than the stores could accommodate. Those who made it inside attempted to sit, while others stood outside. "It was like a gauntlet," said Johnson, with white men surrounding the students, screaming, yelling, and cursing them. They brandished "baseball bats, eggs, angry fists," Johnson said.[39]

Born in Westminster, South Carolina, Johnson was one of fourteen children. His parents brought ten children from previous marriages and had four more together. He had listened as his much older brothers, who worked the Southern Railway tracks, talked about training younger whites to do jobs they themselves wouldn't get because black employees weren't promoted. During high school Johnson found a job pumping gas, but only the white employees were allowed to collect customers' payments. "We were very aware it was a segregated system, but we were not aware we could do anything about it," he said. The sit-ins changed that. "Once we did the first demonstration and saw the reaction we got, you'd think we would be afraid, but it didn't make us afraid. It motivated us to continue in the struggle," he explained.[40]

He marveled at his classmates' nerve. "We didn't know what was going to happen. We didn't know if any of us was going to get back to campus. And we didn't talk about that. We did not think to ourselves, 'What if somebody gets their head cracked open with a baseball bat?' We really didn't discuss those kinds of things." Johnson was sprayed in the face with ammonia, intended to burn his skin and damage his eyes, as he waited outside for his turn inside the five-and-dime. He continued into the store. While the students knew anything could happen, they also knew the silence and stillness of nonviolence that they had employed was resulting, as Plummer said, in "psychological effects" on both the participants and their opponents. The leaflet "CORE Does It This Way!" advised limited contact: "Do we talk to people before they talk to us? Generally not. We always try to avoid talking to antagonistic or excited people." The Rock Hill students took that advice to heart. "After we saw how violently the people were against this, we still went, but we were a little more cautious," said Johnson. "We didn't make eye contact with any-body. We certainly didn't say anything."[41]

This time Woolworth employees roped off the eating area and permitted only white patrons under the ropes. Six black students ducked under and sat together at the counter, where the manager told them they couldn't be served. White patrons continued eating. At McCrory's several students ob-tained seats next to white customers and began reading. As white customers stood and left, employees removed the stool cushions, placing them upside down on the counter, and posted again a "temporarily closed" sign. By the time both stores closed at 1:45 P.M., as many as a hundred black students had crowded into Woolworth to sit at the lunch counter or stand in the aisles.[42]

On Wednesday, when the demonstrators returned, white customers had organized their opposition, as they had on the last day of the Greensboro sit-ins. When students entered Woolworth, white men moved onto any un-occupied stool while others waited in rows to seize vacated seats. When three black students raced for three open seats, a white man tripped one, who fell, striking his head on the counter. Men wrestled a black student off the seat he had just gained and threw him to the floor while a policeman watched. The police then cleared the aisle but ignored the attack by the white man, who stayed on the seat seized. Soon after, the store closed. When Woolworth re-opened at 2 P.M., the black students returned and filled all twenty-three seats until the store closed again after 3 P.M. At McCrory's the white men's plan worked; they relinquished seats only to each other. After the sit-ins ended, three white and three black youths quarreled outside Woolworth. One of the white teens said he was struck, and when he shouted, "There he goes now!" a mob of three hundred charged after a black teen. Police took him into protective custody.[43]

White adults openly met in groups to plan attacks. During the day the men prowled the streets, attacking black adults not involved in the sit-ins. At night cars filled with angry white boys and men cruised through black neighborhoods. A black woman, struck by rocks thrown from a car, was knocked unconscious. Threatening calls rang nonstop on Ivory's phone. He kept a pistol on his nightstand. He sat on his porch, a shotgun on his lap.[44]

"I didn't have any fear," said Johnson. "We were numb to fear. We just knew that in some way we were powerless. There was no way we could fight out of a situation if somebody attacked us. We also knew we weren't leaving." In Chattanooga, Tennessee, where the NAACP asked school authorities for immediate and total integration, violence followed. On February 21 thirty black high school students attempted a sit-in. The following day, a Monday, two hundred black students returned. On Tuesday about a hundred white youths mobbed Kress, throwing sales items—sugar bowls, napkin holders, flowerpots—into the aisles after thirty black students managed to seat themselves. On Wednesday, even though black elders called off a demonstration, black and white youths and adults marched into the business district and fought. Officials authorized the use of riot clubs and fire hoses, the fierce water pressure breaking up a mob of several thousand white people. Throughout the rest of the week, police remained downtown, accompanied by firefighters and their trucks, hoses ready for use again.[45]

Hollings and Rock Hill mayor John A. Hardin asked chain-store managers to set a definite policy on lunch-counter service to white customers only and then to sign warrants against any black person attempting a sit-in. A Greenville legislator proposed modifying trespass laws so that "whites only" signs served as legal notice. Most southern five-and-dimes and drugstores belonged to chains that offered desegregated seating in the North. But southern managers deferred to local custom and said they would continue to do so. They wanted to keep white customers by adhering to the South's segregation of public spaces. On the other hand, they knew defending segregation resulted in sales to black customers plummeting. Selective-buying campaigns, used by the NAACP effectively in the mid-1950s, were sure to damage business further.[46]

Mass arrests of demonstrators at peaceful sit-ins began throughout the South: twelve in Tallahassee; forty-one in Raleigh; thirty-eight in Richmond; eighty-one in Nashville. All those arrested were charged with trespassing after declining to leave stores. CORE sent a telegram to U.S. Attorney General William P. Rogers protesting, to no avail, the use of trespassing laws. Local police and courts enforced a business owner's private practice of segregation in a public space. CORE and the NAACP posited that this violated the Fourteenth Amendment's prohibition of any state action denying individuals equal protection under a state's laws.[47]

Ivory, worried about the violent reactions of whites and unsatisfied with police response since the first sit-in, asked to meet with the mayor and the police chief. Joseph Preston "Pete" Strom, chief of the South Carolina Law Enforcement Division (SLED), also attended. "We were cordially received and also informed that the leaders of such demonstrations would be subject to arrest if the demonstrations got out of hand," Ivory reported to the NAACP. "We assured the officer that we had enough confidence in our students to believe that they would continue to conduct themselves in a dignified manner and that if the situation got out of hand it would come from the other side and not ours." Strom asked Friendship's President Goudlock to stop the students, and Goudlock refused. When reporters asked Goudlock if the school supported the demonstrations, he answered, "Let me put it this way: The students are still demonstrating." Privately he said, "I cannot in good conscience do anything to discourage them. I feel that the cause is just and if they are willing to help remedy conditions, their efforts should not be blocked."[48]

On February 19 members of the South Carolina Civil Rights Advisory Commission divided along racial lines in a discussion of the sit-ins. E. R. McIver, the white chairman, said, "I'm not sure I understand how the students find the time to sit around up town." Dr. Thomas Carr, a black member, said, "Japanese or Hawaiians can eat with whites, and there are no questions about it. But here I am, born in America, but because I am a Negro I can't do it. It doesn't make sense." White-owned media outlets rarely reported viewpoints such as Carr's. However, ample attention was paid the views of WCC members. On February 25, state Senator L. Marion Gressette spoke in Rock Hill to an all-white audience of 350. He said, "No one can be forced to serve. The trespass law is clear. It's up to owners as to whether or not they enforce their right." To applause, he added, "There is no middle ground. You are either for segregation or against segregation." Hollings publicly commended Hardin for shutting down the demonstrations, promising his "complete support."[49]

Plummer and Ivory made speeches statewide, mostly short trips to church meetings, where they promoted sit-ins and sought support. Plummer drove Ivory's Pontiac Chieftain, a long, sleek burgundy missile, and they talked on their drives to and fro. "He was as courageous as any person I've ever seen. He didn't back off anybody," said Plummer. In a public rebuttal to the mayor, senator, and governor, Ivory said, "We are 100 percent in favor of the movement."[50]

On Sunday, February 28, one of many bomb threats was called into Friendship, leading to the evacuation of the school's residence halls. Students stood outside, shivering in their nightclothes, while buildings were searched. Unintimidated, an estimated seven hundred to nine hundred in the black community attended a mass meeting on February 29 at New Mount Olivet African Methodist Episcopal Zion Church (AMEZ). At 5:30 P.M. Plummer discovered he was expected to speak in two hours as student leader. He whipped up a draft in thirty minutes, feeling terrified but assuming he could survive a few remarks. He next discovered he was a featured speaker, and when his turn came and a television camera light came on, he froze. "My mouth was opening and closing, and nothing came out." Luckily the audience filled his silence with a standing ovation, and afterward, "I started on a roll."[51]

Plummer told the audience, "Discrimination in itself is wrong. It makes the white man feel superior; it makes the Negro feel inferior. The Southern white man goes out to tell how the Negro is satisfied, but your being here tonight shows that this group is not satisfied." He cited hostile reactions to sit-ins but said, "We knew at the beginning something had to be sacrificed. We were willing to do this. That's the way you must feel. You must be willing to sacrifice along with us."[52]

Ivory told the crowd, "The history of the South is a list of repeated abuses against the Negro. They've lynched us; they've passed all kinds of silly laws to hold us in check." Ivory refuted claims that "outsiders" sparked and led demonstrations, observing, "These are home people. They are interested in their children and in themselves." Those attending spoke up too. "They say we are going too fast. There is no such thing as going too fast," said Charles Ramseur, an electrical helper and graduate of Virginia's Hampton Institute. "If we go any slower, we go backward. We've got to stop thinking Negro and start to thinking American." Local reporter Virginia Davis noted overwhelming support for a resolution endorsing the student demonstrations. The resolution recommended that black citizens back up the students with pickets and boycotts, protest letters to store managers, and financial support.[53]

Newman wrote afterward, "Negroes of South Carolina feel that the 'Sit-Down protests' is one of the best things that could have transpired. They have a mind to go all out in support of the youthful leaders of the 'Protests.'" A Methodist pastor, Newman helped found the Orangeburg NAACP branch in 1943. He held the state conference's vice presidency from 1948 to 1958, was president for a year, then became field director on January 1, 1960. Dapper and stylish, Newman sported a goatee and was known for his bowties and bowler hat, straight from London's Harrods.[54]

In March closed lunch counters stymied sit-ins, but the students continued to picket. "This game of musical chairs has got to stop," declared Hardin. After meeting about the protests, the SCCHR's board of directors issued a statement advising against repression "by force or by new legislation" and supporting the students: "These actions express not merely the simple desire of these students to use public lunch counters, but are more fundamentally an understandable protest by citizens of South Carolina against continued unequal treatment in the use of public facilities and services."[55]

A seat at the counter was not all the Rock Hill students wanted. "We decided to go to different places around the city," said Johnson. "It became

'Why am I seated in a colored section at the bus station? Why don't I have a right to petition city hall?' and so forth." During a planning meeting at New Mount Olivet on March 7, a cross of two-by-fours soaked in kerosene burned in front of the church. Neighbors smelled the fire and called the church to warn those meeting to get out.[56]

On March 15—in one of several demonstrations coordinated among Columbia, Rock Hill, and Orangeburg students—Rock Hill protesters fanned out across town around noon. Each group had a target. Some students took seats at Good's lunch counter. Others picketed city hall, which was segregated. Others bought bus tickets at whites-only windows and sat in whites-only lobbies in the city's two bus terminals. At Good's, when the manager asked the students to leave, they did, escorted by police. At the Greyhound Bus Depot, Johnson and four other students asked about the schedule at the ticket window in the whites-only waiting room. Johnson bought a ticket to Fort Mill; a classmate bought a ticket to Chester. They took five of the seven seats at the lunch counter and were not asked to leave. Johnson told a reporter, "We came up here to buy a ticket and to get served as the white people do." Next Johnson joined students at city hall. There thirty demonstrators led by Hamm carried signs; one said "Pilate Tried to Wash His Hands, You, Too, Honorable Mayor." They sang "The Star-Spangled Banner," "My Country, 'Tis of Thee," and "America the Beautiful," and they prayed. When police began arresting the male picketers, women paired up with the men and were arrested too. By 1 P.M., police were booking the demonstrators.[57]

At the Trailways bus terminal, Plummer and four classmates took the same steps as Johnson's group. Two students bought tickets at the whites-only window. They entered the terminal at 12:35 P.M., just missing the bus. The next bus didn't leave until 3:40 P.M. Eventually, tired of waiting, they walked uptown to check on classmates. Upon their return the other three students tried to buy tickets at the whites-only window and were refused. The students wanted the tickets to make their presence legitimate. "Our plan was to force them to arrest us so you could get a test case," said Plummer. An NAACP strategy, test cases enabled NAACP attorneys to challenge laws used for an arrest, attacking the role of the state in establishing and defending segregation. If and when the NAACP won, a legal precedent was established in the effort to end segregation.[58]

"If we failed to obey their orders, we were going to get arrested. And that was the plan; that was Reverend Ivory's and the NAACP's plan," said Plummer. The station manager asked the students to leave; the students refused. The manager called for a law officer, who offered to allow the students to leave. Plummer, the spokesman, replied, "We are perfectly happy where we are, so we are not going to leave." The manager agreed to swear out a warrant, and the officer called for reinforcements and transportation. The officer arrested Plummer's classmates, who walked outside, but Plummer remained seated. The officer returned and said, "Let's go," and Plummer replied again, "I'm satisfied right here." Told he would have to leave or face arrest, Plummer replied, "Well, you'll have to arrest me because I'm not leaving." That earned him a ride in a squad car.[59]

In all, police arrested and jailed seventy-one Rock Hill students. Ivory told the local paper, "This was anticipated, expected and hoped for. The machinery was already set up for this situation." The students didn't worry, because they expected their time in jail to be very short. "It had been planned, and when we went to jail we expected the NAACP would post bond," said Johnson. Some proffered celebrities' names at booking. One woman called herself Eartha Kitt, an internationally successful black singer from North, South Carolina. The women were locked up in a large room in the county's office building. Most of the men were locked up in the city jail, where a dozen or more were put in cells meant for three people. "They slammed us all in there and gave us metal drinking cups, and everybody started beating on the bars with the metal cups, and they took them away from us," said Johnson, so they sang "We Shall Overcome" without percussion.[60]

By dinnertime enthusiasm flagged. In their respective cells, Johnson and Plummer fielded complaints from shouting students. Plummer's initial answer: "Just be cool. They're coming to get us out." The singing resumed, "but we didn't have the same enthusiasm that time as when we first got there." At 9 P.M. the complaints turned to threats. Plummer promised again, "Hey, just be cool. We'll get out soon." The reply: "If we don't get out soon, we better not find you when we do get out." Rock Hill officials had decided to accept only cash. Initially bond was set at $100 a student but was reduced to $17 for most, $27 for the fake celebrities, including "Joe Selblock," and $52 for Hamm, identified as leader of the city-hall group. Thanks to Ivory, a professional bondsman, the NAACP, and $1,455, the students left jail around 11 P.M. Plummer and his four classmates at Trailways were charged with trespassing. The other demonstrators were charged with breach of peace.[61]

In Charlotte Ivory met with Thurgood Marshall, chief counsel for the Legal Defense and Education Fund (LDF), the legal arm of the NAACP. Afterward he assured all that Marshall had promised, "They can fill up every jail in the South, and the NAACP can still pay the fines and court cases." *Jet* magazine celebrated the students' persistence in its March 17 issue: "But neither the shotgunning of a 15-year-old Chickamauga, Georgia boy, bomb scares at Fisk University (Nashville) and Friendship Junior college (Rock Hill, South Carolina) nor the resurrection of the KKK in Rock Hill could frighten human beings hungering more for racial equality than a mouthful of toasted cheese."[62]

Roy Wilkins, the NAACP's national executive secretary, announced an "expanded racial defense policy" that included picketing and boycotts of stores practicing segregation. The triggers Wilkins cited for this step included Congress playing "games with the civil rights bill"; arrests of students in Rock Hill, Columbia, Orangeburg, and Atlanta; Hollings's announcement he would "crush" protests; and an announcement by Woolworth, Kresge, Kress, and Grant stores that lunch-counter segregation would continue in the South. The NAACP slogan "Wearing 1959 clothes with 1960 dignity" reminded customers and merchants that withholding what the *Afro-American* newspaper called "the potent dollar" was a tried-and-true response. As the *Baltimore Afro-American* had observed, in a 1956 editorial praising the Montgomery bus boycott, "In a showdown between Southern tradition and Southern pocketbooks, tradition is bound to come out a poor second."[63]

On March 22, in a mass meeting that included Charlotte's Charles Jones and Orangeburg demonstrators as special guests, the Rock Hill students described their arrests. Plummer said police treated the protesters "like we had robbed a bank." Wanda Holland, arrested at city hall, told of a body search by two deputies. Ivory announced, "I had in my hands at my disposal the sum of $10,000," by 5 P.M. on the day of the arrests, proof that local citizens and the NAACP "have faith in what our children are doing." Those attending contributed $450 and vowed to boycott Rock Hill stores whose managers, in Ivory's words, "don't care to have us come around or who are actually hostile."[64]

On March 24 the city tried Leroy Henry first, on breach of peace, for singing at the courthouse. This led to an interesting exchange as defense attorneys Donald J. Sampson and Matthew J. Perry Jr. quizzed Officer John Hunsucker Jr. on his knowledge of music. Defense witnesses described the singing as "sweet" and "moderate." Hunsucker evaluated the singing as in tune but too loud. Asked if the songs were violent, the assistant police chief replied, "No, if they are sung in the proper place and in the proper manner." Perry moved the charges be dismissed on the grounds the city had not proved a crime was committed, saying Henry was engaged in "lawful assemblage of persons for the purpose of giving public expression to officials of government," in the form of patriotic songs. Henry, found guilty, was sentenced to thirty-five dollars or thirty days. Attorney Perry—polite, polished, calm, known for his charm and melodious baritone—had graduated in 1951 from South Carolina State's law school. The NAACP had sued the state for black students' access to a law education, and Perry was the first South Carolina State graduate to clear the next roadblock, South Carolina's first use of a bar exam, intended to stop "Negroes and some undesirable whites" from practicing law, a legislator acknowledged. Perry became chief counsel for the state NAACP in 1957, losing lawsuits locally while making an impeccable trial record that led to wins on appeal to higher courts. The state's hold on segregation made him a master of constitutional rights. As CORE attorney Ernest Adolphus Finney Jr. joked, cases "making right" came their way, not cases "making money."[65]

Members of the city's biracial Council on Human Relations tried applying reason. Rev. Hawley Lynn and three more white Methodist ministers wrote a letter to the editor opposing the city hall arrests, "which don't seem to fit into the pattern of life in this 'home of freedom and justice,' the United States." The ministers wrote that arrests might make sense if the demonstrators carried weapons or made threats. "But to arrest a group acting in non-violent protest because some other group MIGHT BECOME VIOLENT seems to us a restraint upon the wrong citizens." Afterward a complaint to the bishop threatened their employment.[66]

In April the city dropped trespassing charges against Plummer and his four classmates. By then twenty-three of the sixty-five students arrested for breach of peace at city hall had been convicted and fined thirty-five dollars or thirty days in jail. During an April stockholder meeting, this white southern "pattern of life" received confirmation from W. T. Grant Co.'s head. President Louis C. Lustenberger said local custom governed the existence and continuance of variety stores' segregated lunch counters. "Those are customs we can't change."[67]

The *New York Times* asked "whether southern Negroes, already fighting hard in the courts for school integration and voting rights, stand to gain or lose from the more dynamic, more dramatic sit-ins." But black adults' support in Rock Hill remained strong. A mass meeting, on April 12, began with Rev. H. P. Sharper, a Florence minister and president of the NAACP state conference, rattling the windows with a denunciation of the white press and its "10-cent editors." By night's end those attending had approved a letter requesting a meeting with the mayor and other city officials as well as plans for an Easter boycott of any stores that refused service at lunch counters, denied courtesy titles to black customers, used segregated water fountains or restrooms, or denied employment on the basis of color.[68]

During April the teens of the NAACP Youth Council joined Friendship students, picketing fourteen times in front of Grant, Kress, and McCrory's. Police watched, and white onlookers made hostile remarks, but no more attacks or arrests occurred. On one Saturday Hamm directed the picket lines and passed out leaflets explaining the boycott. Three female and three male students carried signs with warnings such as "If we can't buy what we want, we won't buy anything."[69]

Within weeks Rock Hill's black students had become strategists, public speakers, picketers, and marchers, persisting despite threats and assaults. White residents had responded with more WCCs, physical attacks, and cross burnings. City and state politicians had demanded, and gotten, arrests. In an April mass meeting, Ivory blamed the arrests not on the mayor but on the governor. Hollings had asked for store segregation policies, insisting, "We must maintain peace and good order, and when a store fails to do something about demonstrators, we must control it," the "we" meaning local and state government enforcement. Ivory responded, "The word 'jail' has changed its meaning. Jail has become a glorious word, the symbol of sacrifice we have to pay for first class citizenship."[70]

On June 7 Ivory and Hamm made national news with their arrest at McCrory's. Ivory believed he wasn't a full participant without a sit-in arrest. This was a surefire effort. The two visited the store shortly before noon, and Ivory purchased writing paper and a small trash can. They next went to the lunch counter, where Ivory parked his wheelchair, Hamm sat on a neighboring stool, and Ivory asked for service. Officer Hunsucker arrested the two, although Ivory pointed out that he did not occupy a counter seat and had been served twice elsewhere in the store. Charged with trespass, convicted, and sentenced to a one-hundred-dollar fine or thirty days in jail, both appealed.[71]

Hamm graduated from Friendship but remained in town to coach high school students in nonviolent protest. On June 17 he led eleven children, ten to fourteen years old, into Woolworth. They took seats at the lunch counter, were refused service, and remained. No white customers took seats thereafter. The boycott continued, but sit-ins stopped until the fall, when Friendship's new CORE chapter met. The forty-five students attending reviewed rules for nonviolent direct action and reinstated pickets at the five-and-dime stores, starting October 1. On their side stood Pinckney Brown, who owned a pool parlor and worked as a bail bondsman. During the sit-ins of the previous school year, Brown had posted bonds for all the students, charging less than 5 percent of the total cost. He continued his support. The student

CORE, led by Howard Hamer, cooperated with the NAACP youth chapter and earned a reputation as the only group in the Deep South to maintain almost daily sit-ins and picketing. Throughout December, Hamer and others ran picket lines from opening to closing at Woolworth and McCrory's. Managers frequently asked the students and the oft-present Ivory to leave, but no one was arrested.[72]

Claflin University and South Carolina State College, Orangeburg: First Sit-In Held Thursday, February 25, 1960

Resistance to segregation and WCC-led oppression had surged, faded, and surged again throughout the 1950s in majority-black Orangeburg. Black students joined their elders in a selective buying campaign intended to pressure businesses owned by WCC members, including the town's mayor. On their own they sometimes marched downtown to attempt sit-ins at store counters, but once a boycott was fully underway, most black customers didn't enter certain stores for anything. At South Carolina State College, the students added their own food and class strikes—most of the school's 1,100 undergraduates didn't attend classes from April 9 to April 16, 1956—and presented administration and trustees a list of grievances, as well as a vote of no confidence in President Benner Creswill Turner. After the general assembly set up an investigation of NAACP activities among faculty and students, 176 of the college's 177 faculty members and administrators responded with a resolution asserting their constitutional rights, academic freedom, and the legitimacy of the NAACP. Ultimately five faculty members didn't return, fourteen students were suspended, and Fred Moore, the student body president, was expelled, which prevented his graduation. In 1960 South Carolina State remained the only public college for black students in South Carolina, and Turner remained president and subservient to an all-white board of trustees and an all-white legislature.[73]

Attending South Carolina State was almost the death of Charles Frederick McDew. Better known as "Chuck" and "Dews," McDew came to South Carolina in 1959 with a certain swagger, self-described as "a hotshot football player, beloved by all." He quickly found himself "a stranger in a very strange land." McDew grew up in Massillon, Ohio, where he experienced the social and educational freedom of the North: two of his closest friends were white; his schools were integrated, as were the steel mills where many worked, including his father. "Everybody was in the same boat, and judgments of what you could and couldn't do were based on ability," not race, he said. James McDew had graduated from South Carolina State and insisted that his son attend the school, where he had played football under Coach Oliver C. Dawson. A coach of five sports, Dawson led teams to four championships. His successes including the football team's undefeated 1947 season and its participation in the Black National Championship game. James McDew believed his son needed to experience for at least one year this all-black college, Coach Dawson, and a culture of black professionals, as he had.[74]

Muscular with bold features and a bolder, assessing gaze, McDew was a deep thinker and a humorist and jokester who kept a wide smile while talking. None of these traits protected him in South Carolina. During his first term, he spent Thanksgiving in Sumter with one of his four roommates. Several young men attended a party, and they chose the sober McDew to drive home. Sumter police stopped the car, and McDew stepped out to present his license. When the policeman asked him where he was from, and he answered, "Ohio," the officer said, "Didn't they teach you up there to say 'yes, sir,' and 'no, sir'?" McDew thought the man was joking, and "I said so, something like, 'You've got to be jiving.' And he hit me, and I hit him back, and his partner grabbed me, and they beat me." None of his friends stepped out of the car to help him, knowing they might all die. Arrested for the first time in his life, McDew was charged with disturbing the peace and disobeying an officer and jailed with a broken jaw and arm. Allowed medical treatment, he discovered that a beating by police was no more than, as hospital staff told him, "standard operating procedure." His roommate's mother called his parents, who provided bail and ordered him to take a train the sixty-three miles back to campus.[75]

But trains traveling through the South limited seating for black travelers to a Jim Crow car, which often lacked heat, water, or luggage racks, or to the barren boxcar, which held freight and animals. "I was told to sit in the baggage compartment because the 'colored' car was full," said McDew. "I said, 'That's ridiculous.' I was standing in a car with empty seats, so I sat in what was a whites-only car. They called the cops, and I was back in jail." Bailed out again by his parents, McDew reached Orangeburg but made the mistake of taking a shortcut to campus through a park. Only whites were allowed in the park, and he was arrested again, the third time in two days. Southern public spaces, such as parks and libraries, were open only to whites, even though black taxpayers contributed to their existence. McDew's parents ordered him to stay on campus, where he would be safe, until his return home for Christmas.[76]

An arrest interrupted the bus trip home. At a layover in Columbia, Mc-Dew didn't want to enter the depot's segregated waiting room. As he waited outside, a white Ohio friend walked up, and the two decided to pass the intervening hours playing handball at the YMCA. "We had our international YMCA cards. They said he could come in; I couldn't. I could go to the black Y. I said, 'Where's the black Y?' They said, 'It's in Atlanta.'" McDew argued; the Y manager called the police. "I was back in jail for breaking the law for racial mixing. The two of us being friends was against the law."[77]

Thomas Walter Gaither, vice president of Claflin University's student body his senior year and president of the NAACP's youth council both his junior and his senior year, had spent his life in a segregated society. So he knew its rules. Tall and thin, with a distinctively long and narrow face and a dapper narrow moustache, Gaither approached life like a scientist, asking "What is this?" and "What if?" then testing his answers. Why this social order? Was activism the avenue to change? Was he willing to suffer for something he believed in? Intense and intellectual, he found himself studying nonviolence as a protest tactic and sought mentors in that practice.[78]

The oldest of five children, Gaither grew up on a farm near Great Falls, South Carolina, a tiny town founded by Southern Power Company. His parents, Walter and Fannie Gaither, graduated from Friendship Junior College and taught school. The consequences of segregation permeated Gaither's childhood. When Walter Gaither asked white school trustees about the gap between his pay and what he was actually owed, he was fired. Next he took work at a textile mill. As fireman he kept the boilers going with coal, the only mill job available to black job applicants. Black and white employees were prohibited from working together in the state's textile mills. Gaither's connection to union organizers led to another firing, and so he became a handyman and then a brickmason. Thomas Gaither's mother was his teacher for his first seven years in school. The schoolhouse, provided by their Pleasant Grove AMEZ church, consisted of one room. Well water, fetched nearby, sat in a cooler; heat simmered from a fire in a barrel with a stovepipe; two outdoor privies served as bathrooms. His mother provided the only dictionary; white public schools provided hand-me-down textbooks.[79]

In childhood Gaither was aware of the unfairness of his parents' circumstances, and that indignation grew, given his own circumstances as a bright student deprived of almost all resources. In high school all the black students were required to join the New Farmers of America, organized in Tuskegee, Alabama, for southern black youths. Gaither had no intention of becoming a farmer. He didn't want to study "the needs of ducks, the needs of pigs."

He wanted a biology course. He wanted recent Algebra I and II textbooks and a true mathematics teacher. Instead he got out-of-date books that contradicted each other and a busy principal trying to fit math classes into his administrative schedule. "You trained yourself," Gaither said, and so he did, valedictorian of his class.[80]

His parents taught that "the only salvation for you is to study and try to get out." They were registered voters and belonged to the NAACP, both high-risk ventures. As a child Gaither attended NAACP state conferences with them; his father would lift him or his brother above a sea of black folk. Later Gaither traveled solo to Columbia for the mass meetings. Once he was so inspired that he sat on the second-row bus seat for his ride home and, when ordered to move to the back of the bus, disembarked rather than comply. He called the NAACP's Newman to find a ride home.[81]

While McDew found himself beaten into activism, Gaither was attracted by a philosophy. At Claflin he was drawn to McCain and Rev. Glenn E. Smiley; both tutored him in nonviolent direction action. Smiley, a white Methodist preacher and pacifist, belonged to both CORE and the Fellowship of Reconciliation (FOR), an international peace organization founded in 1914. In 1945 Smiley went to prison rather than serve in World War II, declining an exemption as a minister. In 1946, in *Morgan v. Virginia,* the Supreme Court ruled that segregation on interstate buses was unconstitutional, and members of FOR and CORE embarked on the 1947 Journey of Reconciliation, an interracial bus ride from Washington, D.C., through Virginia, North Carolina, Tennessee, and Kentucky. Smiley served as FOR's national field secretary and first came to Orangeburg in November 1955. At the time, despite tensions among black and white residents of Orangeburg—white locals' retaliations for a school desegregation petition, black locals' boycotts and protests at South Carolina State—Smiley got white and black ministers talking to each other, provided information on nonviolent resistance, and convinced the ministers of its efficacy. A few months later, Smiley traveled to Montgomery, Alabama, hoping King could "really be won to a faith in non-violence."[82]

At first Gaither saw nonviolence as compliance, as the behavior he had witnessed among black elders of his childhood and had disavowed. He told Smiley, after hearing him talk at Claflin, "That's precisely why we are in the predicament we are in." However, Gaither also read *Life of Mahatma Gandhi* by Louis Fischer and *The Gandhi Reader* by Homer A. Jack, a CORE cofounder. The leader of India's nonviolent resistance to Great Britain's rule, Gandhi practiced *satyagraha,* or holding onto truth, sometimes translated as "soul power." He distinguished *satyagraha* from passive resistance, which he understood as "a weapon of the weak" that could be characterized by hatred and eventually devolve into violence. *Satyagraha* included civil disobedience and the overlapping refusal to submit to injustice. As Fischer explained it, *satyagraha* returned good for evil until the evildoer tired. *Satyagraha* depended not on numbers of practitioners but on each individual's firmness and consistency.[83]

Gaither decided that nonviolence offered "a high moral plane that the opposition couldn't begin to understand." He recognized something even segregationists commented upon, as jeering whites assaulted stoic sit-in participants: "You became a threat to the system when you sat down to order a Coke or hamburger. When a nice, well-dressed polite person shows up for a hamburger, and you won't serve them, it says something about you, not about the person wanting to be recognized as a human being." He also recognized that nonviolent direction action was neither a simple nor an easy path. Training was required.[84]

Inspired by Greensboro and Rock Hill, Claflin's students wanted to organize their own sit-ins. Gaither turned to CORE's McCain, who had trained the Rock Hill demonstrators. After identifying some interested students, "we met with McCain because we were getting ready to organize sit-ins, but we had no idea how to go about it," Gaither said. "We asked, 'Is there anyone around to train us in the philosophy and strategies of sit-ins?'" McCain came to campus with *CORE Rules for Action.* The guidelines offered more than how-to directions. Also provided was a philosophical and a spiritual rationale requiring of each participant that he or she "will submit to assault and will not retaliate in kind *either* by act or word."[85]

Despite a friendly relationship among student leaders and the NAACP, Gaither did not involve Orangeburg's NAACP, even Rev. Matthew D. McCollom, pastor of Trinity United Methodist Church. An NAACP and Orangeburg movement leader, McCollom had accepted the assistance of FOR's Smiley in the 1950s and was a convert to nonviolence. Gaither believed that "if we had gone to Matthew McCollom and said we want sit-ins, I don't think he would have had any idea how to train us." Instead he believed that McCain was "critical because direct-action protest was not a legacy of the NAACP." While this choice meant training dozens, or hundreds, of students in CORE's practices, "we were interested in nonviolent direct action," said Gaither. "We were not interested in having one student arrested and then having that person be a test case and then getting a court ruling that said, 'Well, you guys can go sit at a lunch counter.'"[86]

In evening meetings at Claflin's Seabrook Gymnasium, students discussed the necessity of stepping past their parents to challenge segregation in person. Because women had a dormitory curfew of 7:30 P.M., most of the leaders were male. Groups of thirty to forty students each met several times to study *CORE Rules for Action* and *Cracking the Color Line,* a thirty-four-page booklet describing CORE's successful desegregation of restaurants, theaters, and swimming pools in the 1940s and 1950s. They also studied King's *Stride toward Freedom,* his 1958 memoir of the Montgomery bus boycott. "In these sessions we emphasized adherence to nonviolence and discussed various situations which might provoke violence. Could each one of us trust our God and our temper enough to not strike back even if kicked, slapped or spit upon?" Gaither wrote.[87]

At South Carolina State, many students remained keenly aware of the 1955–56 conflict with President Turner. Bobby Doctor, a junior, had kept this in mind when he chose the college. He found Turner "more interested in protecting the interests of white folk in the state of South Carolina, particularly whites who were in the legislature, than he was interested in protecting the interests of black students on campus." It was no secret that children of powerful white men led a privileged existence on campus, including Essie Mae Washington, the not-so-secret daughter of Strom Thurmond, former governor and an ex-officio South Carolina State board member until 1952. While Turner experienced the restrictions of a black American in the segregated South, his very light skin and straight hair meant he could pass as white, as could his wife and children, and he was rumored to do so in private life. He had come to South Carolina State in 1947 to start its law school, an underfunded, understaffed, court-ordered substitute for students denied access to the segregated University of South Carolina School of Law.[88]

So Turner was resented for a variety of reasons. "He imposed a number of different policies that were obviously not only offensive but very, very restrictive," said Doctor. Since South Carolina State was a state-supported school, its students were wards of the state. Student body officers were elected from a slate chosen by the administration; women's travel off-campus was limited; expulsion was frequently employed for even minor infractions. The students were not allowed to start an NAACP college chapter, nor could they join the NAACP, which some did anyway. A state law required the college to close if any black student enrolled under court order at any of the state-supported, all-white colleges.[89]

So South Carolina State students joined Claflin's students. This was a continuation of the colleges' entwined histories. Methodist missionaries founded Claflin in 1869, intending to prepare formerly enslaved men and women for freedom and citizenship. Initially Claflin offered students two years of grammar school and three of normal school. In 1872 the state's general assembly established the Mechanical and Agricultural Institute as part of Claflin and provided land-grant funds. Seven years later Claflin graduated its first college class. The state's 1895 constitution separated the two schools, and 1896 legislation created the Colored Normal, Industrial, Agricultural and Mechanical College of South Carolina, which became South Carolina State. Claflin and South Carolina State shared not only a history but also the same portion of town, sitting side by side on Magnolia Street.[90]

Before Greensboro's sit-ins began, Doctor and his closest friends, all social studies majors—James Enos Clyburn, Clarence "Duke" Missouri, and Lloyd Williams—discussed a new campus movement. They wanted to challenge the status quo, challenge again the administration's ruling fist. Clyburn came to the school feeling reverence for Moore and the other student protesters of 1955–56. He joined Claflin's NAACP chapter. While student leaders affiliated with or sought help from CORE, the NAACP, the SCLC, or, later, the Student Nonviolent Coordinating Committee (SNCC, pronounced "snick"), the loyalty of many protesters was first and last to each other, not their schools or organizations. While that may have further divorced students from their elders' experiences, this was their movement, and it was likely helpful that they functioned as free agents, so to speak. From the start of the student sit-ins, the NAACP and CORE engaged in a tug of war for students, publicity, and the expected infusion of new members and funds. Newman wanted demonstrators to affiliate with the NAACP and told Orangeburg students they couldn't belong to both organizations. That earned Newman a letter from Carey remarking on what "seemed to be a rumor" and reminding Newman that CORE and the NAACP had worked "hand in hand for years." When the students planned protests, and when they got on the streets, they often weren't sure or didn't care whether adults in either organization knew what was happening or would back them.[91]

Missouri, Clyburn's roommate at Camden's Mather Academy and now his college roommate, said, "If you wanted us to get in trouble, tell us not to do it. We were rebellious, but in a positive way." The friends called themselves the Broken Dish Society, inspired by a secret organization they learned about in history class. Their initial concerns were campus concerns, but the Greensboro sit-ins turned their attention from school to downtown. "We sat down one night, and we decided, hey, we're going over to Claflin and join them. We had been hesitant at first because South Carolina State being a state-supported school, we didn't know what would happen to us," said Missouri. The friends arranged to meet with Claflin's student leaders.[92]

During the 1955–56 school year, South Carolina State students had gathered regularly at Claflin after Turner prohibited political protest on campus. South Carolina State even erected a chain-link fence in an effort to keep its students from Claflin. But an oak tree on Claflin's campus became the Tree of Freedom, and its gymnasium became a regular rallying spot. With a haven a few steps away, Turner's prohibitions were futile once again, as students cooperated on plans for sit-ins on February 25. "Tom [Gaither] had reading material from CORE; I had never heard of CORE. So we had reading material, and we realized, that's what we're doing," said McDew. Scouts walked downtown to count and measure and make precise, military-like planning possible. "They checked the entrances of the Kress store and counted the number of stools at the lunch counter. The number of minutes it takes to walk from a central point on campus to Kress's was timed exactly," Gaither wrote for CORE. "From our training groups, we picked 40 students who felt confident in the techniques of nonviolence. After further training and some prayer we felt prepared for action."[93]

Classmates invited McDew to participate as spokesperson because he seemed comfortable speaking to whites. However, he felt just fine with his parents' decision, following his many arrests, to remove him from South Carolina State at the end of the school year. He told his classmates no; he wanted to leave the South and leave it alive. But McDew, who had converted to Judaism in his teens when he found himself welcome at synagogues but not segregated Christian churches, returned to the Talmud's admonition: "If I am not for myself, who will be for me? If I am for myself only, what am I? If not now, when?" To refuse was to divorce himself from the suffering of black South Carolinians who lived under oppressive conditions, amply illustrated by his arrests, and "That's terrible. You don't separate yourself from your humanity." He also considered the expectations of his grandmother and his father, who taught him that he was a "race baby," born on the night that "Brown Bomber" Joe Louis knocked out Max Schmeling in one round. To be designated so meant you represented the best of black Americans during Jim Crow. So McDew said yes.[94]

To coordinate their efforts, the students of the two colleges formed the Orangeburg Student Movement Association, somewhat connected to the state association, with Gaither and McDew as copresidents. Other South Carolina State leaders included Clyburn, James Curry, Doctor, Missouri, and Williams. While the meetings and training sessions focused on self-discipline and spiritual confidence, the forces to be met weren't predictable. "We talked about the climate and why it was necessary to do these things," said Gaither. "We continually emphasized these protests had to be nonviolent, and we had to be willing to suffer for something we believed in. We anticipated acts of violence and how you might protect yourself, how you might avoid eliciting violence."[95]

For McDew the choice was pragmatic: "To me, nonviolence was initially don't hit back; if they hit you, don't hit back." He told participating football players, "Your sister will be sitting next to you. If you hit back, they're going to hit her. Understand the nature of the beast you're dealing with. They will get the weakest: the crippled, the lame, and the blind. Don't give them a reason. If you can't do that, you can't participate."[96]

Just what could go wrong was underway in Chattanooga, Tennessee, where February 22 sit-ins were followed by days of violence that media described as a "race riot." Welcome or not, Newman traveled from Columbia to Orangeburg and stayed three days. A methodical man, he made to-do lists, scratching off accomplishments throughout each day. He was at home in Orangeburg, where he had attended high school at Claflin. He earned a bachelor of arts from Clark College and a bachelor of divinity from Gammon Theological Seminary, both in Atlanta. From 1938 to 1950, he served churches throughout the state, including Orangeburg's Trinity Methodist. While in Orangeburg he was president of its NAACP branch before his long tenure in state conference positions. He visited Orangeburg frequently, and the students stayed on his to-do lists. He surely knew that the Orangeburg students had decided, as McDew put it, that "we will do what they did in Greensboro." Just as likely, the student activists didn't consult him. "We started small. And then we brought in other people," said McDew.[97]

In their first try, McDew, Clyburn, and friends stepped into Kress, asked a waitress to serve them, were told they wouldn't be served and should leave—and that's exactly what they did. Undeterred, before noon on Thursday, February 25, about forty-five Claflin and South Carolina State students left their campuses in small groups of three or four, taking different routes but all headed to Kress. The students hoped to escape the notice of campus police, who would warn police downtown. They wanted to surprise store employees. About fifteen students walked into Kress and sat on lunch-counter stools. After the first group sat for fifteen minutes, employees posted signs saying the counter was closed. The initial wave of students left, and another group of about twenty students took their seats. White customers doused them with mustard and ketchup. Some of the white people

S. H. Kress and Co. in Orangeburg removed the seats of its counter stools
to thwart student sit-ins. In 1960 the variety store attributed a national
$4 million loss in sales to sit-ins and boycotts opposing segregation.
Courtesy of Cecil J. Williams. Photograph by Cecil J. Williams

assembling carried weapons, such as large knives, that they brandished. A
woman walked behind those sitting, tapping a baseball bat against the floor.
Others blew smoke from their cigarettes on the students.[98]

In what had become a standard rebuttal, the Kress manager began removing the padded counter seats from their pedestals, one by one. Each student remained seated until the manager approached, then relinquished his
or her seat. Afterward Kress employees strung a rope barrier, intending to
allow in only whites. The Associated Press reported, "About 25 Negroes took
seats briefly Thursday at the Kress store in Orangeburg but departed quietly

when prepared signs were displayed. The signs read, 'Closed in the interest of public safety.' Two Negroes placed $1 bills on the counter, and a third dropped 15 cents in change. One said, 'Thanks for the service we didn't get.'"[99]

The next day about sixty students returned to Kress around 11:30 A.M. As lunchtime approached, employees screwed seats back onto the pedestals, one by one, for white customers. The first group of protesters, about eight students, managed to sit. In their sit-in preparations, said Doctor, "We made it clear we would walk in, we would sit down, we would ask to be served, of course, but we wouldn't respond to anything happening to us in kind." In the afternoon three dozen arrived to sit in at the Kress lunch counter. "We students stood along the rest of the counter until 3:30. By this time, additional students had joined us, so we were several rows deep," wrote Gaither. "For the first time in my life I was really afraid," said Missouri. "To be honest, I could barely feel my legs. I was scared but determined." As Doctor watched his classmates endure harassment, he held a conversation with himself. "I sat there and said to myself, 'I hope like hell they don't come down here.' Here I was trying to get everybody to be nonviolent, but I wasn't absolutely sure I could remain nonviolent if approached by those guys. Luckily, they stayed on the far end."[100]

At 4 P.M. the store closed, briefly locking in the students. Police arrived and asked the students to leave. "We were all kind of anxious and felt we'd made our point," said Missouri. When the Kress doors opened, the students left quietly and returned to campus safely. On their walk back, said Doctor, "there was an old black woman who raised the question, 'Why are you bothering these folk? They aren't bothering y'all.'" Rather than take offense, Doctor thought, "She obviously was so conditioned, so brainwashed to accept the status quo, to accept her position in the system." For some student protesters, such reactions motivated rather than discouraged, serving as proof that the young were required to make the next push for equality. The afternoon visit did result in at least one scuffle. The state NAACP said that several white men jumped a Claflin student and struck him about the head when he tried to sit at the Kress counter. Orangeburg police chief Howell Hall disputed the report, although he did acknowledge that his officers arrested one white and one black adult after "a mild exchange of blows" occurred when students returned to Kress for the second try.[101]

Students also picketed, leaving when Chief Hall told them they couldn't demonstrate without a city permit. The students had sought and obtained clearance from the chief of police, according to Gaither, but as soon as picketing started, police told students to leave or face arrest. Throughout the weekend the students neither picketed nor tried to sit in, but their scouts reported back: Trash cans were stacked atop counters. Black customers were allowed inside, but only two at a time. That was okay; the students were planning something bigger, much bigger. Hundreds of students were training for a mass demonstration. "We were doing what the kids in Greensboro did, and we were a movement," McDew realized.[102]

Orangeburg students had proof, thanks to South Carolina State's expulsion of Moore and others, that activism could end a college career, and Turner did threaten expulsions. That's what the president of North Carolina College did in late February, and immediately thereafter three hundred students defied him with a picket line. At South Carolina State, the success of the sit-in ventures built wide interest on campus, as did news coverage of sit-ins elsewhere. The growing interest added to participants' protection: they had safety in numbers. "They couldn't kick all of us out of school," said Doctor. On March 1, a Tuesday, hundreds of Claflin and South Carolina State students marched into town, following three different routes, to arrive together at 12:30 P.M. at Memorial Plaza. The press estimated four hundred participants; the police chief said six hundred to seven hundred; Gaither's count was more than one thousand. The students carried signs: "All Sit or All Stand." "Segregation Is Obsolete." "No Color Line in Heaven." At the grassy square, garnished with a thirty-three-foot-tall monument to a Confederate soldier, they stopped to sing and pray. It was Missouri's birthday. "I was in ROTC, and everybody said, 'You'll lose your commission.' But you reach a point, the greatest part of it all, when you say, 'The fear is finished; whatever happens happens.'"[103]

Police knew in advance of the march and mustered in force. Police also deputized white bystanders as the students walked by. The Salvation Army offered doughnuts and coffee to the instant deputies. The students were very careful. They waited for red lights. They didn't walk on the grass. They were silent; communication was by hand signals. When they reached the square, SLED chief Strom stepped up to say students would be held responsible for any violence, and if violence occurred, they would be charged with inciting to riot. He also ordered students to furl their signs; they did so. Law enforcement's tactic was to arrest the nonviolent student demonstrators, sometimes all together, when whites indicated any threat of violence or became violent. Cities and the state defended in court this response to sit-ins, picketing, and marches—nonviolent protesters regularly arrested; noisy, disorderly, or violent white bystanders most often not arrested—as appropriate protection for the populace.[104]

In a diversionary move, Doctor, Clyburn, and a few other students entered Fisher's Rexall to stage a sit-in there. "We split off and went around to the other side of the square. We were not expected," said Clyburn. This was where the white power structure met, and "we were going in there to get a cup of coffee," said Clyburn. The manager immediately called the police, who arrived in record time. The students' effort at distraction didn't work; they were arrested before most of their classmates reached the square.[105]

Officers stuffed the young men one by one into the back seat of one squad car. Doctor objected to the rough treatment, but his classmates stayed intent on nonresistance. "We tried to keep him calm, because we figured they were just looking for any excuse to shoot us or something," said Clyburn. "They looked at us and decided, 'Maybe we better search them,'" said Doctor, so the officers ordered the students back out of the squad car, searched them, then stuffed them back in. "I was the last one in, and I remember this big officer begging me to run," said Doctor. Despite the arrests, they were not charged. Also arrested were a black woman and her daughter, observers who engaged in a scuffle during the march.[106]

In the Orangeburg students' view, this was a success. Participation was high. No violence occurred. No one was in jail. *Jet* magazine called the quiet, orderly march the "funeral procession of the week." Next the students initiated a boycott of the stores whose lunch counters were segregated. Orangeburg's *Times and Democrat,* which had ignored the sit-in movement at home and elsewhere, focused its March 2 report not on the local protest but on Mayor Clyde Fair's response. Fair said, "We regret that the situation in Orangeburg has led to a public demonstration in the form of marching students apparently designed to force integration of services to all races at the lunch counter of a local store. As far as we can determine, this student demonstration is the outgrowth of a movement engineered by outside non-Southern organizations to force integration of lunch counter services and to foment troubles that might be used to influence the Senate debate in Washington on the so-called Civil Rights bill."[107]

Fair, like Hollings and Gressette, was unable or unwilling to believe South Carolinians caused such a stir. But Clyburn and Missouri were natives of Camden, Doctor of Columbia, Gaither of Great Falls; McDew was a first-generation Ohioan, his family from Hazelhurst, Georgia, and his father a South Carolina State alumnus. Nor could Fair acknowledge that the students' tactical ability had bested officials. The student leaders were diligent and pragmatic. They met late at night at Claflin. "When we ought to be in the library studying, we were over at Claflin, meeting and planning," said Clyburn. Flyers, slipped under dorm doors in the early morning hours, named the time and date of the next demonstration and its starting point. Each protest contained more than one group; each group had its own leader. Leaders did not identify themselves to participants before or during each event and did not identify themselves to nonparticipants for fear they would be singled out and arrested and their arrests would lead to disarray. Each sit-in or demonstration started with small groups leaving campus along different routes to downtown. During marches students stayed on sidewalks, obeyed traffic signals, and furled or discarded posters when ordered so by police, reducing reasons for arrest.[108]

Fair designed a Catch-22: he used a city ordinance calling for a parade permit but also said public safety required no permits be granted. The mayor announced, "I have ordered the police not to allow another such demonstration in the city of Orangeburg." The state attorney general's office announced that any time a law officer believed a demonstration could produce violence, the officer could end it. Anyone refusing to disperse could be arrested. Hollings said, as youths continued to hold sit-ins throughout March, "There can be no point to any further incidents or demonstrations other than to breach the peace and cause violence." But the students—who had attended and continued to attend segregated schools despite the U.S. Supreme Court declaring segregation unconstitutional—wanted to make a point. Unequal treatment and its concomitant denial of human dignity continued not only in their schools but also in their communities' stores, restaurants, libraries, theaters, parks, pools, golf courses, and beaches.[109]

South Carolina State administrators warned students during a March 2 assembly to end their sit-ins, picketing, and marches. T. J. Crawford, a chemistry professor and the college's activities director, cited the city ordinance banning parades or demonstrations without a permit, said the college couldn't defend students arrested, and promised disciplinary action would follow any arrests. In Columbia plans to march on the State House ended when the governor promised arrests and put pressure on the Allen and Benedict college presidents. But the Orangeburg students expected by this point, even intended, to get arrested. To them, arrests weren't a worrisome threat. State and college officials drew lines that some were determined to cross. "When the mayor made his proclamation there would be no more marches, obviously he had to arrest us," said Doctor. No local or state officials anticipated that they would be overwhelmed by numbers.[110]

Denied a parade permit, Claflin and South Carolina State students marched anyway, more than one thousand strong on March 15. "Part of the nonviolence philosophy is you always reveal what you're going to do," explained Gaither, regarding the useless parade application. "It became a battle between us and the leadership of the city and the city's cops," said McDew. The students—well-dressed and instructed not to bring so much as a fingernail file—intended to walk again to Memorial Square, there to pray for equal rights and sing patriotic songs, then return to campus and class. That's not what happened, and consequently the nation discovered Orangeburg, South Carolina.[111]

"I got in the march as it went by State, marching peacefully. We all knew always that we were to be peaceful and that we were to show dignity," said Loretta Thomas, a tiny freshman, all of 102 pounds. Her father, Charles Thomas, was an education professor at South Carolina State who was active in the local NAACP. "We were just walking, walking to go downtown to the square. More than halfway there we were met by the police, saying, 'Turn around,' and by fire trucks. They told us, 'Stop. Turn around.' We did not. We kept walking, but always peaceful. I could see how the fire trucks were lining up. You could hear some of the students getting fearful, and I was saying, 'Move on. Move on.' We weren't loud, but we did start chanting, 'We will overcome. Freedom! Freedom! We will overcome.'"[112]

Lloyd Williams's group walked just a few blocks past campus, to the local Piggly Wiggly, before firefighters and police told the students to turn around. "I was walking at the head of the line with a young lady," he told the *New York Post*. "The police chief insisted I was the leader. I told him I was not the leader and that I had no right to ask them to turn around." Students behind him shouted, "We are all leaders. If one is arrested, we will all be arrested." Police arrested Williams, then the police chief instructed, "All right, get them niggers," and firefighters turned fire hoses on the group, according to the *Post*. "One student had water hit his ear with such force it began to bleed, and he stood there and took it," Williams said. "No one ran away. The students stood their ground and kept pressing forward. They began to sing, 'Mine eyes have seen the glory of the coming of the Lord.'"[113]

Not only local police but also SLED and other cities' police and firefighters awaited the students, according to an NAACP report. Law officers lobbed tear gas at two groups. Firefighters turned their hoses on three other groups as they approached Memorial Plaza. The powerful spray hit Gilbert "Gigi" Zimmerman and knocked him down. The yearbook editor for South Carolina State, Zimmerman was fewer than four feet tall, and he "spun around like a top" in the surge of water, Thomas said. "The others surrounded him, to save his life, really." The power of the water knocked down Willa Mae

Dillard, a blind, seventeen-year-old South Carolina State student, who was then "swept down the street like a match stem," according to Gaither, who was moving from spot to spot to monitor the protest. The police chief again asked student leaders to step forward and others to disperse. When the marchers didn't comply with either demand, all were arrested. Two officers lifted Cecil J. Williams, photographing the use of fire hoses, from his crouch and shut him in their car, his film and Rolleiflex tossed into their trunk. Left alone and seething about his camera, he disconnected the wires to the police radio, ending the ability to receive or answer calls. Also arrested were ten students attempting sit-ins at the Rexall and Kress stores.[114]

Before they reached the square, Thomas's group was told again to stop, to turn around. When the marchers didn't obey, they, too, were told that they were under arrest. The day was rainy and cold, and the fire hoses' spray soaked to the skin many of the students. Even so, law officers ordered most of the approximately five hundred arrested into the open-air stockade of the county jail, known locally as the Pink Palace or Pink Castle, thanks to its fortresslike appearance. Newspapers throughout the nation published photographs of the neatly dressed students—the men in ties and overcoats, the women in church hats and coats—penned within ten-foot-tall chain-link fencing. Thomas could see her two sisters within the stockade and felt safe until the police pulled her out of the crowd, addressing her as "Dr. Thomas's daughter." They locked her in a jail cell with three other women, one accused of murder, another of prostitution. "I kept saying to myself, 'How long am I going to be in here?' I said, 'I didn't do any of those things. All I did was march and walk and ask for equality and freedom.'" Thomas was horrified by the jail's filth, the rats and roaches, and the company. She felt "fearful with madness." However, her cellmates treated her kindly. "They took me like I was their daughter and protected me." When a meal of mush, grease on top, a biscuit on the side, was shoved through the bars and Thomas refused her portion, her companions told her, "Darling, eat it. You don't know when you're going to get food again."[115]

Students who hadn't been arrested or hadn't participated in the march formed columns and, two abreast, circled the courthouse, continuing until police gathered at the entrance to arrest them. Gaither stood there, talking to Herbert L. Wright, who was the national youth director for the NAACP, a former CORE representative, and a veteran. Told to move, Gaither joined the group circumnavigating. "I was arrested with a group of some 200 students marching around the courthouse in protest over the earlier mass arrests," Gaither wrote. "At first police told us we would be permitted to march if we kept moving in an orderly manner, but then they announced that unless we returned to the campus at once we would be arrested. I was seized first as one of the leaders and was held in jail for four hours." Still more students collected outside the fencing, tossing grapefruit, apples, and doughnuts to friends. Emily England, a South Carolina State student, bought 150 sandwiches from Helen Thompson, owner of the College Soda Shop, who sold them for a total of ten dollars. Thompson also provided free cigarettes, chewing gum, and coffee. Within the stockade the students sang patriotic songs, including "God Bless America" and "The Star-Spangled Banner." They prayed for an end to segregation.[116]

Jailers placed Isaac Arnold, suspected by them of being a student leader, in solitary confinement, where he stood in his wringing wet clothes in water three inches deep. Other students were held in a steamy basement, overheated by the boiler room. Clyburn was there. "They loaded fifty of us in a cell for sixteen," he said. "They had us crammed in like sardines. They had radiators in the ceiling, and the radiators were leaking hot water, so it was almost like torture. We would take turns moving around in the cell so no one would get scalded. You would take your turn under the hot water." Among the constants during training was a promise, said McDew: "If they do anything to any one of us, consider it as done to you. We have to look out for each other." And that's what they did.[117]

While the press reported the day's temperature as forty degrees, Gaither said it was a freezing twenty-eight degrees, following a March 13 all-time low in Columbia of twenty-four degrees. Police prohibited shivering students, stuck in the stockade for four cold hours, from accepting dry clothes and blankets that supporters stripped from dorm rooms and tossed over the fences. Buses lined up in front of the courthouse to transport students to Columbia and the state penitentiary. The students hadn't asked for legal assistance, but it arrived in the person of NAACP attorneys. Gaither said, "On the day of the mass demonstrations, NAACP officers were in Columbia. We didn't even tell them. We reasoned if we needed them to back us, they would." After all, he thought, "the adults didn't have much choice to come to our defense. It would look terrible to be a civil rights leader and say, 'We can't get them out of jail because we didn't tell them to go in the first place.' In Orangeburg the entire movement was without adults; we just did what we had to do." And so did the elders. Newman alerted attorney Matthew Perry, who called in a legal team: Lincoln C. Jenkins, W. Newton Pough, Zack Townsend, and Willie Smith. Newman and the NAACP's current and upcoming state conference heads, Sharper and J. Arthur Brown, traveled to Orangeburg. Initially a cash bond of two hundred dollars each was set. NAACP officers immediately paid one thousand dollars for the release of five students—Brown provided six hundred of that—and began collecting funds from local members and business owners.[118]

With the governor's permission, officials agreed to release the rest of the students on surety bonds, dropped from fifty to ten dollars each. By 8 P.M. most were out of confinement, thanks to signed bonds from a local mortician, a retired farm extension agent, a service station owner, and a South Carolina State professor. Released students collected in the Claflin gym, where Gaither met Perry for the first time. When Perry told Gaither that the NAACP would use its resources to defend the students, that felt like a victory, too, to Gaither, who had hoped the students' actions might force support. Dr. H. V. Manning, Claflin's president, opened the college dining hall and provided students a hot supper, at Newman's request. Herbert Wright arrived and addressed the students. Referring to Willa Mae Dillard, he said, "I am deeply hurt and embarrassed that a group of grown men who profess to be intelligent, civilized human beings, would use a high-pressure fire hose to subdue and beat to the ground by the force of the water, a blind, helpless 17-year-old Negro coed." More than fifty demonstrators needed medical care. When men trained a fire hose on one young woman, knocking her down and holding the water on her, the force broke her kneecap. Another female student, hit in the face by the water, lost three teeth. Still another needed her eyes treated after exposure to tear gas. Several students soon came down with colds, even pneumonia; some were hospitalized.[119]

Ultimately Orangeburg charged 388 students with breach of peace, which carried a maximum fine of one hundred dollars or thirty days in jail. The city intended to move those charged through quick trials of fifteen students at a time, with eleven Columbia-based protesters scheduled for the first hearing. But on Wednesday, March 16, the first trial was postponed through the efforts of the NAACP attorneys, who objected to the wording of the warrants and asked what statutes were violated. On Thursday the defense attorneys— Perry, Jenkins, William W. Bennett, and Cleveland Stevens—delayed the trial again. They objected to the systematic exclusion of black citizens from jury lists and juries and Orangeburg's resulting all-white jury. The day wasn't entirely grim. According to Herbert Wright, some students celebrated tricking the tear-gas-tossing police into gassing themselves.[120]

Turner and Bruce White, the trustees' chairman, vowed disciplinary action, including expulsion. This didn't seem an idle threat. Alabama State College had expelled nine students and placed twenty on probation for their participation in sit-ins and demonstrations. In a press conference, Hollings affirmed his policy of arresting the demonstrators, responding not only to the Orangeburg mass march but to the coordinated protests in Rock Hill, Columbia, and Sumter. Evidently galled by sit-in demonstrators reading Bibles, Hollings said the students appeared to believe that "in a crusade they can violate any law, especially if they have a Bible in their hand. Our law enforcement officers have Bibles, too—but in their hearts, not their hands."[121]

The nation responded with disapproval to South Carolina's use of fire hoses, tear gas, and outdoor imprisonment. A *San Francisco Chronicle* headline read "Southern Police Put 400 Negroes in Outdoor Cage." *Jet* magazine observed, "Students in Orangeburg, South Carolina sang 'God Bless America' after they were arrested and herded, like animals, into a stockade." The *New York Times* said the students sang "God Bless America" after being "herded to a stockade" and ran a front-page photo of stoic, well-dressed young adults confined by a tall chain-link fence. A Canadian reporter visiting Orangeburg after the march wrote, "The ghost of Mohandas Gandhi is walking the red clay of the Bible belt, and the white South is frightened." He noted, "There is something awesome about these Orangeburg boys and girls who have pledged themselves to take blows without returning them and yield to arrest without a fight."[122]

President Dwight D. Eisenhower, in a March 16 press conference, said that orderly and peaceful assemblies were not only constitutional but also "recognized in our country as proper since we have been founded." Asked if the "Gandhi-like passive demonstrations" demonstrated moral courage, Eisenhower said some were "unquestionably a proper expression of a conviction." He added this: "Now let me make one thing clear. I am deeply sympathetic with the efforts of any group to enjoy the rights, the rights of equality that are guaranteed by the Constitution. I do not believe that violence in any form furthers that aspiration, and I deplore any violence that is exerted to prevent them in having and enjoying these rights." Newman telegrammed Eisenhower to applaud his statement and ask that the U.S. Department of Justice join in the arrested students' defense.[123]

Hollings responded with another press conference. He called the president "confused as to the facts and the law." He said it was obvious that "things were getting out of hand." The governor said, "Demonstrators, even though they carried Bibles, were intent on being jailed and promoting violence, and observers were intent on their communities not being taken over by antagonistic groups even under the guise of the Bible and the National Anthem." Eisenhower also had said he supported biracial conferences in every southern city. Hollings didn't like that, either. He said that Eisenhower had done "great damage to peace and good order in South Carolina." He opposed such committees, saying, "I would be taking good colored leaders who are helping us in South Carolina and ruining them."[124]

Next former President Harry S. Truman weighed in. Truman, who ran a Kansas City men's clothing store before entering politics, offered his two cents during a press conference. Asked his opinion of the sit-ins, he replied, "If anybody came to my store and tried to stop business, I'd throw him out." Days later, when Detroit's NAACP branch challenged Truman via telegram, he stuck to his statement: "I would do just what I said I would." But in Florida, Gov. Leroy Collins made a March 20 radio and television address during which he called the use of fire hoses and tear gas during demonstrations "rigid and punitive." He observed, "We can never stop Americans from struggling to be free," and vowed, "I don't care who the citizen is, he is going to be protected in pursuing his legal rights in Florida." He announced a biracial committee on race relations.[125]

The Orangeburg trials began on March 18, with six men on the jury, just one a black juror, their names drawn from a cigar box. The students pled not guilty. Given that 388 students had been charged, Perry earned laughter in the courtroom when he told Julian Wolfe, the solicitor, that he planned to present 388 defense witnesses, maybe more. In the day's only testimony, Chief Hall said he ordered the use of fire hoses when marchers refused to halt. He also termed tear gas, used in the streets, an additional deterrent. The police chief said law enforcement officers arrested the students because "they failed to abide by a city ordinance which I had ordered them to."[126]

During the trial's second day, the assistant police chief and two SLED agents agreed in their testimony that the marchers were well behaved and orderly, except for their refusal to disband. Perry took one law enforcement officer through arrests on Amelia Street. The officer testified that he had told students at the head of a column to halt. They conferred, then continued walking. He announced they were under arrest and ordered them to follow him. They did, two hundred or so students following one policeman to the county jail. Perry believed that "the record was just perfect as a freedom of assembly, freedom of speech case." Defending the use of fire hoses on such peaceful groups, an assistant state attorney general demanded, "Should we wait until some zoot-suited fool, white or colored, stops somebody or cuts somebody, and the roof comes off?"[127]

Perry called three South Carolina State students to the stand: Clyburn, Willie Mattison, and Irene Hazel Brown. All three said they had planned to sing, pray, and petition city officials, who were denying them freedom of speech and the right to peaceful assembly. Under cross examination Clyburn acknowledged that he knew Mayor Fair had said demonstrations would no longer be tolerated. Brown testified that the students wished to express a desire for equality, a desire to live "on an equal basis with any other race." Perry introduced several motions: State evidence should be expunged because it was not linked to the defendants. The defendants were arrested because they failed to obey an order, not because of breach of peace. The state failed to prove that the defendants committed breach of peace or were engaged in unlawful assembly. Perry also introduced a plea to information. It asserted that the defendants were engaged in peaceful and lawful assemblage for the purpose of expressing grievances and petitioning for redress of grievances, activities protected by Article 1 of the South Carolina Constitution and the First and Fourteenth Amendments of the U.S. Constitution.[128]

Wilkins, the NAACP executive secretary, said the state had misused its police powers, employing "storm trooper action." In a telegram to Hollings and in national press releases, he charged South Carolina with damaging the country's image "as a citadel of liberty" through the "cowardly and bestial actions of the Orangeburg police officers who used tear gas and other Nazi-like tactics" against the students. Sharper arranged a March 24 meeting with Hollings and, in a preemptive press release, noted, "We call upon the Governor to recognize that certain laws and customs of South Carolina conflict with stated laws and principles of our federal government. When Negroes study and come to appreciate and love these principles of democracy, they should be far less than intelligent if they continued to labor under this conflict of national ideals and section customs without any protest." Sharper pointed out that fire hoses and tear gas were unnecessary because the students were peaceful and submitted to arrest. Inflamed rather than chastened, Hollings assigned his legal aide and an assistant attorney general to help prosecute the students.[129]

As the Orangeburg trials began, sixty-two southern lawyers gathered in Washington, D.C., at the behest of the NAACP, to plan defense strategies for the South's arrested students. Marshall promised, "We're going to appeal every fine," an expensive vow, given an estimated one thousand southern students had been arrested so far. The national NAACP had raised just forty thousand dollars for defense and appeals, most already spent on bail and legal fees. Now, Marshall promised, "We're pulling out all the stops." Marshall and other LDF attorneys also used the three-day meeting to scrutinize federal rights along with local attorneys. As the meeting wrapped up, Marshall said the commonly used charges—trespassing, parading without a license, violating fire regulations by blocking store aisles, conspiracy to obstruct commerce, and breach of peace—were employed "as means to enforce racial discrimination." He announced that the lawyers agreed that using public force in the form of arrest by the police or conviction by the courts was state enforcement of private discrimination and thus a violation of the Fourteenth Amendment. Therefore NAACP lawyers expected to challenge the student arrests as violations of the amendment, which said, in part, "nor shall any State deprive any person of life, liberty, or property, without due process of law, nor deny any person within its jurisdiction the equal protection of the laws." In Orangeburg Perry was offering exactly that defense.[130]

Marshall followed up his Washington meeting with a trip to Charlotte for an NAACP Freedom Mass Meeting. At a news conference, he promised again that the NAACP would defend anyone brought to court for participating in "a lawful and peaceful demonstration." He said the Orangeburg demonstrators engaged in peaceful assembly; any threat of disorder came from white onlookers, some carrying firearms. He said that sit-in participants could not rightfully be convicted of trespassing. However, he also acknowledged uncertainty as to whether courts would rule that small businesses must serve all races. The uncertainty had to do with the common law expectation of service to all versus an owner's right to refuse service. In other words was racial discrimination constitutional in public accommodations that are privately owned and operated businesses serving the public? Marshall was fully aware that sit-in participants were tired of waiting for legal remedies to inequality; that was why they held sit-ins. "And if you mean, are the young people impatient with me, the answer is yes," he told journalists.[131]

South Carolina's black students had effectively made their points about their rights, their dignity, their ability to remain peaceful under attack—and had been heard nationwide. They had coordinated a tour de force: Rock Hill's sit-ins and city hall demonstration, with 71 arrests; Orangeburg's mass demonstration by 1,000 students, with 388 breach-of-peace charges; sit-ins in Columbia, with 9 arrests; three dozen Morris students singing at Sumter's courthouse, without arrests—and no violence anywhere on the students' part. CORE had offered training; the NAACP had provided bail or bond to get them out of jail. CORE and NAACP attorneys had defended them in court. They had organizational support, but this was the students' show and their triumph.[132]

The NAACP may have felt it barely held a tiger by its tail. Wilkins, in a national memo citing Orangeburg, wrote, "This is a BIG PUSH. Everyone's shoulder should be at the wheel. This job requires youth and enthusiasm. It also requires age and experience. It also requires praying and preaching." Convictions and subsequent appeals ensured that the NAACP would continue a legal attack on segregation in public spaces, so, of course, Wilkins named the NAACP's primary focus: "It also requires legal activism in court." He warned, "Close cooperation is a must. Let's *push forward* not *pull sideways*."[133]

In March in San Antonio, Texas, five of six stores desegregated lunch counters after a month of conversations among business leaders and pastors. The dialogue, started by the executive director of the city's Council of Churches, was independently furthered by Mary Lillian Andrews, the seventeen-year-old leader of the local NAACP Youth Council. In Galveston, Texas, owners voluntarily desegregated after conversations among business, civic, and religious leaders. In Richmond, Virginia, two months of picketing led to four historic-district drugstores desegregating, while downtown department stores did not.[134]

In Orangeburg trials continued, the students appearing before a magistrate in groups of up to thirty at a time. Eventually 373 Orangeburg protesters were found guilty of breach of peace and sentenced to fifty-dollar fines or thirty days in jail. Perry filed appeals. The students barely paused. Three more sit-ins at the Orangeburg Kress resulted in five more arrests and convictions, fines of one hundred dollars, and appeals. The NAACP tried to keep up. Newman reported twenty-seven thousand dollars raised around the state for protesters' defense.[135]

In mid-April, Newman presented the notarized statements of thirteen Orangeburg demonstrators to the South Carolina Advisory Committee on Civil Rights. Newman wanted the committee to investigate a possible violation of the constitutional right to peaceful assembly. Dewey M. Duckett Sr., a black dentist from Rock Hill, read aloud from a student's statement: "A fire hose was turned on me like I was a burning house." However, chairman McIver said, "If they want to picket two or three at a time and engage in a financial boycott, I don't see any objection to that, but if the masses get out of hand we've got anarchy." Gaither and McDew spoke at the next meeting, in May, protesting the use of fire hoses. Barbara Jean Tilly of South Carolina State described a foot injury when fire-hose spray forced her to her knees and a hospitalization for the flu after her drenching. Gaither said the students believed—once their request for a parade permit was denied, as the mayor had vowed—they had no recourse but to march to present their grievances. "We felt we had the right to peaceful assembly," he said. McDew made a similar point. "We must resort to demonstrations when the normal channels for mediating problems are not open to us."[136]

In July the committee wrote Mayor Fair in Orangeburg and the federal Civil Rights Commission in Washington, D.C., to say it supported the right to peaceful protest by all citizens and recommended that local groups be set up to deal with racial tensions. On the other hand, McIver personally believed the students were "unwitting dupes" of the Communist Party. Hollings continued to insist this was so, as did Truman, reiterating in the spring and summer that the sit-ins were communist-inspired.[137]

Ella Baker's assessment differed radically from those in the white and the black power structures. For her the student movement demonstrated homegrown creativity and courage, a group-centered leadership heading in a new, even revolutionary direction. Baker, a former national NAACP field secretary and director of branches, had helped organize the SCLC in 1957. She was leaving her SCLC post as interim executive director, and she proposed the SCLC invest in collecting sit-in leaders at her alma mater, Shaw University in Raleigh. Her conference invitation predicted "great potential for social change." Held April 16–18, the Southwide Student Leadership Conference on Nonviolent Resistance to Segregation brought to life just what Baker hoped, a student organization independent of CORE, the NAACP, and the SCLC. The idea—a student organization spread across southern states—had been brewing among Nashville's activists and took shape during a February retreat at Highlander Folk School in Monteagle, Tennessee. Baker wrote about the students a few weeks later in the *Southern Patriot*, the newspaper of the Southern Conference Educational Fund. She wrote that she believed the students' sit-ins were concerned "with something much bigger than a hamburger or even a giant-sized Coke," that the students felt they had "a destined date with freedom."[138]

McDew attended the Shaw conference, one of five representatives of the Orangeburg movement. The all-male group knew they would meet students from other cities who had held marches. They also knew that they arrived as heroes, participants in what McDew termed "a solid movement" and, better yet, stars of the biggest demonstration so far. "We came with a reputation. We were the people who had coffee dumped on our heads, who faced cops with billy clubs and fire hoses," who stayed true to their vow of nonviolent direct action, said McDew. They rode together in a Claflin student's car, with money for gas, room, and board provided by Reverend McCollom, a founding member of the SCLC. Hamm and Plummer came from Rock Hill; Columbia sent one representative and Sumter two.[139]

At a press conference, Reverend King noted that the students' sit-ins were spontaneous, their activism valuable: "More Negro freedom fighters have revealed to the nation and the world their determination and courage than has occurred in many years." He also noted that the students lacked a national organization. On the conference's second day, SCLC leaders privately discussed subsuming the student movement, which Baker vehemently opposed. Baker, concerned about consequences "when the prophetic leader turns out to have feet of clay," met privately with students to encourage their autonomy. Among the 200 conference participants, 126 of them students, McDew helped develop what came next.[140]

James M. Lawson Jr., who had been expelled from Vanderbilt Divinity School in early March for his role in Nashville's sit-ins, delivered a conference address, describing the students' desire for direct action and their impatience with past strategies. He criticized the NAACP as preoccupied with fundraising and lawsuits and thus failing to develop "our greatest resource: a people no longer the victims of racial evil, who can act in a disciplined manner to implement the Constitution." Lawson had grown up in Masillon, like McDew; their families knew each other. His dedication to a Christian concept of unconditional love and to Gandhian nonviolence helped shape the Nashville participants into what McDew admiringly called "nonviolent warriors." Their approach resonated with McDew and influenced the emergence of a new student organization. Baker also spoke, drawing a line between the old guard's bureaucracy and the students' radical confrontation of segregation. For McDew and others, the weekend's decisions were shaped by trust in Baker and her conviction that the students' all-inclusive activism and group-centered leadership were the hope of the civil rights struggle. McCollom had told McDew to trust Baker, and McDew decided, "Anything Ella Baker says, you can believe with your heart and soul. Anything she can support, you can support."[141]

McDew discovered that he disagreed with King's stance—that the students become a "spearhead" for SCLC, a youth group dedicated to mass and nonviolent direct action—and agreed with Baker's that the students should form an autonomous group in which their vision and energy were neither diluted nor diverted by existing leaders and existing agendas. For McDew autonomy wasn't the only issue; another was King's description of nonviolence "as a way of life." When approached by King, McDew told him that the majority of the Orangeburg participants were "regular people," likely suppressing their own violent nature to get things done. McDew said he didn't want to reject such people. He believed of himself and fellow protesters that

Charles Frederick McDew, at the head of this Orangeburg march,
led combined protests by South Carolina State College and Claflin
University students in 1960. The sign James Reeder held referred
to veterans of World War I and II coming home to segregation,
which denied them full citizenship rights.
Courtesy of Cecil J. Williams. Photograph by Cecil J. Williams

"we are being nonviolent because we have to be; otherwise, they'll kill us."
McDew later said that nonviolent direct action was a useful tactic with a
short life because "you cannot make a moral appeal in an amoral society." He
hashed this out with other young leaders, including Charles Sherrod of Virginia Union University and Diane Nash and James Bevel of Nashville, and
found that he respected the Nashville students' commitment to nonviolence
but resisted the SCLC's interest.[142]

By the end of Easter weekend, a Temporary Student Coordinating Committee existed, with McDew one of the founders. Recommendations that
issued from April's founding stated that "nonviolence is our creed," recognized "the virtue of the movement," and endorsed "the practice of going to
jail rather than accepting bail." This was not just a nod to Nashville. Lawson drafted what became the foundational statement of purpose. It said, in
part, "We affirm the philosophical or religious ideal of nonviolence as the

foundation of our purpose, the presupposition of our faith, and the manner of our action." The students named as their adult advisers Baker, fifty-six; King and Lawson, both thirty-one; and Constance Curry, twenty-three, who was director of the Southern Project for the National Student Association (NSA). Baker set up, in SCLC's Atlanta headquarters, room for what became SNCC.[143]

The established organizations kept trying to get a handle on the student movement and to claim some credit for the students' achievements. A May interagency meeting, held at Penn Center in Frogmore, South Carolina, included CORE, the NAACP, the SCLC, and the American Friends Service Committee (AFSC), a Quaker organization that engaged in antiracism work. Ruby Hurley, the NAACP's Southeast regional director, wrote a report depicting ongoing competitiveness. When conversation turned to the sit-ins, Hurley asked Baker to discuss the Easter conference at Shaw. Baker reported on a developing interest in "moral witnessing" by students willing to go to jail without bail, wrote Hurley. A friend of Baker's, Hurley reacted by describing this as "confusion related to the procedures seeking an end to discriminatory practices in stores and public accommodations." When the group addressed the question of fundraisers, funds, and their recipients, Hurley wrote, "Miss Baker's reply impelled us to have Reverend Newman spell out the costs being borne by the NAACP in South Carolina as a concrete example of who is bearing the brunt of responsibility and, to set the record straight, on the origin of the sit-ins."[144]

It could be argued that multiple approaches by multiple organizations diffused and weakened the attack on Jim Crow. When Marshall spoke at Fisk University in Nashville, he praised the successful sit-ins. Next he told his audience of more than four thousand that refusing bail and staying in jail was a mistake. The right strategy was the NAACP strategy, Marshall said. The NAACP remained focused on its litigation endgame: case by case, legally challenge the practices of Jim Crow; defeat segregation through the Constitution and the courts. The NAACP had prepared the ground the students marched upon and perhaps expected respect and gratitude.[145]

It also could be argued that ending Jim Crow required attacks by all comers from all sides. CORE and SNCC barreled ahead. James Robinson, a cofounder and the executive secretary of CORE, urged that leaders "not be so attached to organizations that we overlook the movement as a whole." He believed what he called "the usual legal method" and nonviolent direct action were complementary, not contradictory. SNCC wanted to create something new, a youth-based collaboration. In its first year, the SNCC founders described themselves as people who refused to accept injustice, who went to jail rather than submit. They decided that SNCC would assist existing local groups "in the intensification of the movement." As their black-and white jacket button said, "Support Southern Students."[146]

Gaither and McDew threw themselves into work for different organizations with differing approaches. A senior at Claflin, Gaither took to the road, sponsored by the NAACP. In February he served as chairman of an NAACP Southeast Regional Conference for youths. In late March he spoke in New York City's churches and in television and radio appearances. In April he attended a training and planning meeting at Penn Center for 125 members of NAACP youth councils and college chapters in the Southeast. In attendance were J. Arthur Brown, H. P. Sharper, Herbert Wright, and Julie Varner Wright, a straight-A Claflin graduate hired by Newman to visit and recruit youth that summer. Also in April, Gaither spoke throughout California's Bay Area, telling an audience of nine hundred at Longshoreman's Hall about the intertwining of Christianity and nonviolent protest. At the University of California, Berkeley, he received a standing ovation. In San Francisco the *Sun-Reporter* called Gaither "one of the heroes of the third American revolution." In late April he made speeches in Indiana. In May, CORE published "Orangeburg: Behind the Carolina Stockade," Gaither's account of Orangeburg's mass arrests. In May he spoke in Englewood, New Jersey, and St. Louis, Missouri. He carried his schoolbooks wherever he traveled so he could keep up with his studies.[147]

McDew participated in SNCC's first meeting in Atlanta in May, during which founders ratified the April statement of purpose; elected as chairman Marion S. Barry Jr., a Nashville movement leader; and established the *Student Voice* as the official newsletter. At the June meeting, SNCC began filling voting memberships, with McDew the official delegate for South Carolina. SNCC's first newsletter announced, "Freedom . . . is to stop living the lie."[148]

Over the summer SNCC introduced itself to the platform committees of the Democratic and Republican national conventions and sent all members of Congress letters urging civil rights legislation. The Republicans' platform reaffirmed "the constitutional right to peaceable assembly." The Democrats' platform supported "peaceful demonstrations for first-class citizenship." South Carolina opposed the Democrats' civil rights plank, which supported sit-ins, voting guarantees, and school desegregation. In July, Hollings flew to Los Angeles to make an emergency appeal to stop the civil rights resolutions. He claimed, "The Southern position is the constitutional way and the American way." During a convention fight, Hollings said that South Carolina police actions were intended to protect black citizens' rights, that the state had allowed sit-ins until "radical groups" from outside the state captured the students. The allowance Hollings alluded to had been short-lived. Barely two weeks after the first sit-in, he publicly pressured merchants to sign trespass warrants. And southern merchants often did. By now about 1,400 students had been arrested throughout the South, their fines totaling more than one hundred thousand dollars.[149]

Neither the promise of violence nor continuing arrests stopped the Orangeburg students. In April and May, they held three more sit-ins at Kress. A May 13 sit-in brought four anonymous bomb warnings. The store closed for forty-five minutes while SLED agents and local police searched the premises. The manager sought advice from national Kress officials and didn't pursue arrest, but on May 16 three students quickly ended their sit-in when the manager told police to eject them if they didn't leave. On May 17, 300 students attended an NAACP-sponsored statewide youth rally at Claflin. In August, McDew and representatives of fourteen other southern colleges attended the Southern Student Human Relations Seminar, which had been supported by the NSA since 1958. White and black students spent three weeks at the University of Minnesota studying racial prejudice and methods that might lead to desegregation. During the NSA National Congress that followed, SNCC requested support of sit-ins; that led to a debate and a 305–37 endorsement by NSA members.[150]

In September, Gaither's dedication yielded an appointment as a CORE field secretary. Traveling among Rock Hill, Sumter, and Orangeburg, Gaither prompted picketing, coached a sit-in campaign in Rock Hill, and helped South Carolina State and Claflin students found a joint CORE student chapter, led by Napoleon Giles with Clyburn as vice president. In Orangeburg, Gaither worried about CORE's ability to pull the student body into the movement again and worried especially about Newman. Gaither wrote that Newman was warning, "CORE would start trouble that the NAACP would have to clean up."[151]

McDew was still enrolled in school, but his focus was civil rights too. He, Jones, Sherrod, and Timothy Jenkins of Howard University decided they would soon drop out of college. They would devote themselves, as McDew put it, to building up SNCC and thus fashioning a movement. When SNCC convened an Atlanta conference on October 14–16, representatives attended from Friendship and Claflin, Morris, Benedict, and South Carolina State. McDew, a workshop leader, found himself among heady company. Speakers at the Nonviolence and the Achievement of Desegregation conference included such notables as Baker, King, Lawson, and Lillian Smith, author of *Strange Fruit* and *Killers of the Dream*. Sen. John F. Kennedy sent an encouraging telegram: "I pledge that if elected president, we will move to make the freedom guaranteed in our Constitution a living reality for all our citizens."[152]

On October 20 police arrested McDew and five Claflin students for a Kress sit-in. In response more than one hundred students marched to the city jail to object. The city responded with its fire trucks, threatening again to douse students with the high-pressure hoses. The students disbanded, but a second Kress sit-in by two students followed, and they were arrested. That night Claflin students gathered, and Julie Wright warned against further demonstrations, saying that the NAACP wouldn't back them without advance notice of demonstrations' dates and purposes. McDew, the four other men, and one woman remained in jail until October 24.[153]

McDew wrote Valerie Brown, of Texas Christian University, on the jail's brown paper towels, "Oh sickness, oh hate. Go and leave the hearts of man. Let me be me, Charles Frederick McDew, man, student, lover of life. I don't want to be that nigger with no personality, no being, just a dark blob. I want to be me with the color that I love, with my eyes, my body, my dreams and inspirations." SNCC reported in its newsletter, "Orangeburg resorted to its usual method and brought out the firehoses to break up the students who were singing in front of the jail."[154]

In November SNCC delegates elected McDew their new chairman. Gaither returned to Claflin in December to lead training in nonviolent direct action. CORE attorney Finney stayed on alert because, as Carey noted, "We obviously can't control what the city of Orangeburg does." McDew and Gaither had graduated from local to national leadership.[155]

Voorhees College, Denmark:
First Sit-In Held Monday, February 29, 1960

Within a few days of Orangeburg's first sit-ins, college students in rural Bamberg County attempted their own. Tiny Denmark, home to two drugstores and one whites-only diner, was also home to Voorhees School and Junior College. In 1897 Elizabeth Evelyn Wright, a graduate of Tuskegee Institute, founded Voorhees as an industrial school. In 1924 the school affiliated with the Episcopal Church and, in 1947, became a junior college. Voorhees, with its campus of two-story brick buildings and tall oak trees, functioned independently of Denmark, two miles away. The distance was emotional as well as physical. For campus residents Voorhees and the rural black community were sufficient. Students seldom walked into town but weren't cut off from the world. Newspapers, television newscasts, and friends and family elsewhere fed them the latest information, so they knew immediately of the Greensboro sit-ins and, within days, discussed holding their own. Cleveland Sellers, a high school student on the campus, worked at the junior college's student union, whose one television offered daily updates on the sit-ins. The first shock was black folk on TV, said Sellers. Then, "As it would unfold each night, showing what's going on, the crowds got larger and larger, and the students began to talk about what are we going to do." The Voorhees discussions continued in meetings of the Student Government Association and the NAACP youth chapter.[156]

Sidney Glee, who grew up in Suffolk, Virginia, talked with older brother George Glee and friend Alfred Robinson about what might happen in their hometown. There the three had worked in privileged positions for the two drugstores, hiring other black youth to make bicycle deliveries of prescriptions and acting as chauffeurs for the white owners' wives and children. The three agreed one of their bosses might have accepted that black customers would want the same treatment as white customers; they weren't so sure about the other. Such speculation led the young men to ask themselves whether they should stage a sit-in. They hesitated. Grateful to be attending college and playing football, they didn't want a misstep that would harm them or the institution. "The school meant a lot to us. We didn't want to do anything that would hurt the school," said Sidney Glee. However, "Two to three days later, it began to have a life of its own." The conversation continued among a select group of campus athletes; soon several young men were meeting. "We decided we would do that in Denmark," said Arthur L. Copeland, a sophomore who grew up in Nansemond County, Virginia.[157]

For Sellers, water boy for the football team and thus privy to the sit-in plans, student activism made sense. Sellers's parents subscribed to the newspapers and magazines of black America—the *Baltimore Afro-American*, the *Pittsburgh Courier*, *Ebony*, and *Jet*—and belonged to the Voorhees educational community. For Sellers the call to action began with the murder of Emmett Till in August 1955, when Sellers was eleven. Two white men kidnapped, tortured, and murdered Till, a fourteen-year-old who was visiting relatives near Money, Mississippi, after he allegedly spoke to and whistled at a white woman in a local store. Three days later his body, trussed by barbed wire to a cotton-gin fan, was pulled from Mississippi's Tallahatchie River and sent home to Chicago. Mamie Elizabeth Till-Mobley insisted on an open casket at her son's funeral, attended by fifty thousand. *Jet* and the *Chicago Defender* published photographs of Till's mutilated corpse. White- and black-owned media followed the September trial. An all-white, all-male jury acquitted Till's murderers, who confessed the following year in *Look* magazine.[158]

"A part of our history would be that we had an obligation as a generation to change a system that allowed a kid, Emmett Till, to be murdered just because he was African American," said Sellers. "Then the other part was we watched the whole judicial system operate, and we contended that justice was just not available for African Americans." Thus the NAACP strategy of pursuing social change through the courts was, for Sellers and many youths like him, "just too slow." He began to believe, "We had an obligation to vindicate what had happened to Emmett Till. Generationally, that was a call to action. The question was 'What do we do, and how do we do it?'" The sit-ins seemed at least a partial answer. Sellers and his older classmates saw peers taking direct action, and this roused them to make their own statement.[159]

The Voorhees students set up meetings through private conversations or notes passed during lunch in the school cafeteria. "We would meet late at night so no one would know what we were trying to do," said Herman Gloster, a freshman on the football team. One student crawled down a dorm wall, cutting his hands on a cable as he made his way to the ground and secret meetings at Menafee Hall, a sprawling dormitory painted white and nicknamed the White House. High school students, including Sellers, participated in the planning, but the group decided only male college students would demonstrate and only those whose parents weren't in danger of losing Bamberg County jobs or store accounts as a result.[160]

In a remote town in an impoverished county, "How would a family get something to eat if they couldn't go to the one grocery store?" asked Gloster. "We didn't want to upset relationships; we didn't want our parents not able to get the resources they had. But when you think about it, you can't have it both ways." For Gloster, a Denmark native, a childhood encounter at a water fountain ensured his activism. He and his brother had come to town, and his brother turned the handle to drink at a water fountain labeled for whites. "A big guy grabbed my brother at the neck and jerked him off the water fountain; the guy just grabbed him at the neck and snatched him away." The harsh instantaneity and impunity of the man's action stayed with Gloster. A few years later, when the lunch-counter demonstrations began, "I thought it was something well overdue. It was time to take a stand." His friends agreed.

"We thought it was our duty to do something," said Sidney Glee. Herman Young, a Fairfield County native who played baseball and ran track for Voorhees, saw it the same way. His parents had taught him, "Whatever you can do to help someone, you have to do that." Besides, the friends knew what one did, all would do.[161]

Discussions focused on staying united and remaining nonviolent: "That was the main thing and not to resist arrest if anything happened because we knew the mentality of the people we were going to get involved with and that could cause the death of someone very easily," said Gloster. "We would all get together and exchange ideas," said Young, Gloster's roommate. "We would talk about the good, the bad, and the ugly. We knew there could be consequences, could be arrests." The conversations were hopeful but also pragmatic, supposing violence, including being shot, according to Young. "We talked about it so much, it was like a pattern. We knew exactly what each and every one was supposed to do."[162]

The meetings did not include their elders; the students made no effort to contact leaders of CORE or the NAACP. They did seek advice from Amos Sherrald, a young professor living in Menafee Hall with them. Sherrald made some calls and then advised the students to be selective in choosing participants, to plan nonviolent reactions to any attacks, and to design an escape. "If you're being attacked, you fall to the ground. You go into the fetal position. We called it 'the baby position.' Curl up so you absorb the blows," said Glee. "You couldn't fight back. You got to remember your name. Repeat it to yourself a million times. Whatever they call you, that's not your name. I don't care what they call you; you've got to be strong and know that's not your name. You don't react to that."[163]

In the midst of the sit-in planning, Copeland's sister called him home to the funeral of a brother-in-law. Copeland's mother had worked as a housekeeper. His father had worked as a railroad trackman and told his children of the towns where the white workers ate in restaurants while he sat outside. When Copeland's parents died, his eldest sister sent him to Voorhees to become a teacher. During his visit home, she warned him not to participate in sit-ins. When he returned to Voorhees, the date for the first sit-in was set, and he was included. He said he couldn't participate. The Glee brothers, Gloster, and others pleaded, persuading him to go along. Copeland felt compelled by memory to disobey his sister. He remembered his childhood walks to school—seven miles—while white students rode by in school buses, throwing trash at them. He remembered his schoolbooks, white students' hand-me-downs that were missing pages, even whole chapters. He wanted the sit-ins combined with boycotts because he wanted to hurt white people in the wallet, with the expectation that "they would have a different thought, a different mind-set."[164]

Similar childhood memories motivated Young. He attended Gethsemane School, in rural Fairfield County. The all-white Monticello School passed down its students' textbooks; the black schoolchildren's first task upon receipt was erasing scribbles and marks until the texts were clean. The children fetched their drinking water by hand from a spring. They walked miles to school, no matter the weather. However, Young's family owned land—the reason his father returned to South Carolina after working in Pennsylvania's steel mills—and achieved success in the local pulpwood business. Young's father was close to a white landowner who controlled pulpwood logging and harvesting in the county. So Young was also pushed by a question: "Wait a minute. Why can't we be close like that to everybody?" Young's parents knew he was considering sit-in participation. "They constantly told me, 'We don't want anything to happen to you.' My parents knew what I was in school for, that I was to get an education, but at the same time, be a role model and do what's right, and if it meant protesting something, then you do that. They would pretty much say that God has your back."[165]

On Monday, February 29, fourteen Voorhees students walked downtown from campus, planning to ask for service at the two drugstores, Talbert's and Carolina Cut Rate. The stores, divided by Coker Street, sat on the east side of a brief stretch of plain brick buildings bordering U.S. 321. The two-lane highway served as the town's main street and connected Denmark and its neighbor Norway to the capital city. Ordinarily the black students purchased school supplies and food at the stores but weren't allowed to sit. The students split into two groups. They planned to buy magazines as proof they were store customers and then sit and read until asked to leave. Anyone hurt "would have to bear with it," said Glee.[166]

On this day barely half got past the stores' doors. "They were waiting for us," said Copeland, referring to the white men at Carolina Cut Rate, who stormed toward the first group of students. When Copeland and one or two fellow protesters made it inside, the white men attacked. "They had ax handles and chased those who were inside back out," using obscenities and threatening swings of the weapons. The first thought flashing through Copeland's mind: "I don't want to get hit."[167]

The second group of students entered Talbert's. They managed to sit. "There was shock," said Gloster. "The waitress came over and said, "We can't serve you.' We ignored her. We had reading material and sat until the police came." The waitress repeatedly requested they leave, said Glee, but the students remained silent, leafing through magazines. For a short time, students traveled back and forth between the two stores until the venture ended in all arrested. The Associated Press described the men's persistence, reporting that fourteen students entered Talbert's six times and each time were refused service. Glee described the arrests as mass confusion. Police said the students were disturbing the peace. They handcuffed Copeland, the first one they arrested. "Fourteen Negro students were held under brief arrest Monday in Denmark after they repeatedly sought service at a drug store counter. Meanwhile, officials in several Carolina cities awaited signs of Negro boycotts against stores who refused to offer them integrated lunch counter service," the Associated Press reported.[168]

Gloster left Talbert's before the arrests, and he, George Glee, and two others decided to sit in at the Denmark Diner, the town's only restaurant, which allowed only white patrons through its plate-glass door. The four students walked north a few blocks and turned the corner, passing the low, plain building's plate-glass windows to reach its door. White men waited, wielding butcher knives. "Guys inside rushed to the door with knives. They looked violent. We realized we were out of sight of everyone, and they had big knives," said Gloster. As those inside the restaurant locked the door, Gloster and George Glee backed up. The four made it back to campus.[169]

The arrested students were surprised. They thought their plans were "top secret," as Gloster put it. Yet the white merchants seemed to have known they were coming and to have prepared for their arrival. However, that wasn't what most worried them during their march to the police station three blocks away. They were busy imagining their parents' reactions, said Copeland, the most cautious member of the group and the only one handcuffed. The police crammed the dozen students into one closet-size cell, "packed in like sardines," said Copeland, for two to three hours. At some point they decided they could ask for a phone call and, if granted a call, would telephone campus. But black community members, including angry alumni inflamed by witnesses to the arrests, had put a rescue in motion. The Reverend Henry Grant, the school's Episcopal priest, arrived, was allowed to talk to the students, and promised to get them out within a day or two. The outcome was much faster. Police Chief W. V. Whetstone agreed to relinquish the students into Grant's custody, without charges, and Grant walked them back to campus.[170]

That was Copeland's first and last sit-in. He called his sister, who told him he was at Voorhees to get an education and couldn't afford to be expelled.

"She told me to make sure I didn't participate in another demonstration." He obeyed. She also told him that "it was a great danger to our lives. I agreed with her. But it was just something we had to do, take a chance on, and pray to the Lord he would be our protector."[171]

In neighboring Barnwell County, the *Barnwell People-Sentinel* editorialized in early March, "Just why anyone regardless of race would want to force themselves upon the company of others is beyond us. Why don't the Negroes, instead of resorting to political pressure, set about earning the equality they claim to desire!" Later in the month, another editorial warned, "In recent years, we have been told on numerous occasions that 'It won't happen here,' the reference being to racial activity trying to break down the segregation custom. We sincerely hope it won't, but in all fairness we must point out that Denmark is only fourteen miles away."[172]

Small groups of three or four students at a time sporadically continued the sit-in effort, walking into Denmark between classes. They sat, read magazines they brought—"Something to look intelligent," said Sidney Glee—then left when asked to do so. No one was injured or arrested. "In my case, I would get up and go," leaving not just the store but town, said Gloster. Sherrald, the biology professor, often retrieved the students and drove them back to class on time. One Sunday morning Gloster and three other students decided to attempt worship at the First Baptist Church. The imposing brick church, its towering steeple a downtown landmark, was established in 1844. The words of Isaiah, "Seek ye the Lord while He may be found," curved over its double doors. "As soon as we started up the steps, the usher came down and said, 'You can't come in here,'" Gloster said. "One of us asked, 'What God do you believe in?' and he said, 'It doesn't make any difference; you can't come in here.'" The students left but continued brief visits to the drugstores that did not end in arrests.[173]

On May 10 lunch counters in six of Nashville's department and variety stores opened to black and white customers for the first time. Negotiations, underway since March, had been punctuated by the April 19 bombing of Alexander Looby's home. Looby, one of two black city councilmen and an NAACP attorney, had defended sit-in participants, two thousand of whom responded to the attack on him by marching on city hall. In a spontaneous question-and-answer on the city hall steps, Mayor Ben West answered yes to Diane Nash's question, "Do you recommend the merchants open their lunch counters to all citizens?" The ensuing May agreement included an end to the six-week-long boycott of merchants practicing desegregation and made Nashville the first southeastern city to desegregate downtown. Winston-

Salem, North Carolina, followed on May 24, also through a biracial committee's negotiations.[174]

However, at Kress's annual meeting in New York City on May 18, chairman Paul Troast had nothing new to say, despite declines in sales and income. He told shareholders that stores, whether owned by individuals or chains, were "local in character." And "if the citizens of any city give reasonable evidence that they are now willing to integrate, we will be glad to make this change with them." James Peck, representing CORE, warned shareholders that boycotts would continue and continue to hurt sales. On Fifth Avenue, CORE pickets marched. "It was happening more and more places, and we participated," said Gloster. "We didn't know what the next step would be."[175]

Allen University and Benedict College, Columbia: First Sit-In Held Wednesday, March 2, 1960

About five hundred students gathered on the eastern side of Columbia's downtown on a dreary Wednesday morning. They were from Allen University and Benedict College, side-by-side historically black colleges just a mile from Main Street, their compact campuses bounded by city blocks. In the morning sleet and rain, about two hundred students marched two by two to the core of the white shopping area. They walked in and out of stores, and at noon small groups converged on lunch counters at Kress and Woolworth. In the weeks before, a carload of Columbia students—including Benedict's Talmadge Neal and Allen's Simon Pinckney Bouie and twin Samuel Preston Bouie—had visited the Greensboro protesters to discuss what the Allen and Benedict students quickly understood was a movement. The Columbia students also consulted CORE organizers and asked for the help of local NAACP leaders. They decided to focus their first sit-in on the capital city's downtown. They met with Claflin and South Carolina State students, too, with the goal of coordinating simultaneous protests, but Orangeburg's students acted early and on their own.[176]

When forty to fifty black students entered Woolworth, the manager had already closed all but two of the seating sections at the lunch counter. As soon as the Columbia students sat, he closed the open sections too. The men and women read textbooks or Bibles for about ten minutes before departing. Protester Jack Simmons told a reporter, "If we can spend our money at the counters, we should be able to eat there, too." The *Columbia Record* reported, "Their stay at the white counter didn't even interrupt a half-dozen

On March 2, 1960, five hundred Benedict College and
Allen University students walked downtown to attempt sit-ins
at Columbia's Kress and Woolworth.
Courtesy of Richland Library, Columbia, South Carolina

white patrons, who kept on drinking their coffee or eating their pie." At Kress
white patrons already occupied most of the seats. Employees had roped off
a dozen or so open seats; a sign said, "This department closed in the interest
of public safety." Students there decided to return to campus. About twenty
white onlookers heckled them.[177]

About three hundred students gathered on Thursday, leaving the campuses around 11 A.M. They marched in pairs, wearing hats and their long all-
weather coats against the cold. They sang "We Shall Overcome" and "Oh,
Freedom," passing occasionally between gauntlets of white observers lining Taylor Street, which led directly from their campuses to the downtown
shopping area.City, county, and state law enforcement officers awaited them,
as did an aide to the governor. The students had selected ten targets. They
stayed on Main Street for about two hours, visiting Woolworth, Kress, Mc-
Crory's, H. L. Green, Walgreen, Eckerd, and Silver's, as well as Tapp's and
Belk department stores and the Greyhound Bus Depot, where they sat quietly, in their overcoats, on the wooden pews of the whites-only waiting room.
Downtown businesses posted signs that said, "Carry Out Service Only" and

"No Trespassing." Tapp's served only its employees in its roped-off dining area. At Woolworth ropes barricaded the lunch space, so students left after a few minutes. At Kress employees had removed counter seats. On the street a group of white men formed a line of their own and marched toward the demonstrators, yelling and laughing, but didn't attack. This time two students managed to obtain service at McCrory's. A young man, described in news reports afterward as a "light-skinned Negro," entered ahead of the students, sat at the counter, told the waitress he was in a hurry, and ordered tea and a hamburger. When served he passed the food along to "a darker companion." The manager closed the counter, turned off the lights, and closed the store for an hour.[178]

These were Milton B. Greene's first protests, and they fit what he considered a well-considered format. "It was Allen and Benedict, and we marched down to Main Street, not to the State House, just to call attention. We went into some of the stores that had lunch counters and attempted to sit. They didn't serve us, and after a while, we left." Robert Devoe, a tall and soft-spoken U.S. Army veteran who served in Germany after his 1953 high school graduation, held faith in the planning as well as the protection of numbers. "I was a little bit skeptical, but I wouldn't say scared. We would march and sing, and that would give us a kind of courage, and when you're with a crowd, a lot of people, that takes away much of the fear." So it was reassuring when, on the second day, participation remained in the hundreds, said Devoe.[179]

City Manager Irving G. McNayr announced that he would not tolerate any more demonstrations. Allen president Frank Veal said he had not anticipated sit-ins occurring in Columbia. Benedict president J. A. Bacoats publicly defended the students, calling demonstrations "an ancient and universal practice" and aptly noting, "Certainly, any college administration should with reluctance and hesitation interpose itself in a way that would seem to identify the college with the status quo and then identify the college as an opponent to progress through social and political change." However, Bacoats privately threatened to expel Rev. David Carter, one of the student leaders. When a reporter asked Carter about SLED officers telling the black colleges' presidents to stop students' protests, he responded, "No college can exist without students, and this is a student movement." Devoe, a cousin of Carter's, explained, "We figured that with all the students at Benedict and Allen, they weren't going to get all of us."[180]

Devoe had grown up on a small Barnwell County farm, where his parents raised cows, pigs, and chickens. He was one of eight boys and eight girls. Aunts raised him after his mother died when he was three years old. Carter had grown up in town and was ahead of Devoe in school because Devoe missed a grade through illness. Devoe had participated in the NAACP as a child because his father, Rhodel Devoe, who had only a few days of school, wanted his children both educated and determined to "bring about a better world." In Barnwell County black residents knew to avoid certain whites who enforced certain customs, such as requiring black people to knock only on the back door and, if offered a drink or food, to sit separately in the kitchen, using utensils set aside only for black people. Rhodel Devoe wanted his children to escape Barnwell and small-town white residents who took advantage of black residents. He taught his son that a college degree and the opportunities of big cities might make this possible. In the 1950s both Devoe and Carter discovered a taste of freedom in the desegregated military. "That gave us a different perspective" about life in the South, said Devoe. He believed that the self-discipline he and his cousin learned in the military served them well in the sit-in movement, helping them adhere to the code of nonviolent direct action.[181]

The Allen and Benedict students agreed at the end of February to plan together and hold combined demonstrations. Classmates elected Simon Bouie as president of the Student Movement of Allen University, also called the Student Committee on Human Rights. Classmates elected Neal as president of the Benedict Student Movement Association. Allen and Benedict students met after the second day of demonstrations, and their next maneuver was a pause. A team delivered a statement to the city hall, the police chief, and *The State*, Columbia's morning newspaper, announcing a protest suspension. The one-page statement said they met their intention, which was to protest "unfair, inequitable, discriminatory treatment at public and transportation services patronized by Negroes" because "services and treatment to all patrons should be the same." The statement predicted that any arrests would build cases for the higher courts, which was certainly the expectation of NAACP attorneys opposing statewide charges of trespass and breach of peace.[182]

The statement's third point got to the heart of the students' motivation: "It is often said by certain political leaders that the Negro in the South graciously accepts segregation and in some instances desires it—that whatever agitation is made against segregation is by outsiders. This demonstration was to indicate that segregation may be here for a long time and the Negro may have to endure and tolerate it, but he does not willingly and voluntarily accept it." The statement ended with thanks to officials, law enforcement, and bystanders for fair treatment and was signed "THE STUDENTS." None of the demonstrators was arrested in these first Columbia forays.[183]

Behind the scenes the how-to was a bit murky. "We were loosely orga-nized," said Bouie. "We just wanted to march." Allen and Benedict faculty supported their students privately while also warning them that anything in-terrupting studies jeopardized scholarships, passing grades, and graduation. Local black attorneys, who had never seen a movement like this in Colum-bia, puzzled over legal footing. NAACP leaders were anxiously supportive privately and publicly. Students found Rev. Frederick Calhoun James, teach-ing at Allen, a particular influence. A graduate of Allen and Howard Univer-sity, James preached at Mount Pisgah African Methodist Episcopal (AME) in Sumter. Black ministers often held multiple jobs to get by. James met on campus with the students, set behavior guidelines, and constantly cautioned them to be orderly and nonviolent so the NAACP would back them up.[184]

Bouie said that many Columbia elders feared that "we were going to really hurt the movement of the past." NAACP leaders reminded the young activ-ists that their predecessors had toiled during and since slavery for freedom and equality. "They didn't mind telling us we've got real battles we're fight-ing in, and 'Y'all have 'put us in the pot,'" said Bouie. Further, they warned, "young people come up and think you're going to change society overnight, and you're really going to set us back." Plus these mass sit-ins had caught all by surprise. This was brand new to everyone, including the students. "After we had organized, we still didn't know any more than before what was to be expected," noted Bouie.[185]

On March 5 close to fifty student leaders from throughout the state gath-ered in Columbia to discuss their future. They formed the South Carolina Student Movement Association and named David Carter its president. One of fifteen children, Carter left South Carolina to serve in the U.S. Air Force, fighting in the Korean War and boxing for the military. He had earned a bachelor's in social studies from Benedict and intermittently worked as a Baptist preacher while earning a bachelor of divinity at Benedict's J. J. Starks School of Theology.[186]

Carter wore close-cropped hair and a trim mustache. He was a short, compact man with intense, fierce eyes, and a deep and often loud voice. He used that voice to dramatic effect, frequently raising his right hand and pointing heavenward to emphasize his points. He worked at knowing and getting along as much as possible with everyone. His age, twenty-eight, and military background likely contributed to his leadership role, as did his so-cial skills and fluency under pressure. Carter fell in love with Vida Pruitt when she was a teen and waited for her father's permission to court and marry her. While he studied religion at Benedict, she majored in education at Johnson C. Smith University. She inspired him by spending her hours out-side of classes standing patiently in lunch-counter aisles during sit-ins or, as she described it, marching around Charlotte with Charles Jones and class-mates.[187]

Privately Carter hoped the protests would lead to negotiations to deseg-regate downtown. That didn't happen. On the other hand, the pause might have been protective. That Friday night white youths were reported burn-ing a cross on Allen University property. Violence among groups of white and black youths lasted into Saturday's early morning hours. Black students patrolled the periphery of their schools. White youths drove down the city streets that boxed in the campuses and threw bricks and bottles from their cars. Next members of black and white groups threw bricks at each other. After midnight two patrons of nearby Mac's Drive-In, which served only whites, reported that a group of black men, armed with sticks and bricks, rushed parked cars and shouted they were going to take over. One white patron, who quickly drove away, reported a car window broken; another re-ported shattered window and windshield glass.[188]

One Allen student arrested that night was convicted of loafing and loiter-ing and fined $10.50. An Allen instructor, speaking for the student in court, said the young man was among a group charged with protecting the campus. No arrests were made among the groups of whites vandalizing the colleges, but on March 18 fifteen more Allen students, all arrested that night for dis-orderly conduct, pled guilty. Nine were fined $100.00, the other six $49.50 as "victims of circumstance." The police chief said he had obtained sworn state-ments that no cross was burned, and the judge claimed direct proof of out-side agitators using students "to create strife among various groups."[189]

Following that weekend some young activists met again, at the invitation of the Richland County Citizens Committee (RCCC), somewhat a shadow NAACP. Others chose to boycott the meeting, objecting to the involvement of pastors and RCCC and NAACP officials whom they deemed the estab-lishment and thus not part of their movement. The hiatus provided time to plan a March 12 pilgrimage to the State House, where students hoped to pray and sing freedom songs. The organizers anticipated 1,600 participants. "The churches, Methodist and Baptist, gave students the chance to come in to talk and strategize for the marches," said Devoe. "The NAACP, they had a chapter on campus. Mr. Newman being field secretary, naturally he had contact with the ministers, and he was a minister too. We said the NAACP was an arm of the church, so naturally the churches, especially the Methodist and Baptist churches, came to the rescue of the students to provide assistance or facilities where we could meet. Usually we would meet late at night to strategize the next time a march would come."[190]

Newman conferred with student leaders not only in Columbia but also in Orangeburg, Spartanburg, and Sumter throughout the month. He wanted to stay informed, influence their plans, and bring them into the fold of the NAACP's youth councils and college chapters. While much of the strategizing and all the protests occurred off the campuses, Benedict students did stage an end-of-segregation funeral on school grounds, carrying a coffin labeled "Jim Crow" and digging a hole for burial.[191]

As the state capital, Columbia was a politically fraught target. Home to the state's first NAACP chapter, established in 1917, to middle-class black businessmen, and to black movers and shakers of previous decades, Columbia held many older black leaders eager to control the student movement and many white leaders determined to squash it. Certainly local civil rights leaders competed for influence. An exchange of verbal fisticuffs in *The State*, South Carolina's largest newspaper, made public the disagreements. First to air public disapproval of the sit-ins was John Henry McCray. In 1960 the fifty-year-old worked as a reporter and editor for the black-owned *Baltimore Afro-American* and *Pittsburgh Courier*. He had worked as editor and publisher of the *Lighthouse and Informer,* a black weekly that ended publication in 1954; organized many of the state's NAACP chapters; and cofounded, in 1944, the Progressive Democratic Party (PDP). The PDP supported a fourth term for President Franklin Delano Roosevelt and, in a first-ever move, challenged the Democratic Party's all-white delegation to the 1944 national convention. Both that challenge and a second one in 1948 failed but influenced black voter participation. Tall and slender, McCray wore his hair slicked back. His bare, high forehead made a long face look longer. His direct gaze, eyes slightly narrowed, warned of his self-described reputation as a "fighting editor" and the "official mouthpiece of all militant movements."[192]

McCray sounded affronted by student activism in an interview and a lengthy published statement. Calling the second day of sit-ins a mass invasion, he criticized the presence of so many black youths downtown: "For close to two hours, mostly unguided young people wandered and roamed about Main Street, a breath away from an ugly explosion." He cited rumors that the anticipated pilgrimage to the State House would be met by whites bent on violently ending such a demonstration. He wrote that segregated dining was a "custom, right or wrong," and changing that required "much more than a sitdown demonstration." He said racial issues should be solved by "the real and responsible community leaders within the two races." Clearly in his mind that didn't include anyone attending high school or college. Without naming any organizations, he wrote, "Negro adults have been trying to take over the student movement" and had launched what he saw as self-serving fundraising. He claimed students' arrests served the venal purpose of organizational fundraising on "a larger and more profitable scale." McCray concluded that the students had made their point, and there was "no further sense in their making new demonstrations."[193]

Rev. William McKinley Bowman immediately answered McCray in a letter to the editor, asking, "When has walking up and down Main Street become a misdemeanor or a crime?" Bowman had grown up in St. George on land settled by a Native American grandfather. Severely injured in a sawmill accident when he was fourteen, the portly, forty-six-year-old minister walked with a swinging limp. Bowman had run unsuccessfully for city council in 1954 and the state House of Representatives in 1958. Misleadingly country sometimes in his manner, Bowman filled many roles: president of the RCCC, pastor of Second Nazareth Baptist Church in Columbia, a founder of WOIC radio and host of its gospel show *Wings of Faith,* owner of the record label Bowman Records, and a newly elected member of the Richland County delegation to the state Democratic convention.[194]

In his letter Bowman defended the many black citizens committees, formed county by county beginning in 1942. Names varied throughout the state—some were concerned citizens, for example—but all aided in the achievement of what charters called "first-class citizenship" and shielded activists from the consequences of NAACP membership. The citizen committees had worked in conjunction with the PDP, which Bowman now declared "dead as a Dodo." Bowman wrote that the current RCCC had put the student protests on its March 7 agenda, invited students, city and business representatives, ministers, and their congregations from Richland and neighboring counties, and reaped 1,500 attendees. This was proof, wrote Bowman, that "the Negro masses as a whole are staunchly behind the student protest movement" and "ready now to use every legal, non-violent means at their disposal" to ensure success.[195]

Perhaps more revealing than the public tussle over the students' activism were the differences between McCray's and Bowman's depictions of segregation. McCray praised "City Fathers" as being ahead of "colored leadership." Bowman disparaged "inching along Negroes" and second-class citizenship. McCray noted the desegregation of city buses; Bowman noted the city was forced into it by Supreme Court decisions. McCray praised the existence of Drew Park for black residents; Bowman pointed out it was the only park available, as all other city parks were segregated. Bowman cited other difficulties—the fight for black police and firefighters and the push for black military police, eventually provided but unarmed—then noted that the city was "trying hard not to determine who incited friction by burning a cross near the colleges, but who got mad when it was burned, not why students went to a near-by white restaurant, and who was running in front of them, but what students dared to become angry."[196]

In an editorial *The State* praised McCray's "courageous and revelatory statement," saying other black residents who "favor racial integrity" dared not speak up. Fault lines were inevitable; so much was at stake. The students did not follow the cautious, methodical, legalistic approach of their elders. They had a different style, a different focus, a different timetable, and, if they persisted, the potential to redirect the civil rights movement. They had already reenergized it. As the SCCHR observed a few months later in its quarterly report, "Someone has said that since students have done in a short time what adults have not succeeded in doing over a much longer period of time, that the adult organizations are trying to capture the student movement."[197]

As the week drew to a close, Hollings promised arrests. He confirmed that he had sent SLED chief Strom to inform Allen's and Benedict's presidents that any assembly at the state capitol would result in arrests for any protesters or bystanders who, even by their presence, "may constitute a threat to peace and good order." He pointed to violence elsewhere: the February 24 clash in Chattanooga, when thousands of white and black demonstrators fought; the February 27 attack in Nashville, when whites beat sit-in participants; the March 1 mass protest in Montgomery, Alabama, when one thousand students sang and prayed at the state capitol to protest the threatened expulsion of Alabama State College students; the March 6 siege in Montgomery, when hundreds of angry whites trapped protesters within Dexter Avenue Baptist Church until armed police came to the rescue.[198]

Like other southern governors, Hollings made no mention of the constitutional protection of free speech and assembly. Instead he said, "Demonstration groups should not be misled by some technical opinion on trespass statutes, parade ordinances or the like." Hollings said that he had proof of participation of "outside, selfish, antagonistic groups," but he did not explain who this might be. A *State* editorial obscurely referred to instigation by "national influences," praised Hollings's "apparent proof," and argued that history threatened to repeat itself. The history? Reconstruction, when, according to the editorial, "the colored people of the state were incited by vicious white carpetbaggers and other interlopers venting hate and humiliation upon the white people."[199]

David Carter's response sounded unshrinking, even sarcastic. He said that he had lived in Columbia for six years and that no one in his group was a member of "outside forces" nor even a dues-paying member of the NAACP. He said, "Evidently our governor has forgotten all the laws of democracy, if he ever knew them." The students would not march on Saturday, March 12, but "the only reason we will not go through with our pilgrimage is because we are law-abiding citizens and not hoodlums and gangsters who will have to be met with brass and guns. No one is calling our bluff. We are not afraid of crowding the jails." That was a fact; filling the jails had become a logical extension of the sit-in movement. On February 27 Nashville police—confronted with hundreds of students participating in the city's fifth sit-in—stopped arresting those involved because the jail was full. Those already packed into cells were released within hours.[200]

The demonstrators understood that their towns and cities weren't equipped with adequate police, jail cells, or magistrates for a flood of arrests. In other words the students knew they could overwhelm the system. Of the pressure on the college presidents, Carter said that the demonstrations were "not a problem for the college presidents and deans to solve." He called Hollings's response "an acute tension attack." Carter's last words on the subject: "We will be back." The following week the students returned downtown.[201]

On Friday, March 11, students held sit-ins without arrests, and on Monday, March 14, Neal, of Benedict, and Bouie, of Allen, entered Eckerd Drug Store on Main Street, the store whose employees they found most prejudiced. The twenty-year-old students were part of a large group but ended up alone inside. "We thought we were going in en masse," said Bouie. "We walked in because we were the leaders, so we walked in, and they remained on the outside, which was wise. But we weren't aware of that until we got all the way to the back." Bouie, the song "We Shall Overcome" in his head, thought, "Y'all get to overcome, and I get to go to jail." The two persevered. "When we got to the counter, there were seats available, and we took our seats," said Bouie. Some white patrons at the other end of the counter stood rather than sit with them. A waitress told them they couldn't be served and had to leave. The manager told them, "'Y'all get out of here.'" Customers began banging their knives and forks on the counter. When the two refused to leave, the manager asked for the police, then told Neal and Bouie, "The law will put y'all out," according to Bouie.[202]

"We prayed," said Bouie. "I was scared as hell, all the white people looking at you with hatred. People sitting there got up." While Neal carried in his pocket typewritten instructions on carrying out a nonviolent sit-in, neither he nor Bouie had engaged in nonviolence training. However, in organizing meetings, said Bouie, "We were told, 'This is a nonviolent effort. Above anything, don't create violence. Don't beat nobody; don't jump on nobody. Just do what you're supposed to do. Go in there, sit down, and let them do what they're supposed to do.'" Assistant Police Chief S. A. Griffith arrived, and, when Bouie said the two wouldn't relinquish their seats, ordered them removed. The six-foot-tall Griffith lifted Bouie by his collar as he marched him to the store's front door. "I tried to get away. I didn't weigh but 125 pounds," said Bouie. Secretly, though, he was glad to go. "Oh, free at last," he thought. "I would rather die outside than die in here."[203]

Neal and Bouie were charged with breach of peace. Bouie's objection to being marched roughly to the waiting police car and then shoved in led to the additional charge of resisting arrest. Newman, "really behind all of it in a skillful way," according to Bouie, was not available to bail out Neal, Bouie, and those who had remained outside Eckerd's entrance. Instead Reverend Bowman came to the rescue. Bouie could hear Bowman telling officials, "These boys, we don't know what got into them. We've been good in the white community; we've been peaceful." Released on a two-hundred-dollar bond, Bouie was sympathetic to what he thought of as Bowman's old-school apologetic approach. He felt nothing but gratitude since Bowman had obtained their release. Bouie went from jail to his job at a Lady Street barbershop. He attended work as if nothing had happened, but the television news came on, and there he was, being hustled into a police car. A white customer told the barber, "That boy up there in that picture looks just like that 'shine' boy." The barber replied, "Oh, no, he's been here all day long," as Bouie kept his head down.[204]

On Tuesday, March 15, Benedict and Allen students attempted several sit-ins downtown, synchronized with protests at Rock Hill, Orangeburg, and Sumter. These simultaneous events did not represent weeks of calendar coordination. Communication was minimal. "We understood that was where our strength was," said Bouie: no central authority existed to be eliminated. "Each school had its own movement independently, but we were interdependent on each other." So Rock Hill students sat in the bus depot and sang in front of city hall; Orangeburg students marched; Columbia students staged a round of sit-ins.[205]

Understanding that whites would retain lunch-counter seats to prevent students sitting and that dime-store and cafeteria employees would refuse to serve them, the Columbia students decided to arrive early in the day and just take up space, preventing white customers from sitting and eating and white merchants from making a profit. "So we started sitting in," said Devoe. "We knew what time the whites would have to go to lunch, so we would go and sit before they would get there. We knew they [waiters or waitresses] wouldn't serve us, but we could keep them from coming and getting a seat." Participants worked around their class schedules or asked professors to allow them to make up missed work.[206]

"We would sit for an hour or more until we knew that those folks had to go back to work," said Devoe of unseated white patrons. He and his friends read or talked quietly among themselves. They would sit and "wait for the waiter or waitress to come, and they never would." For self-protection they always worked in groups. "When you're with a crowd and you've strategized, for some reason it takes, at least with me, the fear out of you. You know the others are with you," said Devoe. "We had a feeling, too, that the whites will never attack you when you're in a larger group. When you're by yourself, yeah. But if you're in a group, they might talk and say things to threaten, but they won't attack you violently."[207]

On March 15 five black students walked into Taylor Street Pharmacy, located midway between the colleges and Main Street. Intent on sitting at the lunch counter, they fully expected arrest. At the same time, three students briefly sat at the Kress lunch counter on Main Street. Five more students sat at the lunch counter within the Union Bus Depot on Blanding Street. At Kress the manager closed the counter and ignored the students, who left. At the bus depot, the students purchased tickets at the ticket window, sat at the lunch counter, and began reading their Bibles. After telling the students, "I'm sorry, we don't serve Negroes," the depot manager stepped aside for police already there, who took the students in for questioning and then released them. But on Taylor Street, the students got the attention of SLED's Strom and the media.[208]

The surprised students walked by waiting television newsmen and six law enforcement officers, wondering who had alerted the authorities. David Carter led the noontime group: Charles F. Barr, Johnny M. Clark, Richard M. Counts, and Milton Greene. All but Clark and Carter belonged to Omega Psi Phi fraternity. The men had decided on their own that they would sit in and had prepared to be nonviolent and to follow Carter's lead. They felt some anxiety as they walked in the large pharmacy's front door, intent on first making small purchases. For Greene the law enforcement officers were a worry and a comfort because he knew the police were there both to arrest the students and to protect them from angry whites. Barr, whose father belonged to the NAACP and whose pastor had been Newman, occasionally engaged as a teen in his own private protests, riding up front on city buses to and from school. White riders objected, but he was never arrested. On this day, Barr said, "We were determined. We were on a mission." Being surrounded didn't stop them. According to Barr, their leader kept them moving. "Carter said, 'That's okay. We're going to still do what we're supposed to do.'"[209]

They did know exactly what to do: Take the first seats available. Respond to no one. Let Carter answer for them. Barr sat next to a blue-eyed blonde and steeled himself for blows. The woman began quietly panicking, "Oh, God. Oh, God." She stood and left. Two men standing behind Barr began a running commentary, calling the students "niggers" and "communists" and asking, "Who do you think you are?" Greene sat next to a man who immediately jumped up and began walking back and forth, wringing his hands. Another woman shrieked, "Eek!" and left her counter seat. Greene and Clark didn't have any money. Counts had agreed to pay for them, if they actually had the opportunity to order food. They held hope in that regard. At Taylor Street Pharmacy, black customers could buy food at the counter but could not sit. They didn't get the chance to order.[210]

The manager had arranged the day before for police in case any students attempted a sit-in. He quickly told the students, "You might as well leave because you won't be served." Carter said loudly, "Keep your seats," and, to the manager, "Okay, we'll just sit, then." The manager left, returned, and again asked the students to go. Carter again told his friends to remain seated. At this point Strom stepped up. He pointed out that the manager had asked them to leave the counter. "We didn't give any back talk at all," said Barr. Strom announced the manager would repeat his statement, this time in the SLED chief's presence, to each of the students. Then Strom told the students, "You heard what the manager told you," and said they were trespassing. Carter said the students would continue to sit and wait because the manager had offered a choice: they could sit and not be served. In response Strom announced the students were under arrest. When an officer grabbed Counts by the arm and shoved him, Strom rebuked the officer. The students walked out, without being handcuffed, and each was put separately into an awaiting car manned by two officers.[211]

Barr felt secretly offended when one of the law enforcement officers tried to strike up a conversation. He told Barr he understood the protesters were "people from the North, outside agitators." All five were tied to South Carolina: Barr was born in Kingstree and raised in Charleston. Clark was from Anderson. Carter, born in Barnwell County, had lived in Columbia for six years. Greene was from Columbia. Counts's parents lived in Washington, D.C., but his grandparents lived in the Waverly neighborhood near Allen and Benedict. At the city jail, as the students were booked, the commentary continued, with officers talking to each other, calling the students "coons," "niggers," "plants from the North," and "outside agitators," according to Barr. The five were charged with breach of peace and trespass.[212]

When the jailer escorted the students into the segregated cell block, they discovered they had the section almost to themselves. Prisoners had been released, all but one; the students felt sure he remained to eavesdrop. That prisoner, a street person whom Barr recognized, did his best to upset them, saying the students thought they were better than anyone else, that they weren't from Columbia, that they were trying to cause unrest in the city, "just crazy things," said Barr. Carter posted bond at 7:30 P.M.; jailers wouldn't release the rest. Newman posted bond for the other four after midnight and fed them a 2 A.M. dinner at the ALBEN restaurant, named for and across the street from Allen and Benedict. Additional NAACP leaders joined the students in a private room, praised them, and warned them they should expect to be in court within a week.[213]

Hollings met with black leaders, including Sharper, NAACP state conference president, after the mass arrests in Orangeburg. But in his public disagreement with Eisenhower, Hollings had ruled out negotiations or mediation by a biracial committee. By this time Savannah, Georgia; Knoxville and Nashville, Tennessee; and Greensboro, Raleigh, and Charlotte, North Carolina had formed such committees. The SCCHR, which counted one thousand black and white contributors and members statewide, urged black and white leaders to form biracial working groups. SCCHR members conducted personal conversations and telephone interviews on the subject. Alice Spearman, the white executive director of the SCCHR, wrote Eisenhower to apologize for Hollings's hostility and to mention her search for those in the state's power structure interested in mediation. The SCCHR did manage to bring together a small group of black and white leaders. "There was such a split in the philosophy of the Negroes that the white people decided to terminate communication," wrote Spearman. Some black leaders attempted personal contact and negotiations with white merchants at the same time that others worked on an escalation, an Easter boycott in conjunction with the national NAACP's "racial defense policy" of pickets and

boycotts at chain stores discriminating against black workers and customers.[214]

During their trial on March 26, Neal and Bouie said they went to Eckerd
to buy food. "I considered it my rights to buy food," Neal said. He initially
refused to answer City Attorney John Scholenberger's question, "Wasn't it
your intention to be arrested when you went there?" Instructed by the judge
to answer, Neal said, "Yes." Bouie testified he went to Eckerd to buy food and
"to get arrested, if it took that." Chief Griffith said that, upon being told he
was under arrest, Bouie replied, "Take your hands off me!" and tried to break
away. Bouie testified, "A small person and a tender one like me wouldn't
resist the sheriff there," pointing at the burly Griffith. The twenty-year-old
students were each fined one hundred dollars; Bouie was fined one hundred
more for the resisting-arrest charge. The judge, in finding them guilty, cited
Charles E. Williams v. Howard Johnson's Restaurant. In that case an Alexan-
dria, Virginia, restaurant refused service to a black Internal Revenue Service
agent. In 1959 the Fourth Circuit Court of Appeals said that a restaurant,
"an instrument of local commerce," could deal with different people in different ways, despite "the substantial inconvenience and embarrassment to
which persons of the Negro race are subjected in the denial to them of the
right to be served in public restaurants."[215]

White judges often warned sit-in students another arrest meant time in
jail. Newman and Perry advised Bouie, as they did other arrested students,
to avoid further protests while his case was under appeal. Attorneys feared
that more than one arrest might lead to not just jail but also prison. Bouie
sat it out for a while, but officials punished his grandmother. An elementary
school teacher who had raised Bouie and his twin brother after their parents'
deaths, she was questioned and reprimanded after Bouie appeared in newspaper accounts of the sit-ins. Next she received notice that she was dismissed
from her teaching post in Mullins, South Carolina, after thirty-four years.
She was one year short of eligibility for full retirement benefits. It was her
pay that enabled Bouie to attend college.[216]

On March 26 the KKK burned two crosses a few miles outside the capital
city. *The State* described the crosses as sizable and the groups of robed men
as small. The next day brought a meeting of 1,500 high school and college
students at Sidney Park Christian Methodist Episcopal Church. The students met under the auspices of the Student Movement Association, eager
to decide next steps. Despite the rallying of students in the capital city, Allen and Benedict lagged behind Claflin and South Carolina State in student
participation. Newman's head count for February through April showed the

difference: 1,200 participants from Allen and Benedict compared to 2,300 from Claflin and South Carolina State. In Columbia NAACP leaders asked students to pace themselves. The NAACP was scraping together money to get students out of jail. The Benedict and Allen leaders felt dependent on their classmates' interest, on momentum, as Bouie said, so they took the local temperature rather than building fervor. And the leaders operated independently, despite the statewide organization. "We did pretty much what we wanted to do at each school," said Bouie.[217]

April brought what one white leader termed the "Easter Scare," rumors that students would shift from a seat at a lunch counter to a seat in the pews. Hollings said he had no advice to offer. The white congregation of the Holland Avenue Baptist Church, across the river from Columbia, voted to refuse admission after the pastor asked the 450-member congregation to "act in a Christian manner." Carter announced his disdain: "We definitely don't intend to destroy our dignity and waste our good time Sunday morning trying to attend a Caucasian congregation." The theology student made the additional point that black students enjoyed their own services too well to be interested in white people's church services.[218]

The Columbia students turned their attention instead to other city facilities. A group tried to register for library cards at the Richland County Public Library's main branch at Sumter and Washington Streets. Librarians turned them away, not because black patrons couldn't use that library but because all black patrons were required to first register at the Waverly branch, in the all-black Allen-Benedict area. The State reported that this requirement eased checks on character, credit, and references. Carter and Moses Javis, who led the library protest, first presented themselves at the mayor's office, where they read a letter objecting to "unjust practices existing in Columbia," including access to the "best libraries," equal protection of the law during protests, and "the privilege of eating as citizens at certain stores." The mayor and city manager dismissed their complaints as invalid.[219]

On May 5 Allen and Benedict students united to march on the State House and the Governor's Mansion. The students reached the capitol grounds as legislators debated school desegregation. SLED's Strom told them that they couldn't demonstrate on State House property, and agents turned away about thirty students, who were chanting, "Down, down, down with segregation." Joined by another fifty students, the protesters marched a mile farther to the mansion, monitored by a matching number of law enforcement officers. The students sang "Give Me the Old NAACP Spirit," "I Shall Not Be Moved," and

"The Battle Hymn of the Republic" outside the boxy white residence, built in 1855 to house officers of a military academy. *The State* reported, "Negro servants at the mansion watched the demonstration from the windows and over the walls." No one was arrested.[220]

Newman compiled a full count into May. He included five high schools and all the higher-education institutions but Clinton. He recorded 41 demonstrations, 4,037 participating students, 586 arrests, $27,000 raised for student defense, $15,110 spent in bail, and $44,671 spent in appeal bonds. Any assumptions the summer would be quiet were wrong.[221]

In June CORE and the NAACP united in a meeting that included Carter, Gaither, and adult advisers McCollom, Newman, and McCain. The last two, who jointly issued the invitation, reported the adults were making "whatever plans that are necessary to further the students' cause and thereby putting ourselves on record to continue the efforts of the student through the summer." In keeping with that outlook, McCain led a discussion on nonviolent direct action, and Newman led one on selective buying. A few days later, Hollings addressed the Sertoma Clubs' convention in Miami. He said that he had run out of the state "the Ku Klux Klan and the scalawags," the latter a Deep South term to describe white supporters of Reconstruction. He vowed the state's "voluntary segregation" would remain.[222]

In Greenville, second to Columbia in population in South Carolina, white residents reacted violently to summer sit-ins. On July 16 eight black teens held what was their third sit-in at the segregated Greenville Public Library. High school and visiting college students sat down in the late afternoon to read newspapers, magazines, and books after a morning attempt ended when police arrived. This time, about an hour into their stay, they were directed to the branch serving only black patrons. When they refused to budge, police arrested them. Within an hour they were released on thirty-dollar bonds each through the efforts of attorney Sampson and the Reverend James S. Hall Jr., pastor of Springfield Baptist Church and an NAACP youth mentor. On Monday, July 18, their trial was postponed, but not before Sampson and the police revealed bomb threats against Sampson.[223]

Downtown Greenville erupted. About seventy-five black adults, who had hoped to attend the trial, and visiting Atlanta students, who filled three cars, attempted sit-ins at Woolworth, where the doors were locked; Green's Variety Store, where they were turned away; and Grant's, where the manager closed the counter. Other sit-ins in Greenville had been ignored, but this time angry white residents gathered. The *New York Times* reported that a white student, an Atlanta native enrolled in graduate studies at Union Theological Seminary, led sit-in attempts and was attacked by waiting whites. Police took him, minus his broken glasses, into protective custody.[224]

That was not the end of it. For three days in a row, Columbia's students sat at lunch counters in Silver's, Walgreen, Kress, and Woolworth. They were led by Gaither, Carter, Javis, and Frank Robinson. At Woolworth on July 20, twenty-five high school students participated. No one was served throughout the three days, and all left safely when the counters closed. Greenville was a different story. On July 22 students held another sit-in at Grant's. When white customers followed ten black protesters into the street, fistfights erupted. Police ended the brawl with three arrests, but peace wasn't restored. On Saturday and Sunday nights, gangs of black and white teens and young men roamed the city and county, throwing rocks, shooting at cars, and fighting at three segregated drive-ins. Sunday and Monday fights at drive-ins involved hundreds and resulted in Greenville City Council on Tuesday setting a curfew for anyone twenty years old or younger.[225]

On Wednesday, July 27, as Greenville cooled, nearby Spartanburg heated up. At Woolworth witnesses reported two white men debating consequences. One asked, "What do you reckon it would cost if I shoved someone off a stool?" The reply: "About $50 to $100." The decision: "Well, it ought to be worth that." When the white men slugged the two black men sitting at the counter, police arrested all four. At Kress about twenty-five black protesters gradually took seats at the counter, careful not to sit next to white customers. As the sit-in demonstrators left the dime store, white men waiting for an opportunity and led on by cheering attacked two white sit-in participants. The Spartanburg mayor announced police would prohibit crowds on city streets and would freely arrest, using disorderly conduct charges. Back in Greenville on Thursday, crowds of whites repeatedly gathered, and police repeatedly ordered them to depart. On Friday a dozen black students held sit-ins at four downtown stores without attacks or arrests occurring. Hollings, who had sent Chief Strom to Greenville, blamed the civil rights platforms of both the Democratic and Republican Parties, saying references to the constitutional right to assemble peacefully were misleading. He defended, instead, "the constitutional right of a private storekeeper to cater to whomever he pleases."[226]

Sharper, challenging Hollings's stance, issued a statement endorsing sit-ins, describing them as "an expression of impatience and resentment with and for segregation." The NAACP conference president said, "Negroes are obligated morally and spiritually to resist segregation." A few months later, evangelist Billy Graham, who prohibited segregation at his revivals, said the opposite when asked about sit-ins: "Laws—even unjust laws—should be obeyed," he said, unless the laws interfered with Christian worship.[227]

In North Carolina, Greensboro had negotiated its way to desegregation. On July 25 the downtown Woolworth and Kress desegregated their lunch counters. In the city where sit-ins had animated the civil rights movement, drugstore managers had accepted the advice to desegregate from the mayor's advisory committee. By August merchants had agreed to desegregate lunch counters in twenty-seven other southern cities, the SRC reported. Not one city reported violence or loss of business afterward. The SRC report nudged white leadership by pointing out that these successes proved that racial discrimination could be eliminated without long periods of tension or violence. However, throughout South Carolina not one lunch counter, restaurant, bus or train terminal, park, or beach had been desegregated.[228]

A library desegregated, though. On July 28 Sampson sued in federal court for desegregation of the Greenville Public Library. On September 2, at the direction of the mayor and city council, all Greenville library branches closed to prevent court-ordered desegregation. "The efforts being made by a few Negroes to use the White library will now deprive all White and Negro citizens of the benefit of a library," declared Mayor J. Kenneth Cass. But white and black people missed their libraries. On September 18 one of the arrested teens wrote, and the *Greenville News* published, a letter explaining the students' stance. "The separate but equal principle is very expensive," wrote Dorris "DeeDee" Wright. "Integration of the libraries is not only morally right, but it is also less expensive as well." On September 19, succumbing to public pressure, the mayor reopened all libraries "for the benefit of any citizen having a legitimate need." The city dropped its charges against the youths.[229]

At its annual state conference in September, the NAACP focused on an "expanded policy of economic and political self-defense," including sit-ins at libraries and state parks. Sit-in participants dominated the conference's last day; two thousand students attended a mass rally, some representing protest movements in North Carolina, Georgia, and Florida. An impromptu one-man sit-in followed the conference. The Charleston Airport's restaurant denied service to Gloster B. Current, director of branches for the national NAACP. He entered the restaurant for lunch before his flight and, when turned away, asked for the manager. Current, who complained directly to the Charleston mayor afterward, said the manager approached him with "fists doubled." Current had been in the same situation at the Greenville Airport in 1959, when he, baseball star Jackie Robinson, and others refused to leave the whites-only waiting area. An NAACP lawsuit was pending against that airport. In 1955 the Interstate Commerce Commission had ruled that facilities at bus and railroad stations and airports couldn't legally discriminate against black interstate passengers. A failure to enforce that ruling meant discrimination continued.[230]

The day before the 1960 presidential election, the *State* ran what was essentially a race-based directive on voting, penned by John Adger Manning, the Columbia-based chairman of the Association of Citizens' Councils of South Carolina, and Farley Smith, the executive secretary. The newspaper published the letter on the front page rather than the op-ed page, the traditional location for readers' missives. Most white South Carolinians had begun voting Democratic during Reconstruction, creating what was known as the Solid South. Manning and Smith focused on those who considered themselves Democrats unwilling to follow the national party. They wrote that the WCC operated to maintain states' rights and "the traditional and well justified separation of the races." Devoting themselves to seven comparisons of Republican and Democratic positions, the authors said that Democrats called for integration "in all areas of community life," supported voting by all persons, would give federal appointments to black citizens, and would legislate federal aid for teachers' salaries. In contrast Republicans would confine integration to public facilities, limit voting to those who had completed sixth grade, and oppose some federal aid to schools because states "should be supreme."[231]

Prognosticators expected Vice President Richard M. Nixon to win South Carolina, thanks to the roles race and religion played in the presidential election. That's not how it turned out. Kennedy won the national election, just barely, with 50.31 percent of the popular vote. Kennedy won in South Carolina, with 51 percent of the popular vote. Not incidental was a federal investigation of black voter registration in the South. During the summer, despite the objections of Hollings and Sen. Strom Thurmond, the FBI had investigated black residents' access to the vote in Clarendon, Hampton, Manning, and McCormick Counties. At the time a mere fifty of five thousand black residents of McCormick County were registered. Reverend King told reporters that he believed "the Negro vote played a significant role" and, consequently, Kennedy "owes something basic to the Negro community."[232]

After the election Gaither visited Allen and Benedict colleges. He reported that, despite previous contacts, complacency impeded continued protests, illustrated by only one student attending a workshop on nonviolent direct action. Carter did keep the sit-ins puttering along. Ten students visited McCrory's on Tuesday, December 13, and sat while two white men finished their lunches. Thirty white men stood behind them, boxing them in. Newman, who attended, described the sit-in as a "wild-cat strike" not promoted by the NAACP. On Wednesday seven students sat for three hours at McCrory's; white patrons stayed in their seats or took seats. On Thursday six students sat at Woolworth's, three at Kress, and four at Silver's. This time McCrory's employees covered the counter with merchandise, the stools with paper bags. Carter promised that sit-ins would continue downtown indefinitely.[233]

Morris College, Sumter: First Sit-In
Held Friday, March 4, 1960

Morris College students held their first sit-ins on Friday, March 4, and police immediately arrested all, charged them with breach of peace, and required one-hundred-dollar bonds. Sumter started tough and got mean. These arrests—along with the arrests of forty-eight Florence youths, engaged in a second sit-in try at a Florence Kress—likely were the earliest South Carolina arrests of sit-in participants. Students at Morris College, a Baptist-supported school, had followed the February protests through their own networks and the red flags of Sumter's *Daily Item*. The newspaper warned in a February 9 editorial that the Greensboro sit-ins meant "the agitators would next probably try to invade the dining rooms and cafes of the Southern states, the churches, even social gatherings."[234]

Invade often functioned as the verb of choice, indicating white South Carolinians' conviction that black South Carolinians attempted to enter, with hostile intent, territory justifiably closed to them. On February 12 the newspaper alerted readers, "Lunch Counter Move Invades South Carolina," when Friendship Junior College students held sit-ins in Rock Hill. And the day before the town's own students walked into its drugstores, the editorial page warned that "proof has been offered time and again that the Communists some 30 or more years ago set about to create racial strife in the South. Their objective at the time was the establishment of a 'black republic' in the South."[235]

Frances DuBose said yes to sit-ins when a classmate approached her during a word-of-mouth selection process. Recruits such as DuBose and volunteers met every night at the school canteen after it closed. There McCain and others trained them for nonviolent protests. "We were told we were expected to remain nonviolent, in the tradition of the Reverend Martin Luther King," she said. "We were told to expect the worst; we knew there would be abuse." Only juniors and seniors were finalists for this first effort, twenty-six students who believed they could endure violence without responding in kind. The night before the protest, they gathered to choose teams and destinations. They discussed "expecting the worst but not retaliating; otherwise, we would lose the true meaning, to bring awareness to the Sumter community," said DuBose, who was twenty years old.[236]

Multiple Sumters existed. White Sumter included downtown shopping, businesses, the segregated hospital, doctor and dentist offices, and white neighborhoods. Eleven miles away a different Sumter existed at Shaw Air Force Base, opened in 1941 to train air cadets and, like all military bases, desegregated after Truman's 1948 executive order ended segregation in the military. A third Sumter, industrial South Sumter, bustled across the railroad tracks, dominated by Williams Furniture Corporation and Korn Industries. Black residents there found crossing the tracks to shop, bank, or visit a doctor an unpleasant chore, a venture into a different and hostile world.[237]

The FBI reported Sumter's WCC membership of four thousand as the highest among the state's fifty-nine councils. Sumter was not only home to the Citizens' Council of Sumter County, Inc., but also headquarters for the Association of Citizens' Councils of South Carolina. Sumter stayed locked up tight by prominent whites who were public and unapologetic in their defense of segregation and their use of the KKK and the WCC as enforcement arms. The WCC's 1957 state chairman, Thomas D. Keels, was from Sumter; its 1958 chairman, B. A. Graham, was from Olanta, twenty-five miles away. The executive secretaries of several years—Farley Smith, of Lee County, and S. Emory Rogers and L. B. McCord, of Clarendon County—were from adjoining counties. Clifton G. Brown, elected mayor of Sumter in 1960, ran the 1960–61 WCC membership drive as general chairman of the Sumter WCC. Ramon Schwartz, who presided over the Sumter recorder's court and heard protesters' cases, directed the annual WCC campaign. The Sumter WCC had recently engaged in an internal struggle as to whether its membership would be "dressed up Klans," according to an FBI report. So sit-in territory was more than just a segregated store's lunch counter but an entire and entirely unfriendly downtown whose white residents freely talked of the sit-in youths as communists, outside agitators, and invaders and responded with violence.[238]

The Morris College students, a third of them women, left campus on March 4 at 11 A.M. to walk a bit more than a mile to downtown lunch counters. When they reached North Main Street and its straight stretch of boxy brick buildings, they entered Kress, Lawson's Pharmacy, and Sumter Cut Rate Drug Store. DuBose ventured into Sumter Cut Rate. "We sat down. A white man sitting at the counter said, 'Uh-uh, uh-uh, no, we're not going to serve you. Get up and leave.' The waitress said, "We don't serve colored people.' She got on the phone and said, 'There are some colored people down here who want to be served, and we're not going to serve them,'" said Du-Bose. "Within a matter of two to three minutes, the law officers came and arrested us." The manager told a local reporter that he hadn't asked anyone to leave before law enforcement arrived. He said the students, who carried Bibles, just started reading. That evidently offended a white customer, who demanded, "What're you doing? Holding church in here?"[239]

At Kress the clerks placed a closed sign on the counter and turned out the lights. Mae Frances Moultrie managed to sit down, as did about a dozen classmates. "We just went to the counters and sat," said Moultrie, twenty-three, fine-boned and slender, with a heart-shaped face. "We had some money and were going to buy whatever we wanted." The minutes ticked by as she had expected. "We knew they would tell you they didn't serve Negroes, and then what would happen was we would just sit there and say we wanted to be served like anyone else. It wasn't long before they called the police." Police arrested all the students before the manager could ask them to leave himself. During CORE training Moultrie had learned that they likely would be arrested and charged with trespassing or breach of peace. "I didn't have a sense of being afraid. Those who weren't afraid had to do what needed to be done."[240]

Seven students also took seats in Lawson's Pharmacy, where they read their Bibles in red-leather booths coveted by white teens after school and on Saturdays. Owner J. H. Lawson locked the door and called Sheriff Ira Byrd Parnell, who announced upon his arrival, "No store in Sumter is going to be closed by these demonstrators." Lawson reported the students held their seats for only a few minutes. "They didn't say a word to us, and we didn't say a word to them."[241]

News spread quickly downtown, and both white and black bystanders watched as police marched those arrested to jail. "They caught us by the arm and walked us down the street to the county jail, where we were booked," said DuBose, charged with breach of peace. "That's when I got my first look into the eyes of a white man. He asked me, 'What color are your eyes?' when he was asking about my age and all this, and I just looked up so he could see, and for both of us, eye contact was established." Saying the stores had been invaded, the *Daily Item* published a front-page editorial calling the quick arrests "a splendid demonstration of how to deal with the lunch counter sit-downs" and published the names and hometowns of all twenty-six jailed. White Citizens' Councils often paid local newspapers to publish the names of anyone signing a school petition or arrested in a demonstration. J. D. Dinkins, chairman of Sumter's WCC, issued a six-paragraph statement published on the front page. It echoed the newspaper's charge of an invasion—"Negro students from a local college invaded three segregated lunch counters"—and praised law enforcement.[242]

Police locked the twenty-six in cells, four or five to a cell in sections segregated by race and gender. DuBose believed that "they didn't expect us to stay." The women compared notes and found that some had been threatened; some had been slapped, struck, and spat upon. Almost all were unsettled upon being locked in. "The horror of hearing the door close on you, steel-on-steel, and someone holds the key and won't let you out," said DuBose. They hadn't given a lot of thought to this part. They just expected a CORE or NAACP representative to bond them out. Nineteen belonged to church choirs, so they spent the afternoon singing. "It got on our jailers' nerves," said DuBose. "'King Jesus is a-listenin' all day long.' One shouted, 'If you don't shut up your noise, I'll throw you in jail,' and that felt humorous. But that steel-on-steel started a reaction in some of the young women, who felt, "I want my mama.'"[243]

Later that day a jokester called the C&W Cafeteria to reserve a table for a "Marshall" supposedly staying at Morris College, playing with the agitation that NAACP counsel Marshall caused segregationists. Newman arrived. The students remained jailed for seven hours, checked on by Reverend James, president of the Sumter NAACP branch. They were finally bonded out, through a $2,600 cashier's check provided by Robert John Palmer, a local funeral home director. Wilfred Mansfield, the college's public relations director, accompanied Palmer.[244]

On March 5 the *Daily Item*'s editorial page fumed, "All of these demonstrators seem to be under the leadership of some 'Rev.'" These ministers were paid a portion of NAACP dues, the editors claimed, "to forget the gospel and devote their full time to promote integration." On March 7 the KKK erected a cross on the Morris College campus and lit it around 9:30 P.M. The campus was not fenced in, and the KKK placed the cross on the back edge, looming near the science building and library, its fire in full view of the women's dormitory. Students and faculty worked quickly to put it out, using water, sand, anything they could find to douse the flames. A Sumter fire truck arrived to assist. The cross still smoked when a caravan of cars and trucks drove onto campus. At the wheels were the black men of the community. "They popped their trunks and said, 'Get what you want,'" said J. Charles Levy Jr., a freshman that spring. The car trunks and pickup beds held revolvers, pistols, rifles, shotguns, and ammunition, and "nobody was taking inventory" as to who took what. "That was a rude awakening for me, not that they'd burn a cross, but that so many black men had guns," said Levy. Soon "we were armed to the teeth," and "we were praying they wouldn't come back." They didn't.[245]

On March 9 someone fired out of a car, wounding a black man in the forearm; again no one was arrested. On March 12 the *Daily Item* carried a quarter-page ad that announced, "If you believe in maintaining RACIAL INTEGRITY STATES RIGHTS LAW AND ORDER JOIN AND SUPPORT YOUR SUMTER COUNTY CITIZENS COUNCIL." On March 15 about thirty Morris College students gathered in front of the courthouse to sing patriotic songs, including "America, the Beautiful," their appearance coordinated with Rock Hill's picketing and singing, the Orangeburg mass march, and Columbia's sit-ins. No one was arrested.[246]

On April 4 the *Daily Item* published another accusation of communist involvement. "All of this talk that the demonstrations have been spontaneous is just so much bunk. They have been organized by agitators." The piece continued: "These demonstrations are part of a revolutionary movement, inspired in the initial states, at any rate, by the communists. To begin with students are being used for the demonstrations. This is an old revolutionary tactic." Consequently black youth were "led to believe that they can do anything now and get by with it."[247]

On April 24 CORE held a mass meeting to raise funds for the students' defense. Speedily printed leaflets asked black customers to stay out of the stores in which students were arrested. Rather than be intimidated by the hostility, the arrests, and a cross burning, 115 black residents accepted CORE's help in registering to vote. "Sit-ins can and do help registration," reported McCain in the *CORE-lator,* CORE's newsletter.[248]

On April 26, when the students came to trial, more than three hundred white and black people filled the court benches. While the students had been charged with breach of peace and trespass, they were tried on conspiracy to breach the peace. Perry, the students' NAACP attorney, objected, without success, to the change in charges. The judge also refused his motion that the charges be dismissed. Sheriff Parnell, the first witness, revealed that he watched the downtown for days because of "tension and apprehension" and was sitting in a car with SLED lieutenant J. L. Dollard when students entered Sumter Cut Rate. Parnell said that he entered Kress to find nearly a dozen students at the counter, and the assistant manager asked him to "get them out of here." Parnell testified that he believed violence would have erupted if the arrests hadn't taken place. Both the Kress assistant manager and the Cut Rate manager testified that they set policies locally and did not allow black customers to sit. Lawson testified that he offered "a colored room" that allowed black customers to sit and eat separately from whites.[249]

Perry called only DuBose to testify. The city attorney asked her why she sat at the lunch counter; did she expect to be arrested? She pointed out that she was allowed to make purchases throughout Sumter Cut Rate and for this reason asked for counter service. DuBose said that she was a citizen and had a right to protest. Asked why she carried a Bible during the sit-in, she answered that she had come from a Bible-study class. The attorney then asked, didn't she know she would get arrested? She answered no. When he asked why she didn't think she would be arrested, DuBose answered that she was an American citizen, so why should she expect to be arrested? She emphasized that point: "There was no reason for my being arrested. I had a right to be there." All the students were convicted of conspiracy to breach peace and sentenced to thirty days or fines of one hundred dollars. The students' four defense attorneys—Perry, Jenkins, Sampson, and Bennett—appealed the convictions.[250]

DuBose had observed throughout childhood the denigration and demands Sumter's white residents placed on black residents. Her mother worked as a maid, supporting herself and three children. Eliza DuBose made $7.50 a week working seven days a week, with the occasional Sunday off. She walked six miles to work, each way. In 1949, when Frances was ten years old, her mother's employer drove up, blew her horn, and asked, "Is Eliza home?" Frances answered, "No, she's not. Miss Eliza is not home." She offended the white woman, who made that clear. A few years later, Frances watched a replay. The employer drove up as Eliza and Dorothy DuBose, a daughter named after the white woman, rocked in a porch swing. The woman wanted her maid, and Dorothy spoke up, saying her mother was busy. The white woman demanded, "You let your child tell you what to do?" And Eliza DuBose answered, "Yes, ma'am. I can't go." This was the first time Frances DuBose had heard her mother speak up to a white person. After that she noticed other consequences to being black in the South. She kept noticing.[251]

When the sit-ins offered DuBose the opportunity to take a stand, she saw a moment that might change her world. "What really stands out in my mind was we wanted to see if we could get the town to literally crack. We wanted to force them to change their policies." White Sumter residents categorized the activists as either radicals or communists, said DuBose, who became publicity chairman for the activists. "You couldn't be a free thinker, a free spirit who wanted to be treated as an equal. You were expected to be subservient; you were not supposed to have feelings about self-worth; you weren't supposed to have goals and aspirations."[252]

Such clear-cut convictions made DuBose not only a determined protester but also an effective witness. "I believed in what I was doing," she said. "I had enough history to know that I had rights and freedoms I didn't think should be abridged because of the color of my skin. We're all God's children." Morris College administrators neither reprimanded nor punished the protesters. In public President Odell R. Reuben chose to be ambiguous in his stance, telling the local paper more than once that he was reserving judgment. In truth the college, founded in 1908 by the Baptist Educational and Missionary Convention, served as home port for McCain, whom DuBose considered a catalyst not just for the students but for the involvement of NAACP leaders, faculty, and other community elders. While the students, who were inspired by Greensboro, believed that emulating the North Carolina AT&T students would lead others to act, it was McCain who "put the fire" under all, said DuBose.[253]

The students met with McCain and Gaither, a May college graduate, to discuss forming a CORE chapter. They did so on May 11, 1960, but Gaither was worrying about the summer hiatus. He was convinced that "we would have to take immediate drastic steps to get the movement started again." Students helped with voter registration, spoke at churches, and joined a committee focused on police brutality. They distributed pledge cards, which asked black shoppers to vow that they would not enter stores where the students had been arrested. On June 15 Frank Robinson, chairman of Sumter CORE, organized a statewide meeting in Columbia attended by 150 adults, including field secretaries Carey and McCain. McCain noted in his engagement calendar that he wanted to prevent "the student movement from reaching a stalemate over the summer." He told the *CORE-lator* that statewide plans included picketing twice a week and a sit-in at least once a week.[254]

Nationally Woolworth still defended segregation. At its annual stockholders' meeting, President Robert C. Kirkwood said the variety stores would continue to adhere to "local customs, established by local people for the conduct of business in their community," given the "deep-rooted convictions of the people in the South."[255]

In Sumter confrontations waxed then waned, but the intensity burned hot on both sides. One of the drugstore owners, determined to keep protesters out, met black youths at the door with an electric cattle prod, said Willie J. Singleton Jr. "Anyone who attempted to come in would be stuck with it," he said. Singleton came to activism in the 1940s. As a child he delivered *The State* and the *Charlotte Observer*, riding his route on a new bicycle. Like many newspaper carriers, he rode on the sidewalk so the papers he tossed would land on porches. One morning two detectives stopped their car, got out, and demanded of him, "Boy, what are you doing riding on the sidewalk?" When Singleton answered, "Delivering the paper," one slapped him, commanding, "Answer the question." Singleton answered again and was slapped again because he hadn't said "sir." Singleton's father, a chauffeur for a prominent white family, had to pay twenty dollars to keep his son out of a cell.[256]

Harassed from then on by the police, "I knew I couldn't stay because the police were making my life miserable. There was nobody to report the police to because the system was just that way." Singleton joined the Marine Corps at seventeen "to outrun the segregated society I lived in" and was the second black recruit to go through training at Parris Island. Sent to the Korean War, he lost an arm to shrapnel. By 1959 Singleton had returned to Sumter, where he opened a pool room, a gas station, and a wrecker service. A member of CORE, he managed the funds raised for protesters and arranged their bail or bond.[257]

The sit-in support led to increased voter registration efforts, which resulted in more arrests. Florence and Sumter police tailed an interracial canvassing team of six, headed by Frank Robinson and including Gaither. While the CORE canvassing was low-key, such as speaking in churches, police harassed the team because white and black activists were working together. The work was hard in another way too. Many of those approached by the team feared reprisals, such as losing their jobs or their housing. When Gaither asked about plans to vote, he often heard no more than a muted agreement that included, "If my reverend says it's okay." The work was not only difficult but unpaid. Frank Robinson was a CORE volunteer; Gaither lived with the Robinson family and subsisted on a stipend from the Southern Conference Educational Fund. On August 24 in Florence and August 26 in Sumter, police arrested team members and held them for questioning before release. Highway troopers stopped Robinson near Sumter and threatened him with the loss of his license. Within weeks he accumulated six tickets or warnings.[258]

Gaither finished his summer way down South, accompanying McCain on a six-hundred-mile trip to Miami in a 1955 Chevrolet. KKK members interrupted their travels in Georgia, stopping traffic to hand out leaflets. Despite the heat, they kept their windows up. In Miami for three weeks in August, CORE held an Interracial Action Institute for thirty-five CORE members, mostly students. Attendees learned the philosophy of nonviolence, how to apply it, how to negotiate, and how to respond peacefully to assault. The six staff members also offered training in negotiation, which was used before any action in the hopes of averting protests. CORE students and staff managed to eat in twenty-three of forty eating places, swim at two white beaches, and gain admittance to five of seven movie theaters during the institute.[259]

However, just three days in, on August 17, police arrested eighteen participants, who didn't leave Shell's City Supermarket at the manager's request. CORE had not expected these arrests. Eight—including Gaither and James Robinson, a CORE cofounder and the executive director—chose to stay in Dade County's jail rather than accept bail. The two white men, Robinson and Tom Roland, were held in the whites-only section, populated by segregationists who beat Roland but later included the two in their "rough-housing, card-playing, cigarette-sharing, and TV-watching," Robinson wrote for the *CORE-lator*. Gaither and five other black activists found themselves living with murderers and rapists for the nine days they were held but discovered "we were sort of celebrities" for their civil rights activism. At trial on August 26, the judge placed each on one-year probation.[260]

Gaither and McCain moved on to New Orleans, where McCain was arrested on September 16 for picketing. The arrests began when a new CORE group ended its first, and New Orleans's first, sit-in on September 9 with the arrest of all seven participants. The Woolworth arrest for "criminal mischief," a new Louisiana law intended to inhibit sit-ins, was followed by CORE picketing, then a citywide ban on picketing, then the arrest of McCain (his first) and five others for continuing to picket. Gaither's resolute belief in and ability to persist in *satyagraha* resulted in CORE's hiring him and a Miami cellmate, Joe Perkins. CORE wanted these youthful veterans of the student movement to strengthen its nonviolence training and support of peaceful protests. Gaither returned to South Carolina, hoping to breathe new vigor into the sit-ins.[261]

With the fall semester and more protests looming, U.S. Attorney General William Rogers reported the end of segregation at lunch counters in sixty-nine southern communities. Rogers had called in representatives of Woolworth, Kress, Grant, and other variety store chains in June, and executives had agreed to urge local managers to work it out. In his August announcement, Rogers said he told the executives that ending the sit-ins through desegregation of their lunch counters was in the national interest, "because the standing of the United States as a leader of the free world suffers as the result of acts of racial discrimination." He also warned that local ordinances requiring local businesses to practice segregation raised serious constitutional questions. Independently a chain called Bus Terminal Restaurants announced the desegregation of its lunch counters in Maryland, Virginia, North Carolina, Tennessee, and Florida. The federal pressure did not result in the desegregation of any lunch counters in South Carolina, Georgia, Mississippi, Louisiana, or Alabama. The *CORE-lator* warned that sit-ins consequently would continue in South Carolina.[262]

The fall semester brought another Sumter sit-in preceded by a solo excursion. Levy, president of the sophomore class at Morris, had felt slighted when he was not among chosen sit-in participants the previous semester. He decided one morning to sit in on his own and convinced roommate John Endicott Toney to stand lookout. Levy stepped into Kress, walked to the counter, and sat. No one spoke to him; the staff cut off the lights and turned their backs. "Everything got quiet; I turned around on my stool, and everybody was gone." No one called the police. Bewildered, Levy left for a nearby diner. Slight and short, he was awestruck by the diner's remarkably tall owner, who announced, "I'm not going to have this in here," and immediately demonstrated what he meant. "He took one hand on my shirt and picked me up like I was a feather and opened the door and flicked me out." He tossed Levy in the direction of a parking meter and, while airborne, "God spoke to me and told me to catch the parking meter; he knew I was way out of bounds," said Levy. He reached, grabbed the meter's head, and whirled, his legs wrapping around the pole. Staggering but undeterred, in his mind he said, "I'll be back," and the same time next day he was. As Levy reached for the door, so did the owner from inside. "He smiled at me. I smiled at him," and that was the end of Levy's solos. "Word went out I was going to get myself killed," thanks to Toney's abandoning his promise of secrecy and told all.[263]

On October 10 what Gaither named Operation Integration began: picketing and sit-ins to regain momentum for Morris College's CORE. The October 10 sit-ins at Kress and Sumter Cut Rate, timed to match Kennedy's presidential campaign stop in Columbia, did not result in arrests. Nor did the October 11 sit-ins. On October 12 Moultrie, Levy, and Rogers Laverne Robinson took seats at the Kress lunch counter around 10 A.M. "There was a big Fruit of the Loom display," said Levy. The large display, placed between the door and the counter, hid the students as they walked to counter seats. Whites already seated had their backs to the door, said Levy. "They turned around, and someone hollered, 'Oh, my God, they're here!'" Staff immediately cut off the lights. Levy asked the waitress frozen in front of him for "a hamburger, hold the onions, and a small Coke." He wanted to place an order before she could disappear. After he spoke "the quiet then in that place was almost deadly." Within minutes the three heard sirens, and Levy thought, "Here they come."[264]

Parnell himself arrested Levy, placing his hand on Levy's head and swiveling him around. When Levy didn't answer the first question with a "sir," the sheriff lectured him, "Answer 'Yes, sir,' boy." Levy complied but was disturbed by the anger he felt and his conviction that, as he'd been taught, anger could not be part of this moment. Parnell asked him, "Did they ask you to leave?" to which Levy responded, "No." To his surprise, Parnell escorted Levy to his car and told him to sit in the front seat. The sheriff asked, "Where are you from?" and Levy answered, "Cheraw." Next Parnell asked, "What does your Daddy do?" and Levy answered, "He's a pastor." Parnell asked, "Do you act like that in Cheraw?" and Levy answered, "Not yet." He took that moment to "say his piece," that he sat down in Kress because "I'm here for the bigger picture. If I can spend money to buy Fruit of the Loom, can I not sit and eat?" Police, who took Moultrie separately to jail, recognized her as a participant in the March sit-ins, as did the *Daily Item,* which referred to her as "the Moultrie woman."[265]

Outside both Kress and Sumter Cut Rate, six students carried signs, one saying, "There's no color line in heaven." The bottom corner of each sign carried the signature "CORE." Police arrested the picketers too. About 11:30 A.M., back at Kress, police arrested Marvin McAllister and DuBose, even though they had yet to take seats. DuBose felt sure the police had expected all the students since they arrived so quickly. She believed they tapped phones in her neighborhood. Despite such concerns, some of the students had decided a sit-in and arrest weren't enough of a statement. They planned to remain in jail, a tactic that CORE advocated. For Operation Integration the Morris College students agreed among themselves to remain in jail for thirty days.[266]

Levy kept a secret, though. Throughout his childhood in Camden and Cheraw, his father, the pastor of Pee Dee Union Baptist Church, and his mother constantly emphasized, "You don't do anything to go to jail." That prohibition crashed down upon Levy, the first to reach the jail, be booked, and taken to the cell block. The bare, stained mattresses repulsed him, and he stood against the wall rather than sit. "The smell got to me." It was so powerful that he thought, "I've got to get out of here." Attorneys Perry and Finney arrived before all the bookings were completed and offered the eleven students the option of posting bail immediately and leaving. Levy instantly raised his hand; he wanted out. "I went back to Morris and burned my clothes."[267]

DuBose said she would stay. "We felt if we stayed in jail thirty days something in Sumter would emotionally and psychologically crack," she said. The cell she stood alone in was tiny and filthy. "That jail cell was really deplorable, hardly enough room in it for a bed, a sink, and a commode. There was a mattress of sorts, but no bedclothes, and it was roach infested. Even that didn't change my mind."[268]

That night a Morris College instructor persuaded DuBose that remaining could endanger others. The instructor came in the late hours, was allowed in, and wept. She told DuBose, "Frances, you have got to come out. I understand there are carloads of whites riding around, trying to find where you live. And your mother is there alone, so you've got to come out." She told DuBose the newspaper had published the family's address. DuBose's mother was in her sixties and lived alone. "I loved my mother. I made the sacrifice," DuBose said. She allowed herself to be bonded out. Four of the eleven students, including McAllister, remained in jail but not for the thirty days of their aspirations. A disappointed McCain discovered that college administrators told the seniors that they would not graduate if they remained.[269]

Choosing jail over bail or bond was a dauntingly complicated decision. Stories abounded of jailers beating and raping and mobs lynching black people. Parents warned their children, as Levy's had, of the terror and shame a stint in jail inflicted on a family. Despite perfectly logical reasons for getting out of jail as quickly as possible, students were reconsidering. Some objected to paying bail or bond, which put money into the governmental system denying them equality. Some were drawn to the dramatic implications of a democracy imprisoning youths for sitting quietly at a counter or praying in a city square. In Nashville eighty-one students chose thirty-three days in the county workhouse over paying fifty dollar fines; the mayor released them two days later. In Tallahassee, after a February 29 sit-in arrest, eight Florida A&M students with CORE chose sixty-day jail sentences over three-hundred-dollar fines. Leon Holt, a CORE field secretary, said the organization was "encouraging those who can undergo the hardships to offer themselves as sacrificial lambs." CORE hoped the Tallahassee students would set a pattern for other demonstrators. If large numbers of students chose this option, they could overwhelm the jails and cost the government in time, resources, and room and board, believed CORE.[270]

The national NAACP adamantly opposed this tactic. If students served a sentence, they forfeited "the right to seek vindication by an appeal." In a position statement, the NAACP advised those arrested to know their rights, know the charges against them, immediately get in touch with a local attorney and local NAACP officials, plead not guilty to the charges, and accept bail. "The only way we will be able to successfully break down the practice of segregation and discrimination and undermine the legal support of these practices through the law is by the process of having such laws and ordinances declared unconstitutional," said the position paper. Accepting jail posed "a great danger to the individual," stigmatized those convicted with criminal records, and was an all-around "ill-advised and ill-considered scheme" inconsistent with NAACP policy and philosophy that rendered "ineffectual our overall legal attack." Whatever attitudes students held about organizations, organizations' philosophies and policies, or effective protest practices, no one disputed the danger. Black South Carolinians knew white law officers often cooperated with or even belonged to the Klan. As Singleton observed, "It's bad when your worst enemy was law enforcement. If you can't call on law enforcement, who do you call? That's what made it so scary."[271]

On October 16 Woolworth, Grant, Kress, and McCrory-McLellan jointly announced that 150 drug and variety stores' lunch counters had desegregated in 112 cities. Not one city was located in the Deep South. The four companies' statement, more than a little defensive, noted that retailers did not have sole responsibility for a solution and that counter service outside the South had never been segregated. The statement sweepingly—and mystifyingly, given the thousands of arrests within stores in the South—said that the chains had been "consistently opposed to causing the arrest or prosecution of students for their sit-in activities." J. Arthur Brown, new president of the state NAACP conference, pointed out that South Carolina stores "refuse to take note of the social changes that are taking place all around us." He warned boycotts would intensify.[272]

Gaither called arrests during sit-ins and picketing "a basic denial of rights" in a telephone interview with the *Daily Item*. He referred to the right to redress the government in a peaceful, nonviolent manner and remarked on the damage that segregation inflicted on the nation's international reputation, especially with African nations joining the United Nations. The Morris College CORE distributed a flyer that said, "This could have been one of your family or you. The management of these stores refuses to allow Negroes to eat at their lunch counters," and "Don't buy from stores which discriminate against you in any way." Clifford Sumner Jr. and James Lewis, cochairmen of the Morris College Student Movement Association, wrote the city manager to say that previous efforts to obtain picket permits had been denied. They again formally requested a permit. "Being firm believers in the democratic process, we should like to call attention to the fact that the right to picket is guaranteed under our Constitution," they wrote. Sumter CORE sent a letter to supporters, asking for financial support and urging, "DON'T SHOP AT KRESS! DON'T SHOP at CUT-RATE!"[273]

On October 27 five of the Morris College students faced trial. The judge asked Levy, before his testimony, if he believed in God. The Kress manager testified that he neither asked the students to leave nor called the police. The three students who asked for service were convicted of breach of peace and each sentenced to thirty days in jail or one hundred dollars. The two who didn't sit had been charged separately and were also convicted of breach of peace. On Saturday, November 5, two counties away, police arrested two CORE members for distributing leaflets that opposed the Sumter sit-in arrests. The Hartsville police chief charged Robert Williams and Horace Watts with distributing leaflets without a license. The two remained in jail until Monday, when the national CORE paid bonds of one hundred dollars each. On November 21 they were found guilty of violating Hartsville's handbill ordinance and fined one hundred dollars each or thirty days in jail.[274]

On November 22 the six students who had carried picket signs—saying "Segregation is America's Shame," "Father, Forgive Them for They Know Not What They Do," and "Don't Buy Where You Can't Eat"—were tried. Freddie Lee Williams and Roosevelt McCullough testified that they wanted the public to know how they felt about segregated lunch counters. Parnell testified that the picket signs offended his beliefs and "could have caused trouble," although he acknowledged under cross-examination that the students were quiet, orderly, and had no physical contact with passersby. The six were convicted of breach of peace, with fines of $100 each. Bond was set at $1,200 total, with the national CORE paying and the local CORE later raising $800 toward the cost. CORE counsel Finney appealed each case.[275]

Newman chastised these students for their demonstrations and argued they should formally disaffiliate from CORE. The students refused, McCain interrogated the Sumter NAACP's executive committee, and all agreed that Sumter should not be split into CORE versus NAACP. McCain confronted Newman later and reported, "This was an opportunity for the NAACP to cash in on an action project," but "as it stands now, we have blown holes in whatever plans Newman might have had in taking our students away from us." CORE printed and the students distributed fifteen thousand "Don't Buy" leaflets, which explained a boycott they expected to last throughout the holidays. CORE students visited churches in both Sumter and Clarendon Counties, and McCain visited nearby towns to include rural residents in the boycott, a relatively safe form of activism since shoppers could participate relatively anonymously through absence and avoid white reprisals.[276]

The geography of sit-ins expanded from drugstores' lunch counters to include sit-ins at libraries, wade-ins at parks and pools, and kneel-ins at churches. CORE, SNCC, and the Atlanta Committee on Appeal for Human Rights started kneel-ins during August, testing the tolerance and Christianity of Atlanta's white churches by seeking admission to Sunday worship services. SNCC described the kneel-ins as students' attempt to "awaken the dozing consciences of white Southerners by carrying the problem of segregation to the church, which they think is the best place for reconciling moral problems." For three Sundays in a row, black worshipers appeared at the doors of Atlanta's white Christian churches. Of nineteen visited, each by three or four people, ten refused the students entry.[277]

On November 20 four Morris College students made their first attempt, with Rock Hill's Hamm as spokesperson and McCain as observer. An usher at First Presbyterian Church turned them away. A police officer followed, stopped the students, and threatened them with arrest if they made another attempt. McCain had heard, through a white minister, that First Presbyterian wanted the arrests of any black churchgoers who came to worship. On November 27 First Presbyterian ushers again stopped students at the door. On their walk back to school, several police stopped them, took their names, but did not arrest them, as CORE had hoped. An officer told McCain, "These students were giving the college a bad name." McCain wrote, "To this statement I made no comment." Some white ministers, disturbed that a church door was barred to Christians, approached the president of the Negro Ministerial Alliance about a joint meeting. The black ministers set terms: they would not meet with white ministers intent on an end to the kneel-ins, but they would meet with any ministers interested in an interracial alliance that focused on ending discrimination in Sumter.[278]

At this point the Negro Ministers Alliance, the Sumter CORE, Morris College's CORE, the Sumter NAACP, and the Sumter County Citizens Committee united to enforce a total boycott of Kress. At church services boosters called for engagement and passed out leaflets. Each morning and afternoon, spotters tallied how many black customers entered the store and, upon their exit, informed them of the boycott. The groups united in their opposition not only to the continuing segregation but also to the continuing arrests. McCain heard that some white residents were arguing for a desegregated stand-up counter or the seated lunch counter's removal, neither satisfactory to the black activists. By December 21 the Ministerial Alliance estimated the boycott's success at 95 percent.[279]

In the meantime another arrest opened up another protest avenue. On December 15 Phillip Cleary took the first seat on the B&H bus headed to Morris College, where he was a junior. He had done this before. On this morning the driver asked him to sit in the back of the bus. Cleary refused; he asked for his money back and said he would disembark. The bus moved on, out of Cleary's community. A plainclothes officer, who was riding the bus, arrested Cleary, charging him with breach of peace. The Morris College president stepped up. Odell Reuben paid Cleary's one-hundred-dollar bond and backed student leaders calling for a bus boycott. The college students made up about 25 percent and the black community as a whole about 80 percent of the fares, so this was a genuine threat. CORE backed the boycott and provided placards to place along the routes, discouraging bus rides. The students started walking. McCain ended his December report this way: "(Smile)."[280]

Year's End: December 1960

The student movement—so persistent, so personal, whether two or three at a lunch counter or hundreds at city hall—surprised everyone: white politicians; black elders; church leaders, white and black; attorneys, white and black; black parents, who thought they were sending their children to study history and found them making it; and black students themselves, who discovered they were willing to put their lives on the line for equality. The *Southern Newsletter* reported that customers' tolerance of desegregated lunch counters negated "predictions that 'the sky will fall in' if Negroes ate alongside whites." As CORE's Gaither pointed out, bolstering such successes was his peers' approach. It differed fundamentally from the efforts of past decades, which had relied most often on lone petitioners and NAACP attorneys.[281]

Gaither called the students' approach—their march tactics, their sit-ins and kneel-ins, their picket signs—a passion. For him the student movement exemplified strength in the active and public involvement of many individuals and their willing endurance of consequent suffering. And the spiritual component of the civil rights movement remained. Many of the students continued to embrace the Christianity of their parents; others were drawn to Gandhi's nonviolent direct action as their spiritual force. As Claflin College's Moultrie pointed out, "I never saw in the Bible that God only loved white people. God made all people and loved the whole world." And as South Carolina State's McDew said, "You don't separate yourself from your humanity."[282]

On December 23 Eisenhower surprised the nation. He had not used his bully pulpit or presidential authority to support the Supreme Court decision in *Brown v. Board.* Yet he devoted most of his holiday message to racism and its harm to the nation's reputation. This was his final presidential lighting of the national Christmas tree, this one a seventy-five-foot Oregon fir adorned with nine thousand lights and ornaments. Many Americans had been prevented from enjoying political and economic opportunity "through bitter prejudice and because of differences in skin pigmentation," the president said. This was "a blot on the brightness of America's image." The nation's laws demanded respect and the support of public opinion if Americans were to live up to Christian and national ideals, he said.[283]

South Carolina's newspaper editors wound up the year with a focus on race too. Responding to a year-end poll by the Associated Press, the white male editors ranked the presidential campaign and Kennedy's surprise win, assisted by black voters, as the top two stories of the year. Ranked third and fourth were lunch counter sit-ins and the "anti-segregation demonstration by 1,000 Negroes in the streets of the usually placid city of Orangeburg." With an offhand nod to "angry punches" in Orangeburg, egg-throwing in Rock Hill, and "some minor shoving in Columbia and a few other cities" as exceptions, the article claimed no violence occurred. Absent from that assessment: tear gas and fire hoses in Orangeburg and the resulting injuries to demonstrators, as well as bomb threats, cross burnings, and assaults throughout the state. The wrap-up story noted this: "The busy year of demonstrations failed to integrate a single Palmetto State lunch counter."[284]

The many-months extension of the NAACP Easter boycott into the adoption of the "No Christmas Gift Buying" drive sustained economic pressure on what *Jet* magazine called "Jim Crow stores." The push invited the participation of older or more conservative black citizens familiar with the selective-buying campaigns of the 1950s. The NAACP state conference urged a boycott of any store that practiced "refusal of lunch counter service, refusal to accord courtesy titles to adult Negroes, maintenance of segregated restrooms and water fountains, and biased employee practices." Newman encouraged black consumers not only to abstain from any Christmas giving but also to donate their holiday money to churches and the NAACP as a protest of segregation and a contribution to "the advancement of the Negro in South Carolina." He did make an exception for gifts to children who didn't know the truth about Santa Claus. SNCC endorsed the campaign and sent appeals to student groups throughout the country. The *Student Voice* celebrated a shopping-season drop in department stores sales in the South, attributed to racial tension and boycotts. SNCC also asked black and white students traveling during the holidays to employ "reverse" seating in buses and use of restrooms, with black riders sitting up front in buses and white riders in the back and white customers using "colored only" restrooms while black customers used "whites only" restrooms.[285]

The Tuskegee Institute, which had been publishing an annual race relations report since 1953, called the sit-ins of 1960 "the major new ingredient." But the report also reiterated a plaint. Previously the institute had noted "a hesitancy by America's citizens to face the moral implications of continued segregation." At the end of 1960, segregation remained, and its "moral underpinnings were largely neglected," according to Tuskegee. But the students exhibited moral outrage, and their politeness, their calm demeanor, their formal clothes, their prayers and patriotic songs, their peacefulness no matter what the affront, all components in the use of nonviolent direct action, made their complaint a moral complaint. "Instead of attacking the legality of segregation, students struck at its morality," wrote Lerone Bennett Jr. in an *Ebony* report on the sit-ins. Bennett quoted Orangeburg's McCollom: "Every protest that makes a point is worthwhile. We've been lying to the white man for years: 'Yassah, Cap'n. Everything's all right.' We have to stop lying to him." Hurley wrote in her regional NAACP report that the sit-ins "brought a reawakening among both Whites and Negroes." She believed that "by the year's end, more Negro adults have turned from their old casual ways to more dynamic action." Carey, of CORE, asserted, "There is a new awareness of the racial problem throughout the country."[286]

Newman did the numbers in his annual field report for the NAACP: "Altogether there have been 80 'protest demonstrations' in South Carolina such as Sit-Ins, Kneel-Ins, Wade-Ins, Picketing and marches." He wrote that the state NAACP had borne the brunt of legal assistance and financial aid for students protesters at a cost of $42,450. Nationally the legal defense arm of the NAACP reported that the organization spent 40 percent of its entire $405,000 budget defending 1,700 cases involving demonstrators.[287]

Harder to measure were the costs to participants: physical injuries, emotional trauma, court appearances, convictions, opportunities blocked by convictions, parents economically punished for their children's actions. McDew, having experienced it all, decided to invest further by dropping out of South Carolina State and working for SNCC full-time. He set himself a five-year plan, both to assure his parents he would return to his studies and "because by the end of that time you'd either be dead or crazy."[288]

South Carolina's students had provided CORE and the SCLC additional proof that nonviolent direct action could protect activists while producing results and speaking powerfully to allies and opponents. The students also had affirmed the long view, the legal view held by the NAACP that Jim Crow could die on the streets of the South, its demise brought about by fervent believers in first-class citizenship and a U.S. Supreme Court acknowledging the U.S. Constitution. *McAllister et al. v. City of Sumter* appealed convictions on breach of peace, convictions despite no crowds, no interference with traffic, no boisterous conduct, no threat or acts of violence. *Henry v. City of Rock Hill* appealed breach-of-peace convictions for singing at city hall. *Bouie v. City of Columbia* and *Barr v. City of Columbia* appealed convictions of criminal trespass for peaceful attempted sit-ins. *Fields v. South Carolina* and *Irene Brown et al. v. South Carolina* appealed breach-of-peace convictions in the Orangeburg mass march. *Hamm v. City of Rock Hill* appealed Hamm's conviction for sitting beside Ivory at McCrory's. Attorneys such as Perry and Finney knew they were making local records for appeals and, as NAACP counsel Carter explained, were using the law "to revolutionize race relations by seeking to have the Thirteenth, Fourteenth, and Fifteenth Amendments given their intended effect."[289]

They won—won them all in the Supreme Court. You might say that Reverend Ivory had the last word. Hamm's conviction for trespass during his sit-in with Ivory had enforced racial discrimination in violation of the Fourteenth Amendment, said the Supreme Court. Convictions for peaceful sit-ins ended with the 1964 Civil Rights Act. The Court ruled in *Hamm v. City of Rock Hill* that the Civil Rights Act abated not only federal convictions but also state convictions under the Supremacy Clause. "The great purpose of the civil rights legislation was to obliterate the effect of a distressing chapter in our history," said the opinion. *Edwards v. South Carolina* had provided an earlier dispensation. In 1961 a mass march on the State House had finally occurred, with students circling the grounds, singing, listening to David Carter's religious exhortations, then marching to jail. Breach-of-peace convictions of 187 of the demonstrators led to a definitive 1963 Supreme Court ruling. The students had exercised "basic constitutional rights in their most pristine and classic form," said the Supreme Court. South Carolina had infringed on their rights of free speech, freedom of assembly, and freedom to petition for redress of grievance. "The Fourteenth Amendment does not permit a state to make criminal the peaceful expression of unpopular views."[290]

White officials seemingly never tired of describing black South Carolinians as satisfied with their lot. But 1960 had begun with an Emancipation Day Prayer Pilgrimage to the Greenville Municipal Airport, organized by McCain and Greenville's Reverend Hall and sponsored by CORE and the Greenville Ministerial Alliance. Between nine hundred and one thousand participants walked almost three miles in a light snow from Hall's Springfield Baptist Church to the airport. A baker's dozen—including Ivory, McCain, McCollom, Newman, Sharper, Brown, and Perry—entered the waiting room to address formally airport management regarding its enforcement of segregation.[291]

Months before, on October 25, 1959, three NAACP greeters left the airport terminal rather than accept the manager's banishment to the "colored lounge" or arrest by an armed guard. They were waiting for Jackie Robinson, flying in to address the NAACP's annual state conference. That evening the manager again attempted to enforce segregation—banned since 1955 on interstate buses and trains and in their terminals' waiting rooms. As the baseball star checked on his departure, Gloster Current, Hall, and Hall's wife, Elizabeth, stood tensely in the main waiting room, listening to the manager order a police officer to arrest them if they sat down. Current said they were willing to go to jail; Hall feared violence. The standoff ended when about a hundred children rushed toward the celebrity, who began signing their baseballs. "God sends angels to have charge over us," said Hall, who believed the children rescued them. On New Year's Day, at the march's snowy end, McCollom said, "We will no longer make a pretense of being satisfied with the crumbs of citizenship." Sharper said, "We are sick of segregation."[292]

A month later young people took the matter into their own hands.

Five

You Thought We'd Say, "Sorry, Boss"

The Charleston Hospital Strike

More than four hundred black women strike. Coretta Scott King leads protesters on marches through the streets of Charleston. National Guard troops don helmets with face shields and clutch rifles with fixed bayonets. The marchers carry signs saying, "Still a Slave" and "We Are Tired of Being Sick and Tired." The marchers chant, "I Am Somebody!" A startling cast of characters shapes the strike's momentum each day: a twenty-seven-year-old black nurse's aide who delivers rousing speeches nationwide, a mattress factory's foreman armed and ready to die, the anxious heir to Rev. Dr. Martin Luther King Jr.'s legacy, a hospital president whose father doctored South African Zulus, a governor tainted by recent shootings of black college students.

This was Charleston in the spring and summer of 1969. Ordinarily the port city reaped millions of dollars by attracting white tourists fond of fresh shrimp, ocean breezes, garden tours, carriage rides past historic houses, and tales of antebellum bliss. But from March through July 1969, a city best known for celebrating the Old South of myths and movies got national media coverage and lost millions of dollars as black women and their supporters picketed two hospitals, asking for better working conditions. For that spring and summer, Charleston was a destination not for tourists but for labor and civil rights activists, the National Guard, and riot police. Charleston was a town slowed not by horses pulling carriages but by daily marches and nightly curfews.

When black women working low-level, low-pay jobs at the Medical College Hospital (MCH) and Charleston County Hospital (CCH) compared grievances and couldn't get a hearing, they shouted on the picket lines, "Soul

Power! Union Power!" Soul power, union power, and woman power merged when nurse's aide Mary Moultrie and licensed practical nurse (LPN) Rosetta Simmons turned to their friends, then to their coworkers, then to the financial and strategic support of New York City's Local 1199, the Drug and Hospital Employees Union, and to the Southern Christian Leadership Conference (SCLC). Their appeals for help led to a strike; months of attention from media, labor, civil rights, and congressional leaders; and the involvement of the U.S. Department of Health, Education, and Welfare (HEW) and the White House.

Moultrie, a strike leader, became the voice of the underpaid hospital workers, a persistent voice demanding attention. With that voice, which combined firmness with irony, which simultaneously sounded melodious and militant, she announced, "You thought we'd just die out after a day or two of marching. You thought we'd say, 'Sorry, boss,' and put those handkerchiefs back on our heads." Moultrie found her voice young, working for Esau Jenkins, a Johns Island community leader and activist. She still recited "The South Awake at Midnight," one of her first speeches under his tutelage: "When change is in evidence it is logical to assume there has been an awakening. Change as we speak of it at this time means a passing from one condition to another." In the 1950s Jenkins and Septima Clark had developed the Citizenship Schools, Sea Island schools where black adults learned to read, write, do math, understand election laws, and thus succeed in registering to vote. While in high school, Moultrie was among the teens accompanying Jenkins to rural meetings of the National Association for the Advancement of Colored People (NAACP) and assisting him in voter registration drives. She also worked in Jenkins's J&P Restaurant on Charleston's Spring Street. He encouraged her, and many others, to speak up.[1]

Upon high school graduation, Moultrie left Charleston to join a cousin in New York City. Charleston held no opportunities for her, she believed. She found a job as a nursing assistant at Goldwater Memorial Hospital, located on Welfare Island in New York City's East River. Through on-the-job training and classes, Moultrie earned certification as an LPN, making four dollars an hour, with benefits such as paid sick leave, holidays, and vacation days. She sent money home to help her parents—her father worked as a laborer at the Charleston Navy Yard, her mother as a housekeeper—and to support her younger brother and two sisters. But she missed Charleston and family and visited frequently. When her mother fell ill, in late 1966, Moultrie came home, but she came home changed. In New York "the hospital was integrated. I was working with people of other races, different nationalities.

I didn't feel the sting of prejudice up there. I felt really comfortable." She returned to Charleston with self-respect and expectations.[2]

Moultrie got a job at MCH, which didn't accept her certification. She was back to being a nurse's aide, her initial pay $0.70 an hour. Over the next few years, her pay reached a peak of $1.33 an hour as her job requirements increased. "We did all the labor, the hard labor," Moultrie said. While the black nurse's aides worked, the LPNs, most of them white, took their ease and drank coffee, she said. Moultrie was responsible for twice as many patients as in New York plus tasks a nurse's aide shouldn't have been assigned, such as giving medication. She took patients' blood pressure and temperature, bathed them, did housekeeping chores, and helped with meals. The hospital expected the nurse's aides—almost all black women—to help train the white nursing students, young women who demanded the honorific "ma'am" while using the older black women's first names.[3]

The white LPNs and registered nurses allowed the hospital's few white nurse's aides to join them in a lounge. Black employees had no lounge. The hospital provided two cafeterias, one for white doctors only, one for other white employees. Some black workers ate in the boiler room, others in their locker room. As late as 1967, the hospital maintained segregated restrooms. However, the Civil Rights Act of 1964 had ended segregation in public facilities. The hospital accepted federal funds, putting it in violation of federal law. The Medical College, which became a state school in 1913 and added a hospital in 1955, enrolled no black nursing students and employed no black doctors. "The nurses would refer to us as 'monkey grunts.' They would call you names, and if you retaliated, your job was at stake. They could fire you at will," said Moultrie. "I just didn't like it. I didn't know how to do what they wanted me to do and not answer back. I got written up all the time and threatened."[4]

In December 1967 five black women who worked as practical nurses and nurse's aides walked off the job. Trouble began around 1:30 A.M. on the neurology floor, said Martha Simmons "M. S." Alston, a practical nurse and one of the five. "We went into work, and we had a new nurse in charge, who really wasn't, I think, quite familiar with everything." Customarily the charge nurse reviewed all patients' conditions and treatments with the aides and practical nurses. "Sitting for a report for thirty-two patients takes about an hour and a half. She decided that was just too much time for us to sit." The charge nurse instructed the women to start taking vital signs without the information session. "She said, 'Would you all go ahead and get started with the vital signs, and I'll give you a report later,'" said Alston.[5]

The women objected. Without the proper instructions for each patient, they might cause harm. Besides, "We weren't going to let anybody put us in the position of destroying our licenses," said M. S. Alston. The charge nurse called in the shift supervisor, who told the women to obey instructions. Convinced this was not only wrong but also dangerous, the women sat for about forty minutes. According to Alston, the charge nurse then said, "Well, if you all don't start doing vital signs now, I'm going to dock you two hours." The standoff ended when the women decided to leave. "We said, 'Don't take two hours; take eight,' because that's our shift. Give her the whole shift." During the elevator ride from Seven East, then the drive home in the dark, they felt elated. "When you know you're right, you have to stand up for it." But the reality that they had walked away from jobs, during the Christmas season at that, cut in quickly. Four of the five women were raising children. "I said, 'Lord have mercy, what will we do?'"[6]

M. S. Alston, who had trained as an LPN in 1967, was among the first black women employed as cashiers on Meeting Street downtown, following civil rights protests in the early 1960s. At the Piggly Wiggly, she was so speedy at her tasks that her boss called her "Alka Seltzer," a reference to the quick relief promised in the antacid's commercials. Her mother, a single parent, was a domestic worker. Alston, married to a contractor and the mother of three, wanted a better life for her family and other black Charlestonians. When she had worked in the hospital's pediatric clinic, she had called HEW about neglectful medical treatment of black children. Now she found herself promising her coworkers, "When my children eat, yours will, too." The next morning the women met at her house for eggs, grits, and sausage and affirmed, "We were tired of being taken advantage of," then asked for the help of their ministers. Pastoral intervention didn't help; the hospital fired them.[7]

The black-owned *Lowcountry Newsletter,* reporting on the firings, noted MCH lacked black secretaries or receptionists, segregated patients, and violated its own regulations by allowing aides to provide patients their medication. "It is clear that the Nurses' Aides, the Orderlies, and the other black staff at the Hospital ought to UNIONIZE, or else what happened to these five Aides will keep on happening to black people who work there," concluded the newsletter, edited and published by William J. Saunders, a Johns Island native.[8]

"It wasn't a chosen mission; it just happened," said M. S. Alston, but the incident served as a slow fuse. Moultrie, when she heard about the walkout and the firings, discussed problems at the hospital with Saunders and others. Saunders, another Jenkins protégé, described himself as militant, although he admired Jenkins's peaceful approach. Tagged a "rebel with a cause" in his *Lowcountry Newsletter* following efforts to improve the segregated schools of Johns Island, Saunders said he wanted "betterment of the poor man, the grassroots man." He saw organizing black unions as one means. Adamant about his beliefs, he used his newsletter to spread his views and aspired to a greater role in the state. He was close to Moultrie, and he saw the women's unrest as an opportunity he could seize for good.[9]

A Korean War veteran, Saunders worked as a foreman at the Weils Mattress Factory in downtown Charleston. Tall, an island lilt to his speech, he sported a Fu Manchu mustache and wore a dashiki or jeans with a blue jean jacket, the attire of 1960s activists. He was an anomaly in Charleston who met with gun-toting gang members and negotiated with suit-and-tie white officials, "looking for another way." He participated in several activist communities: business manager for Jenkins's Progressive Club, an alumnus of the Highlander Folk School in Tennessee, a cofounder of Concerned Citizens for Johns and Wadmalaw Islands, and a member of a local nameless but self-described Black Power group. He read Elijah Muhammad, leader of the Nation of Islam. He was host to Cleveland Sellers and Stokely Carmichael of what was now called the Student National Coordinating Committee (SNCC). In 1966 SNCC changed its focus (and in 1969 its name) from nonviolent direct action to a call for black power. It amused Saunders to no end that a 1967 Carmichael visit, straight from Cuba, convinced opponents that Saunders had to be a communist, a label white politicians often applied to activists in an effort to discredit them.[10]

Saunders got in touch with Reginald Barrett Sr., a black Charleston Realtor. After a May 1965 complaint about segregation at the hospital and an NAACP protest march, HEW named Barrett and four others to a committee charged with monitoring the hospital's compliance with the 1964 Civil Rights Act. Moultrie met with Isaiah Bennett, an employee of the American Tobacco Company's cigar factory and shop steward of Local 15A, Retail, Wholesale and Department Store Union (RWDSU). Round-faced and mustached, Bennett was a devoted union man. He began work at the cigar factory in 1942, served in World War II, then returned. The factory entered Charleston history in 1945 when a strike by tobacco workers, mostly black women, won better wages and working conditions. Now, years later, hospital workers struggled with similar problems. Behind-the-scenes negotiations by Barrett, Bennett, and HEW ensured the five women returned to hospital work after several weeks. However, the larger issue—institutional racism—remained.[11]

"We started having meetings," explained Moultrie, "and that's when we discovered this was not an isolated situation, but this type thing had been going on throughout the hospital"—the inappropriate tasks, the name-calling, the instantaneous firings. That led to the next step: "After we started talking about all the stuff going on, Bill [Saunders] said, 'The doctors have an association. So you all need some kind of an association so you can't be picked off and fired like that.' So we started talking about it at the hospital. We would keep it out of the ears of the whites and just started getting people to come to the meetings. And then every week we'd say, 'You bring someone you can trust real good,' and it started growing like that," said Moultrie. "We decided we needed to do something, but we still didn't think about a union." At the time just 7 percent of the state's workers belonged to unions, the lowest percentage in the nation. South Carolina was one of eighteen "right to work" states; since 1954 state law had forbidden closed-shop unions.[12]

The women's meetings moved from Barrett's real estate office to the tobacco workers' union hall at 655 East Bay Street. The women were meeting on the April 4 evening that King was assassinated in Memphis, Tennessee, during a sanitation workers strike. His presence in Memphis was part of the Poor People's Campaign, begun by the SCLC to highlight economic inequality. Bennett brought them the news the civil rights leader had been shot and then the news he had died. Otis Robinson, the city's Black Muslim leader, told the group, "We've got to hold this thing together for Dr. King."[13]

They did, and their numbers grew until hundreds of black workers, almost all women, from MCH and the CCH were involved. The women considered formally joining Bennett's union. However, Moultrie said, Bennett advised her, "'This is a tobacco workers' union; you need to get somebody that's professional in terms of dealing with hospital workers,' and that's when we got in touch with Local 1199." Moultrie and Lillie Mae Doster, who had participated in the cigar factory strike, wrote to Local 1199, a growing division of the RWDSU. Under founder and president Leon J. Davis's direction, New York City's Local 1199 had provided the SCLC financial support during the 1955–56 Montgomery bus boycott, participated in the 1963 March on Washington, D.C., and opposed the war in Vietnam, as did King. He had named Local 1199 his favorite union, calling it "the authentic conscience of the labor movement."[14]

Doster, too, had attended Highlander and belonged to the Citizens Committee of Charleston County, founded by Jenkins in 1959 to assist black locals. "There were a few people here trying to get things going," said Doster, who wore a pageboy hairdo and cat-eye glasses. During the winter-long

1945–46 strike, she had picketed all but one day. At this point she worked as shop steward and secretary of the Distributive, Office, and Processing Workers' Union, a CIO union. While she didn't know Moultrie well, the hospital workers met where she worked. She became so involved that she was arrested for picketing with them.[15]

Within the previous ten years, Local 1199 had organized forty thousand hospital workers in New York City. Serendipitously Local 1199 recently had formed the National Organizing Committee of Hospital and Nursing Home Employees, with $350,000 in funds, Elliott Godoff as director, and Henry Nicholas as assistant director. With an eye to organizing, Doris Turner, vice president of the local, visited Charleston. So did David White, Brooklyn area director, who was impressed by "the tremendous spirit of the people" and by their determination "to do something to improve themselves." In the meantime local union members provided advice on next steps. Bennett asked everyone interested to pay three dollars in dues so that all were dues-paying participants. This step impressed Nicholas because it proved "buy-in." In October 1968 the energized workers formally organized as a union, electing Moultrie as president; Jack Bradford and Rosetta Simmons, vice presidents; M. S. Alston, treasurer; Ernestine Grimes, secretary; and Jack Coaxum, sergeant-at-arms.[16]

Rosetta Simmons had experienced her own walkout years before. Born in nearby Mount Pleasant, she grew up in Charleston. Her father, David Simmons, was a road worker for the city. He died young. Her mother Loretta Simmons joined forces with an older sister to raise their children. After high school Rosetta Simmons tried "a little bit of this, a little bit of that. Housekeeping was not my calling." At St. Francis Xavier, the city's small Catholic hospital, a nun took an interest in her, and through the Roper School of Practical Nursing, she earned a license as a practical nurse. From 1959 to 1965, she worked at MCH. With her short, straight hair, square face, and strong hands, she conveyed competence, determination, and resolve. But the hospital's racist environment wore her down. "I quit because I was being an agitator," she said. Being a "vocal or aggressive" black employee wasn't tolerated, she said, and when she disagreed with an RN about an assignment, she was told, "'You do what I told you to do or else.' I did the 'or else.' I went home."[17]

Rosetta Simmons next worked at CCH in the intensive care unit and, like so many others, felt unsettled by the unremitting racism. In 1968 she heard about the secret meetings, attended, and began careful forays into other CCH departments to recruit workers. She said the black workers at both hospitals told the same stories of inequities and no recourse. "It was overwhelming, to think of all the unfairness," she said. The order of the day was "Do what I tell you to do," and any objections were "rocking the boat." Simmons decided, "To get fairness, you have to come together as one body."[18]

The Whip

Dr. William Mellon McCord, president of MCH, didn't respond to the workers' repeated attempts at contact, despite what he called "sub-rosa" warnings of unrest and a September invitation by the cigar factory's Local 15A to meet with hospital employees. Instead, in an October 11, 1968, letter mailed to all employees' homes, a letter littered with all-caps statements, McCord issued a warning. He wrote, "WE DO NOT WANT A UNION HERE AT MEDICAL COLLEGE," and "This union bunch is interested in one thing and one thing only. That's MONEY. YOUR MONEY." He vowed, again in all caps, to resist the union with every legal means possible. The mailing included two cartoons depicting the greed of labor unions. One cartoon showed a union organizer who held a fistful of money while shoving an employee into a manager. The other showed a beefy, stogie-chomping, champagne-swilling, money-grabbing "union boss," accompanied by a tiara-wearing blonde and a limousine.[19]

This infuriated the workers, Moultrie said. "A big fat union boss with a cigar and all these champagne glasses and women all over him. It was really an insult." Three days later McCord answered the meeting request made by John Cummings, president of Local 15A. Armed by his board's directions to resist unionization efforts, McCord wrote, "I know that a majority of our employees would not have anything to do with an outfit such as yours." In truth he worried. He knew union organizing had reached a point he called "the strike-rumor stage."[20]

The bow-tied, cigar-smoking first president of MCH was born in Durban, South Africa, in 1907. In 1909 his missionary-doctor father founded the Mc-Cord Zulu Hospital, despite Durban's white residents suing to stop him. McCord's mother worked as the hospital's head nurse while raising six children. The young McCord grew up in a country where white citizens exerted rigid racial control, barring black South Africans from membership in parliament, reserving 90 percent of the country for white land ownership, and using a pass system to restrict black residents' travel and create labor pools. McCord came to the United States in 1924, earned his bachelor's from Oberlin College, a doctorate in chemistry from Yale University, and a medical degree from Louisiana State University, where he taught. In 1945 he joined the Medical College as chemistry department chair, becoming interim president in December 1964 and president in November 1965. Known as "The Whip" by workers, McCord was a big, blustery man who had inherited what his father called "Irish blood" and "Scotch stubbornness."[21]

McCord's autocratic responses led Saunders to believe McCord did more than anyone black or white to inspire workers to organize. Moultrie suspected that McCord believed, if he waited, that the workers' ire would "just go away. But it escalated." She found ironic his warning the union only wanted the workers' money, for a key issue was the black workers' low wages. Among the rebelling women were LPNs such as Edna Johnson, who had worked ten years to reach fifty-two dollars a week. Yet the hospital carried a $1.5 million surplus into 1968–69. Then again Moultrie had not expected McCord to take them seriously. "That was how we were treated all along."[22]

In November another meeting request failed. So Bennett wrote Barrett, asking Barrett to use his HEW clout to arrange a meeting. With no other way to negotiate, the women decided on a high-noon walkout for December 6, 1968, and announced their plans to engaged coworkers. Nurse Louise Burney, seventh floor supervisor, told her staff she would fire anyone extending the lunch break, and Moultrie's reply was, "Well, you'd better get my check ready because I'm going." From noon to 1 P.M., about two hundred workers demonstrated outside the hospital, holding "Union Recognition" signs.[23]

"At high noon, you stop working. It was a beautiful sight; everybody walked toward the outside," said M. S. Alston. "Ain't going to let nobody turn us around." The police arrived as people gathered to watch or join in. "We marched, chanting and singing 'We Shall Overcome,' carrying our signs, and made sure we didn't over-stay our time out there," said Moultrie. At this point, Moultrie said, she didn't worry about being fired. "Didn't care. Didn't give it a second thought."[24]

Hospital administrators collected names and photographed individuals and groups. Both this showdown and businessman Barrett's efforts led to an invitation to meet with two hospital administrators: John E. Wise, vice president for business affairs, and William D. Huff, vice president for development and public relations. Barrett and other members of the local HEW compliance team accompanied Moultrie, Bradford, and M. S. Alston on December 11. The workers told Wise and Huff that white supervisors and coworkers called them names, such as "monkey grunt" and "Miss Sassy-ass." They said they lacked job descriptions. They said supervisors ordered them to clean the white nurses' lounges and stations. Wise and Huff abruptly ended the meeting when Moultrie asked to discuss the union.[25]

Legal advice had led the hospital administrators to equate meeting about a union with recognizing a union. When the women had organized in October, the board of trustees retained the services of Knox Haynsworth, a Greenville attorney known for his anti-union work as counsel for textile companies. Haynsworth, paid a then-princely fifty-dollar-an-hour fee plus retainer and expenses, urged the trustees to "fight this effort to unionize the employees" and thus stop the spread to other hospitals. He warned that employees were claiming discrimination in their disputes with supervisors, that the SCLC had sent assistance, and "any confrontations on the civil rights issue should be avoided."[26]

Historically South Carolina used violence to prevent unions. In 1929 in Ware Shoals, Pelzer, and Greenville, thousands of textile workers struck or engaged in walkouts. Hooded men abducted and beat a local organizer, Clara Holden, and officials praised the local police and the Ku Klux Klan for preventing unions and communism. In 1934 Gov. Ibra Charles Blackwood deputized citizens, declared partial martial law, and ordered the state National Guard to shoot to kill picketers during a national strike by the United Textile Workers Union. On September 6, 1934, at Chiquola Mill in Honea Path, the mill superintendent ordered police and private guards to open fire on workers protesting poor wages and working conditions. Seven mill workers were killed and dozens wounded.[27]

The textile industry—beating back unions not only in the 1930s but also in each following decade—provided more than half of South Carolina's manufacturing jobs, almost all to white workers. In 1956 Roger Milliken closed the Darlington Manufacturing Company after its textile workers voted for a union. While this was a blatant threat to workers at Milliken's twenty-seven other mills, the Supreme Court held that an employer could close an entire business, even when motivated by "anti-union animus." An anti-union stance was a given among the state's politicians—and the hospital's administrators and trustees.[28]

December ended without any other conversations, and January was quiet too. In February picketers protested again in front of the hospital, and fifty workers met at the state capital with Charleston legislators. In March HEW returned to investigate complaints that MCH paid white employees more than black employees. A News and Courier columnist reported Charleston's legislators fretting over the hospital administration's failure "to solve the seething discontent." McCord warned the trustees that impatient union activists planned to "become aggressive." Another hospital workers' letter to McCord promised another high noon, and McCord pledged to answer with firings.[29]

But HEW pressed, as did his board, for a milder response, so McCord agreed to meet with specific employees. He invited seven of the discontented workers plus eight others of his own choosing for a 10 A.M. conversation. "Finally, he agreed that he would meet with us," said Moultrie. "We gave him the names. We got a letter telling us exactly what time and where the meeting would be held."[30]

Those invited understood that attendance was limited to their numbers plus hospital administrators, said Moultrie. They expected to see McCord and maybe a few administrators and trustees at the March 17 gathering in a second-floor classroom. However, "When we walked into the room where the meeting was supposed to be held, wow." McCord had not told them that he had invited his own selection of hospital workers. And word about the meeting had gotten out, resulting in dozens more workers showing up, workers who refused to leave when Huff arrived to announce McCord would meet only with those invited. As numbers grew, the group moved to an amphitheater on the same floor. Moultrie was surprised to see white and black employees known to be loyal to the hospital administration, including "a lot of older blacks who had been with the hospital for umpteen years, who we had tried to convert but couldn't because they were satisfied and afraid. So the place was stacked against us." The women considered leaving but decided, "No, let's see what happens," said Moultrie. Huff then announced that there would be no talk of unions and McCord would not attend. "That's when we walked out," said Moultrie.[31]

The women marched to McCord's office. "When we went in, the receptionist was there, and we asked for Dr. McCord, and she said he wasn't there, so we came on in the office, and she flew into the back." They packed the reception area, president's office, and boardroom. They took command of the telephone consoles. They chanted for union recognition. They ignored Huff's requests that they leave. "We took over the desks and phones. We were singing, and the phone would ring, and we would say, 'Local 1199, signing people up,'" said Moultrie. The crowd grew. "A lot of people who hadn't even signed up came because they wanted to be a part," said Moultrie.[32]

Louise Brown, a seventh-floor nurse's aide, climbed onto a table to dance. "Everybody was saying, 'Go, Brown. Go, Brown. Good, Brown,'" she said. By the time Charleston police chief John F. Conroy arrived, the area overflowed with the curious and the newly converted: janitors, housekeepers, elevator operators, food and laundry workers, more nursing assistants. As many as 350 gathered. Conroy told them to return to work or face arrest.[33]

It was noon. "We didn't have a discussion because it was time to go back to work anyway," said Moultrie. "I was basically in charge, and I just said, 'Let's go.'" Some of the workers met outdoors with the supportive Bennett before returning to their posts. Moultrie jokingly told companions to call her "Madame Pres" as they crowded into elevators to return to their floors. Over the next few hours, the workers from the seventh floor—Moultrie's floor—became the focus of the administration's wrath.[34]

Louise Brown got her call first and consulted with Moultrie, who told her friend, "They call one, they call all." Moultrie explained, "We were supposed to get off at three o'clock, so at a few minutes to three, they called. The phone rang, and the nurse told me they wanted to see me in personnel. I knew right then what was going to happen. . . . We all met down there, and they told us we were fired. Boy, we were happy; okay, thank you; we were waiting for this." Brown heard, "You're fired," and retorted, "With pleasure." The eleven women and one man—two LPNs, nine nurse's aides, and one male attendant—walked straight to the union hall and called a meeting for that night.[35]

"My only thought was that I'm sick and tired of being mistreated. I work hard and do a good job," said Louise Brown. She also felt outraged. "We were overworked and underpaid. All we wanted was a twenty-five cent raise in wages." Moultrie sent McCord a telegram that evening, saying the administration's attitude was racist and the discharges discriminatory and unjustified. She asked for reinstatement of all twelve. Bennett sent a telegram to nurse Burney and administrator Wise saying the firing was "an act of great injustice" and asked for immediate reinstatement. Bennett also sent telegrams to Gov. Robert E. McNair and Charleston mayor J. Palmer Gaillard Jr. asking them to intervene.[36]

Like Moultrie, Louise Brown had seen a better way. A Charleston native, she studied nursing in New York City in the late 1950s, then worked at an NYC hospital for chronic diseases and a nursing home. In 1963, missing her mother, she returned to Charleston and worked in the Medical College's cafeteria until hired as a nurse's aide. Like Moultrie she wanted home to be more like New York City. There, she said, "you were important because you took care of the patients. They didn't see color; they didn't see male; they didn't see female. They saw a worker." In Charleston "They got a slave mentality; that's what they had. I was ready for a change because there needed to be one." The majority of the new union's members agreed with Moultrie and

Brown; they, too, were ready for a change. A call for a March 19 meeting said, "Join the fight for better wages," and "Unionism is the way to end injustice." The workers voted to strike.[37]

Moultrie and Louise Brown were typical of many of the women who voted to strike: single parents with few resources beyond relatives. Moultrie wasn't too worried about the lost income; she thought resolution would come quickly. Besides, at the time she and her two-year-old daughter, Arnise, lived with her mother, Mabel Jenkins Moultrie. Louise Brown was the sole support for her three children, ages ten, four, and two. She also assisted an invalid brother. But she had the encouragement of her mother, also named Louise. The elder Brown had worked at the cigar factory and had walked the picket line in the 1945–46 strike. She advised her daughter, "Do it and make it better. If not for you, it'll help someone else." She pitched in by paying her daughter's rent.[38]

Up and down the East Coast other forces collected. After Reverend King's death widow Coretta Scott King became honorary chair of Local 1199's National Organizing Committee. At the time of the assassination, the SCLC not only supported the Memphis sanitation workers but also had organized the multiracial Poor People's Campaign around issues of poverty, employment, and housing. A union was a natural partner. This also seemed an opportunity to end the South's historic rejection of unions and thus improve the wages of black workers.[39]

Local 1199 hadn't planned to venture to the South so quickly. But conversations among union and SCLC leaders resulted in an agreement that each would send representatives to Charleston. Ralph D. Abernathy Sr., chosen by King as his successor, had considered similarities between Memphis and Charleston. Both southern cities refused to recognize unions. Both cities' black workers had little experience, beyond civil rights protests, in asking for better work conditions. And the workers' troubles, in the view of Local 1199 and the SCLC, combined economic and racial issues. Charleston also provided Abernathy, a year after King's death, an opportunity to step out of King's shadow while honoring his legacy.[40]

Abernathy wasn't the only SCLC member intrigued by Charleston. Charleston pulled Coretta Scott King out of mourning. She left behind her widow's black attire when she joined the marches. After speaking at the first Charleston union meeting, she suggested that the Charleston group be named 1199B, following Local 1199 in New York. Andrew Young Jr., SCLC's executive vice president, also held a strong South Carolina connection. He worked with Septima Clark when, in 1961, the Citizenship Schools became an SCLC program. The SCLC could pull on ties to Citizenship School graduates.[41]

The Charleston workers' demands included the rehiring of the twelve fired employees, better working conditions, lighter workloads, better wages, a grievance process, the right to be a union member, and respect. As Moultrie put it, their desire was simple—"just the right to be treated as human beings." While the city and state officials, the hospital administration, and the union leaders focused on unions, the black hospital workers focused on their dignity and their humanity. The women were tired of being called by their first names or "girl." They were hurt by constant descriptions of themselves as "unskilled" or "nonprofessional" workers. "Don't let anybody tell you that you are not professional," Robinson, the Black Muslim leader, told those attending organizing meetings. "You're with a patient twenty-four hours a day. You feed them. You clean them. You bathe them. You do everything; you are a professional." Often invited to the initial meetings as a motivational speaker, Robinson would ask the workers to repeat after him, "I may be black, but I am somebody." This turn of phrase, coined in the 1940s by an Atlanta preacher, became the strikers' cry: "I Am Somebody."[42]

Strike!

The morning of the first strike as many as four hundred workers stayed away from work. At 5 A.M. on Thursday, March 20, about one hundred MCH employees walked off the job. By 5:30 A.M. around three hundred more people gathered in front of the hospital. "People were driving by to look; some were giving us the victory sign and some giving us the other finger," said Moultrie. Police arrived but didn't arrest anyone. Ninth Judicial Circuit Judge Clarence Singletary granted a temporary injunction prohibiting picketing. The county sheriff read the injunction over a loudspeaker at 7:30 A.M., naming Moultrie and Bennett plus Godoff and Nicholas of Local 1199's National Organizing Committee. In obtaining the injunction, MCH officials refused to enter into collective bargaining and alleged that "threats, cursing, obscenities, acts of intimidation and acts of violence" impaired the hospital's functioning and endangered its patients. The picketers responded by singing "We Shall Overcome," invoking their predecessors. During the 1945 strike, tobacco worker Lucille Simmons had fostered the song's union and civil rights rebirth. Picketing continued until midnight.[43]

At a news conference, Godoff said, "Workers cannot live on $1.30 an hour," and strikers were prepared to go to jail. "This is a question of securing elementary justice," he said. He announced the support of Abernathy and Coretta Scott King and compared the situation to the 1968 Memphis strike. Godoff, Nicholas, and Moe Foner, the union's educational, cultural, and public relations director, decided to stay in Charleston for the long haul. When the twelve workers were fired, Nicholas was traveling for the National Organizing Committee. Told to go straight to Charleston rather than return to New York, he arrived before the first strike. He left his car in LaGuardia Airport, where it sat for six months. Nicholas understood the "different territory" of the South, having grown up in Mississippi. He knew South Carolina was a right-to-work state, so he also knew that "there were going to be problems." On the other hand, at his first meeting with the Charleston workers, he asked how many belonged to a church. "Everybody raised their hand, and then I knew we had something going." The churches became home to rallies day and night. That, Nicholas believed, "created a movement."[44]

In the early 1960s, downtown Charleston had experienced its share of civil rights protests, called the Charleston Movement. Students' lunch counter sit-ins in 1960 were followed by a 1962 "No Buying Strike," boycotts and picketing of King Street stores that depended on black customers but employed no black clerks, office workers, or salespeople. At that point Mayor Gaillard kept the city's response low-key by limiting arrests. The *News and Courier*, led by segregationist editor Thomas R. Waring Jr., refused to report on the "No Buying Strike," nor would the paper run an NAACP ad about the boycott, which lasted from March through May.[45]

In 1963 students, the NAACP, and the Congress of Racial Equality (CORE) joined forces in the Charleston Movement's nightly rallies, mass meetings, marches, and boycotts. The protesters' demands included desegregation of theaters, restaurants, hotels, city parks, and swimming pools; equal job opportunities; and an end to segregationist practices at the Medical College and its hospital. Throughout June and July, hundreds of students stopped traffic downtown, and hundreds were arrested. The sustained effort led to a restraining order to stop marches, a violent protest involving as many as 750 opposed to the racist policies and politics of the *News and Courier*, the mayor asking for state assistance, and the governor sending 125 officers from the South Carolina Law Enforcement Division (SLED). The Charleston Movement ended with the summer. Some merchants changed hiring practices; some lunch counters desegregated, as did the library, a bus station, and a municipal golf course, under court order. In August a court order forced admission of eleven black children to city schools.[46]

Yet in 1969 much remained undone, as the hospital strike proved.

On Friday, March 21, a modified injunction limited picketers to ten persons, each spaced twenty yards from the other. As Moultrie noted during a stadium rally, "According to the injunction we could put only five people on this field from goal post to goal post. I think even the governor, as slow as he is, could get through a picket line like that." It was not in the strikers' interest to accept such a reduced presence, particularly given the enthused initial participation: that day MCH reported that 272 of about 800 service workers didn't come to work.[47]

Hundreds gathered to watch this second day of picketing, singing along to protest songs, such as "We Shall Not Be Moved." Police arrested fourteen picketers during what the local paper called "a wild melee." Striker Naomi White, a five-foot-three-inch redhead, had blocked the path of a woman who worked in housekeeping and the man she brought along for protection. White, a practical nurse, said that she told the pair, "'Look, I don't care how you're getting in there, but you ain't passing me going in there.' And this guy, he said, 'Yes, she is, because I'm here to see she gets in safely.'" The standoff escalated into "'Oh, no, she ain't,' and 'Oh, yes, she is,'" then White grabbed onto the many chains adorning the housekeeper's neck.[48]

As the housekeeper flailed about, police grabbed Naomi White by an arm. She resisted. Two male strikers latched onto her other arm. "The police were pulling me on this side, and the coworkers got me on this side, and I said, 'I guess they're going to stretch me.'" White's scrapping continued after her arrest. At the Orange Street police station, another officer, face scratched, accused her of attacking him. The booking sergeant defended her, pointing to her arrival time in the station. When the officer persisted in his tale, she did scratch him. Just before midnight Charleston police arrested six more picketers for not "spreading out." At 1 A.M. legal help arrived. White was charged with disorderly conduct, creating a disturbance, and striking a police officer with her hand. Upon her release, on a two-hundred-dollar bond, she walked straight to the union hall.[49]

Singletary modified his injunction with the 1963 protests in mind, "a bad summer for all of us," he thought. He believed the hospital administration didn't understand just how bad this summer could get. And he believed the workers "at least had the right to picket in a peaceful fashion and be permitted to petition as any citizen would have the right aside from the merits of the labor issue." Hoping the modified injunction would both protect rights and limit clashes, he arranged a meeting with representatives of the mayor's office, SLED, and city police before signing it. Instead workers violated the injunction by the hour; daily busloads carted picketers to jail.[50]

A rally on Saturday, March 22, drew four hundred of the hospital's service and maintenance workers. A picketing schedule of 7 A.M. to 3 P.M., 3 P.M. to 11 P.M., and 11 P.M. to 7 A.M. guaranteed a constant presence. Moultrie said, "We don't like to strike," but added that picketing would continue "until every hospital worker in the Charleston area is earning a living wage and is not under the yoke of discrimination." That morning the mayor met with the biracial Concerned Clergy Committee, headed by Rev. John Enright of Plymouth Congregational Church. Anxiety brewed. The ministers warned of a potential second massacre. On February 8, 1968, highway troopers had fired on about two hundred unarmed students at South Carolina State College. The gunfire killed three young men and wounded twenty-seven more, most shot in their sides or back as they tried to escape. A grand jury refused to indict nine patrolmen charged in the shootings, which became known as the Orangeburg Massacre.[51]

Given reasonable fears of a long, hot summer, Herbert Ulysses Gaillard Fielding met with Governor McNair. Fielding, president of Fielding Home for Funerals in Charleston, was doing a favor for the NAACP's state field director. Rev. Isaiah DeQuincey Newman wanted Fielding to oppose what he called "Uncle Tom" influence on McNair. The slight, polished Fielding was a U.S. Army veteran and founder in 1965 of the Political Action Committee of Charleston County. He bridged the divide between the black Charleston elite and the largely blue-collar NAACP membership. Fielding told media that McNair, during their March 21 conversation, instructed a SLED officer "no violence in any case" and arrests only when necessary. Despite that assurance, two days later police arrested fifty-seven hospital protesters amid complaints of police brutality. "Women were being beaten in jail," said Louise Brown.[52]

Bennett was worried, given ongoing unrest at the South Carolina State Ports Authority. There Charleston dockworkers had walked off the job, following a sixty-seven-day strike by Local 1422A of the International Longshoremen's Association (ILA). The majority-black dockworkers returned under a state injunction on March 7. They were fired a week later. Mirroring the hospital workers, the longshoremen's local found itself fighting for the rehiring of those fired. "We gave in and went back to work under an injunction, and they fired 150 of us. That's what they call justice," said Bennett, who took a leave of absence from American Tobacco to work as an organizer for 1199B.[53]

At first the strike days seemed predictable. Each day the women gathered before the hospital, just blocks from downtown, in their white nursing uniforms and shoes. On their heads perched the paper, white and blue Local 1199 caps. Some held babies or pushed strollers. Many held the hands of their young children, come to walk with them. Signs supported the union: "We want union and human rights." Signs took jabs at McCord: "In Memory of the Old Slave Tradition, Consult Dr. McCord." By the fourth day, police had arrested seventy-seven demonstrators, including Saunders and about twenty other men packed into one small cell at the county jail.[54]

The state NAACP did not join the fight even though it was clear the civil rights of the strikers were at issue. "We tried to get the local NAACP to respond, but they didn't want to break away from the power structure," said Nicholas. Bennett telegraphed Delbert L. Woods, vice president of the NAACP state conference and a Charlestonian, describing opposition "from legal action against picketing to the brutalization of women workers by police" and asking for aid. But the NAACP stayed mostly silent. Newman, soon to announce his resignation, said publicly only that strikers would be offered any aid required. When 1199B decided formally to invite the SCLC's help, the NAACP objected. "But we were about winning, so we went ahead," said Nicholas.[55]

With encouragement from Local 1199, strikers formally invited the SCLC to Charleston, scheduling Abernathy to speak on Monday, March 31. Quickly the SCLC sent Rev. James Orange, a six-foot-two, 275-pound project coordinator who worked with teens and street gangs. Orange was followed by Robert Ford. A twenty-year-old SCLC fieldworker, Ford had been expelled from Grambling State University for his civil rights activism. He had just worked in Memphis on the Poor People's Campaign. The SCLC charged the two with creating innovative social actions.

By Tuesday, March 25, police had arrested more than 130 protesters, most for violating picket restrictions at MCH, most released under $500 personal recognizance bonds. The 500-bed, ten-story hospital had limited itself to 325 patients and restricted admissions to emergencies. At a Wednesday news conference, Moultrie said strikers would continue to defy the picket limit, would stop posting bail or bond, and would include children in the picketing, a financial as well as a psychological strategy. The union appealed the injunction to federal court. However, U.S. District Judge Charles E. Simons Jr. left the picket limit in effect and ordered the U.S. marshal's office to assist law enforcement, saying, "We have a situation that might be explosive."[56]

As the month drew to a close, County Hospital workers staged their own high noon. Moultrie sent a telegram to that hospital's administrator, Dr.

V. W. H. Campbell, asking for a meeting. Bennett sent a telegram to the chairman of the county council, J. Mitchell Graham. Moultrie also called Campbell, trying to set a meeting deadline. Campbell replied in a letter, "Please be advised that the attorney general of South Carolina has ruled that the state and its agencies may not negotiate with labor organizations." On March 27 Campbell refused to speak to a group of employees outside his office. On March 28 sixty picketers encircled CCH at 5:30 A.M.; the hospital counted seventy-seven employees absent from shift work. Moultrie announced a majority of the hospital's three hundred service workers had joined the union.[57]

Rosetta Simmons and a dozen other workers surprised Campbell in his office. "We said we had grievances we wanted to address," said Simmons. "We caught him off guard. He was hostile, not a man you could talk to. He listened and said there was nothing he could do at the time, and he didn't want this to go any further." The hospital, like MCH, paid its workers well below minimum wage: $0.85 an hour in 1966, $1.15 an hour in 1968, raised to $1.30 an hour a month before the strike. That wage was still $0.30 below the federal minimum of $1.60 an hour. At union headquarters a vote to strike CCH passed. Simmons counted 113 strikers.[58]

Administrator Campbell wrote Bennett that the attorney general's ruling made any meeting for union recognition or collective bargaining "impossible." State Attorney General Daniel R. McLeod decreed, "Collective bargaining by public bodies in this state is not authorized." McLeod said the state could not forbid employees joining unions, but the state and its agencies could not negotiate with employees.He acknowledged that no law prohibited negotiations, but at the same time, no law delegated authority to negotiate. And without this authority state agencies had no power to bargain with unions, according to McLeod.[59]

McLeod was talking about policy, not law. The stance had a Catch-22 quality. Intended to prevent unions from getting a foothold in the state, the no-discussion position forced multiple negotiators into secret meetings, which often ended when the dreaded word *union* led state officials to stalk out. As to unions, another difficulty existed for the hospital strikers: the National Labor Relations Act didn't cover public employees. Some states had added laws allowing labor negotiations and unions, but not South Carolina. By necessity South Carolina did recognize, bargain, and negotiate contracts with unions at Charleston's Ports Authority and Veterans Hospital. However, these chinks in the state's armor weren't a point of public debate until late in the strike.[60]

During the strike's second week, clergy joined the picketers. Children as young as two years old became regular participants. Arrests became standard fare. The modified injunction allowed the picketers ten people; if one hundred showed up, ninety went to jail. "Everybody was raring to go to jail," said Moultrie. "'I'm going to jail today!' To go to jail was an honor." Coretta Scott King told a Charleston audience that she had never been arrested but believed going to jail a "privilege." Daily picketing, nightly rallies, and fundraisers featuring such stars as the Fabulous Drifters or comedian Pigmeat Markham kept enthusiasm high. "Justice must triumph," proclaimed a handbill announcing a mass rally featuring the SCLC's Abernathy and Young.[61]

As the strike and spring warmed up, Governor McNair tangled with three problems, one of which was immutable in his view: the refusal to recognize unions. The second problem was overdue for amelioration, a state government that had yet to engage in twentieth-century employment practices. State departments and agencies operated like private fiefdoms, each determining its own hiring and promotion standards, job ladders, salary schedules, and employee rights. McNair conceded personnel inequities and deficiencies not only at the Medical College and its hospital but throughout state government. He pointed to employee classification and compensation standards going into effect July 1, 1969, with $10 million budgeted to set up the system. He pledged a policy of "like pay for like work." Of course the Civil Rights Act of 1964 already prohibited employment discrimination based on race, color, religion, sex, or national origin. And Executive Order 11246, issued by President Lyndon B. Johnson in 1965, prohibited federal contractors from discriminating on any of those same grounds. At MCH $8 million in construction money and $4 million in grants, no small matter, could be jeopardized by the strikers' claims of discrimination. A third problem couldn't be fixed. The black community had no reason to trust McNair after the student injuries and deaths in Orangeburg.[62]

"Sock It to 'Em"

Moultrie and her coworkers defined the situation not in legal but personal terms. "It was like survival," said Moultrie. These women supported their families as single parents or working wives. Most considered their jobs, despite the poor pay and disrespect, among the better jobs available to black women. Charleston options mostly limited them to teaching in still-segregated schools or to childcare, housekeeping, and kitchen and laundry work in white households. Now 1199B was their job. The job of striker eventually offered a few subsistence dollars. Meals, camaraderie, and informal day care at the union hall accompanied those dollars. Better yet, participation offered respect and a powerful sense of mission.[63]

As the strike continued, "it seemed like it just got into your blood," said Naomi White, who lived downtown. She ventured out each morning with Hermina Traeye, a member of the CCH strikers' committee. "Sometimes I'd say, 'I'm not going,' and I could hear the singing and chanting from different areas," said White. "I'd say, 'Oh heck, I got to go.' It was like the song says, 'I woke up in the morning with freedom on my mind.' That just motivated you." And then there was the united sense of purpose: "The only way you could do this was with unity," said M. S. Alston. "If we were caught at curfew at my house, everybody would just stay over."[64]

Now the strikers provided McNair a new concern: Abernathy was coming to town. McNair responded by putting a National Guard unit on standby and sending in fifty state troopers. Abernathy's March 31 arrival at the Charleston Metropolitan Airport drew hundreds of supporters waving banners saying, "We Remember Dr. Martin Luther King" and "Slave No More." A police motorcade escorted the SCLC president into the city. His eleven-hour visit drew two thousand to the New Tabernacle Fourth Baptist Church on Elizabeth Street. Abernathy offered a promise to the workers and a warning to the power structure. "I've come to join with you in socking it to 'em," he said. Abernathy declared himself "sick and tired of an antebellum society which lives in past history" and vowed, "I am going to tell the people of Charleston we will be saved together as brothers or we will perish as foes." He vowed to return, noting, "I've been to jail 23 times, and I'm just itching to make it 24."[65]

Moultrie, sharing the pulpit with Abernathy and Young, said, "There's a new day coming to Charleston. No more poverty, no more discrimination, no more injustices and no more full-time work for part-time pay." Like Abernathy, she made a promise: the strikers would not surrender until "free from the yoke of poverty." Moultrie and the SCLC sounded this theme—the confluence of race and poverty—regularly. The New York Times connected the Charleston strike to the Memphis strike and to the SCLC premise that "the nature of their work and their race had resulted in an intolerable employer-employee relationship that smacked of racial prejudice."[66]

Race and poverty traveled hand in hand in South Carolina. Historically, white landowners and business owners expected black South Carolinians to provide permanent labor as enslaved people, then as sharecroppers, and always as the muscle for difficult and unpleasant work like that of sanitation workers or nurse's aides. At the decade's start, a quarter of Americans lived below the federal poverty threshold; 45 percent of South Carolinians, and 40 percent of Charleston County residents, did. "I've told these people they have to organize or they will be 20th century slaves," said Bennett. MCH not only paid black workers less than minimum wage, but the state facility also didn't recruit or consider them for jobs at certain levels, as its all-white nursing students, floor supervisors, residents, and doctors proved. As a child's picket sign said, "We Need More Than Bread to Live On."[67]

McCord had skirmished with HEW in 1965, when the Office of Civil Rights held up twenty-eight thousand dollars in federal funds because HEW found segregation in patient visiting hours, room assignments, and eating facilities and an evident refusal to admit black people to psychiatric services. Saunders joked that only white people "went crazy" in Charleston; MCH provided proof through its lack of black patients.[68]

HEW returned in July and August 1968 after another complaint. Since September 1968 the hospital had remained on notice that HEW found it in noncompliance with the executive order banning racial discrimination, a hospital secret that would play an important role in the strike's resolution. Violations included the lack of black physicians, despite their availability in Charleston; white staff physicians practicing segregation; segregation of cafeterias, lounges, and restrooms; job descriptions requiring in-house experience not offered black applicants; black employees being paid markedly less than white employees despite similar training, experience, and length of service; and no training programs to help black workers upgrade skills.[69]

"It was time," said M. S. Alston. "This was what King wanted, what he died for." And as the strike continued, "you felt the strength. The more people came, the more you wanted to rally, the more you wanted to fight." But most white Charlestonians didn't make a personal connection to the racially motivated inequities. Their presence or support was minuscule. A few white nurses' aides did participate briefly in the early meetings before taking jobs elsewhere. The black nurse's aides feared they were spies. Local media and white officials stuck to the long-standing tradition of blaming unrest on "outside agitators" stirring up otherwise happy black citizens.[70]

The Roman Catholic Church broke rank with local white opposition. A few white nuns marched with the strikers; police arrested four white priests for participation. Bishop Ernest Unterkoefler, head of the Charleston Diocese, had marched at the head of a caravan for the Poor People's March when it entered Charleston the year before. He blamed the strike on hospital officials' "constant refusals to communicate" with black workers. He and administrators of St. Francis Xavier Hospital, Charleston's small Catholic hospital, met with 1199B and released a statement recognizing the workers' rights to collective bargaining. St. Francis Xavier administrators announced a readiness to negotiate with the union if asked to do so. At the end of April, Unterkoefler set aside a day of prayer for peace and harmony and defended the "natural and constitutional right of American citizens to organize."[71]

Two biracial groups did participate in strike negotiations: the Concerned Clergy Committee and the Community Relations Committee. Early in the strike, the Concerned Clergy Committee released a Peace with Justice proposal, signed by thirty-four ministers. The proposal recommended that hospital management reinstate the twelve fired workers, allow strikers to return to work, accept a workers' election, and meet with the elected 1199B representatives to settle grievances. A memo by attorney Haynsworth warned trustees that the Concerned Clergy Committee was "stacked against the hospital" and encouraged rustling up telegrams to clergy thought to support the hospital. Haynsworth needn't have worried; no Christian uprising occurred. While the Concerned Clergy Committee repeatedly invited 265 full-time clergy, participation didn't pass 50.[72]

The Community Relations Committee backed up the Concerned Clergy with a resolution that supported Peace with Justice and requested the governor and MCH administration meet with the strikers. The chairman was Rev. Henry Grant, a black Episcopal priest at St. John's Mission Center, which served the poorest of the poor. The committee included prominent white businessmen, such as Hugh C. Lane Sr., president of Citizens & Southern National Bank, and Edward Kronsberg, owner of a chain of variety stores. And the committee included black activists, such as Jenkins, Saunders, and the Reverend Z. L. Grady, whose Morris Brown African Methodist Episcopal Church (AME) became a second strike headquarters. The Concerned Clergy and the Community Relations committees worked with a third, the Concerned Citizens Committee, a long-standing mix of civic and religious groups that included Fielding, Jenkins, and Saunders. The Community Relations Committee put together a leaflet that answered thirteen questions such as "Why do individual workers want to organize?" and "Is it right to strike against a hospital?" and promoted the Peace with Justice proposal.[73]

McCord had so far refused public comment on the strike, but he did answer the Concerned Clergy. He said they were asking him "to accept violence and patient neglect as a means to resolve the present strife." He seemed particularly incensed by the possibility that striking workers could return, citing "acts of harassment, intimidation, verbal abuse and physical violence against employees who have continued to work and who have continued to take care of the sick." In the first weeks of the strike, the hospital reported seven fires in the laundry and two anonymous bomb threats.[74]

McCord vehemently opposed reinstatement of the twelve fired workers, saying, "Those 12 individuals had completely abandoned their assigned duties on the seventh floor of the hospital for more than one hour" and were fired for "completely disregarding patient care." Moultrie made a public rebuttal: "Shedding crocodile tears over the plight of patients will never cover up the exploitation, the horrors of poverty, the $1.30 wage and his refusal to provide a procedure for handling grievances and problems affecting the welfare of workers. By this time everyone knows that he dismissed 12 employees whom he invited to his office for a conference because he later became displeased with the contents of their remarks." Throughout the strike McCord ignored the fact that some of the fired workers left their units through a prior agreement with him to attend an approved meeting. So did local media, regularly repeating McCord's version, even after HEW asserted the twelve were "hastily and vindictively fired."[75]

CCH, which had 103 strikers, began filling its vacant positions. Even with replacements, the County Hospital served half its usual patient load, with sixty-one beds available. This generated widespread concern since it was the area's only hospital offering indigent and twenty-four-hour emergency care. MCH closed more beds, recruited doctors' wives as volunteers, and worked at replacing about half its 425 striking workers. McCord more than once mentioned the possibility MCH could close due to inadequate staffing. "They had hired people who didn't know how to take a temperature or blood pressure. They were putting the thermometer upside down in the patients' mouths," said Naomi White, who kept sources inside the hospital. "We're out here in the sun, baking like potatoes, and they're coming and going, the scabs, and, when they break line, saying derogatory things. That irked me."[76]

Hell Angels

Naomi White, a practical nurse, could claim the title of fiercest striker. Her mother, a Charleston seamstress, had died when White was just a year old. Her grandmother and father, a museum janitor, raised her and sent her to parochial schools. She graduated from Charleston's Immaculate Conception High School in 1943 and, after beauty school training and a job in a relative's salon, worked in New York City and Washington, D.C., living with aunts. In 1961 she took a job as a practical nurse at MCH and worked the graveyard shift in obstetrics and gynecology at the time of the strike. She was the mother of six children.[77]

Naomi White didn't meet Moultrie until an organizing meeting in 1968. But she, too, felt work conditions were unfair. She thought RNs deliberately ordered black technicians or practical nurses to do a prohibited task, anticipating a refusal, with the intention of firing the person for the refusal. Firings occurred without oral or written warnings. "If you did do what you were told to do and something happened to that patient, you're all by yourself. But if you didn't, you were insubordinate, and you could be fired," said White. A fervent participant in the strike, she was arrested several times, remaining in jail once for eleven days, then again for fourteen. She organized the Hell Angels, women willing to haunt the night entrances and confront workers. "I said things had to change, and we had to get out there at night and catch them scabs. We would talk to them and ask them, if they didn't want to come out and participate with picketing, if they just stayed home, it would help. Some of them, their husbands wouldn't let them [strike]."[78]

The SCLC didn't want chaos and riots. Its leaders knew how to maintain discipline, arrange security, organize section leaders, and preach and teach nonviolence. Everyone knew the worst could happen, as it already had: the murders of Medgar Evers in June 1963, of four Birmingham children in the Sixteenth Street Baptist Church bombing in September 1963, of Malcolm X in 1965, and of King in 1968. The labor movement's history overflowed with stories of bloody union busting. Because of his connection to black militants, Saunders found himself in an FBI interview regarding potential dangers. Private bodyguards protected prominent participants. Guarding Moultrie were a member of SNCC, who carried a gun, and Eva Alston, a striker and friend of Rosetta Simmons and Moultrie whose weapon was acid carried in her purse.[79]

Those who continued to work at the hospitals wanted safety too. SLED agents guarded McCord and his wife. The aides and technicians who didn't strike or who filled jobs poststrike told supervisors of harassing phone calls and threats that mentioned the Jackson Street Panthers, a street gang. Strikers surrounded people at bus stops or blocked cars; some threw pepper or salt into people's eyes. Some continuing workers reported to work with paper bags over their heads to avoid recognition or used police escorts or slept in the hospital between shifts. SCLC's philosophy of nonviolence coexisted uneasily with some strikers' desire to confront those continuing to work.[80]

Families divided; relationships ended. The childhood friendship of Louise Brown and Thomasina Washington died in the strike's early days. Brown knocked on her friend's front door one April morning and asked Washington, "How could you be working, and we're out on strike?" Washington answered, "I don't care what you are doing up there; I do have my kids to support," and latched her screen door. Other strikers rushed onto the porch, and when Washington also shut and locked her front door, they pounded on the doors and broke her windows. Washington reported the incident, and the police looked for Brown at the union hall and her home, where she hid under her bed so she wouldn't be arrested in front of her children. She turned herself in, and a sympathetic magistrate admonished her not to break windows anymore and set a small fine.[81]

On Good Friday, McNair met with Concerned Clergy members plus Jenkins, Fielding, and Marjorie Amos-Frazier, an American Tobacco Company employee, union shop steward, and member of the NAACP. Later, during a press conference, the clergy slung a few pointed questions. They asked, "Why is it that no one on the state level can cite a state law which would prohibit a state institution from dealing with an organized body of workers?" and "Why is it that state funds go toward spreading a particular philosophy of labor-management relations?" The clergy wanted the press to investigate state funds being used to convince hospital workers that unions were harmful to their interests. They wanted to know why the state could pay Haynsworth, a nationally recognized anti-union attorney, to strategize against the state's workers.[82]

Despite such challenges, McNair may have felt secure in his stance. An Illinois appellate court had ruled, on March 27, that strikes against nonprofit hospitals were illegal. "The operation of a hospital involves a public interest of such urgency that labor's right to strike must yield to the greater importance of the uninterrupted and efficient operation of hospitals." McNair and McLeod pointed to the ruling as reinforcement and harkened back to a 1919 Boston police strike, during which three-quarters of the force went on strike for better pay and working conditions. Gov. Calvin Coolidge called in the Massachusetts Guard, ending the strike. He refused to rehire the strikers, whose jobs went to returning World War I soldiers. Coolidge proclaimed, "There is no right to strike against the public safety by anybody, anywhere, anytime."[83]

With no end in sight, economic concerns grew, because the thirty-million-dollar-a-year tourist season approached. Who would stroll through historic neighborhoods packed with demonstrators? Following a Memphis speech memorializing King, Abernathy returned to Charleston for an April 4 memorial service and mass march. Papers were served on Moultrie, Bennett,

Godoff, and Nicholas when they met Abernathy at the airport. They faced contempt charges for failing to comply with the picketing injunction. About five hundred marchers, led by Moultrie and Bennett, walked past each of the city's hospitals, a two-hour, almost four-mile walk. Many held portraits of the deceased King. They carried placards saying, "Dr. McCord, bigotry is poor medicine," and "Give us bread, not jail," and "Moultrie for Mayor." One sign insisted, "There will not be any Orangeburg in Charleston." Easter Sunday stayed peaceful as strikers visited eighty black churches, asking for help. A leaflet said, "We are still looking for a resurrection, but our resurrection has justice and dignity attached to it."[84]

Rosetta Simmons missed the Easter march. She was pregnant when the strike began and, on April 2, went into premature labor. "One of the supervisors came in while I was in labor and told me how do I expect them to take care of me, being a striker," said Simmons. But aides at MCH protected her, frequently checking on her welfare. Bodyguard Eva Alston arrived; she claimed she was Simmons's aunt. "I said, 'I'm safe,'" said Simmons. Her child, born with a hole in her stomach, died two days later of complications from surgery. Asked to consent to an autopsy, Simmons insisted a mortician immediately take the body. "Leaving her there wasn't going to happen." In May she returned to the picket line. "As soon as I felt better, I went back out. I just couldn't sit around."[85]

On April 7 Moultrie and three dozen strikers drove to Columbia, after asking for an audience with McNair. They picketed the State House, and they waited in the governor's reception room, playing cards to while away the time. At 5 P.M., when the lobby closed, they perched on the granite steps facing North Main Street and sang. One of their signs read, "We don't want nobody to give us nothing. Open the door. We'll get it ourselves." McNair was in New York, so the protesters spent the night. Moultrie, Bradford, and 1199B's Charleston attorneys, Fred Henderson Moore and George Payton Jr., met with the governor on Wednesday. Said Moultrie afterward, "That was a waste of time." McNair patronized them, Moultrie believed. She said he told her, "You know something, Mary, if I worked at J.C. Penney and the conditions weren't the way I liked, I'd leave and go get a job elsewhere."[86]

Attorney Moore, a five foot, five inch voluble Charleston native, had made his name at South Carolina State College. In 1955–56 Orangeburg's white community used firings and foreclosures to punish black parents petitioning for desegregated schools. The black community answered with a selective-buying campaign, refusing to purchase goods from known members of the Orangeburg White Citizens' Council. Council members used their control of funds, employment, land, goods, and services as bludgeons. Moore, who was student government president, led campus participation in the boycott. Expelled for his activism two weeks before graduation, he finished his bachelor's at Allen University in Columbia and was graduated from Howard School of Law in Washington, D.C. In McNair's office he found himself busy interpreting strikers to officials unwilling to give an inch or a dime. After Moultrie departed, Moore told the governor, "While we want to preserve the peace and engage in peaceful negotiations, the heart of the matter is that people aren't being given fair wages." Moore believed McNair knew that the strikers' complaints of racially biased treatment and inadequate wages were valid. He was right. McNair privately acknowledged conditions were "just terrible."[87]

Publicly McNair didn't acknowledge that long-standing segregationist practices once again had sparked unrest. Neither he nor local officials acknowledged that the women had not chosen a strike as the preferred response; they wished for a conversation among equals. The workers had tried for more than a year, before striking, to obtain that conversation, and those efforts had the support of black community leaders recognized by the white power structure, such as Barrett, Bennett, Jenkins, and Fielding. Now, with a strike and a brand new set of players, the working class was kicking the door. Moultrie said more than once, "All we wanted was someone who would listen to the grievances and who would do justice." Citing the power of the American Medical Association as a lobbying force, Saunders observed, "It seemed to us that it really was becoming a race issue because only poor black people weren't being allowed to organize."[88]

In an impressively tone-deaf choice in that regard, McCord offered workers an additional holiday: Confederate general Robert E. Lee's birthday. And Hugh E. Gibson, a special assignments reporter for the *News and Courier,* wrote a six-part series that compared the strike to the Civil War and McNair to General Lee: "A second union invasion of the South is under way, this time of labor organizers instead of federal troops," he wrote. "The scene again is Charleston and again the plight of the Negro has been invoked as the proximate reason for the Northern crusade." In his stew of metaphors, Gibson called the strike a "black-tipped" spear "deeply embedded in the economic vitals of Charleston." Behind the spear, "providing the brain, the muscle, and the vital financial sinews," stood the SCLC and various unions. And in a paid newspaper ad, Father Leon J. Hubacz objected to Abernathy's critique of antebellum pride, asking, "What of the colored Mammy? Could all your speeches and marches ever replace the glow of pride in her face as she watches, day after day as her little charges grow into a man of importance in the world?" As Abernathy observed, "Few cities represented so clearly the old way of looking at Southern society."[89]

In an April 9 press conference, Moultrie announced at a shift in strategy: no more meetings with officials and administrators. Abernathy would return and direct civil disobedience. She said, "For a long time we had hope that a reasonable approach, that meeting with important people might lead to a solution. We are now convinced that our fight must be intensified in every direction." She promised an economic boycott of downtown stores, street demonstrations, and confrontations on the picket lines. On Thursday strikers shouted "scab," tried to block a worker, and clashed with police at MCH. One woman threw pepper at patrolmen; windows of two cars were broken. At CCH twenty-two strikers picketed. Others collected at bus stops, where they surrounded anyone attempting to go to work.[90]

Judge Singletary signed another injunction, this one limiting pickets at CCH. The order included a summons for relief, saying the union activities were illegal, and invoked the state's right-to-work law, which prohibited picketing that interfered with access to work.[91]

On April 11 police arrested Moultrie in the picket line, along with thirty other strikers. Ordinarily Moultrie's assignment was making speeches, not walking the picket line. But that day's strike strategy included her arrest. "They decided, 'You got to go to jail; we need you in jail,'" and she agreed. Evidently that matched the authorities' feelings. "They were probably looking for me," said Moultrie. "As soon as I got there, they shoved me in a paddy wagon." Bradford, the 1199B vice president, said those arrested would remain in jail. "Neither hunger nor injunctions will stop us from fighting for our rights." The price had gone up for getting out: $500 for the first violation, $1,500 for the second, $5,000 for the third. Moultrie said she would remain in jail "until justice is done." That day's arrests brought the total jailed to 170.[92]

The blue-and-white 1199B cap had become a badge of honor; so had an arrest on the picket line. During the ride to jail, strikers sang, "We're going to jail now, don't want no bail." Jailers placed Moultrie, in her union cap, sunglasses, and a flowered, ruffled dress, in a large cell with thirty other strikers, including M.S. Alston and Naomi White. There they stayed for eleven days. "We would sing, and we would pray, and we would just really have a good time," said Moultrie. "One day they actually turned up the heat on us. One day they took all the bed linens from us. The food wasn't very good. Sometimes the union would bring us fried chicken, and we would never get it."

One meal consisted of butter beans, green peas, and pork and beans. White chose to go hungry. But the strikers didn't go without cigarettes, a toothbrush, or toothpaste; Father William Joyce provided them.[93]

The city released the strikers, without bond or bail, when Singletary called at 7 A.M. on the eleventh day and ordered them let go. "Early that morning they said, 'Judge Singletary said he wants Mary Moultrie and all of her people out of his jail,'" said Moultrie. "They just threw us out. We had to wait outside for rides to come get us. Out of the blue. That morning they announced it on the intercom system." Moultrie believed that "they opened the jail door because Mrs. King was coming," and officials feared another march on the jail, as strikers did upon Moultrie's arrest.[94]

"My Room Blew Up"

While Moultrie was jailed, CCH strikers tried a sit-in during a county council meeting, hoping for an audience with Graham, who resisted their pleas and complained of threatening calls. The hospitals had replaced workers, 250 at MCH, 54 at CCH. City police were investigating forty-one complaints of threats to those working. Louise Brown's landlord forced her out of her home. "I was ducking and hiding," she said. "Mary Moultrie was threatened. I believe some people wanted to kill us." To protect her mother and daughter, Moultrie moved to the Brooks Motel, where the SCLC staff stayed. The motel, at the corner of Felix and Morris Streets, served black travelers. Union organizers stayed at the air-conditioned Holiday Inn. Convinced his phone was tapped, Nicholas also slept at a second motel outside the city. That didn't seem the best solution when, a week after the strike started, his alternate room exploded as he approached in a cab. "Just as I pulled into the motel, just as I made the curb into the yard of the motel, my room blew out the balcony. I turned around and went straight back to the Holiday Inn," said Nicholas. From then on union representatives kept their quarters guarded.[95]

The strike headquarters on East Bay Street—with its clutter of picket signs, infants and children playing in a nursery, strikers sleeping on sofas, and a strike kitchen serving Kool-Aid, rice and beans, turkey necks, and baloney sandwiches—also was guarded around the clock. Local 1199's David White wrote in his strike diary, "We are not permitted to stand in front of union headquarters at night for fear of being shot from a passing car. The local leaders sleep from place to place on different nights. It is not exactly fear, but precautions the local people feel must be observed."[96]

These precautions also involved armed Jackson Street Panthers standing guard at the union hall's windows and doors each night. "Some of the guys in the gang had family members working at the hospital," said Timothy Grant. A high school athlete who turned fifteen the day the strike started, Grant joined his older brother in the gang. "We were like a family, and we protected one another. Some of the older guys said, 'Let's protect our women.' We knew our presence would make a difference." This also meant serving as covert bodyguards and deliberately seeking arrest to accompany protesters to jail. "Wherever they go, we go," the gang members decided. And this meant stepping between protesters and police batons. Grant remembered a march halted by the highway patrol on King Street, in front of Condon's Department Store. "They had sticks taller than us," he said. "We were singing, 'Ain't gonna let nobody turn us around.' We heard screaming; we saw the batons. We got in front of the ladies, and you-know-what broke out. They carted us off to jail." Arrested several times, Grant spent some days penned up outside with other teens; the city used Harmon Field. "They would put you in the hot sun all day and wouldn't give you any water. They were trying to discipline you so you wouldn't march again." He spent some nights in the city jail, locked up with adults, released the next morning without a charge. None of this discouraged the Jackson Street Panthers; instead they recruited more participants.[97]

Strike reports regularly made national print and television news. Compelling television footage showed police shoving women into paddy wagons. In March, Moultrie had requested help from Shirley Chisholm, the nation's first black congresswoman. In her telegram Moultrie cited "unrestrained intimidation and violence." She said she wanted national attention to end "poverty wages and discriminatory practices." In April, Chisholm and actor and activist Ossie Davis wrote the *New York Times*, asking, "How long must the inhumanely paid Charleston hospital workers be forced to strike and suffer jailings before they are treated as first-class citizens?" For the first time since King's death, civil rights leaders united again publicly for a cause, with thirteen signing a statement by Coretta Scott King that called the Charleston strike a "fight for human rights and human dignity."[98]

The widow sent the strikers a telegram to be read at an April 21 rally to be followed by a march the next day. In it she said, "You in Charleston are demonstrating that my husband's dream still lives." At the rally, attended by two thousand, Abernathy proclaimed, "We will deliver plague after plague upon the power structure of this city and state." He said those arrested would remain in jail. Moultrie said they were going to live by the words "An injury to one is an injury to all." The next morning Abernathy locked arms with Moultrie and Cleveland Robinson, president of the Negro American Labor Council. SCLC organizers had built support in Greenville, Columbia, Florence, and Beaufort, so participation kept growing. The trio led close to a thousand, including schoolchildren, on a sixteen-block walk. Abernathy clasped his jail gear: a toothbrush, toothpaste, and his thirty-year-old Bible. He expected arrests, including his own, which didn't occur. Upon reaching MCH the participants knelt in prayer. On the return march, Abernathy called out to hospital employees leaning out windows, "Come on down; we're marching for you."[99]

The *Evening Post* editorialized, "Mr. Abernathy has led his march and departed, taking with him the toothbrush that he packs along as some kind of symbol of his willingness to martyrdom." Within the malicious or tone-deaf referral to martyrdom, some truth lurked: Abernathy wanted to be arrested, certain his jailing would guarantee national attention. He flew in and out of the city, appearing at rallies and marches as an exclamation point. Young stayed in Charleston, coordinating community activities. The union's Godoff, Nicholas, and Foner also stayed in Charleston, focused on the rank and file and later on involving their many powerful labor and government connections. As to strategic decisions, said Nicholas, "We had a single vision of where we were going."[100]

On April 23 MCH trustees concluded an all-day meeting, held in Columbia with the governor, by reiterating a no-yield stance. As to union recognition, McNair said, "Somebody is victimizing a lot of people with an issue that is moot." That night more than four hundred students attending a rally at New Tabernacle Baptist, where the SCLC's Carl Farris vowed, "We're going to violate the law openly and before everyone in Charleston and before God. We are going to go to jail and stay until the fuzz turns us loose." The somewhat-peaceful aspect of the strike was over.[101]

On April 25 Ralph and Juanita Abernathy and Moultrie led a post-rally morning march of several city blocks, this time accompanied by Local 1199 president Davis and three thousand marchers singing and clapping. This time the march ended in Abernathy's arrest and the arrest of one hundred others, mostly teens. When the first few hundred marchers reached MCH, they stretched into a picket line bordered by police officers. Abernathy, dressed in the denims and sneakers he wore when expecting arrest, led as many as five hundred protesters back and forth. Fifty broke through the police lines, raced to a hospital entrance with police on their heels, tried to get through the locked doors, then sat on the steps. Police Chief Conroy

Rev. James Orange, a project coordinator with the Southern Christian
Leadership Conference, worked in Charleston throughout the hospital
strike. He trained participants in nonviolence and helped strikers illustrate
their dignity and worth through actions such as prayer on the picket line at
Charleston's Medical College Hospital and Charleston County Hospital.
Courtesy of Bill Barley. Photograph by Bill Barley.

called in the National Guard. They arrived wearing helmets with plastic face
guards, carrying rifles with fixed bayonets. When the seated protesters refused to move, Conroy allowed Abernathy and Moultrie to walk onto the
hospital grounds and lead the group back to the street. Conroy personally
arrested Abernathy.[102]

While reporters crowded around to listen, the two engaged in a philosophical debate, with Abernathy announcing, "You must do your duty to
enforce the laws, and I must do my duty to disobey unjust laws." Abernathy
rode to jail in an unmarked car, while fifty others rode in white prison buses.
Officers also arrested Local 1199 president Davis and 1199B vice president
Bradford. Later police arrested fifty-one more protesters on the picket line,
packing them into a prison bus, its metal-hatched windows allowing a hand-
drummed backbeat to "Ain't Nobody Going to Turn Us Round." Five hundred National Guardsmen took over the streets. At Morris Brown AME,

the start and end point of the march, an armored personnel carrier pulled up, and troops blocked the cross streets to prevent an additional late-night march.[103]

The weekend brought out more young people. Photos published nation-wide showed teens confronted by soldiers who wore tear-gas masks, tow-ered atop tanks, and lined downtown streets, their rifles with fixed bayonets pointed outward. "I was frightened to see all those guns and big tanks on Morris and King Streets," said Louise Brown. "You don't know what they're going to do. Are they going to shoot us?"[104]

At a morning rally at Central Baptist Church, Young told teens the pub-lic would say, "Now why do they need that kind of power for these beauti-ful people?" Throughout the morning soldiers and police pinned students within a two-block area so they couldn't march. In the afternoon, with en-couragement from the SCLC's Farris, they walked toward a street corner and Conroy, ignoring his bullhorn order to disperse. Dozens sat on the sidewalk and chanted; all were arrested. Among them were sixty protesters sixteen or younger. They were ordered to march behind the officers to a nearby police station, which they did. "It's a concentration camp; that's what it is," said one student. For the next several days, school absences tripled. Police arrested as many as a hundred students a day, the show of force by governor's or-der. "We encouraged the young people to participate in their freedom," said the SCLC's Ford. "They learned more than in school, and they loved it."[105]

James Jones, of Bonds Wilson High School, said, "We feel since we are the leaders of tomorrow, we should do all we can to help the poor of the commu-nity." So it seemed too little, too late, that CCH announced an upcoming in-crease in minimum pay, from $1.30 to $1.50 on July 1 or that the two hospitals offered to take back striking workers—without union recognition, and only those without arrests, and only if all picketing and demonstrating ended.[106]

The presence of troops angered Charlestonians, white and black. Also on duty were the FBI, Army Intelligence, and Joseph Preston "Pete" Strom, chief of SLED. Strom stayed in Charleston throughout the strike and regularly met with Saunders about upcoming events, as he had in earlier years with the NAACP's Newman. Strom and Conroy depicted their personal outreach as partnering rather than information gathering, a tactic with limited value given unfamiliar participants from Local 1199 and the SCLC. And perhaps sincerity seemed lacking with nearly a thousand guardsmen now assigned to duty within the six-mile peninsula.[107]

A march following a Sunday rally grew to a thousand. At MCH march-ers knelt to pray. They answered "yes" to the question, "Do you want to be arrested?" Police and SLED agents arrested close to four hundred that weekend, including two Roman Catholic priests, Richard Sanders of Illinois and Thomas Duffy, director of the local Catholic Charities and chaplain for the county jail. Most of those arrested joined Abernathy at the crowded city jail, where he spent the morning preaching cell to cell.[108]

Another police blockade that Sunday night at Morris Brown AME prevented a march of 600. It seemed obvious the strike approached a dire phase, what the *New York Times* called "the growing danger of a racial explosion." On Monday students skipped school with plans to march downtown but were blocked again at Morris Street by police, state troopers, and the National Guard. A refusal to disperse resulted in 140 arrests, including Catholic priests William Joyce and Leo Croghan and 99 students. The city confined the students at Stoney Field, the city football stadium used by all-black Burke High School. Adults were locked up at the Charleston County Prison Farm. Joyce reported that he, Croghan, and fellow inmates were held in cages, fed "a lot of rice and a little grease," and, on the last of the priests' five-day stay, tear-gassed.[109]

Newspapers nationwide published photos of Fathers Joyce and Croghan behind police compound wire and of children lined up in a police station yard. The *News and Courier* editorialized about "professionals in community disruption," "spurious leaders imported from outside," and "outside disruptionists" creating a "hysteria that breeds violence, discord and confusion." The *New York Times* offered a different take: "The strike of hospital workers in Charleston, S.C. has become the country's tensest civil rights struggle— one involving values as fundamental as those in the original battles for school desegregation and equal employment opportunity." Connecting the Memphis and Charleston strikes, the *Times* editorial described both as "national rallying centers for a coalition of union and civil rights groups, rightly angered by the systematic exploitation public agencies were practicing against underpaid black workers at the bottom of the skill ladder," and called for intervention by President Richard Nixon.[110]

The poignant Memphis slogan "I am a man" had broadened by necessity to Charleston's more inclusive statement: "I am somebody." Edrena Johnson, a twenty-two-year-old job trainee who marched in support of the strikers and was among those arrested with Abernathy, wrote in her diary, "We, as black people in South Carolina, have awakened to the fact that we are no longer afraid of the white man and what we want is to be recognized, not because of our race, but because we are human beings and we have a right, a right which we shall fight and go to jail for."[111]

Said Moultrie, "Whenever Rev. Abernathy or especially Mrs. King was coming, we had beaucoup of people. Sometimes you couldn't get to the church because there were people inside and out." Moultrie herself had become a national somebody, an iconic presence: in her simple dresses, walking shoes, and union cap, she daily linked arms with the famous. Her demure short curls had expanded into an Afro; in the summer sun, she wore stern-looking sunglasses. The National Organizing Committee sent her traveling and provided her coaching in speaking and writing. She spoke in Philadelphia and Washington, D.C., in New York and Florida. She met Golda Meir, Israel's first and the world's third female prime minister. She met performers such as Cicely Tyson, Harry Belafonte, Ruby Dee, and Ossie Davis. At the 1199 General Delegate Assembly, Moultrie told her audience, "We're asking to be treated equal and as human beings," and the women listening cried.[112]

Her travels reduced intimate connection with other strikers and decreased opportunities for heat-of-the-moment training. But Moultrie continued to see herself as "rank and file all the way." She said, "My job was to get out on the picket line and do what I was asked to do." Her experiences differed from those of the other strikers, though. She didn't regularly walk the picket line; she led marches. She didn't make do at home; she stayed in the Brooks Motel, where the strike's celebrities, such as Coretta Scott King or gospel singer Mahalia Jackson, stayed. Or she stayed in hotels on the road, her needs covered. Other strikers, including other 1199B officers, often couldn't pay their rent or buy food. They turned to food stamps, to the Charleston Clergy Emergency Fund, to union emergency aid, and, late in the strike, to union strike pay of fifteen dollars a week. Moultrie's mother took care of her daughter. Other women on strike went home to children missing their mothers and to disgruntled husbands missing their wives' companionship and paychecks.[113]

While a star promoter—she brought back twenty-five thousand dollars from one AFL-CIO speech in Michigan—Moultrie was not directing the revolution. "A lot of the meetings I was someplace else," she said, fulfilling a role as spokesperson and promoter. "The men were the leaders, more or less. Some people had to tell me, 'You are a leader.' I did know in order to get everybody else to do more, I had to do more." Moultrie quite ably enhanced the directions of the local and imported men, who made decisions and chose the words and actions to express those decisions. Her job became inspiration, and that stayed the arrangement for the rest of the strike. The striking women, including Moultrie, saw the men as, if not their leaders, at least their strategists. They deferred to experience. "We needed them; we needed their help," said Louise Brown.[114]

The women walked the pavement and carried the signs and went to jail. Of course some male hospital employees, mostly orderlies and janitors, served as foot soldiers, too, but estimates put their numbers at a few dozen. "Those four hundred women were quick learners," said Nicholas. "It was the best militia you would ever want to be at war with. They had courage. They were articulate, and they could make things happen." The strikers were grateful that professional organizers cared what happened to them. As Moultrie said, the union knew about workers' rights and organizing unions; the SCLC knew about rallies, demonstrations, and marches. Both Local 1199 and the SCLC were providing for the long term their staff, even their leaders, in a shared cause, this melding of workers' rights and civil rights. The union and the SCLC provided order by holding daily meetings and setting responsibilities and schedules. The union and the SCLC worked connections, attracting notables and celebrities and the national media so that the strikers' cause stayed in the news. This was not altruism: the Charleston strike might breathe life into their own futures while breathing new life into Charleston. That, at the time, was okay. "Everybody fell into place; everybody wanted to be involved; everybody wanted to be a picket," said Rosetta Simmons.[115]

That didn't mean it wasn't scary. "It was hard to go to jail," said M. S. Alston.[116]

As April drew to a close, prominent white Charlestonians warned not of union blue but of the Red Menace: communism. In 1940s congressional investigations, Local 1199's Russian-born Davis was accused of communist ties. While Davis said the congressional committee had no right to investigate his personal beliefs, he stated publicly that he was not a communist. Even so the Charleston papers reported and editorialized on what local reporter Gibson called "a thin red thread . . . stretching back to the New York local." A full-page ad in both Charleston papers, addressed to the Concerned Clergy and signed by fifty-nine local businessmen, said, "We are hereby putting you on notice that you are contributing to a long established plan to create discord and destruction in our community, to use the Negro people as cannon fodder in a bloody and violent revolution, a plan which is designed to dismember and destroy freedom in the U.S. and convert this country to a Communist dictatorship."[117]

Abernathy responded with a half-page answer in both Charleston newspapers a few days later. In his "Letter from the Charleston County Jail," a conscious echo of King's 1963 "Letter from a Birmingham Jail," Abernathy focused on the duty to assist the poor. He pointed to organizations for doctors, nurses, and hospital administrators, to the Chamber of Commerce, then to objections to a union for "poor hospital workers." He asked, "Is it simply because they are poor, or is it because all poor, black and white, brown and yellow and even red are getting together and this represents a force too powerful for you to deal with? Are you afraid that, 'You are going to reap what you have sown?'" Pitching the Poor People's Campaign, he wrote of organizing the poor, of a nonviolent revolution. And he addressed the communism charge: "We want no and will have no part of a godless, atheist, totalitarian form of Communism. But neither will we have a dictatorial, repressive so-called Democracy."[118]

Abernathy wrote Nixon, due to visit the state capital. He cited the arrests of hundreds of black and poor workers as proof of a crisis requiring federal intervention, but Nixon ignored requests for a meeting. The Nixon administration just wanted this to go away. Under pressure from Sen. Strom Thurmond and other southern politicians and in debt to what was deemed the "Southern strategy" for getting him elected, Nixon was stalling on school desegregation. He did so despite a 1968 U.S. Supreme Court decision ending "freedom of choice" plans that had allowed white students to stay in majority-white schools. And then there was the conservative distaste for labor; the administration didn't want to appear friendly to unions. On May 13 Abernathy got his say in a brief Washington meeting with Nixon that focused on poverty. Afterward he told the press the president "said nothing" when asked to use his influence on the strikers' behalf. On May 16 Abernathy announced the end of the Poor People's Campaign, a human rights project, which could not reach its myriad goals.[119]

Charleston, South Vietnam

On Tuesday, April 29, Coretta Scott King returned to town. Among those meeting her at the airport were M.S. Alston and her son, who presented roses; droves of reporters; and Local 1199's Foner. Foner heard a reporter say, "Mrs. King, Welcome to Charleston, South Vietnam." The night before her arrival, an arsonist burned up two private planes and a car at Johns Island's airport. In downtown Charleston firebombs hit a grocery store, two tire companies, an electric company, and Berlin's, an upscale King Street clothing store. A laundry, a five-and-dime, a restaurant, and another clothing store were pelted with rocks; windows throughout the city were broken.

A Greek merchant on Calhoun Street put up a sign saying, "Joey ain't mad at nobody," and escaped the rocks and Molotov cocktails. The "Burn, baby, burn" fires of 1965's urban summer riots inevitably came up in conversations. "They didn't want violence, and they didn't want businesses burned," said attorney Moore of strike organizers. However, Moore also remembered someone saying, "'You know how to get these white people to the table? If some of these damn buildings burn, they'd bring their ass to the table.'" Moore added, "And, then, you know, Berlin's burned." He acknowledged, "We realized that was an impetus for bargaining."[120]

King visited the two hundred plus jailed protesters and spoke at a night rally at Emmanuel AME Church attended by four thousand. In her speech and a letter to the strikers, she said, "My husband used to say that hospital workers were forced to work full-time jobs for part-time pay. May I add that $1.30 an hour is not a wage, it is an insult." She compared the strikers to Harriet Tubman, Sojourner Truth, Rosa Parks, and Fannie Lou Hamer. She told the crowd, "If my husband was alive, he would be with you right now, joining in your struggle," and won a standing ovation.[121]

The next day, stately in her union hat, beads, and an orange knit dress, King led 1,500 from Morris Brown AME to MCH. A third of the city's black students skipped school to join her. Her aides released a statement linking Charleston to Memphis and Selma as a "national test of purpose with tremendously important implications for decent-minded Americans everywhere."[122]

The city hit a saturation point. The new million-dollar jail, built to hold four hundred, overflowed. Parking arrested students on a football field and transferring adult protesters to the prison farm didn't end the problem of more arrests than cells. The city reopened the former county jail, rickety enough to have earned the nickname Sea Breeze Hotel. The main downtown hotel, the Francis Marion, reported it had lost sixty thousand dollars in canceled conventions. In a public statement, Mayor Gaillard called on MCH, state officials, and striking workers to "sit down and have some very serious discussions," then he turned to the Community Relations Committee. County Council Chairman Graham objected, formed his own committee, and reiterated a refusal to meet with strikers or their representatives. At one point, given Graham's resistance, peacemaker Jenkins asked a Navy Yard minister to drive him to the McClellanville home of Graham's uncle, where he asked the uncle to apply family pressure for the strike's end.[123]

Frank B. Gilbreth Jr., aka Ashley Cooper, wrote in his popular "Doing the Charleston" newspaper column that "a group of outside Northern dissenters have been able to cause a free city in a free country in a free world to be taken over by bayoneted troops." He proposed that "if the hospital workers are promised a little more money and maybe future union recognition—so what?—everybody will probably find a way to save face and we'll be able to get the Rev. Ralph Abernathy and the other paid protesters plus the National Guard out of Charleston." Many white residents longed for any bargain that would send away the troops and the SCLC, particularly after Abernathy's promise that the mass demonstrations would make "Birmingham and Selma look like picnics."[124]

Concerned about sporadic violence that began with his arrest, Abernathy ended his eight-day stay in jail the night of May 2. The streets were probably safer than the jail. Saunders surrounded Abernathy with local men chosen to guard him. J. Arthur Brown—a former NAACP branch and state conference officer and a successful real estate and insurance broker—signed the five-hundred-dollar surety bond. Seventeen others arrested, including Local 1199's Davis, paid bond after the court refused to release the protesters on their own recognizance. The jail stay did provide Abernathy a laugh in speeches. He would proclaim, "Man, they've been serving us macaroni and cheese—without the cheese." Columnist Cooper responded, "If you think our macaroni is bad, Preacher Abernathy, you ought to try our okra."[125]

Godoff made public a willingness to settle for less than state recognition of the union. Better working conditions, a grievance process that permitted the attendance of workers' representatives, and recognition of a "workers' committee elected by workers" would suffice. However, an elected workers' committee combined with a grievance procedure that allowed workers to elect representatives amounted to collective bargaining, as McNair knew.[126]

Charleston's four state senators, all Democrats, announced that state employees had a constitutional right to join unions, even if South Carolina didn't recognize unions as a bargaining agent. They said a union could function like a state association—they offered the example of the South Carolina State Employees Association—and present the workers' grievances. The AFL-CIO sent William Kirchner, a troubleshooter and top aide to its president, George Meany, to Charleston. Twenty members of the U.S. House of Representatives—but no member of the South Carolina delegation—urged Nixon to settle the strike. After Reverend King's assassination, President Lyndon B. Johnson had done just that in Memphis. On May 6 Nixon directed U.S. Attorney General John Mitchell to send federal observers to Charleston.[127]

But South Carolina's white politicians preferred obduracy. Their stance hardened. The legislature affirmed the governor's position. The governor dug in further. He said what had started as a local labor dispute had, thanks to "outside influences," become a civil rights movement—evidently worse in his books. McNair proclaimed, "No surrender." He declared a state of emergency in Charleston and set a 9 P.M. to 5 A.M. curfew, at the request of the mayor and county council chairman. He also said the Charleston citizen committees had no right to settle the strike. He increased the number of troopers and National Guardsmen to 1,200.[128]

The *News and Courier's* Gibson clung to a combat parallel, writing about a "long siege," the governor's "ace in the hole" of martial law, and the governor's laying down "a demand for an unconditional surrender," all under a headline that said the governor fought "insurrectionists." In a following Sunday column, he wrote, "So the issue now becomes this: Whether South Carolina will knuckle down to the invaders and accept the terms of surrender or stand firm behind the governor." This was the third month of the strike. Yet several hundred black women, marching on the streets in their white uniforms, asking to be treated with dignity and paid a human wage, could not overcome the obsession with outside influences as the only possible reason black citizens might oppose discriminatory practices.[129]

The state was spending eight thousand to ten thousand dollars a day to "stand firm" and keep the National Guard on duty. Rudolph A. Pyatt, the *News and Courier's* first black reporter, wrote in his Washington report, "It doesn't take a genius to conclude that it has cost the state more in one week to maintain that force in Charleston than it would have to pay each of the 400 strikers $1.65 an hour for the same time period." Pyatt believed that the governor's stance helped the SCLC: "A crisis in leadership, waning influence as a viable civil rights organization and a scarcity of funds had the SCLC floundering." Charleston came to the rescue, wrote Pyatt, offering a "much-needed rallying point."[130]

The new curfew led to even more arrests, six hundred within a few days, many for curfew violations. Over time almost all those arrested on curfew violations were black, leading to complaints that this was a "racial curfew." Merchants stayed in their stores all night, on guard with guns and rifles. False alarms, firebombs, and fires kept fire trucks on the road. Gunfire hit a fire truck and a patrol car.[131]

The numbers of protesters continued to grow. For many the hardships and danger inspired rather than deterred. Naomi White surprised herself and others when she changed from "just a quiet person" to a Hell Angel. "They said a lot of us were very militant. I guess when you let them see that regardless of what they do you are not going to be intimidated by the tactics they are using, they say you're militant." Her family backed her. Her oldest two children marched with her. Her stepmother lived with them and helped out. Her husband, a barber, provided free haircuts to strikers.[132]

At the next Abernathy-led rally and march, on May 4, Moultrie said, "The city is in crisis, but McNair fiddles while Rome burns." In his speech Abernathy issued McNair an ultimatum, saying the SCLC would put forth a national call if the state didn't immediately begin negotiations. Abernathy said that violence discredited the movement and poverty discredited South Carolina. Privately he worried about young participants who were not trained in nonviolence and, he feared, were responding in kind to the National Guard or were taking advantage of unrest to vandalize. Even so he asked for a school boycott: "Go back home and tell your mother and father you are a traitor if you go to school. You can learn more by standing up and marching with Local 1199B than you can in any schoolroom in Charleston."[133]

The SCLC's Reverend Orange preached, "We got to do it peaceful," to teens such as Timothy Grant. "He was always talking, always encouraging us. He was relentless," said Grant. The SCLC held Citizenship School for youth and even took some of the young men to Penn Community Center on Saint Helena Island. There the Charleston teens learned about civil rights organizing. "A couple of guys wanted to do their thing, Molotov cocktails, and we told them, 'You don't want to do that. That's you; you're on your own. Don't use the Jackson Street Panthers,'" said Grant. While armed with pistols when on guard, the Jackson Street Panthers practiced nonviolence on the marches. "Big Orange was the one who kept our violence down," said Grant, referring to Reverend Orange. The teen believed, "That's the SCLC, what they stood for, a nonviolent movement. We understood if we go against the grain, the whole SCLC credibility is shot."[134]

White-owned media did not interview strikers or report on strikers' injuries, although the black community talked constantly about the women being "manhandled." Moore believed increasing violence was not a response to Abernathy's arrest but to increasingly rough treatment of the women. Police beat a striking nurse's aide, Thelma Buncum. Moultrie told Abernathy that Buncum was "arrested without cause on the picket line, thrown into the back of a patrol wagon and beaten by a policeman." A National Guardsmen pressed his bayonet to Naomi White's throat during a march. "It looked like a war zone with the tanks on King Street," said White. "They're telling us where you could go and to go back. He held his knife at my throat, and I told him, 'You do what you have to do because I'm sure going to do what I have to do.'"[135]

Many strikers feared the National Guard and agreed with Young, who called the new curfew "stupid." He said, "It's giving license to an angry and frustrated National Guard to persecute the Negro community." Timothy Grant believed Chief Conroy allowed the police to be rough. But the *Evening Post* quoted a television reporter's description of Conroy as "tough as nails and cool as a cucumber," resulting in the nickname "Mr. Cool." A Niagara Falls, New York, native, Conroy had served twenty years in the Marine Corps; he was hired as police chief in 1968. When Orange's brand new blue Ford LTD, parked in front of Morris Brown AME, was beaten to junkyard status, Conroy punished the transgressors in the police force.[136]

Long, Hot Summer

The Charleston strike followed the nation's "long, hot summers," a series of riots in racially divided cities: Harlem in 1964; Los Angeles in 1965; Cleveland in 1966; Cincinnati, Newark, Detroit, and Tampa in 1967. Upon King's assassination in 1968, race riots broke out in more than one hundred U.S. cities. The riots brought out looters, arsonists, snipers, armed police, and the National Guard. In Chicago 350 people were arrested and 162 buildings destroyed; there was no official death count. In Baltimore 6 died; more than 1,000 small businesses were looted or set on fire. In Washington, D.C., 13,600 federal troops took over. Marines mounted machine guns on the steps of the Capitol. Twelve died, 1,097 were injured, 6,100 were arrested, and 1,200 businesses burned. Overall the riots resulted in more than a hundred deaths, the majority black people; thousands injured; thousands arrested; and millions of dollars in property damage. In February 1968 the National Advisory Commission on Civil Disorders, known as the Kerner Commission, said that discrimination in education, employment, and housing were at the root of the unrest, concluding, "Our nation is moving toward two societies—one black, one white, separate and unequal."[137]

As Charleston simmered, white businesses and civic organizations joined in a statement supporting McNair's refusal to engage, and the State Employees Association passed a resolution backing the governor. McNair did agree to meet with Moultrie again. She was accompanied by labor representatives, including Bennett, Godoff, and Kirchner of the AFL-CIO, as well as Alvin Heaps, secretary-treasurer of the RWDSU, and Sinway Young of the South Carolina Labor Council of the AFL-CIO. Afterward the labor representatives had nothing good to say. For his part McNair followed the meeting with a South Carolina Bar Association speech in which he said, "In a sense, this is not simply a test of will or a test of strength. It is a test really of our whole governmental system as we have known it in South Carolina."[138]

On May 6 the *Evening Post* reported that MCH might close. McCord said he might close the hospital that weekend; it was operating at half its capacity, and he feared patient care was inadequate. On May 8 MCH trustees attempted a meeting with the 1199B officers, including Moultrie, but Graham dodged three tries by CCH strikers to meet with him. At that point the Medical College's settlement terms refused recognition or bargaining with the union and agreed only to rehire "up to capacity" and to reveal its wage scales and its reasons for firing the twelve. Any conversation with 1199B's officers was a begrudged concession. McCord had decreed in December that no one in an official capacity at MCH could talk with any union representative.[139]

The brief meeting inflamed all participants. Trustees claimed they arrived to find prohibited Local 1199 organizers in wait. Godoff said that they were advisers and had been told they could be nearby on call yet, upon arrival, were told to sit out the meeting in the restrooms of the small bank building or leave for a nearby firehouse. The strikers stalked out. David Prosten, of the National Organizing Committee, complained afterward that the trustees refused to find another location, expecting the union representatives to "sit on the john until we finish our meeting." Meanwhile the curfew pressed on all sides, limiting rallies and meetings for strikers and restricting nighttime work and events for city residents, business for merchants, and activities for tourists. The SCLC planned to apply even more pressure through a Mother's Day March, May 11, starring the strikers and thousands more. This was phase two of the strike, fitting neatly into the economic focus that the deceased King had dubbed phase two of the civil rights movement. A national march had been set for the nation's capital but was now a Charleston event.[140]

South Carolina had never seen anything like this. A warm-up—a four-hour rally at County Hall—was attended by four thousand, including five congressmen, various East Coast union representatives, Kircher of the AFL-CIO, and Walter Reuther, president of the United Automobile Workers, his collar unbuttoned and tie loosened in the hot auditorium. He presented Abernathy five hundred dollars and pledged five hundred a week to the SCLC, presented a check for ten thousand dollars to Moultrie, and promised, "We are going to have the governor of this state jacked up into the twentieth century." Gloster B. Current, director of branches for the national NAACP, proclaimed, "We say to the government and city officials we are greater in numbers and power and political influence than you, and we will not stop marching until hospital workers have won their demands." Moultrie hit her stride: "In tomorrow's papers we're going to read about outside agitators who come here to mess up Charleston. I'll tell you something. We've got more in common with you hospital workers from New York . . . packing house workers from Chicago . . . steelworkers from Pittsburgh. We've got more in common with all you so-called outsiders than we'll ever have with those fat cats in Columbia and those hospital trustees in Charleston."[141]

Flourishes added to the sense of ceremony. Walter Fontroy, head of the SCLC's Washington, D.C., office, sang "The Impossible Dream." Rosa Parks, renowned for her 1955 refusal to give up a Montgomery bus seat, presented roses to Alberta Williams, a technician at MCH who supported nine children on her $1.30-an-hour wage. Young proclaimed Williams "the first black mother of the year," a reference to a state and national celebration of motherhood begun in 1935 that honored only white mothers. Before Abernathy started the march, he promised those inside and the several thousand waiting outside that "we're going to march this afternoon, we're going to march around the walls of Charleston till those walls come tumbling down." Shortly before 7 P.M., the police forced the rally's end, worried the four-mile march would extend past the 9 P.M. curfew. After strikers and dignitaries left the auditorium, more and more people joined, block by block, pulled from their houses by the singing. "They were like tributaries coming into a large river until it becomes swollen and overruns its banks," Abernathy later wrote.[142]

The SCLC had recruited nationwide; participation estimates ranged from ten thousand to fifteen thousand. The Operation Breadbasket Band from Chicago played jazz, spirituals, and freedom songs. The Rangers, a security force astride horses, wore dazzling red Stetsons, red and black kerchiefs, and white boots. Rev. Jesse Jackson, a Greenville native and director of the SCLC's Operation Breadbasket, took the march's lead after Abernathy left for Atlanta. The participants made their way to MCH, where they prayed. Reuther said, "Black is beautiful. White is beautiful. But black and white marching together is more beautiful." The union's Foner, bringing up the rear, asked SCLC's Young if they might win, and Young replied, "I don't know if we'll win, but we sure can't lose."[143]

Foner was thrilled: tanks, gas-masked soldiers, bullhorns, marching children threatened with jail, the national networks' cameras rolling, and money. While Meany, the AFL-CIO's president, didn't attend, he later donated twenty-five thousand dollars. So did the Auto Workers-Teamsters Union. The forty thousand New York City workers of Local 1199 began contributing a dollar each during each week of the Charleston strike. They must have felt

Leaders of the 1969 Mother's Day March in Charleston included, from left, Rosetta Simmons, strike leader at Charleston County Hospital; Walter Reuther, president of the United Automobile Workers; Mary Moultrie, strike leader at Medical College Hospital; Rev. Ralph Abernathy, president of the Southern Christian Leadership Council, and wife Juanita Jones Abernathy; and Rev. Joseph E. Lowery, an SCLC founder, and wife Evelyn Gibson Lowery. Courtesy of Cecil J. Williams. Photograph by Cecil J. Williams

sympathy as well as camaraderie; Charleston workers earned what they had in 1959.[144]

During this march and others, Moultrie and Rosetta Simmons walked in the front row, locking arms with national leaders. "That was where I supposed to be," said Moultrie: at the front, sometimes wearing a nursing uniform and shoes, sometimes wearing a plain cotton or knit shift, always wearing the Local 1199 cap. Her favorite marching dress was blue with white ruffles. "I felt good that I was up there with them, and I was leading, and there were people there to help me. I felt I was where I was supposed to be, doing what I was supposed to do."[145]

The Mother's Day March ended peacefully. However, a bomb threat delayed the takeoff of union officials' chartered plane. When Foner visited the press room afterward, reporters greeted him with warnings. They told him, "'You're going to die in Charleston, all of you. You're never going to get out of there alive. You're going to crawl out. McNair's never going to move. He's too tough. They're rednecks.' They were afraid that things were going to get out of control, that it was a losing battle."[146]

Nonviolent direct action required such a delicate balancing act. Young acknowledged publicly, "The nonviolent protest philosophy of the SCLC is on trial in Charleston. It is getting harder for people to adopt this philosophy now." He told Jules Loh of the Associated Press that he and Abernathy had met with "revolutionaries who appeared bent on destroying the city." They had asked Young, "'Are you going to go the old way of Martin Luther King or keep up with the times?'" Many of the protesters, male and female, carried guns, usually a .38. On the other hand, the strikers' security unit threw a firebomb maker, rope attached, into the Ashley River and wouldn't let him out until he promised to leave town. And then there was the suspected government agent who shot his revolver into the union hall's floor during a confrontation with a member of SNCC, saying, "The next time you come messing with me, one of us is going to die." Hustled out of the hall by Bradford, he left Charleston under the guard of federal agents.[147]

It seemed possible this labor–civil rights alliance could implode or explode. In an editorial the *New York Times* said that unions and civil rights groups had "put aside their differences to help a wretchedly underpaid workforce." The editorial suggested the coalition had a role to play "in easing the plight of the exploited black worker." The Charleston County Medical Society disagreed, passing a resolution stating the union had "focused its attention upon aspects of the dispute of its own creation, i.e. race and poverty, which are not cogent nor crucial to the issue." Proclaimed the *News and Courier*, "It was Fort Sumter and the Civil War siege of Charleston all over again."[148]

The strike and military occupation had destroyed spring, and likely summer, tourism, and the SCLC's Ford and Orange made sure downtown became even less hospitable, day and night, with or without curfews. A rally was held at the Hanging Tree on Ashley Avenue, an oak where enslaved people and, perhaps, Denmark Vesey rebels were hanged. Another was held at the Old Slave Mart on Chalmers Street, once a slave auction gallery. Long lines of protesters staged shop-ins, strolling in and out of stores, handling merchandise but not buying anything. Teens blocked traffic by dribbling basketballs down King Street. Strikers let chickens loose at the corner of King and

Calhoun streets. At rush hours cars deliberately disabled by flat tires or dead batteries blocked the Grace and Pearman Bridges over the Cooper River.[149]

More important, the strikers didn't flag. Vera Smalls, among the twelve fired with Moultrie, had fallen behind on her rent. Her furniture was in danger of repossession, thanks to the strike and her husband's assembly-line layoff. The mother of two said, "I need my job so we can live decently. But I won't go back until they realize black people are entitled to a union, too." Virgie Lee Whack, who accrued two months of jail time with her sister Donna, said, "South Carolina is a sick society, and maybe a strike like ours was God's way of making his people realize that." She added, "In church the one thing I did learn was that salvation didn't come on a silver platter. There would be suffering and sacrifice like what Jesus spoke of and if you wanted victory you had to work for it and hold out to the perfect end."[150]

Magnolia Curtain for a Banana Republic

Following the Mother's Day March, seventeen U.S. senators asked for federal mediation, a request that incensed McNair and Thurmond. Despite Nixon's hands-off attitude, behind the scenes HEW had continued investigating the strikers' charges of racial discrimination. Hugh Brimm, of the Atlanta office's civil rights division, had interviewed the twelve, as well as McCord and other hospital administrators in April. In statements the fired workers cited McCord's invitation to talk and named aides, LPNs, and nurses who remained on the seventh floor's various units during the March 17 disturbance. McCord insisted that he faced "an incipient riot," and "I stopped it. Now the HEW team is attempting to force me to repudiate my action at that time."[151]

Atlanta recommended a full-scale investigation. Owen Kiely, HEW's chief of federal contract compliance, headed to Charleston. Given that HEW had been investigating racism at the hospital since 1965, it seemed time for action. However, S.C. representative L. Mendel Rivers wrote U.S. Attorney General Mitchell to suggest demonstrators had violated the civil rights of Charleston merchants. He wrote HEW Secretary Robert H. Finch to say the strike was a personnel and union matter and not a civil rights issue. William Vanden Heuvel, a prominent New York attorney who worked with the family of former president John F. Kennedy, met with Charleston bankers and pushed McNair for a settlement. CCH remained at two-thirds capacity, MCH at half its capacity. The *Washington Post* described a standoff: "The union still has not won recognition. The hospitals still are crippled in their operation, and the city is still under curfew and business is still off."[152]

Banker Hugh Lane continued to believe the Community Relations Committee deserved a role. He also believed Washington had more to do. Lane's involvement led to a phone call from Washington, asking that he listen to an FBI assessment that included concerns the strike could "explode out of Charleston and be a nationwide hospital problem." To a request for advice, he responded: tell HEW Secretary Finch "to quit being a wimp," to pick up the phone and give the hospital its marching orders. For Lane that meant telling McCord, "Now get on the ball, or we're going to cut the federal funds off, right like that," with "right like that" illustrated by a finger snap.[153]

The strike was taking a toll on Local 1199 and the SCLC too. Godoff estimated the National Organizing Committee was spending about twenty-five thousand dollars a week in Charleston. Donations to the SCLC had increased right after King's death then declined. Some SCLC staffers felt too many had stayed too long and cost the organization too much. Hotel stays, transportation, and food for thirty-five to forty staffers and organizers over many weeks cost more than the SCLC could afford, according to Ford. And then there was the cost of strikers' and staffers' bail; Ford alone was arrested five times.[154]

The longer the strike, the greater the toll all around. Boycott pressure included strikers quizzing shoppers before they entered stores. Strikers restricted themselves to purchasing only medicine and food and then only from supportive merchants. As the SCLC's Young warned, "Only at the time you keep the same crisis on the community as exists in the daily life of the worker is the strike settled." Handbills asked, "Which side are you on? You either join the freedom fight or you 'Tom' for Governor McNair," then declared, "Buy only food and medicine. Support our Soul Power with your Green Power!!!!" Experience throughout the 1950s and 1960s had taught civil rights activists that, as Young preached, "whites understood green," as in money. Twenty-eight businessmen in North Charleston petitioned McNair, asking him to lift the curfew before their businesses went under. The local *Catholic Banner* accused white Charlestonians of pulling "a Magnolia Curtain down over their heads and eyes" and cited the consequences. "We have a curfew, militia and policemen making a great show of force, and all kinds of balderdash, to protect us from a few strikers, most of them very mild women indeed. One sometimes wonders whether South Carolina thinks it is a State of the Union or a banana republic."[155]

Obviously a stalemate was not a solution. As Moore pointed out, "Union negotiations in the context of a typical union situation up North ain't the equivalent of negotiating on behalf of a union down South with right-to-work laws." Foner reflected later, "South Carolina was not New York. We knew we weren't going to get that law changed." The union's Godoff again announced scaled-back requirements to end the strike: reinstatement of the twelve; better wages, working conditions, and benefits; a grievance process; and an elected workers' committee able to negotiate conditions. "We're not holding out for formal union recognition," he told journalists. The push for much better pay remained, with Godoff calling "inadequate" the $1.45 an hour minimum McNair promised, which was all of $58.00 a week. In New York City, Local 1199 had achieved a $74.00-a-week minimum in 1966 and a $100.00 minimum in 1968.[156]

Moultrie told the *Afro-American*, "I feel Dr. McCord is racist and has no feeling whatever about the welfare of black people. There will be no progress unless someone takes this matter out of his hands," an accurate forecast.[157]

As May drew to a close, a South Carolina jury acquitted the nine patrolmen charged by the Department of Justice with violating the civil rights of the slain and injured South Carolina State students. And in Charleston another try at face-to-face negotiations occurred. The governor flew to Moncks Corner to meet with McCord and J. Edwin Schachte, MCH board chairman. A strikers committee that included Moultrie, Bradford, Moore, and Saunders traveled to meet with Schachte and other hospital trustees, hospital administrators, and Earl Ellis, director of the state's new Personnel Division. On the agenda were the strikers' demands from the earlier failed meeting: reinstate all workers with back pay, drop criminal and civil charges from the picketing and marching arrests, improve wages, and provide fringe benefits, a credit union, and grievance procedure. The strikers wanted this set forth in a memorandum of agreement endorsed by all. Union recognition was not on the list. The strikers narrowed to a "committee assigned by the workers, to discuss grievances and working conditions."[158]

Schachte reminded the group the minimum wage for all state employees would increase July 1, as part of the Personnel Division's new employee compensation and classification plan. "Miss Moultrie said that was all well and good, but she was not going to wait until July 1 and what could be done now to end the strike," Huff wrote in his notes. In a civil conversation that followed, the trustees pulled out chairs for the women strikers, listened, and accepted the majority of the strikers' demands. Who would be rehired remained the sticking point. Schachte said the board would not rehire workers fired or arrested—unless HEW insisted. The meeting ended with both sides believing progress was made.[159]

Coretta Scott King returned for a fried chicken lunch and conversation with strikers, followed by a rally at Stoney Field attended by 4,500. She read a telegram promising the "wholehearted support" of Ethel Kennedy, the widow of Sen. Robert F. Kennedy, assassinated in 1968. She also announced a two-hundred-dollar donation from Jacqueline Kennedy Onassis, widow of President John F. Kennedy, assassinated in 1963. King spoke about the plight of the strikers, calling them the heroines of 1969 and saying the strike had added woman power to black power and soul power. "These women and their leaders are displaying the kind of great determination that can move mountains," she said, noting that the nation's hospitals depended on the work of poor women and that Charleston's were the poorest paid of all. "All of them are poor. Most of them earn as little as $50 to $60 a week. They are sick and tired of working full-time jobs at part-time pay." King asked, "When is the federal government going to do its duty and expose this injustice?"[160]

Leon E. Panetta was working on it. He was the director of the Office for Civil Rights at HEW, an appointment he accepted in March 1969 after saying, "No one in his right mind should take it—and besides, it should be a black." Ruby Martin was working on it. A civil rights activist, she had served as director of the Office for Civil Rights from 1967 until her resignation when Nixon took office. James Farmer was working on it too. The former director of CORE, he accepted a Nixon appointment as an HEW assistant secretary after losing a New York congressional race. All wanted the Atlanta HEW office to enforce hospital desegregation. In a secret meeting outside Charleston, HEW's Brimm revealed to Foner and others that, in addition to investigating civil rights violations, HEW was investigating the twelve firings.[161]

As Foner later explained it, "Apparently, HEW had evidence that the hospital falsely accused the twelve workers of leaving patients to attend a union meeting. If this were true, the hospital, which received federal funds, would have run afoul of HEW regulations by falsifying documents about how those funds were used." Foner, who informed an HEW contact almost daily about events in Charleston, hoped the HEW investigation would provide the deus ex machina, the unexpected solution to an intractable problem. But first, as SCLC's Young accurately warned, "We are really going to have to dig in for another month or so."[162]

On June 4 HEW came to town. HEW's Brimm and Kiely met with the hospital's McCord, Schachte, and Huff. Brimm and Kiely made the HEW position clear: rehire the twelve fired workers. On June 5 the MCH board met, and Schachte told them HEW had sufficient examples of discrimination over time, particularly in hiring and promotion. HEW had added the "blanket firing" of the twelve to the list. McCord still wanted to fight it out. But on-the-spot checks with HEW's Washington office and with Brimm, still in town, resulted in the dread word *sanctions* and a potential funds cut-off date. The trustees asked Brimm to force their hand, to put it in writing.[163]

Brimm did just that. His June 5 letter said HEW investigators had examined personnel and payroll records and interviewed the twelve fired workers, as well as supervisors and administrators. Brimm wrote, "This investigation established one basic fact, which is that the Medical College of South Carolina together with its hospital facility is not in compliance with the requirements of Executive Order 11246," the presidential order requiring fair employment practices by federal contractors. The HEW letter warned that an affirmative action program was required. The first step: reinstate the fired workers without penalty and with back pay. Follow that with programs to recruit, hire, and promote on a nondiscriminatory basis. The *Washington Post* described the HEW directive as good news for the state, "an opportunity to back down under federal pressure without losing face." A few days later, all state employees benefitted from the strikers' staying power. The state announced its new minimum wage, effective July 1, would match the federal minimum, $1.60 an hour. McNair had wanted $1.45 an hour, saying a greater increase would alter the state's wage structure.[164]

Very quietly, very behind the scenes, a complicated web of conversations spun, likely too complicated. McNair took pride in setting groups against one another: the local Saunders versus the national labor organizers, the local Reverend Grant versus the national SCLC staff. This likely added to the weeks and weeks of negotiations. Communication happened in relays: Young and Foner talked to Washington contacts, who talked to the governor. Saunders secretly met in the early morning hours with Huff, who talked to the governor. Schachte met with the governor and attorney general, then wrote fellow trustees that they were advised to rehire the twelve, but the offer could be made by Huff rather than McCord.[165]

Young had observed earlier that the real dispute was not union recognition but human recognition, thanks to white officials' inability or refusal to deal with black people as equals. He told the *Afro-American*, "Until this old southern paternalism is broken, this situation will not be resolved." South Carolina paternalism grudgingly acknowledged only familiar black elites, such as the NAACP's Fielding and J. Arthur Brown. In fact McNair wanted state NAACP leadership involved in the strike's ending, which greatly angered Saunders and Reverend Grant. The white leadership did not want to acknowledge the existence and certainly not the power of homegrown activists such as Moultrie nor the effectiveness of out-of-state leaders such as Abernathy. Oddly, then, Saunders, the homegrown militant, and Young, the suave outsider, ended up moving negotiations to an endpoint.[166]

Assisting a finale were mounting lost dollars: $12 million in federal funds to MCH, many millions more if longshoremen closed the port, not to mention the millions in downtown shopping and tourism dollars. Working against the strikers were union-busting attorneys, a state government determined not to recognize unions or, for that matter, civil rights, and the state's years of practice at keeping a lid on activism. And then there was fear: editorials warned of a "racial explosion" or "another tragedy." The nightly fires and gunplay provided a sampling, perhaps a warning.[167]

Banker Lane and Kronsberg of the Community Relations Committee, still in the mix, arranged for the governor to meet secretly with Saunders and Reverend Grant at Hawthorne Aviation in Charleston. McNair flew in and, it seems, found common ground. On June 8 he and the MCH trustees met in Columbia, and McNair reported that Saunders and Grant wanted resolution on a local level, minus the SCLC and the union, which was what he and the hospital's Schachte wanted too. McNair said the strike resolution would be "without union recognition, no memorandum of agreement, no elected committee or other union subterfuge," in other words, a whimper of a wrap-up that did not protect the strikers.[168]

McNair insisted rehiring the twelve was not too big a price for settling the strike. Besides, according to McNair, the key issue was not what happened to the twelve. The key issue was avoiding a union as well as a tourist haven in flames, which Saunders and the FBI forecast. McNair got the MCH board to authorize the rehiring, saying this was at HEW's behest. On June 9 an offer was made through Saunders, with SLED's Strom standing by as witness. On June 10 McNair met in Charleston with MCH faculty and made it clear that rehiring the twelve rested on the hospital and not the state. Some booed and then telephoned Republican Party stalwarts to object.[169]

It seemed the strike was over—at MCH.

In a mood to celebrate, attorney Moore took Young, Godoff, and Foner on a tour. There hadn't been time for sightseeing before. Moore drove them to Magnolia Plantation and Gardens, the oldest public gardens in the nation. In town he drove them past the John Rutledge House, relevant to history because Rutledge was a signer of the Declaration of Independence, relevant to Moore because his mother, who had sold vegetables on the street, was born there. He drove around the Battery, a promenade edged by antebellum homes, and past Rainbow Row, a string of eighteenth-century commercial buildings converted into colorfully painted homes. He drove past the Old Exchange Building, with its dungeon. The men ate seafood at Harbor House, a restaurant on the waterfront.[170]

Bad news waited. The crew returned to their motel to find a note slipped under Foner's door. Earlier in the day, McCord had written Huff a six-point memo that concluded, "In view of the fact that an imminent emergency has developed which indicated the hospital would be forced to close, the offer of reemployment for the twelve is rescinded." There wasn't an emergency, but the agreement's brief life was over. That evening, as Moore had played tour guide, a SLED officer had hand-delivered to Saunders a one-sentence letter from McCord: "Please be advised that the offer to employ the twelve discharged workers made 9 June 1969, is now withdrawn as of Thursday, June 12, at 5 P.M." McCord reneged on his own. He did not inform Schachte, his board chairman. He did not inform McNair, in Florida for a meeting.[171]

Evidently the HEW letter had transformed from a face-saving boon to an invitation to white medical faculty and employees to resist. Thirty-two white nurses wrote resignation letters. Another forty white nurses threatened to resign, as did up to two dozen white doctors. Others, more powerful, resisted too. Sen. Ernest Hollings announced he had demanded the facts behind the HEW discrimination findings. Rivers invited HEW Secretary Finch to a private early morning breakfast and then called reporters to say Finch agreed that MCH had not violated strikers' civil rights. Thurmond called McCord, and then Thurmond announced that Finch had assured him no funds would be terminated, pending a "thorough personal investigation." Finch escaped to a vacation in Bermuda, where messages could reach him only by boat.[172]

Panetta, director of the civil rights office, was juggling more than enough hot potatoes, including about six hundred unresolved school desegregation cases. But as his boss backpedaled into the Atlantic Ocean, Panetta stepped forward, saying he would proceed. The ILA stepped forward, too, threatening to join the strike and close Charleston's port, the nation's fourth largest and a half-billion-dollar business for South Carolina. The threat was real. Kircher met with ILA leaders and members at their June convention, and the convention delegates pledged support. And Foner was working on a commitment from Lane Kirkland, a South Carolina native and the secretary-treasurer of the AFL-CIO, to put "the whole labor movement on record," as Nicholas described it.[173]

Tempers frayed. The strike leaders' public response warned, "We have marched. We have protested. We have gone to jail. We are prepared to make any sacrifices, no matter what the cost to achieve our just goals." Abernathy promised night marches, which the city prohibited. Moultrie led sixty-five protesters to the homes of Rivers and Hollings. After demonstrators tied up King Street, playing basketball, jumping rope, and singing, seven of those arrested were given thirty-day jail sentences. Arrest-and-release for youths had reached an end.[174]

On June 20 Apollo 11 landed on the moon, and McCord held his first press conference. He defended himself, and two mediators from the Federal Mediation and Conciliation Service, an independent government agency, came to Charleston. So did Abernathy, to lead a rally and night march. Police had stopped an earlier night-time attempt; officials feared riots would follow. Fielding, serving as emissary for the governor, came to the Brooks Motel to put Saunders and McNair in touch by phone. McNair wanted Saunders to announce at the rally that the strike would end the following day. Saunders responded, "Send me a telegram, and I will go to the church and read the telegram for you." McNair hung up to consult. When he called back, he said he couldn't provide written proof but still wanted Saunders to make an announcement. Saunders refused and informed Abernathy, lying atop a car hood and reading.[175]

Despite handbills advertising an Abernathy-led night march, the SCLC president felt ill and was considering taking the night off. The speaking role had fallen to Hosea Williams. Young considered Williams part of the SCLC "wrecking crew." He explained, "When we say a wrecking crew, we mean that when you take apart the economy of a town, you don't have to burn it down." Abernathy's night off ended when he heard the crowd two blocks away at Morris Brown AME. Their "amens" for Williams yanked Abernathy off the car and back into the fray.[176]

Played Around Long Enough

Williams called himself the SCLC's "battering ram." A Purple Heart veteran of World War II and a former research chemist, he had come to speak, march, then depart. He came thinking Charleston "too small an item" for the SCLC and the strikers too friendly with police. At the rally that night, Williams told the crowd, "White folks are crazy; white America is insane. We have played around with Charleston long enough. We're going to march in Charleston tonight, or we're going to die." On Mary Street afterward, Williams and Abernathy decided to stay put and refuse to disperse the crowd of about four hundred, violating the curfew. Williams, whose colleagues called him "a bull in the china shop," began preaching in the street.[177]

Abernathy and Police Chief Conroy went head to head. Abernathy told Conroy, "We are not engaged in a march. We are engaged in a prayer vigil." Conroy replied, "This is a night march in the streets of Charleston regardless of what you call it." The SCLC hadn't applied for a parade permit for the evening; the city did not issue permits for any parade after 8 P.M. Abernathy and Williams countered by sinking to their knees to pray. "We thought the chief was the most sane official in the city, and he has turned his back on us and won't let us go to our praying ground," Abernathy prayed aloud. He told Conroy, "We are going to practice civil disobedience in Charleston as it has never been practiced before." Conroy raised his bullhorn and ordered, "Break it up." Abernathy and Williams kept praying in the middle of the street. According to Abernathy, "The crowd turned quiet, and then I heard someone cry out, 'All right, grab him.'" Conroy was done. "Suddenly two policemen appeared on either side of me, and I felt myself being borne through the air, my knees still bent in an attitude of prayer." Arrested with Abernathy were Williams and Charlestonians David Bright and Elijah Pearson.[178]

Outraged to see their leaders carried away mid-prayer, young participants yelled and shoved police. Protesters threw bricks and bottles. Police pushed back, nightsticks braced across their chests. The armed National Guard stepped forward. Reverend Orange sent marchers back to the church. Those who stayed were angry. A brick thrown through a car window injured a UPI reporter. Six police and a firefighter were injured; several cars were overturned. Abernathy and Williams were charged with inciting a riot, which was a felony, and bail was set at an eye-popping fifty thousand dollars each. Abernathy had now been arrested twenty-five times, twice in Charleston, but never before charged with a felony or hit with a bail higher than a few hundred dollars.[179]

On Saturday McNair set another 9 P.M. to 5 A.M. curfew and added more National Guard and highway patrol. During a preliminary court hearing, aides said Abernathy was ill from his ulcers and fatigue, but Abernathy and Williams refused to post bond. Moore announced the two men would stay in jail, on a hunger strike, and "would remain fasting, until death if that be necessary, until the hospital workers have been secured a living wage and a grievance procedure which includes meaningful representation."[180]

During a thwarted attempt at a noon march, some of the 150 demon-strators lay down on King Street. Others resisted arrest or resisted entering paddy wagons. Patrolmen pushed, carried, and dragged demonstrators and beat at least one woman bloody, a response that roiled the black community and led to vows of an escalation of violence. At the union hall, Young said, instead, "White folks ain't had no religion in their churches for a long time. Let's bring some soul to them." On Sunday strikers in their union caps arrived for worship at all-white downtown churches. At St. Michael's Episcopal Church, forewarned ushers seated the women in the front pews. At Citadel Square Baptist Church, ushers kept strikers outside the church's wrought-iron fence.[181]

Young took Rev. Martin Luther King Sr. and Rev. A. D. King to visit Abernathy in jail. Afterward Young told reporters he feared the SCLC wouldn't be able to control young people intent on violence. Juanita Abernathy, in a fervent public statement at an SCLC press conference, denounced the violence as a "tragic, unwise mistake," dangerous to the hospital workers' cause. She deplored her husband's arrest as "the insanity of condemning the philosophy of nonviolence—the philosophy which holds out the only sensible hope for saving this nation from ruin and destruction—with a phony charge and an exorbitant bond." Abernathy had planned to stay in jail but was upset that he now had no choice; one hundred thousand dollars for Williams and himself was too high—deliberately so—to pay. Suffering from stomach pains, Abernathy continued a modified fast after Saturday treatment at CCH. He listened to the Major League Baseball *Game of the Day* on a radio he was permitted; he planned a family reunion. Allowed movement throughout the jail, he ministered to "mostly drunks, brawlers, and disturbers of the peace."[182]

In town little peace existed in the four nights following Abernathy's arrest. Firefighters dealt with a dozen fires, including one damaging the historic Faber-Ward House, and were hit by bricks and bottles as they worked. Gunfire was reported on Meeting Street, an important downtown thoroughfare. While the sound of gunfire continued into a fourth night, no one was reported shot. In the midst of this, McCord wrote Finch both to deny discrimination and to argue that HEW did not have jurisdiction. The hospital trustees met and unanimously supported McCord. Word on the street promised more violence. Evidently some of the federal urgency was related to covert information the city would burn, igniting another of the nation's violent summers—seemingly irrelevant to McCord and his trustees.[183]

The strikers felt dismay, not only that bricks were being thrown and fires were set but also that the violence was blamed on them. Naomi White, who canvassed merchants for support along with friend Hermina Traeye, was shocked when furniture store owner Morris Sokol beseeched them not to burn down his King Street store. "I told him setting fires was not a part of what we are about," said White, who was his customer. The women feared that the lawless sought opportunities to settle grudges. Reverend Grant warned officials of plans to shut down the city and to burn anything owned by Schachte, a real estate broker. The FBI interviewed Saunders, who said, "We would never have a riot in Charleston. We would have a war. Everybody will suffer, not just the black community." Saunders said that his core group of a dozen men were armed, trained, and, he said, "willing to die." As he pointed out, "This is South Carolina. Everybody has at least two to three guns."[184]

Foner called Daniel Patrick Moynihan, a Nixon adviser, and told him, "This city is going to go, and if you don't do something you'll have it on your hands." Moynihan promised the involvement of U.S. Labor Secretary George P. Shultz, who came to Charleston. Shultz met with union leaders and, according to Foner, vowed, "We're going to reinstate the settlement," then talked to McCord. Harry Dent, former chairman of the South Carolina Republican Party and a presidential adviser, called McCord and pressed him to accept the help of federal mediators and end the strike. At long last HEW told the Medical College that its nine months of ignoring the noncompliance notice were over. An affirmative action plan was due. Finch called McCord; federal funds would be withheld.[185]

Young managed a telephone conversation with Huff, who arranged for Young and McCord to meet. During an initial forty-five-minute tirade by McCord, Young allowed him to "blow off steam" and blame the SCLC, as Young later described it, for "leading a virtual slave rebellion." Afterward McCord agreed to a series of conversations with Young. Once McCord "got all the anger and frustration off his chest," they met as "one Christian talking to another Christian," according to Young. In the larger world, Kirchner ratcheted up financial pressure; he announced for the AFL-CIO that maritime unions had been given authority to close Charleston's port in support of the hospital strikers. Perhaps Charleston needed "to suffer a little more economically," Kirchner said. He was in Charleston to arrange just that.[186]

The SCLC and Local 1199 put pickets at textile companies' New York headquarters. Hugh Lane repeated warnings that the interest rate on state municipal bonds could go up 1 percent. McNair met with Wise, the State Ports Authority manager, and Ellis, the state personnel director, then telephoned McCord and demanded a settlement. More than $12 million had already been lost in tourism dollars. Now McNair faced the disappearance of far more than the hospital's $12 million in federal dollars. Teddy Gleason, president of the longshoreman's union, said he was ready to ask Charleston Local 1422 to stop unloading or to turn around ships in Charleston, Port Royal, and Georgetown. The most recent waterfront strike had cost the country $250–300 million. McNair faced an economic disaster that could hurt the nation. [187]

A Settlement and a Declaration of War

After almost a week of building pressure and after a daylong meeting between McCord and federal mediators, on Thursday, June 26, the MCH strike seemed over. Following meetings for faculty and staff throughout Friday, McCord publicly announced that MCH had agreed to a settlement, although he did not participate in the in-house meetings or hold a press conference. The union was not recognized. All striking workers would be rehired. The strikers' minimum wage would be $1.60 an hour as of July 1, the day the state's minimum wage increased and the day Medical College strikers could return to work. The pay of aides, food workers, and technicians would go as high as $2.10. On that same day, through legislation, MCH officially would become the Medical University of South Carolina (MUSC), with accreditation pending. The medical university and its hospital would provide a credit union that could accept union funds, and the new grievance procedure would allow a worker to choose a personal representative for support during a several-step process.[188]

On the strikers' side, Saunders publicly announced the end, as Jenkins and Reverend Grant stood by. At the union hall, strikers received the news with hugs, kisses, dancing, and singing. Moultrie did not participate in the windup; she was in New York, speaking for the union. "I was so hurt when they came to my hotel to tell me the strike had ended in Charleston. I couldn't believe it," she said. "It broke my heart. I wanted to be a part of that." No striker signed the agreement because there was no memorandum of agreement to sign, as McNair wished.[189]

The CCH strike was not resolved. So that same afternoon, when circuit court reduced Abernathy's bond to five thousand dollars, not much changed for him. He held meetings in his cell until visiting hours ended, listening to the opinions of clergy, SCLC and union workers, and strikers. Foner described a cell "stinking with heat." When Abernathy asked the union and SCLC men to kneel in prayer, Godoff's pants ripped. Foner and Godoff exchanged a grim look. Foner obsessed, as the prayer went on and on, "It's so hot in here. I'm going to die here. I'm going to die. If this doesn't stop I'm going to die." As people came in and out, a CCH striker revealed that the county still resisted hiring back all strikers. Abernathy agreed with Young and his wife—she said, "Ralph, you can't go!"—that he should stay in jail until the county workers also achieved a settlement.[190]

Graham said he would meet with Young and Rosetta Simmons, leader of CCH strikers and the 1199B vice president. Young provided the now-familiar list of requirements: All striking employees would return to their jobs, without "recriminations or reprisals." The hospital would provide job classifications, better wages, holidays, and a credit union that could accept union funds and would allow a grievance procedure and an employees' committee. But the CCH strike dragged on. The hospital had filled sixty of the ninety strikers' jobs and resisted hiring back more than thirty-seven strikers or any striker with criminal charges. Rosetta Simmons had been arrested once but quickly released without charges because the jail was so crowded. That was not true of so many others.[191]

At this point arrests totaled close to two thousand, meaning most strikers wouldn't be rehired. Graham called any rehiring a "reward" to strikers. He said, "Council will stand firmly behind those who had the guts to cross the picket line." Young contended that striking workers had invested years in their jobs. Saunders contended that all would return to work or no one would. For three days running, Graham met with Young and Rosetta Simmons. Then Saunders and Reverend Grant intervened again. The two said discussions should be left up to locals, meaning themselves, according to Graham's notes. County Council suggested placing strikers in jobs at other medical facilities. Saunders and Grant countered: shift to other facilities the sixty workers who replaced the strikers. Graham said no.[192]

As July began, 280 of the 300 plus MCH strikers received mailed notifications to return to work. Within a few days, 230 had returned. Moultrie vowed that the returning workers would use any free time to picket and march for their fellow CCH strikers. On July 2 they did so, with 100 protesters marching in front of the CCH emergency room entrance, shouting "scab" at those who crossed the picket line. Abernathy, bail reduced and county negotiations at a standstill, left jail for Atlanta on July 3, issuing a statement that his departure was "a further display of good faith."[193]

But county negotiations remained tense and unfriendly. A count had determined that sixty-nine strikers wanted to return to their jobs. Saunders said CCH must rehire thirty-seven immediately and the remainder on a regular timetable. County Council, using the services of textile attorney Haynsworth, said no. Haynsworth's advisory role had officially ended in April, when press reports revealed he had been paid $13,850. His reappearance was not surprising; to increase pressure the SCLC was angling for a national boycott of the textile industry. When a federal mediator came to Charleston, requesting a meeting, Graham declined and threatened to stop all negotiations if Abernathy returned.[194]

On Friday, July 11, the County Council issued its "final" offer. Union activity on the job was prohibited. CCH would keep its existing credit union, would raise its $1.50 minimum wage to match the state's $1.60, but would not change its grievance process to allow an employee to bring a representative to hearings. The hospital would rehire thirty-seven workers immediately but would not set a timetable for rehiring others nor would it rehire anyone with pending criminal charges or convictions from the strike. Council also issued an ultimatum: meet the terms by next Friday. Any strikers who didn't agree to return by then would be permanently replaced. A joint statement by Abernathy, Godoff, and Rosetta Simmons called this "an open declaration of war." Both sides said they stood on principle. Graham said he wouldn't dismiss workers who had cared for the sick, especially to replace them with strikers. Abernathy said, "They struck for a chance to obtain dignity as a human in the eyes of the other people at the hospital." He added that obtaining that respect and returning to work were as important to the strikers as other bargaining terms.[195]

On Monday, Rosetta Simmons announced strikers would picket council members' homes and businesses, and on Tuesday and Wednesday, a strikers' committee met with Graham and county manager Richard Black. On Thursday a two-hour meeting ended when Simmons walked out after disconnecting an unacknowledged recording device under the conference table. She was unhappy with the stalemate, but she also knew Graham was being pressured from above to settle.[196]

On Friday, July 18, six hours past a scheduled press conference, the CCH strike ended. The hospital rehired immediately forty-two of the strikers and promised the rest jobs within ninety days. The hospital dropped its refusal to rehire anyone with convictions or charges pending. Job classifications would be provided employees on request. The existing credit union and grievance process remained in effect. Minimum wage increased to $1.60. County Council and strike committee members signed the one-page list of conditions. Rosetta Simmons sat beside Graham to announce the strike's end publicly to television cameras. "I am happy that strife and turmoil in the streets of Charleston has ended," said Graham. Simmons read a statement that concluded, "We are confident that all workers will be reinstated in much less than the ninety days mentioned in the agreement," an important statement to make publicly, even though her confidence wasn't there.[197]

The many, many days—100 for MCH, 113 for CCH—cost the state at least $1 million for the National Guard, SLED, and the highway patrol and $15 million in lost business and tourism. The port hadn't closed. No one had died. And the city hadn't burned. Why hadn't it burned? Not just because of the SCLC's promotion and use of nonviolence but because of the striking women's insistence on nonviolence. As Rosetta Simmons told angry strikers who wanted to whack scabs with two-by-fours, "No, we don't do it that way." They understood, as the SCLC's Hosea Williams taught, "Nonviolence is a weapon of the strong. You just have to learn to have patience." They believed, as Juanita Abernathy said, "Violence is most dangerous of all to the hospital workers' cause and to women and children in Charleston." And this was the peninsula, a small, tight community where everyone was someone's mother, sister, aunt, or cousin, where "burn, baby, burn" would hurt those the strikers loved.[198]

The long-lasting resistance of South Carolina officials resulted in the stories of the black women and their SCLC and Local 1199 partners reaching the world. Even *Pravda,* the official newspaper of the Soviet Union, wrote about them. But the workers themselves had asked for very little: a living wage and recognition of their humanity. To get that took stopping a city for a summer.

"We Were Forgotten Women"

McNair had what he wanted: no union. All state employees got something long delayed, a higher minimum wage, a grievance procedure, an employee classification system, and, in 1972, conceding the civil rights impetus, a Human Affairs Commission to "eliminate and prevent unlawful discrimination" in employment, housing, and disability.

Local 1199 got what it wanted: expansion—just elsewhere. The New York union had received two hundred thousand dollars in donations for the strike. Throughout the Charleston strike, Local 1199 was organizing in other cities, and the Charleston publicity paid off, sparking inspiration in hospital workers and fear in hospital administrators. Foner later pointed out that Local 1199 had not intended to go into the South that early and wanted to return to its "normal base." The union did so to its benefit. Charleston had sped up its campaign along the East Coast. Thanks to the SCLC-union alliance, the fear of another Charleston, and the continued involvement of Young and Coretta Scott King, Local 1199 soon had in Philadelphia the ten-thousand-member 1199C and in Baltimore the seven-thousand-member 1199E. These successes were followed by 1199P in Pennsylvania and 1199J in New Jersey. Thanks to Charleston, "they almost had the white flag in hand," said Nicholas.[199]

Local 1199 had needed the SCLC. At the Charleston strike's end, Foner told the press, "We learned that the SCLC can organize the community, and we can organize the hospital. We have shown that there can be an effective link between civil rights and labor, and that was the dream of the late Dr. Martin Luther King Jr." Union president Davis wrote in the Local 1199 magazine, "Without this alliance, a union would be looked on as an outside force attempting to impose itself on black workers." Just so, the SCLC had needed Charleston. Young believed the Charleston strike saved the SCLC from "the jaws of total disintegration" after King's death, because the strike forced the staff to focus on work rather than fights about succession. Abernathy knew the SCLC, weakened after King's death and the end of the Poor People's Campaign, needed "to win something big in order to reestablish the credibility of nonviolence." And Abernathy himself needed Charleston and a win. He believed his role there provided him "a personal victory" that silenced doubters. But no greater successes followed for the SCLC.[200]

The Charleston strikers had needed the savvy labor and civil rights organizers to pull off such a massive effort, and at first success seemed theirs too. Rosetta Simmons, during the county's settlement announcement, said, "We gained recognition as human beings in this community." Moultrie, who addressed delegates at the 1969 AFL-CIO convention, the first black rank-and-file delegate to do so, said, "We were forgotten women, second-class citizens. We worked as nurse's aides. We cleaned the floors. We prepared the food in the hospitals. And if it had not been for the union, we would still be forgotten people. We have demonstrated to the city of Charleston, to the state of South Carolina and to the people all over America that we can and we will overcome. And nobody, just nobody is going to turn us around."[201]

But neither hospital recognized Local 1199B. In a July press release, the SCLC called the settlement terms "a form of recognition of the union." Foner later described the resolution as "a pseudo-recognition kind of thing." Even that was a positive spin. Moore said that, thanks to an agreement not to include union attorneys in negotiations, the results were merely letters of intent. His reaction was "Y'all don't have anything. You've been bamboozled." The hospitals were in "a position not to honor anything," said Moore. "We let Bill Saunders and Andy Young know they were duped." The union's Nicholas and David White did remain in Charleston for three months, but, as Nicholas later pointed out, "We had no enforcement mechanisms. It takes two to continue to agree." In July 1969 MUSC established a grievance procedure but limited the number of times any one employee could accompany another through the process. In other words workers weren't allowed repeated help from union representatives.[202]

In August, Moultrie and the eleven other fired workers wrote the administration to complain of discrimination. They had been rehired as "new employees" and had discovered that plans for the credit union did not include an automatic dues deduction for union membership. In September HEW's Brimm wrote McCord to ask once again about an incomplete affirmative action plan. Brimm also asked about back pay, which HEW had named an affirmative action step, along with the rehiring. The strikers did not get back pay. McCord obtained an attorney general's opinion that MUSC didn't have the authority to make retroactive payments. When granted a charter in April 1970, MUSC set up a credit union without a dues check-off.[203]

The aftermath at CCH was similar. Young, who coached Rosetta Simmons during negotiations and wrote the strikers' proposals, was gone. Essentially so were most of the promised benefits. The forty-two strikers rehired at the strikes' end were the only ones, besides Simmons, rehired. "We made this agreement that's not worth the paper it's written on," said Simmons. She had used up her savings, accumulated in anticipation of maternity leave, and needed her job back. For three months CCH told her no jobs were available. When a former supervisor provided her proof of an LPN position filled in October, she confronted administrator Black, was granted a job, and reported back to work in November. Simmons was intent on keeping her post, which wasn't easy. Supervisors moved her from unit to unit during the workday, required her to work three different shifts in one week, and suspended her twice. "It made me more patient," she said. "Rather than fight, I locked my jaws."[204]

The fight was gone in other ways too. None of the Charleston strikers knew how to run a union local. The office at 220 Rutledge Avenue was not regularly staffed and thus often closed. Without a dues check-off, it was easy to quit paying union dues, and that's what former strikers did. Moultrie, dogged by security at the hospital, couldn't collect dues at work. Without dues Local 1199B couldn't do much, including pay rent. Moultrie used her own money to pay bills, but she didn't know how to run a union. Nicholas believed that Moultrie had been "a star on stage, the voice of the organization," but he also believed she wasn't ready for the "nuts and bolts" of sustaining a local. Lacking staff, training, money, and an operating plan, Local 1199B died within three years. Moultrie resigned before an election she was sure to lose. Rosetta Simmons acknowledged that she herself "just dropped out."[205]

At MUSC, Moultrie did not get back her former job. Her new location was the psychiatric unit, so an eye could be kept on her, she was sure. She missed being "out there," working the strike, and, after a while, wished she hadn't returned to the hospital. Many of her coworkers acted uncomfortable around her. Fellow strikers—finally earning minimum wage, buying cars and houses they didn't want to lose—saw her in the halls and turned away. And many of the white supervisors freely showed hostility. The strikers heard through the grapevine, unsurprisingly, "the twelve had to go." Louise Brown returned and was placed on the pediatric floor. "One nurse told me she would stay on my back. Every day she'd find something to pick on me about. I didn't have a good day when I went back, not one good day." Brown filed several grievances but was fired before a year had passed. "I wasn't the only one," she said. "They stayed on you: 'You're black; you're a striker; we're going to teach you lessons.'" Naomi White endured shift and unit changes until a supervisor told her to "shut up." Edna Johnson, falsely accused of sleeping on the job, refused to sign the write-up, finished her shift, and didn't return.[206]

Moultrie lasted longer but dreaded every day of work. "I would feel really good until I got to the door of the hospital, and then all of a sudden I'd get a stomach-ache. Sometimes my feet would swell. I would have to go to the doctor, and one day he said to me, 'I'm really sorry about what they're doing to you.'" She stayed at MUSC until 1975. Chronically late because she would take a last few minutes to steel herself, Moultrie was warned she would be let go because of tardiness. Unwilling to press a grievance, "I left and never went back." The strikers' last moment of fame came through a thirty-minute documentary, *I Am Somebody*, commissioned by Local 1199, filmed by Madeline Anderson, and released in 1970.[207]

Essentially from then on the women were, in Moultrie's words, "forgotten." The rank and file, as they had called themselves, moved among the other hospitals or found other low-level jobs in a city still resisting desegregation and smarting from what white residents described as a partial "surrender." The lead strikers' lives did not materially change. M.S. Alston stayed in nursing until 1983, when she returned to school for a business degree. Louise Brown became a private nurse but really wanted to open a nursing home. Mary Moultrie dreamed of the back pay no one received. After retiring from a city parks job, she tried unsuccessfully to organize sanitation workers, joined by Rosetta Simmons, who had completed twenty-nine years of hospital work, and Naomi White, who had completed twenty-seven. Said White, "We helped everybody but ourselves."[208]

Conclusion

How important a role did South Carolina play in the civil rights movement? James M. Hinton Sr.'s pursuit of lawsuits to achieve first-class citizenship enhanced the NAACP's legal strategy of the 1940s and 1950s. Summerton's *Briggs v. Elliott,* which led to *Brown v. Board of Education,* undeniably changed the nation, albeit slowly, when the Supreme Court declared segregation in public schools unconstitutional. The 1960 arrests of thousands of peaceful students during sit-ins increased national discomfort with segregation and reinforced the power of nonviolent direct action.

The hospital strike dramatized the confluence of race and poverty and the intense desire for human dignity at least as successfully as the Poor People's Campaign. Grassroots leadership stood the test in Summerton, where petitioners persisted after Rev. Joseph Armstrong DeLaine's forced exit; in Rock Hill, where student activism continued after Rev. Cecil Augustus Ivory's death; and throughout the student movement, where group-centered leadership protected the survival and likely extended the longevity of college-town protests.

But achieving equality in South Carolina? Segregationist governors and legislators from the 1930s through the 1960s anchored South Carolina in last place. The state was last to hold a white primary. The state was next to last to desegregate higher education, preceding Alabama by months in 1963. The state was a holdout in public school desegregation. Not until February 1970, and under order of the Fourth Circuit Court of Appeals, did South Carolina's final twelve school districts desegregate.

Despite the 1964 Civil Rights Act and 1965 Voting Rights Act, segregation and the conflicts it generated remained in South Carolina. That truth was horrifically reinforced in 1968 when troopers opened fire at South Carolina State, killing three and wounding twenty-seven young men in what became known as the Orangeburg Massacre. As with lynchings of previous decades, a grand jury refused to indict the troopers. As had happened before, the federal government stepped in; troopers were charged with summary judgment without due process. As in the past, the jury acquitted all. The only conviction? Cleveland Sellers, a black power advocate and program director for SNCC who was wounded in the shootings. Labeled an outside agitator by Gov. Robert E. McNair, the Denmark native was convicted of rioting and sentenced to a year in jail.

It's fair to say South Carolina functioned as a crucible. Even so, many South Carolina activists' commitment to racial justice stayed steady and took them to the national stage.

Cecil J. Williams, who photographed the *Briggs* petitioners with mentor E. C. Jones when he was twelve, worked for *Jet* magazine and black-owned newspapers by the time he was fourteen, documenting each moment of the South Carolina movement. His work, exhibited in institutions and museums, fills civil rights books. Thomas Walter Gaither, while a CORE field secretary, joined with Gordon Carey to propose the 1961 Freedom Rides, scouted the routes, and escorted riders to safe havens. South Carolina State's Charles Frederick McDew and Charlotte's J. Charles Jones helped found SNCC, and McDew served as its second chairman. Jones joined the Freedom Rides, and the two worked on voter registration in Mississippi. Julie Varner Wright became an NAACP youth field secretary for the Southeast; worked with Medgar Evers, murdered in 1963 in Mississippi; and developed and ran two of the nation's earliest African American research libraries. James Enos Clyburn became the first black adviser to a South Carolina governor, joined Congress in 1993, and has served as majority whip twice. Clyburn's friend Bobby D. Doctor worked for the U.S. Civil Rights Commission as director of the southern regional office. Mae Frances Moultrie Howard became a missionary in Liberia, Mexico, and Canada.

Matthew J. Perry Jr., the students' NAACP counsel, became the Deep South's first black attorney appointed to the federal judiciary and, in 1979, South Carolina's first black U.S. district judge. Ernest Adolphus Finney Jr., the students' CORE counsel, became the state's first black circuit judge since Reconstruction, joined the state Supreme Court in 1985, and, in 1994, became its first black chief justice since Reconstruction.

Such staying power worked generation to generation in South Carolina; like griots the activists passed along deep knowledge. Before Clarendon County's black residents signed petitions for desegregated schools in the 1950s, brothers Levi and Hammett Pearson fought for a school bus for the children. The Pearsons, born in the 1890s, showed parents a generation younger how to step up, resist fear, and withstand pressure.

Before South Carolina's black college students sat on counter stools in 1960, James Thomas McCain taught them the lifesaving rules of nonviolence. Activism had cost McCain, born in 1905, not only jobs but his profession, yet there he was, teaching a new generation peace and perseverance.

Before Charleston's black hospital workers formed a union and went on strike, Lillie Mae Doster and Isaiah Bennett did so. Doster and Bennett, born in the 1920s, belonged to Local 15, a CIO affiliate. They sought pay withheld during World War II and challenged racial and gender discrimination at the American Tobacco Company. In 1946 they got their back pay and a raise. There they were, in 1969, coaching Mary Moultrie and Rosetta Simmons.

Here's a more recent story: In 1993 forty school districts sued the state in *Abbeville County School District v. State of South Carolina,* saying inequitable state funding resulted in marked differences in educational opportunities. Inevitable comparisons were made to *Brown v. Board of Education.* Three Clarendon County school districts were among the original *Abbeville* plaintiffs. When *Abbeville* finally made it to trial, the 101 days of testimony and argument occurred in Clarendon County Courthouse in Manning. While race was excluded from consideration at the trial, 86.5 percent of the plaintiffs—narrowed to students in eight school districts—were black, and 88.8 percent lived in poverty.

In 1999 the lawsuit reached the South Carolina Supreme Court. The South Carolina Constitution's education clause says, "The General Assembly shall provide for the maintenance and support of a system of free public schools open to all children in the State." That wasn't much to work with. The court asserted that the constitution required the General Assembly provide each child the opportunity to receive a minimally adequate education. Notice the words *each* and *minimally adequate.* To squeeze out that meager obligation, the court claimed interpretation of the constitution among its duties. This small victory came from Chief Justice Finney, born in 1931.

The impressively slow progress and paltry outcome might seem familiar too. *Abbeville* didn't make it to trial until 2003. In 2014 the South Carolina Supreme Court, in *Abbeville II,* said the state had failed in its constitutional duty to provide a minimally adequate education but provided no remedy. In 2017 the court said it had previously stepped beyond its judicial powers, could not set a qualitative standard, and ended its jurisdiction.

Missing from that recounting are nameless children: the first graders at East Elementary School, who had just stepped out of their classroom when the ceiling collapsed, crushing their desks; the child who brought a dead bat from the schoolyard to illustrate the letter *B;* the teens at Estill High School whose 1940s library books predicted some future moon landing; the teens whose science teacher, lacking school funding, scooped up roadkill for them to dissect; the seven of every ten Lee County teens who didn't graduate from high school.

Why one more story of struggle? We all want upbeat, finite stories, a way to segment life and history itself into obvious beginnings and happy endings. South Carolina is forever at the beginning. But bright threads run through. Someone from before, who didn't give up, teaches someone now.

Besides, human rights movements don't ever end. This book does, with names. Eliza Gamble Briggs. Frances DuBose. Thomas Walter Gaither. Mae Frances Moultrie. Rev. Cecil Augustus Ivory. James T. McCain Sr. Charles Frederick McDew. Rev. Isaiah DeQuincey Newman. Mary Moultrie. Rosetta Simmons. Cecil J. Williams.

Please add your own.

Notes

One: Fearless Leader

Notes. Newspaper headlines are truncated. The *Afro-American* was founded in Baltimore, Md., by John Henry Murphy Sr., formerly enslaved. The newspaper grew to include regional editions in Washington, D.C.; Philadelphia, Pa.; Richmond, Va.; and Newark, N.J. The edition's location was used in the masthead, hence the varied newspaper names.

1. American Map Company, *Lynchings by States and Counties, in the United States, 1900–1931*, research department, Tuskegee Institute, https://www.loc.gov/resource/g3701e.ct002012/ (accessed 18 November 2019); J. H. Moore, *Carnival of Blood*, 211–12, 223, 224; Equal Justice Initiative (EJI), "African American Lynching Victims by State, 1877–1950," in *Lynching in America*, https://lynchinginamerica.eji.org/report/ (accessed 18 November 2019). EJI, Supplement: Lynchings by County, South Carolina, *Lynching in America*, https://lynchinginamerica.eji.org/explore/south-Carolina (accessed 18 November 2019). The EJI documented 4,084 "racial terror lynchings" in the twelve states and updated that number to 6,500 in a subsequent report. "EJI's Reconstruction in America Report Changes Picture of Lynching in America," EJI, 17 June 2020, https://eji.org/news/reconstruction-in-america-report-changes-picture -of-lynching-in-america/ (accessed 26 June 2020).
2. Wells, *Crusade for Justice*, 64.
3. Rodney Hinton, interview by the author, June 2004; "Rites Held," *Palmetto Post*, 27 November 1970; Testimonial Honoring James Myles Hinton Sr., 26 February 1965, John Henry McCray Papers, South Caroliniana Library, University of South Carolina; John H. McCray, "Ten Feet Tall," *Charleston (S.C.) Chronicle*, 5 October 1985, McCray Papers.
4. Modjeska Simkins, "State NAACP Closes," *Columbia (S.C.) State*, 17 June 1942, 3; "Hinton Re-elected," *Columbia (S.C.) Record*, 13 June 1944, 14; John H. McCray, "And So Exits," *Washington Afro-American*, 28 October 1958, 4; Lau, *Democracy Rising*, 110, 117; Lau, "Mr. NAACP," 152; Grammar and mechanics are Byrd's. Hinton to I. DeQuincey Newman, 3 September 1959, 3, McCray Papers.
5. "Advancement Group," *Columbia (S.C.) State*, 19 June 1941, 16; John H. McCray, Clarendon County Address, 21 June 1955, 2, McCray Papers. McCray dates formation of the Negro Citizens Committee to 1942, with a goal of raising funds for an NAACP voting lawsuit. Burke, *All for Civil Rights*, 4; "Sumter Branch," 1964, 2, Isaiah DeQuincey Newman Papers, South Caroliniana Library, Columbia; Myers, *Black, White and Olive Drab*, 52, 53; Lau, *Democracy Rising*, 132–33.

6. "May Invest Military Police," *Columbia (S.C.) State*, 12 January 1941, 1; "Use of MP's," *Columbia (S.C.) State*, 13 January 1941, 1; James M. Hinton, "Asks Uniform Treatment," *Columbia (S.C.) Record*, 6 March 1941, 12; "Officials Seek Conference," *Columbia (S.C.) Record*, 27 March 1941,1, 6; 'Washington Man Probes," *Columbia (S.C.) State*, 4 May 1961, 40; "Bloodshed Rampant," *Columbia (S.C.) State*, 6 September 1941, 5; Myers, *Black White & Olive Drab*, 34, 36, 40–44; Lee, *Employment of Negro Troops*, 350.

7. "2,000 Hear Klan," *Columbia (S.C.) State*, 22 August 1941, 11; "KKK Plans Parade," *Columbia (S.C.) Record*, 20 August 1941, 1, 2; Early, *One Woman's Army*, 63.

8. Noble Cooper Sr., interview by the author, 2004.

9. "Leaders Look," *Columbia (S.C.) Record*, 4 January 1942, 10; "Negro Soldier Center," *Columbia (S.C.) State*, 15 February 1942, 19. All military branches, blood bank supplies, and United Service Organization facilities were segregated. "Council Thanked," *Columbia (S.C.) State*, 16 July 1944, 26; Hinton to Bethune Chief of Police, 28 April 1946, McCray Papers; Hinton to Bethune Police Chief, 3 November 1946, McCray Papers; Hinton to Belk's Department Store, 1 December 1946, McCray Papers; Hinton to Frank Owen, 17 January 1947, McCray Papers; Hinton to Graham Seibels, WIS-Radio, 9 June 1947, McCray Papers. Capitalization is Hinton's.

10. Levi G. Byrd to McCray, 7 March 1946, McCray Papers; "Colored Group Asks," *Columbia (S.C.) State*, 18 June 1941, 14; Alston v. School Board of City of Norfolk, 112 F.2d 992 (4th Cir. 1940).

11. Charron, *Freedom's Teacher*, 150, 153, 157; Thurgood Marshall to Walter White, memo, 17 June 1942, part 26, series A, reel 18, frame 450, NAACP Papers.

12. "Negroes Head to Court," *Columbia (S.C.) State*, 4 March 1943, 14; "Negro Teacher Suit," *Columbia (S.C.) Record*, 23 April 1943, 1, 9; Viola Louise Duvall v. J. F. Seignous et al. Case No. 1082 (1943); Charron, *Freedom's Teacher*, 163–64; "Negroes Get Equality," *Columbia (S.C.) Record*, 14 February 1944, 1.

13. Thompson v. Gibbes, 60 F. Supp. 872 (E.D.S.C. 1945); Charron, *Freedom's Teacher*, 170–73; "You Can Help," *Lighthouse and Informer*, 3 June 1945, McCray Papers; Hon. James E. Clyburn, Tribute to Viola Duvall Stewart, *Congressional Record*, vol. 156, no. 183, Government Publishing Office.

14. Smith v. Allwright, 321 U.S. 649 (1944); "Negroes Take Effort," *Columbia (S.C.) State*, 5 June 1946, 11; "Few Negroes Cast," *Columbia (S.C.) State*, 21 April 1948, 1; "Court Voids Ban," *Columbia (S.C.) State*, 31 December 1947, 1; Gergel, *Unexampled Courage*, 181.

15. Charron, *Freedom's Teacher*, 167–68; "Negroes Will Seek," *Columbia (S.C.) Record*, 28 April 1944, 1–2; "Negroes Will Send," *Columbia (S.C.) Record*, 18 May 1944,1, 8; "All-White South Carolina," *Columbia (S.C.) State*, 18 July 1944, 1, 9; "Negro Party Picks," *Columbia (S.C.) State*, 31 August 1944, 3; "November 7," ad, *Columbia (S.C.) State*, 6 November 1944, 7; "Constituting No Threat," *Columbia (S.C.) Record*, 11 December 1944, 6; "Group Dismisses Protest," *Columbia (S.C.) State*, 15 February 1944, 5, 11; Sullivan, *Lift Every Voice*, 284–85.

16. "Negroes Seek to Take Part," *Columbia (S.C.) State*, 19 September 1942, 17; Marshall to White, memo, 17 June 1942; "Negroes Seek Ballot," *Columbia (S.C.) Record*, 6 June 1942, 7; "Negroes Set Up," *Columbia (S.C.) State*, 25 May 1944, 1; McCray, "Manner of

Men," *Charleston (S.C.) Chronicle,* 17 March 1984, McCray Papers; Hinton to Members of the 87th General Assembly of South Carolina, 7 February 1947, McCray Papers; McCray, interview by William Gravely, June 1983, Gravely Collection, South Caroliniana; "Negroes Protest Removal," *Columbia (S.C.) State,* 14 July 1944, 1, 2. Accompanying Hinton were Rev. E. A. Adams, Dr. R. W. Mance, John C. Artemus, Dr. O. J. Champion, C. L. Lillewood, and, in uniform, Pvt. Harold R. Boulware, serving in the Army Air Corps.

17. Deanna Pan and Jennifer Berry Hawes, "An Undying Mystery," *Charleston (S.C.) Post and Courier,* 25 March 2018; Teddy Kulmala and Bristow Marchant, "SC Executed," *Columbia (S.C.) State,* 16 June 2019; Mark Warren, "Stinney Makes," *Columbia (S.C.) Record,* 13 June 1944, 1; "NAACP Hits Electrocution," *Columbia (S.C.) State,* 12 June 1944, 2.

18. "Ministers, Unions Protest," *Columbia (S.C.) Record,* 19 June 1944, 3; David Bruck, "Executing Teen Killers Again," *Washington Post,* 15 September 1985; "Not to Interfere," *Columbia (S.C.) State,* 11 June 1944, 1. Stinney was the youngest person in the nation, from the twentieth century on, to be put to death; in 2014 his conviction was vacated.

19. Hinton to U.S. Attorney General, 21 December 1945, McCray Papers; Hinton to Honorable Thurman Smith, Civil Rights Division, U.S. Department of Justice, 1 December 1946, McCray Papers.

20. McCray, speech draft, 14 May 1962, 18–19, McCray Papers; McCray, "They Laughed," *Charleston (S.C.) Chronicle,* 2 August 1980, 8–10, McCray Papers.

21. McCray, "They Laughed."

22. "Negro Files Suit," *Columbia (S.C.) Record,* 21 February 1947, 1; "Debate Limit," *Columbia (S.C.) Record,* 2 June 1947, 9; "Hearing Planned," *Columbia (S.C.) State,* 13 March 1947, 18; "Hearing Today," *Columbia (S.C.) State,* 3 June 1947, 7; "Court Hears," *Columbia (S.C.) Record,* 3 June 1947, 1; Elmore v. Rice et al., 72 F. Supp. 516 (E.D.S.C. 1947); "Negroes Assail," *Columbia (S.C.) State,* 4 June 1947, 1; "Decision Promised," *Columbia (S.C.) State,* 7 June 1947, 1, 4; Hinton to 87th General Assembly, McCray Papers. Capitalization is Hinton's.

23. "NAACP Wants Amendment," *Columbia (S.C.) State,* 13 July 1947, 1, D1; "Negro Party Delegates," *Columbia (S.C.) State,* 17 July 1947, B8. Grammar and mechanics are Hinton's and Elmore's.

24. Simkins, *Journal and Guide,* 4 October 1947, 2, Modjeska Simkins Papers, South Caroliniana; Burke, *All for Civil Rights,* 172–73; Rice v. Elmore, 165 F.2d 387 (4th Cir. 1947). Columbia's Forest Lake Country Club did not accept a black member until 2017; see Andy Shain, "First Black Member Joins," *Charleston (S.C.) Post and Courier,* 18 August 2017.

25. "Few Negroes Cast"; "Negroes Expect," *Columbia (S.C.) State,* 14 June 1949, B1; McCray, "Thanks to Yaschick," *Charleston (S.C.) Chronicle,* 19 March 1983, McCray Papers.

26. Brown v. Baskin, 78 F. Supp., 933 (E.D.S.C. 1948); R. J. Moore, "Beatrice 'Bea' McKnight," 184; Lau, *Democracy Rising,* 178–79.

27. Carolyn Click, "One Man's Sacrifice," *Columbia (S.C.) State,* 3 March 2003, 1; "Elmore Seeks," *Columbia (S.C.) Record,* 4 November 1953, 7. Unremitting death threats contributed to Laura Elmore's long-term hospitalization. George Elmore lost his

businesses, his house, and his own health and died in 1959. He was fifty-three. "Negro Says He Was Knifed," *Columbia (S.C.) Record*, 23 August 1948, 13; "Calhoun Falls Negro Charges," *Columbia (S.C.) State*, 24 August 1948, 3; "Constabulary Told," *Columbia (S.C.) State*, 28 August 1948, 12; "Election Day Beating," *Columbia (S.C.) Record*, 23 September 1948, 3.

28. Sullivan, *Lift Every Voice*, 157, 159.

29. Murray v. Pearson, 169 Md. 478, 182 A. 590 (1936); Missouri ex rel. Gaines v. Canada, 305 U.S. 337 (1938); David Stout, "A Supreme Triumph," *New York Times*, 11 July 2009, 19; "Negro Applies at University," *Columbia (S.C.) State*, 23 August 1938, 11; Burke and Hine, "South Carolina State College Law School," 27–29.

30. "Solomon Blatt Declares," *Columbia (S.C.) State*, 29 August 1938, 3; William Peters, "A Southern Success," *Redbook*, June 1960, 41, 99–105; Baker, *Paradoxes*, 66–70; "Trustees File Brief," *Columbia (S.C.) State*, 16 October 1947, 1.

31. "Negro Sues," *Columbia (S.C.) State*, 9 January 1947, B3; McCray, "Lawyer Boulware," *Charleston (S.C.) Chronicle*, 12 February 1983, McCray Papers; Stonewall M. Richburg, interview by the author; Baker, *Paradoxes*, 77.

32. Wrighten v. Board of Trustees, 72 F. Supp. 948 (E.D.S.C. 1947); "New Angle Reported," *Columbia (S.C.) Record*, 7 June 1947, 1; "University Trustees," *Columbia (S.C.) State*; Baker, *Paradoxes*, 82; Hine, *South Carolina State University*, 190–93.

33. Marshall to Hinton and Boulware, 30 September 1947, part 26, series A, reel 18, frame 454, NAACP Papers; Marshall to Wrighten, 29 September 1947, part 26, series A, reel 18, frame 454, NAACP Papers; "Negro Law School Wins," *Columbia (S.C.) State*, 13 July 1948, 10. The school did graduate black lawyers who fought segregation. By the 1966 closing, its fifty-one graduates included such alumni as Wrighten; Matthew Perry, state NAACP counsel and the first black federal judge in the Deep South; and Ernest A. Finney, Congress of Racial Equality (CORE) state counsel and the first black chief justice of the S.C. Supreme Court. Sweatt v. Painter, 339 U.S. 629 (1950); Sipuel v. Board of Regents of University of Oklahoma, 332 U.S. 631 (1948).

34. Noble Cooper Sr., interview by the author; "NAACP to Renew," *Columbia (S.C.) Record*, 7 June 1950, 3; "Jim Crow's Last Stand," *Washington Afro-American*, 9 March 1954, 1, 3; Simkins, *Journal and Guide*, 27 December 1947, 2, Simkins Papers; "Sheriffs' Stand," *Spartanburg (S.C.) Herald-Journal*, 30 September 1948, 4.

35. Orson Welles, "Affidavit," 28 July 1946, "The Place Was Batesburg," 25 August 1946, in Orson Welles Commentaries, Internet Archive, https://archive.org/details/1946 OrsonWellesCommentaries; "Criminal Information Filed," *Columbia (S.C.) State*, 27 September 1946; Myers, *Black, White and Olive Drab*, 59–62; Gergel, *Unexampled Courage*, 14–23, 119–32.

36. Gravely, *They Stole Him*, 23; Yarborough, *Passion for Justice*, 48–53; "Batesburg Located," *Columbia (S.C.) State*, 18 August 1946, 1; Welles, "Affidavit," "Batesburg"; McCray, "Isaac Woodard Story," n.d., 1–2, McCray Papers; "Aiken Mayor," *Columbia (S.C.) State*, 10 August 1946, 1; Alex Billet, "Woody Guthrie," *International Socialist Review*, no. 85, https://isreview.org/issue/85/woody-guthrie-songs-prove-you-your-world (accessed 17 April 2020); "Negroes Want Governor," *Columbia (S.C.) State*, 20 August 1946, 14.

37. EJI, "Moore's Ford Bridge," *Lynching in America*; Gergel, *Unexampled Courage*, 72–73; "Criminal Information Filed," *Columbia (S.C.) State*, 27 September 1946, 1, 2; "Ready to Testify," *Columbia (S.C.) State*, 28 September 1946, 1.

38. "Federal Jury Acquits," *Columbia (S.C.) State*, 6 November 1946, 1; Sullivan, *Lift Every Voice*, 330; "Bus Passengers Testify," *Columbia (S.C.) State*, 12 November 1947, 17; "Negro Loses," *Columbia (S.C.) State*, 14 November 1947, 1; "Vindication for Shull," *Columbia (S.C.) State*, 7 November 1946, 4; "NAACP Head Disagrees," *Columbia (S.C.) State*, 10 November 1946, 14.

39. "Federal Action Urged," *Columbia (S.C.) Record*, 21 August 1946, 4; Hinton to Newman, 3 September 1959, 3, Newman Papers; White to McCray, 17 September 1946, McCray Papers; McCray to Wilbert Walker, 12 September 1946, McCray Papers; McCray to unknown, 12 September 1946, McCray Papers; "McCray Did Not See," *Columbia (S.C.) State*, 17 August 1946, 10; Madison S. Jones to McCray, 9 September 1946, McCray Papers; McCray to Ruby Hurley, 11 September 1946, McCray Papers; McCray, "Way It Was," *Charleston (S.C.) Chronicle*, 3 April 1982, McCray Papers.

40. McCray, interview by William B. Gravely, Gravely Collection; Gravely, *They Stole Him*, 17, 83, 122; "Hurd Denies Shooting," *Columbia (S.C.) Record*, 15 May 1947, 1, 2; "Negro Lynched," *Columbia (S.C.) State*, 18 February 1947, 1; "Special Lynching Court," *Columbia (S.C.) Record*, 22 February 1947, 1; "Officers Hunt," *Columbia (S.C.) State*, 23 February 1947.

41. "Lynch Inquest," *Columbia (S.C.) State*, 4 March 1947, 1; "Crowded Court," *Columbia (S.C.) Record*, 13 May 1947, 1, 5; "How Mob Killed Negro," *Wilmington (N.C.) Sunday Star-News*, 18 May 1947, 16.

42. "25 Men Take Him," *Columbia (S.C.) Record*, 17 February 1947, 1; "SC Governor Speaks," *Columbia (S.C.) Record*, 19 February 1947, 11; "SC Constables Help," *Columbia (S.C.) State*, 18 February 1947, 1; "FBI Enters," *Columbia (S.C.) State*, 18 February 1947, 1; "Pickens Lynching," *Columbia (S.C.) Record*, 18 February 1947, 4; "Anti-lynching Law," *Columbia (S.C.) Record*, 19 February 1947, 4; Gravely, *They Stole Him*, 40–44, 61, 70; "Lynch Statements Signed," *Columbia (S.C.) Record*, 21 February 1947, 1, 7; "Special Lynching," *Columbia (S.C.) Record*, 22 February 1947, 1; "Double Lesson," *Columbia (S.C.) State*, 24 February 1947, 4.

43. "Federal Anti-lynching Law," *Columbia (S.C.) Record*, 19 February 1947, 4; "No Need," *Columbia (S.C.) State*, 27 February, 4; "No Federal Intervention," *Columbia (S.C.) State*, 2 March 1947, 4; Gravely, *They Stole Him*, 35–37, 49, 75, 127; "Lynch Inquest Slated," *Columbia (S.C.) State*, 28 February 1947, 1; "Omission Won't Halt," *Columbia (S.C.) State*, 5 March 1947, 1; "Lynch Cases," *Columbia (S.C.) Record*, 5 March 1947, 1; "Coroner's Verdict," *Columbia (S.C.) State*, 6 March 1947, 4; "Test Will Come," *Columbia (S.C.) Record*, 7 March 1947, 4; "Double Lesson."

44. "Here and There," *Columbia (S.C.) State*, 3 March 1947, 10; Gravely, *They Stole Him*, 70, 115, 132; "31 Plead Innocent," *Columbia (S.C.) Record*, 12 May 1947, 1, 6.

45. Gravely, *They Stole Him*, 128, 136, 144; "Suspects Place Finger," *Wilmington (N.C.) Morning Star*, 5 March 1947, 3; "Eighth Suspect Accuses," *Columbia (S.C.) Record*, 16 May 1947, 1; "Lynch Details," *Columbia (S.C.) State*, 16 May 1947, 1; "State Nears Conclusion," *Columbia (S.C.) State*, 17 May 1947, 1, 7; "Judge to Charge Jury," *Washington*

(D.C.) Evening Star, 21 May 1947, 4; "Martin to Rule," *Columbia (S.C.) State*, 19 May 1947, 1, 9. Hurd was also identified as "Herd."

46. "Northern Vote Charge," *Washington (D.C.) Evening Star*, 20 May 1947, 1; Rebecca West, "Opera in Greenville," *New Yorker*, 14 June 1947; "Lynch Defense," *Columbia (S.C.) Record*, 1, 7.

47. Gravely, *They Stole Him*, 164, 166; "Northern Votes," *Washington (D.C.) Evening Star*, 20 May 1947, 1; "Biggest Miscarriage," *Arizona Sun*, 30 May 1947, 1; West, "Opera in Greenville"; "All 28 Acquitted," *New York Times*, 22 May 1947, 1, 27; "Mixed Reactions," *Columbia (S.C.) Record*, 22 May 1947, 1, 5; "Newspaper Comment," *Washington (D.C.) Evening Star*, 23 May 1947, 2; "Best Lynching Deterrent," *Richmond (Va.) Afro-American*, 9 August 1947, 1.

48. West, "Opera in Greenville"; Gravely, *They Stole Him*, 77, 152, 159; "Mother of Lynch Victim," *Washington (D.C.) Evening Star*, 26 May 1947, 4; "State Chapter of NAACP," *Columbia (S.C.) State*, 25 May 1947, 1; 9. By 2019 passage of a federal anti-lynching law had failed more than two hundred times. On February 26, 2020, the U.S. House passed the Emmett Till Anti-Lynching Act, which awaits Senate action.

49. S. M. Richburg, interview by the author; "NAACP Asks Full Investigation," *Columbia (S.C.) Record*, 11 February 1949, 2; "Constabulary Joins," *Columbia (S.C.) Record*, 16 May 1949, 5; "Fine Treatment," *Columbia (S.C.) Record*, 19 January 1950, 3; "City Democrats," *Columbia (S.C.) State*, 19 January 1951, 5.

50. S. M. Richburg, interview by the author; Joseph Lewis, branch history, 9 December 1964, box 3, Newman Papers. Grammar and mechanics are Lewis's.

51. Earl M. Middleton, interview by the author, 2004; Middleton, *Knowing Who I Am*, 55–63, 65–66; W. B. Hildebrand to Hinton, 27 April 1948, McCray Papers; "Local Whites" to Hinton, 27 May 1947, McCray Papers. Grammar and mechanics are letter writers'.

52. "Hinton Reports," *Columbia (S.C.) State*, 23 January 1949, 2; "Constables Advised," *Columbia (S.C.) Record*, 26 January 1949, 3; Montgomery to Gloster B. Current, Report for March 1949, 21 April 1949, part 26, series A, reel 19, frame 78, NAACP Papers.

53. "Negro Admittance," *Columbia (S.C.) State*, 29 January 1949, 5; "Morrison Hits," *Columbia (S.C.) State*, 30 January 1949, 10; Hinton to Marshall, 9 June 1949, part 15, reel 9, frame 62, NAACP Papers; "Assembly Elects," *Columbia (S.C.) Record*, 23 March 1949, 1, 15; Baker, *Paradoxes*, 69–70; "Charleston College," *Columbia (S.C.) State*, 2 February 1949, 1, 8; "Negro Urges," *Columbia (S.C.) Record*, 23 February, 3; "Negroes Again Seek," *Columbia (S.C.) Record*, 14 March 1949, 1, 10.

54. Hinton to Marshall, 26 May 1949, part 26, series A, reel 19, frame 73, NAACP Papers.

55. Ibid.; "Death of NAACP Official,'" *Jackson (Miss.) Advocate*, 5 January 1952, 1, 6; "Jim Crow's Last Stand," *Washington Afro-American*, 9 March 1954.

56. "Our Peerless Leader," conference program, 14 October 1950, part 26, series A, reel 19, frame 272, NAACP Papers; Bernard Taper, "Meeting in Atlanta," *New Yorker*, 17 March 1956, 110; Hinton to Marshall, 26 May 1949, NAACP Papers; "Hinton Says Kidnappers," *Columbia (S.C.) Record*, 22 April 1949, 1, 8; "Hinton Freed," *Columbia (S.C.) State*, 23 April 1949, 1, 5.

57. "Our Peerless Leader"; Franklin B. Washington and Everett L. Dargan, interview by the author, 2007; Highlights, 1939–1962, Twenty-First Annual State Conference, Simkins Papers; Dargan, interview by the author, 2004; "Negro Leaders Deny," *Columbia (S.C.) State*, 23 April 1949, 2; Novella Hinton Turner, interview by the author, 2004.

58. Marshall to George Daniel Grice, 2 June 1949, McCray Papers; "Our Peerless Leader"; Marshall to Montgomery, 29 December 1949, part 26, series A, reel 19, frame 160, NAACP Papers; "Hinton Honored," *Columbia (S.C.) State*, 30 December 1949, 13.

59. Sullivan, *Lift Every Voice*, 353, 385.

60. "Slain Officer Wore Robe," *Columbia (S.C.) Record*, 28 August 1950, 1, 9; "Klan Blasted," *Columbia (S.C.) Record*, 29 August 1950, 1; "Klan Chief," *Jackson (Miss.) Advocate*, 16 September, 1, 8; "Charlie's Place," *Charleston (S.C.) Post and Courier*, 10 September 2017; Newman, *Carolina Stories*; Beacham, "This Magic Moment," 132–37.

61. "NAACP to Defend," *Columbia (S.C.) State*, 31 August 1950, 8; "DC Conference," *Columbia (S.C.) State*, 6 October 1950, 9; "Klan Needs," *Columbia (S.C.) State*, 31 August 1950, 2.

62. "Horry Sheriff Holding," *Columbia (S.C.) State*, 2 September 1950, 1; "Klan Member Loses," *Columbia (S.C.) State*, 2 September 1950, 1; "Klan Records Turned," *Columbia (S.C.) Record*, 4 September 1950, 11; "Violence Victim Fined," *Columbia (S.C.) Record*, 8 September 1950, 1, 9.

63. "Klan Leader, Others," *Columbia (S.C.) Record*, 6 October 1950, 3; "Klan Will Tell," *Columbia (S.C.) State*, 2 November, 3; "FBI to Halt," *Columbia (S.C.) Record*, 10 November 1950, 1; "Dragon Says," *Columbia (S.C.) State*, 12 November 1950, 1, 10; "Sheriff's Report," *Columbia (S.C.) State*, 12 November 1950, 1, 11; "Horry Grand Jury," *Columbia (S.C.) Record*, 2 October 1950, 1; "Sasser Says Foes," *Columbia (S.C.) State*, 17 November 1950, 1, 8.

64 "Dragon Says"; "Hamilton Denies Inciting," *Columbia (S.C.) State*, 3 September 1950, 1; "Byrnes Asks Separate," *Columbia (S.C.) Record*, 16 January 1951, 1; "NAACP Sets," *Jackson (Miss.) Advocate*, 10 February 1951, 1, 6.

65. "NAACP Lawyers Laud," *Jackson (Miss.) Advocate*, 16 June 1951, 1, 2; "Negro Group Will Battle," *Columbia (S.C.) Record*, 7 October 1947, 16; "Hinton Asserts," *Columbia (S.C.) Record*, 17 July 1951, 6.

66. "Miscellaneous," *Crisis*, February 1952, 119; "Leader Sees End," *Columbia (S.C.) Record*, 30 January 1952, 10. Delaware had two cases, *Belton v. Gebhart* and *Bulah v. Gebhart*, which were consolidated. Secretary of NAACP to Hinton, 11 January 1952, McCray Papers; Seventh Annual Meeting, South Carolina Conference of the NAACP, 19–20 October 1947, part 26, series A, reel 18, frame 649, NAACP Papers; "Clarendon Community," *Columbia (S.C.) Record*, 15 December 1952, 1, 12; "33 Teachers," press release, 9 April 1953, part 25, series A, reel 16, frame 535, NAACP Papers.

67. Brown v. Board of Education of Topeka, 347 U.S. 483 (1954); Brown v. Board of Education of Topeka, 349 U.S. 294 (1955); Lighthouse Publishing Company, Inc., minutes, 20 March 1954, McCray Papers; "'Big Lie Exposed!,'" ad, *Columbia (S.C.) State*, 27 May 1954, 6; Tax Collector's Sale, State of South Carolina, County of Richland,

Columbia (S.C.) Record, 16 May 1953, 12; "Lighthouse Sale," *Columbia (S.C.) State,* 7 February 1955, 6; "SC Negro," *Columbia (S.C.) State,* 3 December 1955, 7.

68. "NAACP Secretary," *Columbia (S.C.) State,* 20 March 1954, 5; "Put Yourself," *Columbia (S.C.) State,* 21 August 1955, 11.

69. "NAACP Legitimate," *Columbia (S.C.) State,* 25 August 1955, 15; "New Mixing Protests," *Columbia (S.C.) Record,* 26 August, 1, 9; "Hinton Assails," *Columbia (S.C.) Record,* 22 October 1955, 1.

70. Tom Nebbia, "Bullet Holes," *Columbia (S.C.) State,* 20 January 1956, 33; "Shotgun Blast Fired," *Columbia (S.C.) State,* 20 January 1956, 33; R. Hinton, interview by the author, 2004.

71. Lau, *Democracy Rising,* 109–10. Grammar and mechanics are Byrd's. Taper, "Meeting in Atlanta," 86. Grammar and mechanics are Byrd's.

72. "Interposition Resolution," *Columbia (S.C.) State,* 15 February 1956, 1; Hinton to Members of Congress, 31 January 1956, part 20, reel 10, frame 829, NAACP Papers.

73. "Wilkins Hits," *Columbia (S.C.) State,* 25 February 1956, 20; "U.S. Asked," *Jet,* 20 May 1954, 10; "NAACP Leader Answers," *Columbia (S.C.) State,* 31 March 1956, 11; Jones-Branch, "Modjeska Montieth Simkins," 233–34; Simkins, "Oral History Interview."

74. Bass and Thompson, *Strom,* 162–64; "New Political Trends," *New York Times,* 18 March 1956, 188.

75. "Waring Helps Collect," *Columbia (S.C.) State,* 18 March 1956, 1, 2; "Public Jobs in SC," *Columbia (S.C.) State,* 18 March 1956, 1, 2; Lau, "NAACP," *SC Encyclopedia,* 660–661; S. M. Richburg, interview by the author; Taper, "Meeting in Atlanta," 110; "NAACP Promises," *Columbia (S.C.) State,* 22 March 1956, 18.

76. "Around the State House: Thousands," *Columbia (S.C.) State,* 15 March 1956, 4; "Public Jobs," *Columbia (S.C.) State,* 18 March 1956, 1; "South Carolina Anti-NAACP," *Jackson (Miss.) Advocate,* 7 April 1956, 1, 4; "Wilkins, Hinton Condemns," 22 March 1956, part 20, reel 10, frame 833, NAACP Papers.

77. Bryan v. Austin, 148 F. Supp. 563 (E.D.S.C. 1957); "Judges Defer Decision," *Columbia (S.C.) State,* 23 October 1956, 1, 8; C. S. Brown, *Ready from Within,* 36.

78. "Segregation Lines Held," *Columbia (S.C.) Record,* 31 December 1957, 3; J. C. Williams to All Pastors, 15 June 1957, Eugene Avery Adams Papers, South Caroliniana Library; NAACP v. Alabama, 357 U.S. 449 (1958); Louisiana ex rel. Gremillion v. NAACP, 366 U.S. 293 (1961); NAACP v. Button, 371 U.S. 415 (1963).

79. "Sees Barratry," *Columbia (S.C.) State,* 10 February 1957, 35; "NAACP's Role," *Columbia (S.C.) Record,* 29 November 1957, 4.

80. Lau, *Democracy Rising,* 210–11; "Hinton May Retire," *Columbia (S.C.) Record,* 25 September 1958, 12; "Progress toward Goals," *Columbia (S.C.) State,* 19 October 1958, 32.

81. Funeral services for James Myles Hinton Sr., Second Calvary Baptist Church, 25 November 1970; Hinton to Marshall, 26 May 1949; McCray, "Don't Blame It," *Charleston (S.C.) Chronicle,* 18 January 1964, 2, McCray Papers.

82. Cooper, interview by the author.

Two: No Such Thing as Standing Still

1. Ferdinand Pearson, interview by the author, April 2003; Joseph A. DeLaine Jr., interview by the author, April 2003; Phynise "Piney" Pearson Witherspoon, interview by the author, 2004.
2. F. Pearson, interview by the author, 2003.
3. Ibid.; Ophelia DeLaine Gona, *Dawn of Desegregation*, 20–23. A few family records spell Hammett Pearson's given name with an *i*, as "Hammitt." His funeral program used "Hammett." In Remembrance, Mt. Zion AME Church, 24 July 1977, Joseph A. DeLaine Papers, South Caroliniana Library, University of South Carolina.
4. Jesse Pearson, interview by the author, 2003; P. Pearson Witherspoon, interview by the author. Jesse Pearson's obituary uses "Jessie," although his family early on used "Jesse," which also was the spelling used for his son's name.
5. "Building Survey for Summerton," box 8, file 204, Robert McCormick Figg Jr. Papers, South Caroliniana; "Survey of Schools," box 8, file 205, box 7, Figg Papers; Dobrasko, *South Carolina's Equalization Schools;* Bartels, *History of South Carolina Schools.*
6. Andrew Lee Ragin, interview by the author, 2003.
7. Mass meeting, 15 October 1949, part 26, reel 19, frame 131, NAACP Papers; Bartels, *History of South Carolina Schools;* Constitution of the State of South Carolina, Article 11, Section 7, 4 December 1895; Rosenwald Schools, S.C. Department of Archives and History, Columbia. The Julius Rosenwald Fund built five hundred schools in South Carolina between 1917 and 1932.
8. John Wesley Richburg, interview by the author, 2003; Deloris Ragin, interview by the author, 2003; A. L. Ragin, interview by the author.
9. Normel Georgia, interview by the author, 2003.
10. Edgar, *History of Santee Cooper*, 7, 10; *South Carolina: Educational Attainment of the Population 25 Years and Over: 1940–2000*, U.S. Census Bureau.
11. Late James W. Seals, 23 March 1973, DeLaine Papers; Hinton to Ella Baker, 2 July 1945, part 26, reel 18, frame 589, NAACP Papers; E. E. Richburg to DeLaine, 15 October 1956, DeLaine Papers.
12. J. A. DeLaine Jr., Brumit B. DeLaine, interviews by the author, 2003, 2004. Gona, *Dawn of Desegregation*, 14. In most documents, including personal ones, Joseph Armstrong DeLaine spells "DeLaine" without a space between the "De" and "Laine." However, Ophelia Gona separates the particle from the family name.
13. J. A. DeLaine Jr., B. B. DeLaine, interviews by the author, 2003, 2004; Gona, *Dawn of Desegregation*, 15–16; B. B. DeLaine, "Prelude to Opposition," n.d., DeLaine Papers.
14. J. A. DeLaine Jr., interview by the author; B. B. DeLaine, interview by the author; Gona, *Dawn of Desegregation*, 15, 20; DeLaine, "Prelude to Opposition," DeLaine Papers; Annual Report, Clarendon County Citizens Committee, 1942, part 26, reel 18, frame 317, NAACP Papers; Annual Report, Clarendon County Citizens Committee, 12 January 1943, DeLaine Papers; DeLaine to Nationwide NAACP Membership Campaign, 16 December 1946, part 26, reel 18, frame 270, NAACP Papers.

15. DeLaine to Mary Overton, NAACP Membership, 17 January 1943, part 26, reel 18, frame 316, NAACP Papers.

16. Carter, *Matter of Law,* 58.

17. Thurgood Marshall to White, Wilkins, and Morrow, 17 June 1942, part 26, reel 18, frame 450, NAACP Papers; Jesse J. Pearson to W. A. Schiffley, 6 July 1946, DeLaine Papers.

18. "School Desegregation Case," 1954 pamphlet, file 7, DeLaine Papers; DeLaine, "Prelude," DeLaine Papers; DeLaine, "School Segregation Case," *AME Church Review,* part 26, reel 18, frame 409, NAACP Papers; DeLaine to John McCray, 14 December 1961, John H. McCray Papers, South Caroliniana Library.

19. J. A. DeLaine Jr., interview by the author; F. Pearson, interview by the author; B. B. DeLaine, interview by the author; James Morris Seals, interview by the author.

20. Kluger, *Simple Justice,* 4; Lochbaum, "Word Made Flesh," 30, 43; P. Pearson Witherspoon, interview by the author.

21. J. Pearson, interview by the author, 2003; Harold Boulware Sr. to DeLaine, 29 July 1947, DeLaine Papers; R. Hinton, interview by the author, 2003; Viola Louise Duvall et al. v. J. F. Seignous, Case No. 1082 (1943); Thompson v. Gibbes, 60 F. Supp. 872 (E.D.S.C. 1945); Wrighten v. Board of Trustees, 72 F. Supp. 948 (E.D.S.C. 1947); Elmore v. Rice, 72 F. Supp. 516 (E.D.S.C. 1947).

22. S. M. Richburg, interview by the author, 2004; Earl Middleton, interview by the author, 2004; Georgia Montgomery, interview by the author, 2004.

23. "Negro Movement Progresses," *Columbia (S.C.) State,* 1 September 1963, A4; "Negro Voting Right," *Columbia (S.C.) Record,* 15 May 1947, A1, 12; Harolyn Boulware, interview by the author, 2004; Harold Boulware Jr., interview by the author, 2004; Marion Boyd, interview by the author, 2004; Harold Boulware Sr., "Quest for Civil Rights: Judge Harold R. Boulware Sr."

24. F. Pearson, interview by the author.

25. Boulware to Vander Stukes, 5 November 1947, Clarendon County Board of Education Papers, S.C. Department of Archives and History; Membership of S.C. Branches, 10 October 1947, part 26, reel 18, frame 451, NAACP Papers; Stukes to Boulware, 20 November 1947, Clarendon County Board of Education Papers; S. Emory Rogers to McCord, 20 November 1947, Clarendon County Board of Education Papers; Boulware to Stukes, 5 November 1947, Clarendon County Board of Education Papers; Pearson to Boulware, 16 December 1947, DeLaine Papers; Stukes to Boulware, 13 December 1947, Clarendon County Board of Education Papers. Grammar and mechanics are Pearson's.

26. Gloster B. Current to Hinton, 9 September 1947, part 26, reel 18, frame 628, NAACP Papers; Annual meeting in Georgetown, 24 October 1947, part 26, reel 18, frames 642, 650, 655, NAACP Papers.

27. Annual meeting in Georgetown, 24 October 1947, part 26, reel 18, frame 656, NAACP Papers. Grammar and mechanics are Hinton's. "Negro Group Will Battle," *Columbia (S.C.) Record,* 17 October 1947, 16.

28. "Integration Sparkplug," *Washington Post,* 5 June 1955, E3; Juan Williams, "Many Masks of Thurgood Marshall," *Washington Post,* 31 January 1993, C1; Marshall to

White, Wilkins, and E. Frederick Morrow, 17 June 1942, part 26, reel 18, frame 450, NAACP Papers; annual meeting, 24 October 1947, part 26, reel 18, frame 643, NAACP Papers.

29. DeLaine to Current, 25 August 1947, part 26, reel 18, frame 273, NAACP Papers; De-Laine to Hinton, 5 February 1948, DeLaine Papers; Hinton to DeLaine, 10 February 1948, DeLaine Papers; DeLaine to Boulware, 6 March 1948, DeLaine Papers.

30. Burke and Hine, "South Carolina State College Law School," 18; Hinton to Levi Pearson, 12 March 1948, DeLaine Papers; DeLaine to Boulware, 6 March 1948, DeLaine Papers.

31. James Pearson v. County Board of Education for Clarendon County, 17 March 1948, S.C. Department of Archives and History. Named defendants also included E. G. Stukes, District 26 chairman; L .B. McCord, Clarendon County board chairman; and J. T. Anderson, state superintendent of education.

32. "Negroes Seek Free," *Columbia (S.C.) State,* 18 March 1948, B10; "South Carolina's Educational Revolution," State Education Finance Commission, box 7, file 202, Figg Papers; DeLaine to Boulware, 9 April 1948, file 2, DeLaine Papers; F. Pearson, interview by the author; "About Us," Levi Pearson Scholarship Fund, https://www.levipearsonscholarshipfund.org/admissions (accessed 18 November 2019).

33. Pearson v. County Board of Education for Clarendon County, Memorandum on Behalf of County Board of Education for Clarendon County, 1948, box 7, file 202, Figg Papers; Boulware to Pearson, 28 May 1948, note added by DeLaine, DeLaine Papers, file 7.

34. DeLaine to Boulware, 16 February 1948, file 2, DeLaine Papers; F. Pearson, interview by the author, 2003; P. Pearson Witherspoon, interview by the author, 2003; Alfreda Pearson, interview by the author, 2003; Claudia Smith Brinson, "No Longer Separate," *Columbia (S.C.) State,* 9 May 2004, 5.

35. F. Pearson, interview by the author; P. Pearson Witherspoon, interview by the author; A. Pearson, interview by the author; Sandi Chaney, "Pearson Proud," *Sumter (S.C.) Daily Item,* 12 May 2004, 1, 7.

36. F. Pearson and J. Pearson, interview by the author, 2003; P. Pearson Witherspoon, interview by the author, 2004; "Billie Fleming, NAACP Pres., Manning Branch," *Road Trip! Through SC Civil Rights History,* S.C. Educational Television.

37. J. Strom Thurmond, keynote address, States' Rights Democratic Convention, Jackson, Miss., 10 May 1948, box 8, file 204, Figg Papers. Executive Order 9980 set regulations regarding fair employment practices in the federal government. Executive Order 9981 abolished discrimination in the armed forces.

38. Resolution Adopted by S.C. Conference of the NAACP, 9–11 October 1948, part 26, reel 18, frames 801–2, NAACP Papers.

39. J. Pearson, interview by the author, 2004; J. A. DeLaine Jr., interview by the author, 2004; B. B. DeLaine, interview by the author, 2004; Boulware to DeLaine, 8 March 1949, DeLaine Papers. Levi, Hammett, Willie, Jesse, Ferdinand, and Charlotte Pearson and Ravenell Felder attended. Montgomery, Report for March 1949, part 26, reel 19, frame 78, NAACP Papers; J. Pearson, interview by the author; McCray, "The Clarendon County Story," 12 April 1957, 9, McCray Papers.

40. Montgomery to Currant, 21 March 1949, part 26, reel 19, frame 35, NAACP Papers. Montgomery, Report for March 1949, NAACP Papers; J. Pearson, interview by the author.

41. J. M. Seals, interview by the author, April 2003; E. E. Richburg to DeLaine, 15 October 1956, DeLaine Papers; Hinton to Current, 13 July 1948, part 26, reel 18, frame 724, NAACP Papers; Montgomery, "Quest for Civil Rights: Eugene A. R. Montgomery"; Montgomery to Current, 21 March 1949, part 26, reel 18, frame 589, NAACP Papers.

42. Montgomery to Hinton, Report for May 1949, part 26, reel 19, frame 67, NAACP Papers.

43. Daisy Oliver Rivers, interview by the author, 1 July 2014; Gardenia Stukes Hightower, interview by the author, 2003; J. Pearson, interview by the author.

44. Montgomery to Hinton, 13 June 1949, part 26, reel 19, frame 67, NAACP Papers; DeLaine, fifty-second installment, *AME Christian Recorder*, DeLaine Papers.

45. E. E. Richburg, "Senior Class and Parents Meeting," 8 June 1949, file 3, DeLaine Papers; Committee on Action to Trustees of District 22, 9 June 1949, Clarendon County Board of Education Papers.

46. DeLaine, "An Open Letter," January 1950, file 5, DeLaine Papers; P. Pearson Witherspoon, interview by the author, 2004; Parents Committee on Action, 9 June 1949, Clarendon County Board of Education Papers.

47. DeLaine to County Board of Education, 9 July 1949, DeLaine Papers; Robert Georgia, Edward Ragin, and DeLaine to County Board, 2 September 1949, Clarendon County Board of Education Papers; DeLaine to Jack Greenburg and All Concerned, "History Leading Up to the U.S. Supreme Court's Decision," 17 May 1974, 2, DeLaine Papers; Gona, *Dawn of Desegregation*, 61, 194; Carrie Richburg Nelson, interview by the author, August 2014; R. M. Elliott, Board of Trustees of School District no. 22, regarding 24 June 1949, Clarendon County Board of Education Papers; Robert Georgia, Edward Ragin, and DeLaine to Board of Trustees, 19 August 1949, Clarendon County Board of Education Papers; J. A. DeLaine Jr., interview by the author, 2003; Undersigned Parents to Superintendent and Trustees, District 22, 25 July 1949, Clarendon County Board of Education Papers.

48. R. Georgia, E. Ragin, and DeLaine to Board of Trustees, 19 August 1949, Clarendon County Board of Education Papers; L. B. McCord, After Considering the Evidence, 1 October 1949, Clarendon County Board of Education Papers; Gona, *Dawn of Desegregation*, 71–77; DeLaine, "Open Letter."

49. Gona, *Dawn of Desegregation*, 56; DeLaine, "History Leading Up to the U.S. Supreme Court's Decision," 2, DeLaine Papers; DeLaine, "School Segregation Case," *AME Church Review*, part 26, reel 18, frame 412, NAACP Papers.

50. J. Pearson, interview by the author, 2003.

51. Harry Briggs et al., to the Board of Trustees for School District no. 22, Clarendon County Board of Education, 11 November 1949, DeLaine Papers; Eliza Briggs, interview by the author, 1994.

52. Nathaniel Briggs, interview by the author, 14 March 2013.

53. Ibid.

54. Briggs v. Elliott, petition, 11 November 1949, S.C. Department of Archives and History.

55. Montgomery to DeLaine, 14 November 1949, DeLaine Papers; "Negro Patrons Ask Clarendon," *Columbia (S.C.) State,* 13 November 1949, 8; "Negro School Test Slated," *Columbia (S.C.) Record,* 14 November 1949, 7; DeLaine, "Things That Happened Since Nov. 11, 1949," DeLaine Papers; A. L. Ragin, interview by the author, 2003.

56. E. Briggs, interview by the author, 1994; William Greider, "Landmark City," *Washington Post,* 3 September 1970, 1; Lochbaum, "Word Made Flesh," 33.

57. Beatrice Brown Rivers, interview by the author, 2003.

58. Annie Gibson, interview by the author, 1994.

59. N. Georgia, interview by the author.

60. N. Briggs, interview by the author; A. L. Ragin, interview by the author.

61. Rebecca Richburg, interview by the author, 1994; J. Richburg, interview by the author, July 2014.

62. D. Oliver Rivers, interview by the author, 2003.

63. Learnease Trammell, interview by the author, 2003.

64. G. Stukes Hightower, interview by the author, 2003.

65. Gona, *Dawn of Desegregation,* 87; Carl T. Rowan, "Reprisals Fail to Cow," *Afro-American Magazine,* 6 March 1954, 3, 13.

66. J. M. Seals, interview by the author; DeLaine to Chairman and Board of Directors, NAACP, 10 January 1955, DeLaine Papers; Saphronia Richburg Clark, interview by the author, July 2014;DeLaine, "Things That Happened."

67. DeLaine, "Clarendon County School Segregation Case," *AME Church Review,* part 26, reel 18, frame 407, NAACP Papers; N. Georgia, interview by the author; E. Briggs, interview by the author.

68. D. Oliver Rivers, interview by the author; N. Georgia, interview by the author; Gona, *Dawn of Desegregation,* 78, 95.

69. J. A. DeLaine, thirty-sixth installment, *AME Christian Recorder,* DeLaine Papers; J. A. DeLaine, "History Leading Up to the U.S. Supreme Court's Decision," 3, DeLaine Papers; Gona, *Dawn of Desegregation,* 99–102; DeLaine, "Essay, 1973," 7, 8, DeLaine Papers. In this 1973 handwritten draft, DeLaine tells the story slightly differently than in the AME series.

70. "History Leading Up to the U.S. Supreme Court's Decision," 3, DeLaine Papers; Gona, *Dawn of Desegregation,* 117, 133–34.

71. G. Stukes Hightower, interview by the author.

72. Anonymous, "Warning Benson," 4 March 1950, DeLaine Papers. Grammar and mechanics are original. Gona, *Dawn of Desegregation,* 124–26.

73. FBI, File # HQ 44–3077, 8 April 1952, 15, DeLaine Papers; FBI, File # HQ 44–3077, 5 May 1950, 16–17, DeLaine Papers; J. A. DeLaine Jr., interview by the author; anonymous, interview by the author, 2004.

74. J. A. DeLaine Jr. and B. B. DeLaine, interviews by the author; Gona, *Dawn of Desegregation,* 127, 134.

75. N. Briggs, interview by the author; D. Oliver Rivers, interview by the author; J. M. Seals, interview by the author.

76. Decision of the Board, Harry Briggs et al., 20 February 1950, private collection of Julian Wiles, Dock Street Theatre, Charleston, South Carolina; Plessy v. Ferguson, 163 U.S. 537 (1896); "Suit Charging Discrimination," *Columbia (S.C.) State*, 18 May 1950, 16.

77. "Klansmen Slate," *Columbia (S.C.) State*, 18 May 1950, 16; Gona, *Dawn of Desegregation*, 128.

78. Yarborough, *Passion for Justice*, 121; "U.S. Judge Outlaws," *Richmond (Va.) Afro-American*, 19 July 1947, 1.

79. "Man They Love to Hate," *Time*, 23 August 1948, 17; "Waring Home Pelted," *Lewiston (Penn.) Daily Sun*, 10 October 1950, 1; "Social Snubs in Carolinas," *Washington Afro-American*, 26 September 1950, 6; Joint Resolution, 14 February 1950, S.C. Department of Archives and History; "Johnston, Thurmond at It," *Columbia (S.C.) State*, 24 May 1950, 1, 7.

80. Yarborough, *Passion for Justice*, 17–21, 96.

81. "'Head-On' Attack," *Washington Afro-American*, 21 March 1950, 8; "Force Is Only Way," *Columbia (S.C.) Record*, 1; "Impeachment of Waring," *Columbia (S.C.) State*, 7 April 1950, 1, 12.

82. T. C. Callison to Figg, 8 February 1951, box 8, file 220, Figg Papers.

83. Sweatt v. Painter, 339 U.S. 629 (1950); McLaurin v. Oklahoma State Regents, 339 U.S. 637 (1950).

84. Henry Lee Moon, "Clarendon County, S.C. School Case," part 3, reel 3, frame 210, NAACP Papers; "History of the Clarendon Case," part 26, series A, frame 345, NAACP Papers; Woods, "Modjeska Simkins," 110; William B. Williams, "Negro Movement Progresses," *Columbia (S.C.) Record*, 1 September 1963, 1, 4; Gergel, *Unexampled Courage*, 218–19.

85. DeLaine, "School Desegregation Case," file 7, DeLaine Papers; DeLaine to Roy Wilkins, 28 November 1961, file 11, DeLaine Papers.

86. E. Briggs, interview by the author; Carter, *Matter of Law*, 97–98; DeLaine, "Things Don't Just Happen," DeLaine Papers, 2. Close to two hundred volunteered to sign petitions, according to Mazie Solomon, Rebecca Richburg, and Arlonial DeLaine Bradford in 1994 interviews with the author. "Climax Approaches," *Columbia (S.C.) State*, 10 May 1951, 11.

87. Pearson et al. v. Murray, 182 A. 590, 169 Md. 478, 103 A.L. R. 706 (1936); Ashmore, *Hearts and Minds*, 186; "Opening Gun," 22 December 1950, file 7, DeLaine Papers.

88. James Byrnes, inaugural address, 6 January 1951, box 7, file 202, Figg Papers; "South Carolina's Educational Revolution."

89. G. Stukes Hightower, interview by the author.

90. "Byrnes Asks Attorney General," *Columbia (S.C.) State*, 3 February 1951, 2; C. E. Anderson, *Eyes Off the Prize*, 70; Byrnes, Address of James F. Byrnes, 16 March 1951, box 8, file 204, Figg Papers; Moon, 21 May 1951, part 3, series 3, reel 3, frame 210, NAACP Papers.

91. Hinton, memo, 21 May 1951, part 3, series 3, reel 3, frame 210, NAACP Papers; "Suit Testing Segregation," *Columbia (S.C.) State,* 28 May 1951, 1; Harry Giamaris, "Lake City Pastor Threatened," *Columbia (S.C.) State,* 10 October 1955, 1, 10; FBI, File # HQ 9–28873, 1955–1956, 37, DeLaine Papers.

92. Carter, *Matter of Law,* 93–96.

93. Celestine Parson Lloyd, interview by the author, 2003, 2004.

94. Figg, correspondence, January–June 1951, box 7, file 181, Figg Papers; Special Bulletin, 22 May 1951, part 26, reel 19, NAACP Papers.

95. DeLaine, fifty-fifth installment, *AME Christian Recorder,* DeLaine Papers; N. Briggs, interview by the author; J. Pearson, interview by the author.

96. Annie Gibson, interview by the author; reprint, *Lighthouse and Informer,* 16 June 1951, part 26, series A, reel 19, NAACP Papers; "S.C. School Case Ends After Two Days," *Washington Afro-American,* 5 June 1951, 1, 2..

97. Briggs v. Elliott, 342 U.S. 350 (1952), Testimony at Trial, 28–29 May 1951, private collection of Julian Wiles, 2–3, 7.

98. Figg to Julian Mitchell, 6 June 1951, file 183, Figg Papers; *Briggs,* 342 U.S. 350, Testimony, 10.

99. *Briggs,* Testimony, 35–45, 51.

100. *Briggs,* Testimony, 73–74.

101. *Briggs,* Testimony, 89–92.

102. *Briggs,* Testimony, 168–69, 174, 176.

103. *Briggs,* Testimony, 127–28; Tom McMahan, "State Admits Inequalities," *Columbia (S.C.) State,* 29 May 1951, 1, 5, 9; "Segregation or Close," *Columbia (S.C.) Record,* 17 March 1951, 1; "House Endorses Byrnes," *Columbia (S.C.) Record,* 20 March 1951, 3; "Suit Opens in SC," *Columbia (S.C.) State,* 27 May 1951, 1.

104. *Briggs,* Testimony, 227–32, 235. Marshall referred to the following cases: Missouri ex rel. Gaines v. Canada 305 U.S. 337 (1938); Sipuel v. Board of Regents, 332 U.S. 631 (1948); Sweatt v. Painter, 339 U.S. 629 (1950).

105. *Briggs,* Testimony, 239–41, 242, 246, 248, 249; *Briggs,* Brief for Defendants at 43, 23 June 1951, box 8, file 209, Figg Papers; "Judges Get Segregation," *Washington Post,* 10 May 1951, 9.

106. *Briggs,* Testimony, 250–53, 260.

107. *Briggs,* Testimony, 261–62, 265.

108. *Briggs,* Memorandum Brief for Plaintiffs at 13, 5 June 1951, box 8, file 210, Figg Papers; *Briggs,* Brief for Defendants, 28 May 1951, box 8, file 209, Figg Papers.

109. Testimonial Honoring Parent Plaintiffs and Their Children, 17 June 1951, part 26, reel 19, frames 343–44, NAACP Papers. Capitalization is from the program. Gona, *Dawn of Desegregation,* 147; Briggs v. Elliott, 98 F. Supp. 529 (E.D. S.C. 1951).

110. Gong Lum v. Rice, 275 U.S. 78 (1927); *Briggs;* Tom McMahan, "School Segregation Sustained," *Columbia (S.C.) State,* 24 June 1951, 1; "Text of Opinion Upholding," *Columbia (S.C.) State,* 25 June 1951, 6.

111. *Briggs.*

112. Ibid. Italics are Waring's.

113. "Order of Argument in the Case, Brown v. Board of Education," U.S. National Archives, Washington, D.C.

114. Austin Adkinson, "Suit Opens in SC," *Columbia (S.C.) State*, 27 May 1951, 1, 10. "Byrnes Lauds," *Columbia (S.C.) Record*, 12 May 1951, 1; R. Beverley Herbert to Figg, 16 October 1952, box 7, file 186, Figg Papers; "McCray Replies," *Columbia (S.C.) State*, 11 November 1960; "Sit Down Threat," *Afro-American*, 6 October 1951, 4; Southerlin, Building Survey for Summerton, S.C. Educational Finance Commission, July 1951, box 8, file 204, Figg Papers.

115. *Briggs*, Statement as to Jurisdiction, at 13, 21, 20 July 1951, box 8, file 210, Figg Papers; *Briggs*, Appeal on Jurisdiction at 8, October 1951, box 8, file 210, Figg Papers.

116. Figg to John W. Davis, 4 September 1951, box 7, file 182, Figg Papers; Patterson, *Brown v Board of Education*, 5; Davis to Figg, 10 October 1951, box 7, file 182, Figg Papers.

117. Hinton, "Democracy and Equality Are Inseparable," Eleventh Annual Meeting, Sumter, South Carolina, 13–14 October 1951, part 26, reel 19, frame 382, NAACP Papers; Legal Redress, part 26, reel 19, frame 426, NAACP Papers.

118. B. B. DeLaine, interview by the author; FBI, File # HQ 44–3077, 24 March 1952, 26–28, DeLaine Papers; Gona, *Dawn of Desegregation*, 154; DeLaine, "Essay, 1973," 7.

119. *Briggs*, Report of Defendants Pursuant to Decree, 21 June 1951, box 8, file 210, Figg Papers.

120. *Briggs*, Appeal from the U.S. District Court for Eastern District of South Carolina, no. 273, 28 January 1952, box 8, file 211, Figg Papers; Waring, 8 January 1952, box 8, file 211, Figg Papers; Yarborough, *Passion for Justice*, 213.

121. *Briggs*, 103 F. Supp. 920, Decree at 3, 5, 13 March 1952, box 8, file 211, Figg Papers; *Briggs*, Order Allowing Appeal from Final Decree, 9 May 1952, box 8, file 211, Figg Papers.

122. Patterson, *Brown v Board*, 31, 35.

123. Davis to Figg, 29 September 1952, box 7, file 185, Figg Papers; *Briggs*, Oppose Jurisdiction and Motion to Dismiss or Affirm at 7, box 8, file 211, Figg Papers.

124. "Judge Hands Body Blow," *Baltimore Afro-American*, 8 April 1952, 1, 8.

125. Davis to Figg, 9 October 1952, file 186, Figg Papers; "Byrnes Position," *Columbia (S.C.) State*, 3 November 1952, 1; "Voters Favor," *Columbia (S.C.) State*, 5 November 1952, 1, 11; Roberts and Klibanoff, *Race Beat*, 209. Only 25 percent of Deep South black residents were registered to vote in the 1950s, due to racist voter requirements and violence.

126. *Briggs*, Reply Brief for Appellants at 1–2, October 1952, box 8, file 211, Figg Papers; Rogers and Taylor, *South Carolina Chronology*, 78; Brown v. Baskin, 174F 2d 391.

127. *Briggs*, Brief for Appellees at 7, 13, 28, 35, October 1952, box 8, file 211, Figg Papers.

128. "200 Negroes Enrolled," *Detroit Tribune*, 20 November 1950, 10; "Order Applies," *Columbia (S.C.) State*, 16 May 1950, 1; George McMillan, "South Surprisingly Calm," *Washington Post*, 21 June 1953, B2.

129. *Briggs*, Brief for the United States as Amicus Curiae at 6, 8, 17 October 1952, box 9, file 219, Figg Papers.

130. George McMillan, "Suit Revolutionizing," *Washington Post,* 23 December 1951, B3; N. Briggs, interview by the author; D. Oliver Rivers, interview by the author; E. Briggs, interview by the author.

131. Chalmers M. Roberts, "Court Arguments Begin," *Washington Post,* 8 December 1952, 1; *Briggs,* Oral Arguments at 4, 14, 9 December 1952, box 9, file 219, Figg Papers.

132. *Briggs,* Oral Arguments at 18–19, 9 December 1952, box 9, file 219, Figg Papers.

133. *Briggs,* Oral Arguments at 40–42, 9 December 1952, box 9, file 219, Figg Papers.

134. *Briggs,* Oral Arguments at 51–52, 9 December 1952, box 9, file 219, Figg Papers; Louis Lautier, "Capital Spotlight," *Washington Afro-American,* 16 December 1952, 6; Carter, *Matter of Law,* 124.

135. *Briggs,* Oral Arguments at 55, 59; Tom McMahan, "School Segregation Hearing," *Columbia (S.C.) State,* 30 May 1951, 1, 8.

136. Davis to Figg, 5 September 1953, box 7, file 188, Figg Papers; Caldwell Withers for Alex McCullough, 9 September 1953, file 188, Figg Papers.

137. Hinton, copy of check, part 26, series A, frames 531–33, NAACP Papers; Kluger, *Simple Justice,* 623, 641.

138. Warren, *Memoirs,* 4, 148; Kluger, *Simple Justice,* 260, 656.

139. Kluger, *Simple Justice,* 656.

140. Warren, *Memoirs,* 667.

141. J. Williams, *Thurgood Marshall,* 225.

142. Figg to Eugene S. Blease, 10 December 1953, box 7, file 189, Figg Papers.

143. Warren, *Memoirs,* 291; Wicker, *Dwight D. Eisenhower,* 55–56.

144. Warren, *Memoirs,* 3; *Brown v. Board,* 347 U.S. 483 (1954).

145. *Brown v. Board;* Warren, *Memoirs,* 3.

146. "45-Year Fight Vindicated," *Columbia (S.C.) State,* 18 May 1954, 1–2; "17 State Attorneys General," *Columbia (S.C.) State,* 20 May 1954, 2; "'Wait-and-See' Attitude," *Columbia (S.C.) State,* 18 May 1954, 1; W. D. Workman, "S.C. Is Depressed," *Charlotte Observer,* 18 May 1954, 1; "Hinton Offers," *Columbia (S.C.) Record,* 17 May 1954, 2.

147. Brinkley and Dyer, *American Presidency,* 353; "'Wait-and-See' Attitude"; "South Loses," *Columbia (S.C.) Record,* 17 May 1954, 1; "House Passes Bill," *Columbia (S.C.) State,* 19 March 1954, 7; "Action Is Uncertain," *Columbia (S.C.) Record,* 17 May 1954, 1; "Refreshing Candor," *Washington Post,* 20 May 1954, 14.

148. "Reaction of South," *New York Times,* 18 May 1954, 1, 20; Saul Pett, "'Deep South' Still Divided," *Washington Post,* 13 June 1954, B8.

149. Frank R. Kent Jr., "Justice Asks 90 Days," *Washington Post,* 25 November 1954, 1; 'Figg Urges Remanding," *Columbia (S.C.) State,* 13 April 1954, 15; "No School Change," *Columbia (S.C.) State,* 3 June 1954, 4; "NAACP to Petition," *Columbia (S.C.) Record,* 25 May 1954, 11.

150. "Court Told Quick 'Mixing,'" *Columbia (S.C.) State,* 13 April 1955, 15; Kluger, *Simple Justice,* 730–32; "Segregation Hearing," *Columbia (S.C.) State,* 19 May 1955, 2.

151. Brown v. Board of Education, 349 U.S. 294 (1955).

152. Reese Daniel and Bill Winter, "3-Judge Court Fixes," *Columbia (S.C.) State,* 16 July 1955, 1; "Petition School Boards," *Columbia (S.C.) State,* 25 May 1954, 1; Reese Daniel,

"Summerton Citizens Want," *Columbia (S.C.) State,* 28 June 1955, 1; "NAACP Sets Quick Action," *Columbia (S.C.) State,* 1 June 1955, 1; James L. Hicks, "Marshall Sets One-Year," *Baltimore Afro-American,* 28 June 1955, 1; "Negroes Petition," *Columbia (S.C.) State,* 30 June 1955, 1; NAACP, "Program to Implement."

153. "Court Did All It Could," *Pittsburgh Courier,* 2 July 1955, 2; "Summerton Board May Close," *Columbia (S.C.) State,* 2 June 1955, 1; "Group Backs Byrnes," *Columbia (S.C.) State,* 12 June 1954, 1.

154. "500 More Plaintiffs Sought," *Columbia (S.C.) State,* 10 July 1955, 1; "NAACP Meets on Clarendon," *Columbia (S.C.) State,* 11 July 1955, 1; DeLaine to Dr. Nolen, n.d., McCray Papers.

155. "Full Text of Segregation Arguments in Columbia," *Columbia (S.C.) State,* 16 July 1955, 6.

156. *Briggs,* 132 F. Supp. 776 (E.D.S.C. 1955); Evelyn Cunningham, "No Race Tension," *Pittsburgh Courier,* 2 July 1955, 2; "NAACP Attorney Denies," *Columbia (S.C.) Record,* 12 September 1955, 1.

157. Carlton Truax, "Fight for Segregation," *Columbia (S.C.) Record,* 15 August 1955, 1, 11; "Elloree Puts Pressure," *Columbia (S.C.) State,* 16 August 1955, 19; "State Leaders Urge," *Florence (S.C.) Morning News,* 21 August 1955, 3; "Elloree Aids," *Florence (S.C.) Morning News,* 17 August 1955, 4; "NAACP Challenged," *Sumter (S.C.) Daily Item,* 22 December 1989, 9B; "Sumter Schools Petitioned," *Columbia (S.C.) Record,* 2 September 1955, 1; "Parents Ask Entry," *Columbia (S.C.) State,* 30 June 1955, 1; "No Race Tension," *Pittsburgh Courier,* 2; "NAACP to Petition," *Columbia (S.C.) State,* 25 May 1954, 1.

158. "In Clarendon," *Columbia (S.C.) State,* 23 August 1955, 24; "New Anti-integration Groups," *Columbia (S.C.) Record,* 24 August 1955, 16; Bob Pierce, "Racial Tensions Mount," *Columbia (S.C.) State,* 28 August 1955, 1, 8.

159. Greider, "Landmark City"; "New Klan Meets Openly," *Washington Post,* 13 June 1955, 8; Elizabeth Geyer, "The 'New' Ku Klux Klan," *Crisis,* March 1956, 147; McMillen, *Citizens' Council,* 74–76; "Citizens Council Groups," *Columbia (S.C.) State,* 29 August 1955, 5; Cohodas, *Strom Thurmond,* 279.

160. "White Advocates," 1 August 1955, *Rome (Ga.) News Tribune,* 24; "Court Did All It Could," *Pittsburgh Courier.*

161. No headline, *Manning (S.C.) Times,* 10 August 1955, private collection of J. Pearson; McCray to Donald P. Gross, 28 April 1957, 1, McCray Papers; "Progress Report," *Baltimore Afro-American,* 17 September 1955, 27.

162. "Names Off Petitions," *Columbia (S.C.) State,* 18 August 1955, 1, 10; Al Keuttner, "Post-Integration Status," *Hendersonville (N.C.) Times-News,* 1 September 1955, 2; "Three Fired Teachers," *Washington Afro-American,* 4 October 1955, 19.

163. C. Richburg Nelson, interview by the author, August 2014; Yvonne Nelson Means, interview by the author, August 2014; S. Richburg Clark, interview by the author, July 2014.

164. McCray, "Council 'Squeezes,'" *Afro-American,* 1 October 1955, 18.

165. Ibid.; B. Brown Rivers, interview by the author; McCray, "Clarendon County Story."

166. B. Brown Rivers, interview by the author; D. Oliver Rivers, interview by the author, 1 July 2014.

167. A. C. Redd to Clarence Mitchell, 21 June 1956, part 22, reel 13, frame 57, NAACP Papers; "Progress Report," 3 September 1955, *Afro-American*, 9; "White Councils," *Afro-American*, 10 September 1955, 21; "Negro Church Burns," *Columbia (S.C.) Record*, 6 October 1955, 1; Geyer, "New Ku Klux Klan," 140; Gona, *Dawn of Desegregation*, 168–72, 175–76; "S.C. Whites Burn," *Jet*, 20 October 1955, 3–5; DuBose, *Road to Brown*, 10–16; FBI, File #HQ 9–28873, October 1955, 22, 25, 34, DeLaine Papers.

168. "J. A. Delane," 7 October 1955, DeLaine Papers; Fordham, *True Stories*, 69–72; Chestnut, *Lynching*; "J. A. Delane." Original's grammar and mechanics are duplicated, except the word *final* is underlined four times.

169. B. B. DeLaine, interview by the author; J. A. DeLaine Jr., interview by the author; "Still Missing," *Columbia (S.C.) Record*, 13 October 1955, 1.

170. "DeLaine to Fight Return," *Columbia (S.C.) Record*, 21 October 1955, 1; "Militant South Carolina Minister," *Jet*, 3 November 1955, 6–8; "Pastor Flees," *Washington Post*, 20 October 1955, 28; "Fugitive Pastor," *Washington Post*, 21 October 1955, 51.

171. FBI, #HQ 9–28873, 15, 32, DeLaine Papers; J. A. DeLaine Jr., interview by the author; S. DuBose, *Road to Brown*, 27–30; Mattie Belton DeLaine, interview by McFadden.

172. "Still Missing"; "Minister Involved," *Columbia (S.C.) State*, 13 October 1955; "Minister Cleared in 1955 Case," *Jet*, 30 October 2000, 3, 30, 31; FBI, #HQ 9–28873, 13 October 1955, 44, DeLaine Papers; "Get Hands on Minister," *Afro-American*, 29 October 1955, 1, 17; Gona, *Dawn of Desegregation*, 181–89. Gona offers a day-by-day description of the October events. FBI, #HQ 9–28873, 13 October 1955, 41, DeLaine Papers. Grammar and mechanics are DeLaine's. B. B. DeLaine, interview by the author; "Militant S.C. AME Minister Tells," *Jet*, 3 November 1955, 6; "Tells of Carolina 'Terror,'" *Washington Post*, 21 October 1955, 51.

173. "Hollings Reproaches NAACP," *Columbia (S.C.) Record*, 11 October 1955, 3; General Session Court, Assault and Battery True Bill, 4 October 1955, DeLaine Papers.

174. "Still Missing"; FBI, File #HQ 9–28873, October 1955, 32, DeLaine Papers; "DeLaine Furniture Moved," *Columbia (S.C.) Record*, 15 October 1955; "DeLaine Guarded," *Columbia (S.C.) Record*, 19 October 1955, 1; "Shoots Two," *Jet*, 27 October 1955, 6; "Shot in Self Defense," *Afro-American*, 22 October 1955, 1–2.

175. "Extradition," *Columbia (S.C.) Record*, 20 October 1955, 1; FBI, File #HQ 9–28873, Price to Rosen, 11 November 1955, 59–60, DeLaine Papers; "Fight Extradition," *Afro-American*, 5 November 1955, 3; "Militant Pastor Shoots," *Jet*, 27 October 1955, 7; "Minister Tells," 8; "Fight against Return," *Washington Afro-American*, 29 November 1955, 8; Essay, "After Being Fingerprinted," 3 December 1955, DeLaine Papers; FBI, HQ #44–9481, "Until Jan. 16 on DeLaine Case," 32, DeLaine Papers; "S.C. Backs Down," *Afro-American*, 7 January 1956, 16; "Governor May Not Ask," *Columbia (S.C.) State*, 29 December 1955, 1; "Accused by DeLaine," *Afro-American*, 14 January 1956, 3.

176. Quint, *Profile in Black and White*, 25, 47, 83; "Segregation Biggest Issue," *Spartanburg (S.C.) Herald-Journal*, 29 December 1955, 2; "Schools Opening," *Columbia (S.C.)*

Record, 5 September 1955, 1; "Board May Close," *Columbia (S.C.) State,* 2 June 1955, 1; "Rev. L. B. McCord," *Columbia (S.C.) Record,* 6 September 1955, 1, 7.

177. "White Councils"; "Militant Pastor Shoots," 7; Geyer, "'New' Ku Klux Klan," 144–45; McCray, "Shotgun Blasts Hit," *Afro-American,* 1 October 1955, 18.

178. Bob Pierce, "Racial Tensions Mount," *Columbia (S.C.) State,* 28 August 1955, 1, 8; Pierce, "Draw Lines," *Columbia (S.C.) State,* 21 September 1955, 13, 18; "Orangeburg Negro Fund," *Columbia (S.C.) State,* 24 August 1957, 1, 13; "Citizen Councils Grown," *Columbia (S.C.) Record,* 7 September 1955.

179. George Minter, "New Segregation Controversy," *Columbia (S.C.) State,* 1 September 1955, 1; Roy Wilkins, "War against the United States," *Crisis,* December 1955, 582–83.

180. "May Close Schools," *Columbia (S.C.) State,* 2 June 1955, A1; "'Minority Rights,'" *Columbia (S.C.) Record,* 20 May 1954, 4; "Clarendon Case Admittedly," *Columbia (S.C.) Record,* 2 September 1955, 1; "Hinton Assails," *Columbia (S.C.) Record,* 22 October 1955, 1.

181. "Courier Exposes," *Pittsburgh Courier,* 17 September 1955, 4.

182. Robert A. Willis, "Segregation Biggest Issue," *Spartanburg (S.C.) Herald-Journal,* 30 December 1955, 2; "New Schools Cited," *New York Times,* 13 March 1956, 22.

183. "Interposition Resolution," *Columbia (S.C.) State,* 15 January 1956, 1; Concurrent Resolution, part 20, reel 10, frame 927, NAACP Papers; "NAACP Called Subversive," *Columbia (S.C.) State,* 23 February 1956, C2.

184. "Public Jobs in SC Barred," *Columbia (S.C.) State,* 18 March 1956, 1; "Interposition Resolution Signed," *Columbia (S.C.) State,* 15 January 1956, 1; Concurrent Resolution, part 20, reel 10, frame 927, NAACP Papers; McMillen, *Citizens' Council,* 307–8.

185. "Reprisals Fail to Cow," 3; Current to Wilkins, 10 October 1956, part 20, reel 10, frame 649, NAACP Papers; DeLaine to Board of Directors, NAACP, 10 January 1955, DeLaine Papers; J. M. Seals, interview by the author.

186. McCray, "Council Pressure Unites," *Afro-American,* 15 December 1956, 22; I. DeQuincey Newman Annual Report, 1960–61, part 25, reel 30, frame 483, NAACP Papers; L. A. Blackman to Ruby Hurley, 26 November 1956, part 20, reel 10, frame 882, NAACP Papers. Grammar and mechanics are Blackman's.

187. Bob Pierce, "Citizens Council, NAACP Draw Lines," *Columbia (S.C.) State,* 21 September 1955, 13; "Students Hit Surveillance," *Columbia (S.C.) State,* 12 April 1956, 1.

188. "All Squeeze Victims," 26 January 1956, part 20, reel 10, frame 825, NAACP Papers; Woods, "Modjeska Simkins," 112–14; John A. Morsell to Henry Lee Moon, "Racial Reprisals," 10 February 1960, part 20, reel 10, frame 668, NAACP Papers; "Food Caravan," *Columbia (S.C.) State,* 18 March 1956, 1.

189. Shirley McDonald Patterson, interview by the author, 2003; "Waring Helps Collect," *Columbia (S.C.) State,* 18 March 1956, 1; McCray, "Council Pressure Unites."

190. McCray, "Hate Boycott Boomerangs," *Afro Magazine,* 15 October 1957, 8; Wilkins to DeLaine, 11 December 1961, part 20, reel 10, frame 770, NAACP Papers; McCray, "Answer to Boycott," *Washington Afro-American,* 21 May 1957, 7.

191. "Boulware Withdraws in Clarendon Case," *Columbia (S.C.) State,* 4 April 1956, 15; "Integration Goal," *Pittsburgh Press,* 3 August 1958, 7; "New Integration Attempt,"

Columbia (S.C.) State, 2 August 1958, 2; "Integration Petitions Answered," *Columbia (S.C.) State,* 20 August 1958, 1.

192. "Regrettable Move," *Columbia (S.C.) State,* 5 August 1958, 4; Jim Laxson, "Resistance to School Integration," *Columbia (S.C.) State,* 31 August 1958, C10.

193. "SC Negro Pupils Seek," *Columbia (S.C.) State,* 31 August 1959, 1; "Names Told," *Columbia (S.C.) State,* 2 September 1959, B2; "Hollings Says Lots of Talk," *Columbia (S.C.) State,* 2 September 1959, 10.

194. "Integration Spreading," *Washington Afro-American,* 8 September 1959, 2; "Gressette Group and Governor," *Columbia (S.C.) State,* 9 September 1959, 15.

195. DeLaine to Roy Wilkins, 28 November 1961, part 20, reel 10, frames 561–63, NAACP Papers. Grammar and mechanics are DeLaine's.

196. N. Briggs, interviews by the author, 2013, 2014; McCray, "Clarendon County Story."

197. Current to Wilkins, 24 January 1962, part 20, reel 10, frame 573, NAACP Papers; Current to Hinton, 24 January 1962, part 20, reel 10, frame 579, NAACP Papers; Current to Mrs. Myers, Lincoln Hospital, part 20, reel 10, frame 576, NAACP Papers; Current to Harlem Hospital of Nursing, part 20, reel 10, frame 577, NAACP Papers; Current to Harry Briggs Sr., 29 January 1962, part 20, reel 10, frame 579, NAACP Papers; Wilkins to Current, 29 January 1962, part 20, reel 10, frame 584, NAACP Papers; "Things to Do RE Harry Briggs," part 20, reel 10, frame 603, NAACP Papers; Current to Wilkins, 11 January 1962, part 20, reel 10, frames 573–74, NAACP Papers; Voucher, 24 January 1962, part 20, reel 10, frame 575, NAACP Papers.

198. Levi Pearson to DeLaine, part 20, reel 10, frame 783, NAACP Papers; Chaney, "Pearson Proud"; DeLaine to Wilkins, 3 October 1962, part 20, reel 10, frame 782, NAACP Papers. Grammar and mechanics are the Pearsons' and DeLaine's.

199. John Morsell to Henry Lee Moon, 10 February 1960, part 20, reel 10, frame 668; Wilkins to Briggs, 1 February 1962, part 20, reel 10, frame 586, NAACP Papers.

200. Scott's Branch High, National Center for Education Statistics, U.S. Department of Education; Dobrasko, *South Carolina's Equalization Schools.* In Brunson v. Board of Trustees of School District no. 1, 244 F. Supp. 859 (1965), forty-two plaintiffs filed on April 13, 1960, for admission to enjoin Clarendon County from operating a compulsory segregated school system. The lawsuit was filed by McQueen Brunson, father of Bobby, Elizabeth, and Ellis Brunson. Levi Pearson was among the adult plaintiffs. In 1965, only nine of the minor plaintiffs remained of school age: Charles Hilton, Rita McDonald, Mary Oliver, Henry Jeff Ragin, Lucretia Ragin, Willie Jerome Ragin, Rochelle Stukes, Marcian Stukes, and Idella Tindal.

201. Robert M. Ford, "Desegregation Effort," *Lodi (Cal.) News-Sentinel,* 27 December 1967, 6; S. DuBose, *Road to Brown,* 114–16; John Osborne, "Asks Aid Again," *Washington Post,* 20 February 1966, M5; WIS Staff, "SC Woman Remembers Integration Struggle," WIS-TV, 17 May 2014. https://www.wistv.com/story/25544895/on-60th -anniversary-of-brown-v-board-woman-remembers-integration-struggle/.

202. Elaine Whittenberg v. Greenville County School District, 298 F. Supp. 784 (D.S.C. 1969); Green v. County School Board of New Kent County, 391 U.S. 430 (1968); "Doubtful Clarendon Plan," *Spartanburg (S.C.) Herald-Journal,* 1 July 1970, 19; Earl

Caldwell, "Schools Remain Closed," *New York Times,* 4 September 1970, 11; Bonnie L. Blackburn, "All White to All Black," *Sumter (S.C.) Daily Item,* 7 October 1990, 4; "Scott's Branch Graduates Leave," *Sumter (S.C.) Daily Item,* 5 June 1994, 1, 12; Alan Richards, "Stuck in Time," *Education Week,* 21 January 2004, 30–34. In the 2019–20 school year, the high school remained 96 percent black.

203. Wayne King, "SC Segregation: A Curious Legacy," *Lexington (N.C.) Dispatch,* 18 May 1979, 2; N. Briggs, interview by the author.

Three: Forward Motion

1. Tara Wilson and Kimya Dawson-Smith, "Mary Allen College," Amistad Research Center, University of Illinois at Urbana-Champaign; Emily Ivory, interview by the author, 23 July 2003.

2. E. Ivory, interview by the author; Harbison Agricultural College Photograph Collection, South Caroliniana Library, University of South Carolina, 23 July 2003; "Cecil A. Ivory: Presbyterian Leader and Activist," Presbyterian Historical Society, National Archives of the Presbyterian Church (USA), https://www.history.pcusa .org/blog/2018/02/cecil-ivory-presbyterian-leader-and-activist (accessed 10 April 2020).

3. E. Ivory, interview by the author; "Dr. C. A. Ivory" scrapbook, Ivory private collection, 23 July 2003; Fred Roukos Sheheen, interview by the author, 2005.

4. Barry Yeoman, "A Taste for Tolerance," 1 May 2004, http://barryyeoman.com/2004 /05/taste-for-tolerance-charlotte/.

5. Currie, "Before Rosa Parks"; Plessy v. Ferguson, 163 U.S. 537 (1896); "Case Appealed," *Columbia (S.C.) State,* 24 May 1955, 1.

6. Currie and Virginia L. Vroegop, "Sarah Mae Flemming, 1933–1993" in "Before Rosa Parks," 83; "Bus Segregation Appealed," *Columbia (S.C.) State,* 24 May 1955, 1; "Appeals Seating Ruling," *Columbia (S.C.) Record,* 21 June 1955, 1, 6; Flemming v South Carolina Electric Gas Company, 128 F. Supp. 469 (E.D.S.C. 1955). Grammar and mechanics are Timmerman's.

7. Henderson v. United States et al., 339 U.S. 816 (1950); *Flemming,* 224 F.2d 752 (1955); "Bus Company Appeals," *Columbia (S.C.) Record,* 15 September 1955, 13; "Bus Ruling Right," *Columbia (S.C.) State,* 25 April 1956, 7; "Timmerman Again Dismisses," *Baltimore Afro-American,* 19 June 1956; "PSC Says," *Columbia (S.C.) State,* 11 May 1956, 1, 2; "Still Legal," *Pittsburgh Post-Gazette,* 11 May 1956, 2; Robert Pfarr, "All Segregation 'Illegal,'" *Columbia (S.C.) Record,* 15 December 1956, 1, 8; John H. McCray, "SC Jury Rejects," *Washington Afro-American,* 4 June 1957, 1; "Loses Bus Case," *Columbia (S.C.) State,* 11 June 1957, 1, 12.

8. Browder v. Gayle, 142 F. Supp. 707 (M.D. Ala. 1956); Gayle v. Browder, 352 U.S. 903 (1956); Luther A. Huston, "High Court Rules," *New York Times,* 14 November 1956, 1, 22; E. Ivory, interview by the author, November 2005.

9. "Bus Boycott," *Columbia (S.C.) State,* 2 August 1957, D1; "Jottings," *Jet,* 25 May 1961, 11; Addelene Austin White, interview by the author, November 2005.

10. White, interview by the author.

11. "Reported Results," *Charlotte Observer,* 2 August 1957, B1; Trezz W. Anderson,

"Boycotters Buy Second," *Pittsburgh Courier,* Ivory private collection; Anderson, "Woman behind Start," *Pittsburgh Courier,* 14 September 1957, Ivory private collection; Dr. Horace Goggins, interview by the author, 2005; Ray Chandler, "1950s: Protesters Challenge," *Rock Hill (S.C.) Evening Herald,* 16 April 2002, E31.

12. "Pastor Threatened," *Washington Afro-American,* 6 August 1957, 13; Darnell Ivory, interview by the author, 2005.

13. Anderson, "Boycotters Buy Second"; White, interview by the author; "Bus Boycott"; Chuck Hauser, "Ruin for Bus Line," *Charlotte Observer,* 3 August 1957, B1; Chandler, "1950s: Protestors."

14. Handwritten notes, Ivory private collection.

15. Anderson, "Boycotters Buy Second"; "Urge Full Observance," *Charlotte Observer,* 6 August 1957, 11; White, interview by the author.

16. "32-Passenger Bus," *Rock Hill (S.C.) Evening Herald,* 26 August 1957, 1; "Deny NAACP," *Columbia (S.C.) State,* 3 August 1957, B1; E. Ivory, interview by the author, November 2005.

17. "Boycotters Buy Second," *Pittsburgh Courier;* Bus Drivers, n.d., Ivory private collection; Goggins, interview by the author; E. Ivory, interview by the author, 2005; Sheheen, interview by the author, November 2005.

18. "Boycotters Explore," *Rock Hill (S.C.) Evening Herald,* 27 August 1957, 1; White, interview by the author.

19. E. Ivory, interview by the author, November 2005; D. Ivory, interview by the author, 12 September 2006; "Negroes Struggle," *Arizona Sun,* 5 September 1957, 1.

20. Willoughby, *Good Town,* 211–12; Ivory to Mayor, 3 August 1960, Ivory private collection; Goggins, interview by the author.

21. Willie T. Buckingham to Rev. C. A. Ivory, 22 August 1957, Ivory private collection; "Listen," 9 June 1960, Ivory private collection; Anonymous to Hon. Bob Hayes and York County Delegation, 23 October 1957, Ivory private collection. Mechanics, grammar, and underlining are letter writers'.

22. "New Klan," *Rock Hill (S.C.) Herald,* 22 August 1957, 1; "Klan Recruiting," *Columbia (S.C.) Record,* 22 February 1957, 2; E. Ivory, interview by the author, 23 July 2003.

23. Anderson, "Boycotters Buy." Italics are the reporter's. "Mixed Bus Operation," *Washington Afro-American,* 21 January 1958, 17; "Negroes Struggle," *Arizona Sun.*

24. Ivory to *Rock Hill (S.C.) Evening Herald,* 8 December 1959, Ivory private collection; Ivory, "Need for a Patrol Wagon," *Rock Hill (S.C.) Evening Herald,* 26 May 1959, Ivory private collection. Grammar and mechanics are Ivory's or the newspaper's.

25. Ray Chandler, "Stand on Civil Rights," *Rock Hill (S.C.) Evening Herald,* 16 April 2002, E32.

26. Cecil Ivory to South Carolina Conference NAACP, Summary of Sitdown Demonstrations, Rock Hill, South Carolina, Ivory private collection.

27. Ivory, Summary of Sitdown.

28. Sheheen, interview by the author; E. Ivory, interview by the author, 23 July 2006; D. Ivory, interview by the author; Willie McCleod, interview by the author, 2005.

29. Sheheen, interview by the author; Chandler, "Stand on Civil Rights."

30. Special citation, Cecil Augustus Ivory, 30 May 1960, Ivory private collection.

31. "Crippled Minister Arrested," *CORE-lator,* June 1960, 1, reel 49, frame 120, CORE Papers, Thomas Cooper Library, University of South Carolina; "Ivory, Hamm Arrested," *Rock Hill (S.C.) Evening Herald,* 7 June 1960, 1; Ivory to Donald Sampson, 8 June 1960, Ivory private collection.

32. Ivory to Lawrence Still, *Jet,* 8 June 1960, Ivory private collection; "Invalid NAACP Leader," 9 July 1960, part 21, reel 22, frame 286, NAACP Papers; City of Rock Hill v. Hamm, 128 S.E.2d. 907 (S.C. 1962).

33. "Does Not Appear," *Columbia (S.C.) State,* 15 July 1960, 16; "Two More Sit-Ins," *Columbia (S.C.) State,* 20 July 1960, 14; NAACP Special Citation, June 1960, Ivory private collection; NAACP Certificate of Merit, 24 September 1960, Ivory private collection; Goggins, interview by the author.

34. E. Ivory, interviews by the author, 23 July 2003; 12 September 2006.

35. Clarence Graham, interview by the author; Cecil A. Ivory to Thomas Gaither, 14 February 1961, Ivory private collection; James Farmer to C. A. Ivory, 27 February 1961, Ivory private collection.

36. Carlton Truax, "Citizens Council Credited," *Columbia (S.C.) State,* 14 February 1961, 1, 2.

37. Cecil A. Ivory, undated personal notes, Ivory Private Collection; E. Ivory, interviews by the author, November 2005; 23 July 2003.

38. E. Ivory, interviews by the author, November 2005; 23 July 2003; Cecil Ivory to Levi G. Byrd, 1 March 1961, Ivory private collection.

39. A. T. Brown Jr. to Cecil Ivory, 23 March 1961, Ivory private collection; "Council Again Refuses," *Rock Hill (S.C.) Evening Herald,* 11 April 1961, 1.

40. Boynton v. Virginia, 364 U.S. 454 (1960). The court had already ruled in *Morgan v. Virginia,* 328 U.S. 373 (1946), that segregation of interstate and intrastate carriers placed undue burdens on interstate commerce. Gaither, interview by the author, 2019.

41. Lewis, *Walking with the Wind,* 141–42; Arsenault, *Freedom Riders,* 121–22. In 2009, Elwin Wilson apologized to U.S. Rep. John Lewis privately and publicly for attacking Lewis and other 1961 Freedom Riders in Rock Hill. Lewis said Wilson's apology was the first personal apology for a specific attack that he had ever received. See https ://www.youtube.com/watch?v=Y77fUFUfk9I.

42. Lewis, *Walking with the Wind,* 143; Arsenault, *Freedom Riders,* 124, 457. Mob violence in Anniston and Birmingham, Alabama, led CORE to end the first Freedom Ride, but SNCC members and students nationwide continued the rides. The Interstate Commerce Commission ruled on November 1, 1961, that segregation on interstate buses and facilities was illegal. At year's end black and white testers were served without incident in Charleston, Columbia, Greenville, Rock Hill, Spartanburg, and Sumter.

43. "2 Negro Girls," *Columbia (S.C.) State,* 16 May 1961, 10; Memorial Services, 11 November 1962, Rev. J. Herbert Nelson private collection.

44. E. Ivory, interviews by the author, November 2005; 23 July 2003. The Supreme Court ruled in Hamm v. City of Rock Hill, 379 U.S. 306 (1964), that the Civil Rights Act of 1964 prevented federal prosecution of individuals attempting to use public accommodations and applied retroactively to state prosecutions. Ivory's appeal ended with his death.

Four: "Whatever They Call You, That's Not Your Name"

1. Marvin Sykes, "Woolworth Made Target," *Greensboro (N.C.) Record,* 2 February 1960, B1; Sykes, "AT&T Students Launch," *Greensboro (N.C.) Record,* 2 February 1960, B1; Wolff, *Lunch at the 5 & 10,* 11–35; "Negroes in South," *New York Times,* 3 February 1960, 22.

2. Farmer, *Lay Bare,* 103–8; "Student Protest Movement," Southern Regional Council, 25 February 1960, 3–4; Herbert L. Wright, Special Report of Sitdowns, n.d., part 22, reel 22, frame 70, NAACP Papers; District of Columbia v. John R. Thompson Co., Inc., 346 U.S. 100 (1953); Cecil J. Williams, interview by the author, 14 November 2019. Mary Church Terrell was a cofounder and the first president of the National Association of Colored Women and a charter member of the NAACP. Initially a sit-in was commonly called a "sitdown," a term used by labor unions to describe occupying a workplace but not working. That was inaccurate, thus the shift to "sit-in."

3. "Dime Stores Cooperate," *CORE-lator,* January 1951, reel 49, frame 33, CORE Papers, Thomas Cooper Library, University of South Carolina; "Good Work," *CORE-lator,* January–February 1954, reel 49, frame 70, CORE Papers; Shirley Zoloth, "Miami CORE Story," *CORE-lator,* Summer 1959, reel 49, frame 111, CORE Papers; Gordon Carey, "Action Institute Aids," *CORE-lator,* Fall 1959, reel 49, frame 111, CORE Papers.

4. Special Report of Sitdowns, part 21, reel 22, frame 081, NAACP Papers; Blair Jr., *Who Speaks,* 4 March 1964, https://whospeaks.library.vanderbilt.edu/interview/ezell-blair-stokely-carmichael-lucy-thornton-and-jean-wheeler (accessed 18 November 2019); "AT&T Students Launch," *Greensboro (N.C.) Record;* Wolff, *Lunch at the 5 & 10,* 11–35; Jim Schlosser, "Four Men Summon," *Greensboro (N.C.) Record,* 27 January 1985; Farmer, interview by Baker.

5. "AT&T Students Launch"; Perry Mullen, "Greensboro Incident," *Gadsden (Ala.) Times,* 26 April 1960, 2; "Movement by Negroes Growing," *Greensboro (N.C.) Daily News,* 4 February 1960, B1; Claude Sitton, "Negro Sitdowns Stir Fear," *New York Times,* 15 February 1960, 1, 18; Sitton, "Negroes Press," *New York Times,* 21 February 1960, 143.

6. Wolff, *Lunch at the 5 & 10,* 35–55; "Aid Given," *Greensboro (N.C.) Daily News,* 5 February 1960, B1; "White Men Arrested," *Greensboro (N.C.) Daily News,* 6 February 1960, B1; "Counters to Remain Closed," *Greensboro (N.C.) Daily News,* 8 February 1960, B1; Chafe, *Greensboro, North Carolina,* 79–86; "White Students Act," *New York Times,* 5 February 1960, 12.

7. "Klan Tries to Halt," *New York Times,* 6 February 1960, 20; "Negro Protests Lead," *New York Times,* 7 February 1960, 35; Jonathan Murray, "Greensboro Sit-In," *North Carolina History Project: An Encyclopedia of the Old North State,* http://northCarolinahistory.org/encyclopedia/greensboro-sit-in/ (accessed 18 November 2019); Special Report, part 21, reel 22, frame 72, NAACP Papers.

8. "Negroes' Sitdown Hits," *New York Times,* 9 February 1960, 16; Sitton, "Negroes Extend Sitdown Protest," *New York Times,* 10 February 1960, 21; "Store Closed," *Greensboro (N.C.) Record,* 8 February 1960, 1; Sitton, "Negroes Extend Store Picketing," *New York Times,* 11 February 1960, 22; Almetta Cooke Brooks, "Lunch Counter Strikes," *Greensboro (N.C.) Daily News,* 12 February 1960, 1.

9. "Negro Protests," *Greensboro (N.C.) Daily News,* 12 February 1960, 10; "Segregation Protest Spreads," *Columbia (S.C.) State,* 10 February 1960, 1; "Protest at Charlotte," *Greensboro (N.C.) Daily News,* 10 February 1960, 3.

10. "Negroes Splattered," *Greensboro (N.C.) Daily News,* 11 February 1960, 1.

11. "41 Negroes Charged," *Greensboro (N.C.) Daily News,* 13 February 1960, 1; Teresa Leonard, "February 1960 Sit-Ins Move to Raleigh, N.C.," *Durham (N.C.) News & Observer,* 13 February 2013, https://www.mcclatchydc.com/news/special-reports /polygraph-files/article24744823.html; "South Is Warned," *New York Times,* 28 February 1960, 46; "Action in the South," *CORE-lator,* March 1960, reel 49, frame 116, CORE Papers; CORE to Dear Friend, 11 February 1960, administrative, general, January–February 1960, SCCHR Papers, South Caroliniana Library, University of South Carolina; Blair, *Who Speaks.*

12. "Seating Row," *Columbia (S.C.) State,* 9 February 1960, 7; "Lunch Counter Move," *Sumter (S.C.) Daily Item,* 12 February 1960, 1; "Rock Hill Stores," *Sumter (S.C.) Daily Item,* 12 February 1960, 1; "Rock Hill Bomb," *Sumter (S.C.) Daily Item,* 13 February 1960, 1; "41 Negro Demonstrators Arrested," *Columbia (S.C.) State,* 13 February 1960, 1, 14; "Gressette Cites Laws," *Columbia (S.C.) Record,* 26 February 1960, 1; "NAACP Man," *Columbia (S.C.) Record,* 27 February 1960, 1; "Peaceful Sitdown Explodes," *Sumter (S.C.) Daily Item,* 24 February 1960, 1; "Three Negroes Stage," *Columbia (S.C.) State,* 24 February 1960, 13.

13. Farmer, *Lay Bare,* 192; Sitton, "Negroes Extend Store Picketing"; I. DeQuincey Newman, Sitdowns at Orangeburg, part 20, reel 10, frames 683–90, NAACP Papers; "Students Organize," *New York Times,* 6 March 1960, 43; Wayne A. Wiegand, "8 Negroes Sit-In," in "Desegregating Libraries in the American South," *American Libraries,* 1 June 2017, American Library Association, https://americanlibrariesmagazine .org/2017/06/01/desegregating-libraries-american-south/ (accessed 18 November 2019).

14. "Picketing Disbanded," *Sumter (S.C.) Daily Item,* 26 February 1960, 1; "26 Negroes Arrested," *Sumter (S.C.) Daily Item,* 4 March 1960, 1; "Negroes Jailed," *Columbia (S.C.) State,* 5 March 1960, 1; "Cross Burned," *Sumter (S.C.) Daily Item,* 7 March 1960, 1; "BB Shot Fired," *Sumter (S.C.) Daily Item,* 9 March 1960, 1; "Sit-In Backed," *New York Times,* 6 March 1960, 45; "South Carolina," *Student Voice,* August 1960, Civil Rights Movement Veterans, 6, http://www.crmvet.org/docs/sv/sv6008.pdf (accessed 18 November 2019).

15. Sitton, "Negroes' Dissatisfaction," *New York Times,* 6 March 1960, E3; "26 Negroes Arrested"; "South Is Warned"; "Voices Lifted," *Columbia (S.C.) State,* 22 February 1960, 1; Sitton, "Negroes Press"; "Student Protest Movement," SRC; "Aimed at Negro Sitdowns," *Sumter (S.C.) Daily Item,* 2 March 1960, 7.

16. Carey, interview by Judith Vecchione.

17. James R. Robinson, "Meaning of the Sit-Ins," CORE, 1960, 2, https://www.crmvet .org/docs/60_core_sit-ins.pdf (accessed 18 November 2019).

18. Claudia Smith Brinson, "Quiet Man Helped Change," *Columbia (S.C.) State,* 4 May 2003, D1.

19. "Weekend of Cross Burnings," *Sumter (S.C.) Daily Item,* 28 March 1960, 11.

20. "Dixie Lunch Counter Strike," *Jet,* 3 March 1960, 4.

21. "No Let Up Seen," *Sumter (S.C.) Daily Item,* 21 March 1960, 1; "Why Violence Fails," *Jet,* 17 March 1960, 14–15; "NAACP Lawyers," *Columbia (S.C.) State,* 22 February 1959, 32; "Revolt of Negro Youth," *Ebony,* May 1960, 36–40.

22. "Four Negro Demonstrators," *Columbia (S.C.) State,* 13 February 1960, 1; "Rock Hill Stores"; "Negroes' Protest Spreads," *New York Times,* 13 February 1960, 1, 6.

23. Cecil A Ivory to S.C. Conference NAACP, Summary of Sitdown Demonstrations, Rock Hill, South Carolina, scrapbook, Darnell Ivory private collection; Peck, *Freedom Ride,* 95; *CORE Rules for Action,* CORE, 15 April 1963, https://www.crmvet.org /docs/corerules.pdf (accessed 18 November 2019).

24. Carey, "Nonviolence and the Sit-Ins," *CORE-lator,* March 1960, reel 49, frame 115, CORE Papers; "New Leader," *Jet,* 25 May 1961, 11; Carey, interview by Judith Vecchione.

25. James T. McCain Sr., interviews by the author, February 1994 and May 2003.

26. McCain, interviews by the author; Brinson, "Quiet Man Helped Change."

27. McCain, annual calendars, James T. McCain Papers, South Caroliniana Library; McCain, interviews by the author; Patricia Stephens Due, interview by the author, 2003; Brinson and Roddie Burris, "McCain Dies at 98," *Columbia (S.C.) State,* 6 June 2003, B1.

28. Abe Plummer, interview by the author, 1 August 2010.

29. Plummer, interview by the author; Brinson, "Learned Ways of Gandhi," *Columbia (S.C.) State,* 4 May 2003, D1.

30. "'Wait and See,'" *Rock Hill (S.C.) Herald,* 11 February 1960, 1.

31. Plummer, interview by the author; Martin Leroy Johnson, interview by the author, 6 June 2011.

32. Ivory, Summary, scrapbook; "Estimated 100 Quietly Take Seats," *Rock Hill (S.C.) Evening Herald,* 12 February 1960, 1.

33. Ivory, Summary, scrapbook; "Estimated 100 Quietly Take Seats"; "41 Negroes Charged." After the presidential inauguration of Barack Obama, Elwin Wilson apologized to Rock Hill protesters for his racist actions.

34. "Farley Smith Calms," *Columbia (S.C.) State,* 24 February 1960, 11; Carlton Truax, "Averting Race Riot," *Columbia (S.C.) State,* 14 February 1961, 1, 2; FBI, "Delegates of 11 States Form CCA," 9 April 1956, https://archive.org/stream/CItizensCouncil Movement/Citizens%20Councils%20of%20America-HQ-1_djvu.txt; FBI, Citizens Councils, Savannah Division, 8 January 1957, https://archive.org/stream/CItizens CouncilMovement/CitCouncils-Savannah#page/n3/mode/2up/search/South +Carolina; FBI, Citizens Councils, Savannah Division, 27 December 1958, https:// archive.org/stream/CItizensCouncilMovement/CitCouncils-Savannah#page/n75 /mode/2up/search/South+Carolina%3B.

35. "White Groups Asks," *Rock Hill (S.C.) Evening Herald,* 13 February 1960, 1; Sitton, "White Group Acts," *New York Times,* 14 February 1960, 31; Alice Spearman to Rabbi David S. Gruber, 19 February 1960, administrative, general, January–February 1960, SCCHR Papers; "Negroes' Protest Spreads," *New York Times,* 13 February 1960, 1.

36. "Hollings Raps," *Rock Hill (S.C.) Evening Herald,* 17 February 1960, 1; "Lunch Counter Bill," *Rock Hill (S.C.) Evening Herald,* 17 February 1960, 1; "Citizen Council Leader," *Rock Hill (S.C.) Evening Herald,* 17 February 1960, 1.

37. Bill Mahoney, "'Sitdowns' Likened," *Columbia (S.C.) State,* 1 March 1960, B1; Sitton, "Negro Sitdowns Stir Fear."

38. Newman, Ivory attachment, Summary of Sitdown Demonstrations, part 20, reel 10, frame 680, NAACP Papers; Plummer, interview by the author; "Interracial Fighting," *Columbia (S.C.) State,* 24 February 1960, 1; Branch, *Parting the Waters,* 276; Carey, "Nonviolence and the Sit-Ins"; "Near Riots Mark," *Columbia (S.C.) Record,* 17 February 1960, 1; "Bricks and Bottles Fly," *Sumter (S.C.) Daily Item,* 17 February 1960, 1.

39. Martin Leroy Johnson, interview by the author, 6 June 2011; "Rock Hill Police Rescue," *Columbia (S.C.) State,* 24 February 1960, 3.

40. Johnson, interview by the author; "All-Out Riot Marks," *Columbia (S.C.) Record,* 24 February 1960, 1.

41. Johnson, interview by the author; "CORE Does It This Way!," November 1959, McCain Papers.

42. "Lunch Counter Sitdown," *Rock Hill (S.C.) Evening Herald,* 23 February 1960, 1.

43. "Rock Hill Negroes," *Rock Hill (S.C.) Evening Herald,* 24 February 1960, 1; "Rock Hill Police Rescue."

44. Gaither, "Students on a Road Gang," 96; Spearman to Paul Rilling, 17 February 1960, administrative, general, January–February 1960, SCCHR Papers.

45. Johnson, interview by the author; "Interracial Fighting," *Columbia (S.C.) State,* 24 February 1960, 1; "Racial Strife Cooled," *Columbia (S.C.) State,* 25 February 1960, 1; "Chattanooga Faces," *New York Times,* 24 February 1960, 27; Sitton, "Race Crisis Eased," *New York Times,* 28 February 1960, 50.

46. "Governor, Rock Hill Mayor," *Rock Hill (S.C.) Evening Herald,* 25 February 1960, 1; "Hollings Has No," *Rock Hill (S.C.) Evening Herald,* 27 February 1960, 1; "Carter Bill," *Columbia (S.C.) State,* 2 March 1960, 7.

47. "Firehoses Cool Off," *Rock Hill (S.C.) Evening Herald,* 25 February 1960, 1; "North Carolina Negroes," *Columbia (S.C.) State,* 26 February 1960, 2; Sitton, "Negroes' Protest Spreads," *New York Times,* 13 February 1960, 1; "Police Break Up," *New York Times,* 21 February 1960, 57; "38 More Arrested," *New York Times,* 23 February 1960, 38; Halberstam, *Children,* 133.

48. "Sitdowns Continued," *Columbia (S.C.) State,* 27 February 1960, 3; Ivory, Summary; James H. Goudlock to Charlotte Hickman, 18 February 1960, administrative, general, January–February 1960, SCCHR Papers.

49. Rip Wilder, "Members Tell," *Rock Hill (S.C.) Evening Herald,* 19 February 1960; "Gressette Says," *Orangeburg (S.C.) Times and Democrat,* 18 February 1960, 8; "Rock Hill Praised," *Columbia (S.C.) State,* 27 February 1960, 1.

50. Plummer, interview by the author; "Sitdowns Continued," *Columbia (S.C.) State,* 27 February 1960, 3.

51. "Bomb Threat Evacuates," *Rock Hill (S.C.) Evening Herald,* 29 February 1960, A1; Plummer, interview by the author.

52. Plummer, interview by the author.

53. Virginia Davis, "Rock Hill Negroes," *Rock Hill (S.C.) Evening Herald,* 1 March 1960, 1; James H. Goudlock to Spearman, 2 March 1960, administrative, general, January–February 1960, SCCHR Papers.

54. Newman, Summary of Sitdown Demonstrations, part 20, reel 10, frame 680, NAACP Papers. Grammar and mechanics are Newman's. Biographical Sketch of I. D. Newman, ca. 1980, Isaiah DeQuincey Newman Papers, South Caroliniana Library; Mrs. J. E. Williams to James Peck, 15 January 1960, reel 42, frame 1197, CORE Papers.

55. "Lunch Counters Closed," *Rock Hill (S.C.) Evening Herald,* 27 February 1960, 1; "Human Relations Council," *Columbia (S.C.) State,* 7 March 1960, administrative, general, March–April 1960, SCCHR Papers.

56. Johnson, interview by the author; "Cross Burned," *Rock Hill (S.C.) Evening Herald,* 8 March 1960, 1.

57. Johnson, interview by the author; "At Least 40," *Rock Hill (S.C.) Evening Herald,* 15 March 1960, 1.

58. Johnson, interview by the author; Plummer, interview by the author.

59. "At Least 40"; Johnson, interview by the author; Plummer, interview by the author.

60. Johnson, interview by the author; Newman Reported, March 1960, part 20, reel 10, frame 687, NAACP Papers; "Trials Postponed," *Rock Hill (S.C.) Evening Herald,* 16 March 1960, 1; "Ten Negro Demonstrators," *Columbia (S.C.) State,* 29 April 1960, 39; "County Wide Mass Meeting," 22 May 1960, Ivory scrapbook; "Outdoor Cage," *San Francisco Chronicle,* 16 March 1960.

61. Johnson, interview by the author; Plummer, interview by the author; "Trials Postponed."

62. Gloster B. Current to Wilkins, 16 March 1960, part 21, reel 22, frame 137, NAACP Papers; Alex Poinsett, "Why Violence Fails," *Jet,* 17 March 1960, 14.

63. "Adults Map," *CORE-lator,* June 1960, reel 49, frame 120, CORE Papers; Wilkins to All Officers, "Expanded Racial Defense Policy," 16 March 1960, https://www.crmvet.org/docs/60_naacp_sitins.pdf (accessed 18 November 2019); "Sympathy Boycotts," *Afro-American,* 23 April 1960, 5; "Lesson Not to Be Forgotten," *Baltimore Afro-American,* 15 June 1956, 3.

64. Davis, "Leadership Seeking Boycott," *Rock Hill (S.C.) Evening Herald,* 22 March 1960, 1.

65. "Lengthy Trial," *Rock Hill (S.C.) Evening Herald,* 24 March 1960, 1; George Evans, "Student Guilty," *Rock Hill (S.C.) Evening Herald,* 25 March 1960, 1; Brinson, "Council Honors Judge," *Columbia (S.C.) State,* 14 June 2001, 1, 7; Hine, *South Carolina State University,* 272.

66. Hawley Lynn, Jackson W. Carroll, A. M. Fisher, M. Eugene Mulliken, "Voice of the People," *Rock Hill (S.C.) Evening Herald,* 19 March 1960, 4. Grammar and mechanics are the ministers'. Tina White to Spearman, 15 April 1960, administrative, general, March–April 1960, SCCHR Papers.

67. "Ten Negro Demonstrators," *Columbia (S.C.) State,* 29 April 1960, 39; "W.T. Grant Defends," *New York Times,* 27 April 1960, 49, 51.

68. Davis, "Rock Hill Negroes," 13 April 1960, *Rock Hill (S.C.) Evening Herald,* A1; White

to Spearman, SCCHR; "NAACP President Speaks," *Sumter (S.C.) Daily Item,* 15 April 1960, 4.

69. "Sit-Downs," *New York Times,* 3 April 1960, 191; Follow-Up to Student Demonstrations in June Meeting, part 21, reel 22, frame 102, NAACP Papers; "Negro Students Form," *Columbia (S.C.) State,* 24 April 1960, 24.

70. Mahoney, "Sitdowns Likened," *Columbia (S.C.) State,* 1 March 1960, B1; Davis, "Leadership Seeking Boycott," *Rock Hill (S.C.) Evening Herald.*

71. "Crippled Minister Arrested," *CORE-lator,* June 1960, 1; "Rev. Ivory, Hamm," *Rock Hill (S.C.) Evening Herald,* 7 June 1960, 1; "Sitdown Trial," *Columbia (S.C.) State,* 8 July 1960, 17; Ivory to Donald Sampson, 8 June 1960, Ivory private collection; "Another Is Convicted," *Columbia (S.C.) State,* 15 July 1960, 16; "Invalid NAACP Leader," 9 July 1960, part 21, reel 22, frame 286, NAACP Papers.

72. "Children in Sit-In," *New York Times,* 18 June 1960, 11; Gaither, "Rock Hill, South Carolina," 29 September–1 October 1960, reel 42, frames 1181–82, CORE Papers; "Friendship Junior College," reel 42, frame 1238, CORE Papers; Gaither to Peck, "Student Movement Act II," reel 42, frame 1193, CORE Papers.

73. C. J. Williams, *Freedom and Justice,* 97–122; Williams, interview by the author; Hine, *South Carolina State University,* 234, 240–42. Four of the faculty members resigned. The fifth, Florence Miller, appealed to the American Association of University Professors when her contract was not renewed. Trustees authorized a one-thousand-dollar settlement.

74. Charles Frederick McDew, interviews by the author, April 1993, 7 November 2017.

75. Brinson, "Voice of Dignity," *Columbia (S.C.) State,* 22 April 1993, D1; McDew, interview by Mosnier, Civil Rights History Project, Library of Congress.

76. Brinson, "Voice of Dignity"; McDew, Civil Rights History Project.

77. McDew, interviews by the author, 1993, 2017.

78. Gaither, interview by the author, February 2003; Gaither, interview by the author, 13 December 2008.

79. Ibid.

80. Ibid.

81. Gaither, interview by the author, February 2003; Gaither, interview by Mosnier, Civil Rights History Project.

82. Gaither, interviews by the author, 2003, 2008; Morgan v. Virginia, 328 U.S. 373 (1946); Tracy, *Direct Action,* 88–91; "Smiley, Glenn E.," *King Encyclopedia,* Martin Luther King, Jr. Research and Education Institute, https://kinginstitute.stanford.edu /encyclopedia/smiley-glenn-e (accessed 18 November 2019).

83. Gandhi, *Gandhi,* 318; Fischer, *Gandhi: His Life,* 35–36.

84. Gaither, interviews by the author, 2003, 2008.

85. Ibid.; *CORE Rules for Action,* 3; "Application for Affiliation," 23 January 1959, reel 42, frames 1197–98, CORE Papers. Italics are CORE's.

86. Gaither, interview by Mosnier, Civil Rights History Project; C. J. Williams, *Freedom and Justice,* 146.

87. Gaither, interview by the author, 13 December 2013; Gaither, "Orangeburg," 9; Zinn, *SNCC,* 28.

88. Bobby D. Doctor, interview by the author, 7 July 2010; Richard Reid, "Benner C. Turner," *Orangeburg (S.C.) Times and Democrat,* 11 June 2008, https://thetandd.com /news/s-c-state-s-fourth-president-dr-benner-c-turner/article_17ea5764-a15e-5630 -9440-6733ffd465bd.html; Boyce, "I Am Leaving," 295. Turner's 1988 death certificate listed his race as white. Bass and Thompson, *Strom,* 95. Washington attended South Carolina State from 1947 through the summer of 1949; Thurmond visited her there.

89. Doctor, interview by the author; "Civil Rights Group Gets," *Orangeburg (S.C.) Times and Democrat,* 19 February 1960, 1.

90. Meriwether, "History of Higher Education," 124–26; U.S. Bureau of Education, *Industrial Education,* 226–27; Burke, "South Carolina State," 17–18.

91. Carey to Catherine Peppers, 1 November 1960, reel 42, frame 1172, CORE Papers; Carey to James Clyburn, 1 November 1960, reel 42, frame 1173, CORE Papers; Gaither to Carey, 12 October 1960, reel 42, frame 1173, CORE Papers; Gaither, "Orangeburg, South Carolina," 8–11 October 1960, 8 November 1960, 1–3 December 1960, reel 42, frames 1176–78, CORE Papers; Carey to Newman, 11 November 1960, reel 42, frame 1127, CORE Papers; Doctor, interview by the author.

92. Clarence Missouri, interview by the author, 7 June 2010; Clyburn, interview by the author, 11 August 2008; Gaither to Carey, 12 October 1960, reel 42, frames 1170–71, CORE Papers; Gaither, "Orangeburg, South Carolina."

93. Gaither, interview by the author, 13 December 2013; Gaither, "Orangeburg Story," draft for CORE, Gaither personal papers.

94. McDew, interviews by the author, 1993, 2017; SNCC, tape 9, Fortieth Anniversary, 21 April 2000, Rubenstein Library, Duke University.

95. Gaither, "Orangeburg Story"; Gaither, interview by the author, 2013; McDew, interview by the author, 7 November 2017; Clyburn, *Blessed Experiences,* 66.

96. McDew, interview by the author, 2017.

97. Logan, "Isaiah DeQuincey Newman," in *Spirit of the Activist,* 16–19; Newman, appointment book, 1960, Newman Papers; McDew, interview by the author, 2017.

98. "Sitdown Erupts," *New York Times,* 24 February 1960, 28; "Chattanooga Quells," *New York Times,* 25 February 1960, 1, 14; McDew, interview by the author, 2017; Gaither, "Orangeburg Story"; Newman Reported, part 20, reel 10, frame 683, NAACP Papers.

99. "Negro Picket Line," *Rock Hill (S.C.) Evening Herald,* 26 February 1960, 1; "Orangeburg Sitdown," *Columbia (S.C.) State,* 26 February 1960, 1; Gaither, "Orangeburg Story."

100. Doctor, interview by the author; Missouri, interview by the author; Gaither, "Orangeburg Story"; "Racial Strife Cooled."

101. Doctor, interview by the author; "Orangeburg Chief Labels," *Sumter (S.C.) Daily Item,* 27 February 1960, 1; "Second Demonstration Ends," *Columbia (S.C.) State,* 27 February 1960, 1; Newman Reported, part 20, reel 10, frame 683, NAACP Papers.

102. "Sitdowns Continued," *Columbia (S.C.) State,* 27 February 1960, 3; McDew, interview by the author, 2017.

103. "Mayor Issues Warning," *Orangeburg (S.C.) Times and Democrat,* 2 March 1960, 1;

Special Report of Sitdowns, part 21, reel 22, frame 75, NAACP Papers; "Negro Sit-down Held," *Columbia (S.C.) State,* 2 March 1960, 1, 7; Doctor, interview by the author; Missouri, interview by the author.

104. Doctor, interview by the author; Gaither, "Orangeburg Story."

105. Doctor, interview by the author; Clyburn, interview by the author.

106. Clyburn, interview by the author; Doctor, interview by the author; "Orangeburg Mayor Cites," *Columbia (S.C.) Record,* 2 March 1960, 2.

107. Gaither, "Orangeburg Story"; "Funeral Procession," *Jet,* 24 March 1960, 29; "Mayor Issues Warning," *Orangeburg (S.C.) Times and Democrat.*

108. Missouri, interview by the author; Doctor, interview by the author; C. J. Williams, *Freedom and Justice,* 146.

109. "Second Demonstration Ends," *Columbia (S.C.) State,* 27 February 1960, 1; "Negro Sitdown," *Columbia (S.C.) State,* 2 March 1960, 1; "Governor Warns Negro," *Columbia (S.C.) State,* 11 March 1960, 1.

110. Gaither, "Orangeburg Story"; "Governor Warns Negro"; "State Professor Says," *Orangeburg (S.C.) Times and Democrat,* 19 March 1960, 1; Doctor, interview by the author.

111. Gaither, interview by the author, 13 December 2013; McDew, interview by the author, 2017.

112. Loretta Hammond Thomas, interview by the author, 20 July 2010.

113. William V. Shannon, "Sitdowns in the South," *New York Post,* 1 April 1960, 39; "Police Chief Says," *Rock Hill (S.C.) Evening Herald,* 19 March 1960, 1.

114. Current to Wilkins, part 21, reel 22, frame 136, NAACP Papers; Hammond Thomas, interview by the author; Clyburn, "Gilbert 'Gigi' Zimmerman," *Congressional Record,* 10 October 2002, 20578–79; "Student Cases," *Columbia (S.C.) State,* 18 March 1960, 13; Thomas Fleming, "'3rd Revolution's' Leader," *San Francisco Sun-Reporter,* 9 April 1960; Lezlie Patterson, "One Photo at a Time," *Columbia (S.C.) State,* 22 February 2017, https://www.thestate.com/news/local/civil-rights/article134415459.html; "Student Cases Delayed," *Columbia (S.C.) State,* 18 March 1960, B1.

115. Hammond Thomas, interview by the author.

116. Clyburn, interview by the author; Gaither, interview by the author; Gaither, "Orangeburg; Behind the Carolina Stockade," in *Sit-Ins: The Students Report,* 10, https://www.crmvet.org/docs/60_core_sitin.pdf; 13 December 2013, 13 February 2019; Clyburn, interview by the author; Clyburn, *Blessed Experiences,* 68; "425 Negro Protesters," *Columbia (S.C.) State,* 18 March 1960, 1, 5. Clyburn met Emily England when he was released from confinement that day. She offered him half a hamburger; they married eighteen months later.

117. Clyburn, interview by the author; McDew, interview by the author, 2017.

118. Clyburn, interview by the author; Gaither, interview by the author, 14 December 2013, 13 February 2019; Moore, "Civil Rights Advocate," in *Matthew J. Perry,* 157; Current to Wilkins, part 21, reel 22, frame 136, NAACP Papers.

119. Newman Reported, part 20, reel 10, frames 683–85, NAACP Papers; "Police Brutality," reel 30, part 25, frame 493, NAACP Papers; Fleming, "'3rd Revolution's' Leader"; Gaither, interview by Mosnier, Civil Rights History Project; Gaither, "Orangeburg," in *Sit-Ins,* 9–11; Bynum, *NAACP Youth,* 108.

120. "Over 400," *Orangeburg (S.C.) Times and Democrat,* 17 March 1960, 1; "Demonstrators' Trial Put Off," *Orangeburg (S.C.) Times and Democrat,* 18 March 1960, 1; Current to Wilkins, part 21, reel 22, frame 137, NAACP Papers.

121. "Students Are Warned," *Columbia (S.C.) State,* 18 March 1960, 1; "Alabama Expels," *New York Times,* 3 March 1960, 15; "Warnings Followed," *Columbia (S.C.) State,* 16 March 1960, 1.

122. "Outdoor Cage"; Saunders Redding, "Sit-In Student Freedom Fighters," *Jet,* 21 April 1960, 13; Harrison E. Salisbury, "350 Negro Student Demonstrators," *New York Times,* 16 March 1960, 1, 27; "Canadian Newsman Says," Gaither scrapbook, Gaither personal collection.

123. Anthony Lewis, "President Advises South," *New York Times,* 17 March 1960, 1; "Transcript Indicates Ike," *Columbia (S.C.) State,* 18 March 1960, 1; "NAACP Appeals," *Columbia (S.C.) State,* 18 March 1960, 11.

124. "Hollings Rips," *Columbia (S.C.) State,* 17 March 1960, 1; "Warning by Hollings," *New York Times,* 17 March 1960, 37; "Biracial Panels Active," *New York Times,* 17 March 1960, 37.

125. "Truman Would Throw," *Columbia (S.C.) State,* 20 March 1960, 1; "NAACP Queries Truman," *Columbia (S.C.) State,* 25 March 1960, 1; Collins, "Statewide TV-Radio Talk," 350–353.

126. Frank K. Myers, "Defense Plans," *Orangeburg (S.C.) Times and Democrat,* 19 March 1960, 1; "Negro Picked," *New York Times,* 19 March 1960, 8.

127. R. J. Moore, "Matthew J. Perry," 131; "15 Students Found Guilty," *Orangeburg (S.C.) Times and Democrat,* 20 March 1960, 1; Bob McHugh, "Negro Demonstrators," *Columbia (S.C.) State,* 20 March 1960, B1.

128. "15 Students," *Orangeburg (S.C.) Times and Democrat;* McHugh, "Negro Demonstrators"; Clyburn, *Blessed Experiences,* 70.

129. "Federal Intervention Sought," 17 March 1960, part 21, reel 22, frame 229, NAACP Papers; H. P. Sharper, "Negro Citizens Who Were Invited," 24 March 1960, part 21, reel 22, frame 239, 1, 46; NAACP Papers; "NAACP Plans," *New York Times,* 18 March 1960, 23; "Lawyers Agree," *New York Times,* 20 March 1960, 1, 46; "Negroes Plan Tests," *New York Times,* 20 March 1960, E8.

130. "NAACP Plans," *New York Times,* 18 March 1960, 23; "Lawyers Agree"; "Negroes Plan Tests."

131. "Doubts on Sitdowns," *Columbia (S.C.) State,* 21 March 1960, 1.

132. "Protests Mass Arrests," 17 March 1960, part 21, reel 22, frame 227, NAACP Papers; "Economic Boycott," *Sumter (S.C.) Daily Item,* 23 March 1960, 8; James Feron, "NAACP Plans," *New York Times,* 18 March 1969, 23.

133. Wilkins, memorandum to NAACP Branch Offices, n.d., part 21, reel 22, frames 33–35, NAACP Papers. Capitalizations and italics are Wilkins's.

134. "Lunch Counters Integrated," *New York Times,* 20 March 1960, 1, 48; "Lawyers Agree," *New York Times,* 20 March 1960, 1, 46; "Galveston Takes Integration," *New York Times,* 6 April 1960, 27; "4 Richmond Stores," *New York Times,* 8 April 1960, 19.

135. Report of the Southeastern Regional Secretary for May Meeting, part 21, reel 22, frame 103, NAAACP Papers; Current, "NAACP Units Continue," 21 April 1960, part 21, reel 22, frame 253, NAACP Papers; Hine, *South Carolina State University,* 262.

136. "27 More," *Columbia (S.C.) State,* 1 April 1960, 1; "Use of Tear Gas, Hose," *Columbia (S.C.) State,* 15 April 1960, 33; "Acted 'with Restraint'" *Columbia (S.C.) State,* 20 May 1960, 22.

137. "Discuss Racial Friction," *Columbia (S.C.) State,* 22 July 1960, 28; "Rights Group Hears," *Sumter (S.C.) Daily Item,* 20 May 1960, 4; "Truman Repeats Charge," *New York Times,* 13 June 1960, 20.

138. McDew, interview by the author, 2017; "Youth Leadership Meeting," April 1960, http://www.crmvet.org/docs/6004_sncc_call.pdf (accessed 18 November 2019); Ransby, *Ella Baker,* 239–46; Butler, "What We Were Talking About," 43; Baker, "Bigger Than a Hamburger," *Southern Patriot,* May 1960, https://www.crmvet.org/docs/sncc2.htm (accessed 18 November 2019). Highlander, founded in 1932, focused on labor, adult education, and race relations.

139. McDew, interview by the author, 2017; Delegates to Youth Leadership Conference, April 15–17, 1960, 2 June 1960, Southern Christian Leadership Conference, Inc., https://www.crmvet.org/docs/600417_sclc_delegates.pdf (accessed 18 November 2019); Delegates to Youth Leadership Conference, 21 April 1960, SCLC, Inc., https://www.crmvet.org/docs/6004_shaw_delegations.pdf (accessed 18 November 2019).

140. Ransby, *Ella Baker,* 239–46; King, "Statement to the Press," 15 April 1960, King Research and Education Institute, https://kinginstitute.stanford.edu/king-papers/documents/statement-press-beginning-youth-leadership-conference#ftnref9 (accessed 18 November 2019); Sitton, "King Favors," *New York Times,* 16 April 1960, 15; Sitton, "Racial Problems," *New York Times,* 18 April 1960, 21.

141. Sitton, "Negro Criticizes," *New York Times,* 17 April 1960, 32; Sitton, "Racial Problems"; Ransby, *Ella Baker,* 6, 139, 244–245; McDew, interview by the author, 2017.

142. McDew, interview by the author, 2017; McDew, interview by Mosnier, Civil Rights History Project.

143. "Statement of Purpose," 17 April 1960, SNCC, https://www.crmvet.org/docs/600417_sncc_statement.pdf (accessed 18 November 2019); Recommendations of the Findings and Recommendations Committee, April 1960, SNCC, https://www.crmvet.org/docs/6004_shaw_recommendations.pdf (accessed 18 November 2019).

144. May Meeting, part 21, reel 22, frames 100–101, NAACP Papers.

145. Lewis, *Walking with the Wind,* 113.

146. James Robinson, "Meaning of the Sit-Ins," CORE Papers, 3; "Founding of SNCC," SNCC 50th Anniversary Conference, https://www.crmvet.org/info/snccfoun.htm; Recommendations Passed by SNCC, 14–16 April 1960, SNCC, https://www.crmvet.org/docs/6010_sncc_decs.pdf (accessed 18 November 2019); Baker, Report of the Committee on Finance, 13 May 1960, SNCC, https://www.crmvet.org/docs/6005_sncc_cc-rpt-r.pdf (accessed 18 November 2019); "We Are Activists," November 1960, *Student Voice,* 7, https://www.crmvet.org/docs/sv/sv6011.pdf (accessed 18 November 2019).

147. Special Report of Sitdowns, part 21, reel 22, frames 76, 98, NAACP Papers; M. E. Brown, "NAACP Years," 66; Willie Thompson, "Student Leader Here," *Golden Gater,* 5 April 1960; "Gaither Travels," *Claflin College Panther,* May 1960, Gaither scrapbook.

148. "What Is SNCC?" *Student Voice,* June 1960, 2, http://www.crmvet.org/docs/sv/sv60 06.pdf (accessed 18 November 2019); "Present Status of SNCC," *Student Voice,* June 1960, 2. Original uses ellipsis.

149. SNCC to the Platform Committee of the National Democratic Convention, SNCC, 7 July 1960, https://www.crmvet.org/docs/6007_sncc_demconv-platform .pdf (accessed 18 November 2019); Republican Party Platform of 1960, 25 July 1960, https://www.jfklibrary.org/asset-viewer/archives/JFKCAMP1960/1036/JFK CAMP1960-1036-008 (accessed 18 November 2019); 1960 Democratic Party Platform, 11 July 1960, https://www.jfklibrary.org/asset-viewer/archives/JFKPOF/098a /JFKPOF-098a-001 (accessed 18 November 2019); "Civil Rights Mission," *Columbia (S.C.) Record,* 7 July 1960, 27; "10 Southern States Wage," *New York Times,* 13 July 1960, 1, 21; Follow-Up to Student Demonstrations in June Meeting.

150. "Role of the NAACP in the 'Sit-Ins,'" May 1960, part 21, reel 22, frame 299, NAACP Papers; Smith, "Casey Hayden," 364–65; Curry, "NSA's Southern Rights Initiative," 446, 452; "Five Negro Students," *Orangeburg (S.C.) Times and Democrat,* 14 May 1960; "Negroes Get Short Stay," *Orangeburg (S.C.) Times and Democrat,* 17 May 1960.

151. Gaither to Carey, 12 October 1960, CORE Papers; Gaither, "Orangeburg, South Carolina," reel 42, frames 1176–78, CORE Papers; Carey to Clyburn, 1 November 1960, reel 42, frame 1173, CORE Papers.

152. McDew, interview by the author; "SNCC Conference," *Student Voice,* October 1960, 1, http://www.crmvet.org/docs/sv/sv6010.pdf (accessed 18 November 2019); "Orangeburg," *Student Voice,* October 1960, 2, https://www.crmvet.org/docs/sv/sv6010.pdf (accessed 18 November 2019); "Nonviolence and the Achievement of Desegregation," 25 September 1960, SNCC, https://www.crmvet.org/docs/6010_sncc_conf_agenda .pdf (accessed 18 November 2019); "Recommendations Passed by SNCC," 14–16 October 1960, SNCC, https://www.crmvet.org/docs/6010_sncc_decs.pdf (accessed 18 November 2019); "Kennedy Praises Sit-Ins," *Columbia (S.C.) State,* 16 October 1960, 49.

153. McDew, interview by the author, 2017; "Six Arrested," *Columbia (S.C.) State,* 21 October 1960, 36; Gaither, "Orangeburg, South Carolina," reel 42, frame 1177, CORE Papers; "News from States," *Student Voice,* December 1960, http://www.crmvet.org /docs/sv/sv6012.pdf (accessed 18 November 2019).

154. Curry, "Wild Geese to the Past," 20; Minutes, 25–27 November 1960, SNCC, https:// www.crmvet.org/docs/6011_sncc_min.pdf (accessed 18 November 2019).

155. "November Meeting of SNCC," *Student Voice,* December 1960, 1, https://www.crm vet.org/docs/sv/sv6011.pdf (accessed 18 November 2019); "Tom Gaither," SNCC Digital Gateway, SNCC Legacy Project and Duke University, https://snccdigital.org /people/tom-gaither/ (accessed 18 November 2019); Carey to Napoleon Giles, 30 November 1960, reel 42, frame 1174, CORE Papers; Carey to E. A. Finney, 30 November 1960, reel 42, frame 1248, CORE Papers; "Orangeburg," *Student Voice,* October 1960, 2, https://www.crmvet.org/docs/sv/sv6010.pdf (accessed 18 November 2019).

156. Cleveland Sellers, interview by the author, 9 June 2010; Lare, "Cleveland Sellers," 136.

157. Sidney Glee, interview by the author, 20 December 2010; Arthur Copeland, interview by the author, 16 July 2010.

158. William Bradford Huie, "Approved Killing in Mississippi," *Look,* 24 January 1956, 46–50. In *The Blood of Emmett Till,* by Timothy B. Tyson, Carolyn Bryant disavowed portions of her court testimony about Till.

159. Sellers, interview by the author.

160. Herman Gloster, interview by the author, 28 June 2010.

161. Gloster, interview by the author, 12 November 2010; Glee, interview by the author; Herman Young, interview by the author, 28 June 2010.

162. Gloster, interview by the author; Young, interview by the author.

163. Glee, interview by the author, 20 December 2010.

164. Gloster, interview by the author; Copeland, interview by the author; Glee, interview by the author, 12 November 2010.

165. Young, interview by the author.

166. Glee, interview by the author, 12 November 2010.

167. Copeland, interview by the author, 20 December 2010; Glee, interview by the author.

168. "Denmark Police Arrest," *Columbia (S.C.) State,* 1 March 1960, 1.

169. Gloster, interview by the author.

170. "Negroes Invade," *Greenville (S.C.) News,* 1 March 1960, 1; Copeland, interview by the author.

171. Copeland, interview by the author.

172. "Eating Places Can Pick," *Barnwell (S.C.) People-Sentinel,* 3 March 1960, 2; "It Won't Happen," *Barnwell (S.C.) People-Sentinel,* 17 March 1960, 2.

173. Glee, interview by the author, 12 November 2010; Gloster, interview by the author.

174. Follow-Up to Student Demonstrations in June Meeting; "Thousands of Negroes," *Columbia (S.C.) State,* 20 April 1960, 1; "Nashville Integrates," *New York Times,* 11 May 1960, 1, 15; "Sit-In Results," *New York Times,* 15 May 1960, 188; "Bombing Sets Off," *New York Times,* 20 April 1960, 1, 25; "Lunch Bias to End," *New York Times,* 24 May 1960, 42.

175. "Kress in Defense," *New York Times,* 18 May 1960, 59; Gloster, interview by the author.

176. Simon P. Bouie, interviews by the author, 22 May 2010, 7 January 2019; "Negroes Press Protest," *New York Times,* 4 March 1960, 11.

177. "Negroes Stage Protest," *Columbia (S.C.) Record,* 2 March 1960, 1; Joe Barrett, "Short Sit-Downs," *Columbia (S.C.) State,* 3 March 1960, 1.

178. "Negroes Again March," *Columbia (S.C.) Record,* 3 March 1960, 1; "Showdown Due Today," *Columbia (S.C.) State,* 4 March 1960, 1.

179. Milton B. Greene, interview by the author, 21 July 2008; Robert Devoe, interview by the author, 16 July 2013.

180. "Short Sit-Downs," *Columbia (S.C.) State;* "Showdown Due Today"; Vida Carter, interview by the author, 21 June 2013; "Negro March Called Off," *Columbia (S.C.) State,* 12 March 1960, 6; Devoe, interview by the author.

181. Devoe, interview by the author.

182. "Columbia Sitdowns," *Columbia (S.C.) State,* 5 March 1960, 1, 3.

183. Ibid.; "Cars Battered," *Sumter (S.C.) Daily Item,* 5 March 1960, 1. Grammar and mechanics are the students'.

184. Bouie, interview by the author, 2019.

185. Ibid.

186. "Negro Leader Urges," *Columbia (S.C.) State,* 11 March 1960, 9; "Students Organize," *New York Times,* 6 March 1960, 43; Carter, interview by the author.

187. Carter, interview by the author; Newman, Summary of Field Secretary's Report, 1 January 1960–22 September 1960, Modjeska Simkins Papers, South Caroliniana Library.

188. "Columbia Sitdowns," *Columbia (S.C.) State,* 5 March 1960, 1; Devoe, interview by the author; "Negroes Invade Drive-In," *Columbia (S.C.) Record,* 5 March 1960, 1; "Brief Racial Disturbance," *Columbia (S.C.) State,* 6 March 1960, 1, 2.

189. "First Arrest Here," *Columbia (S.C.) Record,* 7 March 1960, 1; "Fifteen Students Fined," *Columbia (S.C.) State,* 19 March 1960, 1; "No Cross Burned," *Columbia (S.C.) State,* 19 March 1960, 1, 2.

190. Devoe, interview by the author; Simkins, "Oral History Interview."

191. Newman, appointment book, 1960, Newman Papers.

192. "Progressive Democratic Party," John Henry McCray Papers, South Caroliniana Library; "Negro Leader Urges," *Columbia (S.C.) State,* 11 March 1960, 8, 9; "Negroes Will Seek Seats," *Columbia (S.C.) Record,* 28 April 1944, 1–2; "Johnston Pleased," *Columbia (S.C.) Record,* 20 July 1944, 2; "McCray Says SC Party," *Columbia (S.C.) State,* 15 July 1948, 19; Frederickson, *Dixiecrat Revolt,* 124–28.

193. "Negro Leader Urges."

194. Rev. William McKinley Bowman, "Fund-Raising Committee Says," *Columbia (S.C.) State,* 15 March 1960, 10.

195. Ibid.

196. "Negro Leader Urges"; Bowman, "Fund-Raising Committee Says."

197. "More than a Fad," *Columbia (S.C.) State,* 15 March 1960, 4; SCCHR Quarterly Report, June–August 1960, administrative staff, general, SCCHR Papers.

198. "'Don't' Hollings Says," *Columbia (S.C.) Record,* 10 March 1960, 1.

199. Ibid.; "Repeat of History," *Columbia (S.C.) State,* 12 March 1960, 4.

200. "Negro March Called," *Columbia (S.C.) State,* 12 March 1960, 6; Lewis, *Walking with the Wind,* 101–3.

201. "After Being Warned," *Columbia (S.C.) Record,* 11 March 1960, 1; "Negro March Called."

202. Bouie, interview by the author, 22 May 2010; "Allen University Group," *Charleston (S.C.) News and Courier,* 18 February 1961, 2; "State Reports: South Carolina," *Student Voice,* August 1960, 6, https://www.crmvet.org/docs/sv/sv6008.pdf (accessed 18 November 2019); "Two Negroes Arrested," *Columbia (S.C.) Record,* 14 March 1960, 1.

203. Bouie, interviews by the author, 2010, 2019; "Columbia Police Jail," *Columbia (S.C.) State,* 15 March 1960, 1.

204. Bouie, interview by the author, 2010; "Columbia Police Jail."

205. Bouie, interview by the author, 2019.

206. Devoe, interview by the author.

207. Ibid.

208. "Five Sitdowners," *Columbia (S.C.) State,* 16 March 1960, 1.

209. Ibid.; Greene, interview by the author; Charles F. Barr, interview by the author.

210. Barr, interview by the author; Greene, interview by the author.

211. Barr, interview by the author; Greene, interview by the author; Barr v. City of Columbia, 378 U.S. 146 (1964); Motley, "Memory," 228.

212. Barr, interview by the author; Greene, interview by the author.

213. Barr, interview by the author; Greene, interview by the author; "Warnings Followed," *Columbia (S.C.) State*, 16 March 1960, 1; "Five Sitdowners." Owner Ozzie Jackson Sr. designed the abbreviated and all-capitals ALBEN name.

214. Spearman to Ira Kay, 22 March 1960, administrative, general, February 1960, SCCHR Papers; Spearman to Claude Evans, 18 March 1960, administrative, general, March–April 1960, SCCHR Papers; Spearman to President Dwight Eisenhower, 22 March 1960, administrative, general, March–April 1960, SCCHR Papers; Spearman to Lawson, 23 April 1961, administrative, general SCCHR Papers; "NAACP Asks Boycott," *Rock Hill (S.C.) Evening Herald*, 17 March 1960, 1; Quarterly Report, March 1960–May 1960, SCCHR Papers; Executive Director Reports, 1960–63, SCCHR Papers; "South's Mood," *New York Times*, 26 March 1960, 184.

215. "Two Negroes Arrested," *Columbia (S.C.) Record*, 14 March 1960, 1; "Student Admits Sitdown," *Columbia (S.C.) State*, 26 March 1960, B9; Charles E. Williams v. Howard Johnson's Restaurant, 268 F.2d 845 (4th Cir., 1959).

216. Bouie, interview by the author; Spearman to Barbara Moffett, 2 August 1960, administrative, general, August–September 1960, SCCHR Papers; Spearman to Rev. J. Herbert Nelson, 2 August 1960, administrative, general, August–September 1960, SCCHR Papers.

217. "1,500 Negro Students," *Columbia (S.C.) State*, 28 March 1960, 2; Newman, Statistical Report, Student Protest Demonstrations in South Carolina, 6 May 1960, reel 42, frame 1138, CORE Papers; Bouie, interview by the author, 2019.

218. "Cross-Burnings Are Reported," *Columbia (S.C.) State*, 27 March 1960, 52; "We'll Attend," *Rock Hill (S.C.) Evening Herald*, 13 April 1960, 1; Quarterly Report, March 1960–May 1960, executive director reports, 1960–63, SCCHR Papers.

219. "Demonstrations Resumed," *Columbia (S.C.) State*, 29 April 1960, 39.

220. "State House March Held," *Columbia (S.C.) State*, 6 May 1960, 6; Follow-Up to Student Demonstrations in June Meeting.

221. Follow-Up to Demonstrations in June Meeting; Newman, Statistical Report.

222. Newman and McCain to Dear Fellow Citizens, 13 May 1960, administrative, general, May–July 1960, SCCHR Papers; State-wide Strategy Meeting of Negro Leaders, 15 June 1960, administrative, general, May–July 1960, SCCHR Papers; "Hollings Says Watch Reds," *Columbia (S.C.) State*, 24 June 1960, 38.

223. "8 Arrested," *Columbia (S.C.) State*, 17 July 1960, 24. Among those arrested was Jesse Jackson, who founded Operation PUSH and the Rainbow Coalition and campaigned for the Democratic presidential nomination in 1984 and 1988. "White Student Roughed Up," *Columbia (S.C.) State*, 19 July 1960, 13.

224. "White Student Roughed Up"; "White Youth Leads," *New York Times*, 19 July 1960, 17.

225. "Greenville Race Fights," *Columbia (S.C.) State*, 27 July 1960, 1, 5; "Whites and Negroes Brawl," *New York Times*, 22 July 1960, 24; "Curfew Imposed," *New York Times*, 27 July 1960, 19; "New Sit-Down Demonstrations," *Columbia (S.C.) State*, 23 July

1960, 14; "S.C. Students in New," part 21, reel 22, frame 296, NAACP Papers; "So. Carolina Students," *Detroit Tribune,* 20 July 1960, 1.

226. "Negroes Punched," *New York Times,* 28 July 1960, 20; "Spartanburg Acts," *New York Times,* 29 July 1960, 49; "Trials Today at Greenville," *Columbia (S.C.) State,* 29 July 1960, 32; "Negroes Sit-In," *New York Times,* 30 July 1960, 8; "Hollings Says Platforms," *Columbia (S.C.) State,* 29 July 1960, 32.

227. "Views on Segregation," *Columbia (S.C.) State,* 4 August 1960, 32; "Graham Asked," *Columbia (S.C.) State,* 28 November 1960, 5; "Bias Fight Urged," *New York Times,* 15 September 1956, 7.

228. "Sit-Ins Victorious," *New York Times,* 26 July 1960, 1, 19; "Twenty-Eight Cities," *New York Times,* 7 August 1960, 43; "Newport News," *Columbia (S.C.) State,* 9 August 1960, 6.

229. George M. Eberhart, "The Greenville Eight," *American Libraries,* 1 June 2017, American Library Association, https://americanlibrariesmagazine.org/2017/06/01/greenville-eight-library-sit-in/ (accessed 18 November 2019); "DeeDee Wright Recalls," *Salisbury (N.C.) Post,* 23 October 2018, https://www.salisburypost.com/2018/10/23/wright-recalls-time-when-greenville-eight-were-arrested-not-celebrated/ (18 November 2019).

230. "Expanded Integration," *Columbia (S.C.) State,* 23 September 1960, 42; "Negro Lauds," *Columbia (S.C.) State,* 24 September 1960, 13; "NAACP Leader Threatens," *Columbia (S.C.) State,* 25 September 1960, 25; "Negroes Rally," *Columbia (S.C.) State,* 26 September 1960, 16; Sarah Keys v. Carolina Coach Company, 64 MCC 769 (1955); Henry v. Greenville Airport Commission, 175 F. Supp. 343 (1959).

231. "Citizens Council Lists," *Columbia (S.C.) State,* 7 November 1960, 1, 2.

232. Democratic candidate John F. Kennedy was Roman Catholic, and South Carolina had the lowest percentage of Catholics in the South. "Kennedy Wins," *Columbia (S.C.) State,* 9 November 1960, 1, 7; "Kennedy Wins Election," 9 November 1960, UPI Archives, https://www.upi.com/Archives/1960/11/09/Kennedy-wins-election-by-slim-margin/5835485152054/ (accessed 18 November 2019); "Hollings Hits Vote," *Columbia (S.C.) State,* 18 May 1960, 15; "Thurmond Calls Probe," *Columbia (S.C.) State,* 9 June 1960, 35; "Clarendon Books Eyed," *Columbia (S.C.) State,* 17 June 1960, 23; "King Says Jack," *Columbia (S.C.) State,* 15 November 1960, 11.

233. Gaither, "Orangeburg, South Carolina," frame 1178, CORE Papers; "Carolina Sit-In," *New York Times,* 14 December 1960, 25; "'Wildcat' Sit-In," *Columbia (S.C.) State,* 14 December 1960, 24; "Negro Group Sits," *Columbia (S.C.) State,* 15 December 1960, 26; "Continue 'Indefinitely,'" *Columbia (S.C.) State,* 16 December 1960, 21.

234. "Must Halt Racial Agitators," *Sumter (S.C.) Daily Item,* 9 February 1960, 6; "Communists Must," *Sumter (S.C.) Daily Item,* 3 March 1960, 6.

235. "Negroes Jailed," *Columbia (S.C.) State,* 5 March 1960, 1, 30.

236. Frances DuBose Singleton, interview by the author, 2006; Rev. Mae Frances Moultrie Howard, interview by the author, 2003; J. Charles Levy Jr., interview by the author, 24 August 2018.

237. Rev. Ralph Waldo Canty Sr., interview by the author, 21 March 2018.

238. "Sumter Council," *Columbia (S.C.) State,* 3 May 1959, 35; "Refuse to Integrate,"

Columbia (S.C.) State, 11 November 1959, 15; "Citizen Council Drive in Sumter," *Columbia (S.C.) State,* 14 August 1960, 48; FBI, *Citizens Council Movement,* 53–54, 75–76, 154, https://archive.org/stream/CItizensCouncilMovement/CitCouncils -Savannah#page/no/mode/2up (accessed 18 November 2019).

239. "26 Negroes Arrested"; F. DuBose Singleton, interview by the author.

240. M. Moultrie Howard, interview by the author; "Sit-Down Effort," *Sumter (S.C.) Daily Item,* 5 March 1960, 1.

241. "Sit-Down Effort."

242. F. DuBose Singleton, interview by the author; "Sit-Down Effort"; "White Citizens' Council," Mississippi Civil Rights Project, https://mscivilrightsproject.org/hinds /organization-hinds/the-white-citizens-council/ (accessed 18 November 2019).

243. F. DuBose Singleton, interview by the author.

244. "Quietus Put," *Columbia (S.C.) State,* 5 March 1960, A13; "Sumter Residents Urged," *Columbia (S.C.) State,* 6 March 1960, 13; "Mayor Stands Firm," *Sumter (S.C.) Daily Item,* 5 March 1960, A1; Newman, appointment book, 1960, Newman Papers.

245. Levy, interviews by the author, 21 August 2018, 24 August 2018; "Cross Burned Near Morris," *Sumter (S.C.) Daily Item,* 7 March 1960, 1.

246. "BB Shot Fired," *Sumter (S.C.) Daily Item,* 9 March 1960, 1; "Racial Integrity," advertisement, *Sumter (S.C.) Daily Item,* 12 March 1960, 10; "350 Negro Marchers Free," *Sumter (S.C.) Daily Item,* 16 March 1960, 1. Capitalization and mechanics are the WCC's.

247. "Communist Planning," *Sumter (S.C.) Daily Item,* 6 April 1960, 8.

248. "Sitdown Trials Begin," *Sumter (S.C.) Daily Item,* 26 April 1960, l; "Adults Map Summer," *CORE-lator,* June 1960, reel 49, frame 120, CORE Papers.

249. "Sitdown Trials Begin"; "Negroes Sentenced," *Sumter (S.C.) Daily Item,* 27 April 1960, 1, 15.

250. "Negroes Sentenced," *Sumter (S.C.) Daily Item,* 27 April 1960, 1; McCain, 1960 Peace Calendar, McCain Papers; F. DuBose Singleton, interview by the author.

251. F. DuBose Singleton, interview by the author.

252. Ibid.

253. Ibid.; "Mayor Stands Firm"; Levy, interview by the author, 24 August 2018.

254. Gaither, interview by the author, February 2003; "Adults Map Summer"; McCain, 1960 Jane Addams Centennial Engagement Calendar, McCain Papers.

255. "Woolworth Posts Sales Gains," *New York Times,* 19 May 1960, 55.

256. Willie J. Singleton Jr., interview by the author, 2004.

257. W. Singleton, interview by the author. In 1963 Singleton became the Sumter movement's treasurer.

258. "Carolina Cops Harass," *CORE-lator,* September 1960, 4, https://www.crmvet.org /docs/core/core6009.pdf (accessed 18 November 2019); Gaither, interview by the author, 13 December 2013, 14 December 2013.

259. "Institute Will Teach," *New York Times,* 24 April 1960, 1, 43; Gaither, interviews by the author, 2008, 14 December 2013; Carey, "Intensive Three Weeks," *CORE-lator,* September 1960, 2, https://www.crmvet.org/docs/core/core6009.pdf (accessed 18 November 2019).

260. "Eighteen Given," *New York Times,* 27 August 1960, 7; "CORE Fights Florida," *Detroit Tribune,* 19 November 1960, 1; "Three Week Course," *New York Times,* 28 August 1960, 150; James R. Robinson, "Jail Not Bail," *CORE-lator,* September 1960, 3; Carey, "Intensive Three Weeks."

261. Robinson, "Jail Not Bail"; Carey, "Intensive Three Weeks"; "McCain Arrested," *CORE-lator,* September 1960, 1, https://www.crmvet.org/docs/core/core6009.pdf; "CORE Adds Two," *Detroit Tribune,* 24 September 1960, 1; "CORE Has Just Hired," *CORE-lator,* April 1960, 2, https://www.crmvet.org/docs/core/core6004.pdf (accessed 18 November 2019).

262. "Executives Meet," *New York Times,* 11 August 1960, 14; "Six Months," *CORE-lator,* August 1960, 1, reel 49, frame 124, CORE Papers.

263. Levy, interview by the author, 21 August 2018.

264. Gaither to Carey, 10 October 1960, reel 42, frame 1169, CORE Papers; Gaither to Carey, 12 October 1960, reel 42, frames 1170–71, CORE Papers; "Five Negroes Convicted," *Columbia (S.C.) State,* 28 October 1960, 37; Levy, interview by the author, 24 August 2018.

265. Levy, interviews by the author, 21 August 2018, 24 August 2018; "11 Jailed in Sit-Ins," *Sumter (S.C.) Daily Item,* 12 October 1960, reel 42, frame 1229, CORE Papers.

266. Gaither to Carey, 10 October 1960, CORE Papers; "11 Jailed in Sit-Ins"; F. DuBose Singleton, interview by the author; "Sumter Sit-In Trials," *Columbia (S.C.) State,* 13 October 1960, 31.

267. F. DuBose Singleton, interview by the author; Levy, interview by the author; "Sumter Sit-In Trials."

268. F. DuBose Singleton, interview by the author.

269. F. DuBose Singleton, interview by the author; "Your Financial Support," reel 42, frame 1222, CORE Papers; Gaither, Sumter, South Carolina, 3 October–20 October, 25 October–1 November 1960, reel 42, frames 1225–27, CORE Papers; Report of McCain, 17 October–1 November 1960, reel 42, frame 1230, CORE Papers; "Sumter Sit-In Trials Today," *Columbia (S.C.) State,* 13 October 1960, 31.

270. "Sumter Sit-In Trials Today"; "South's Mood"; Lewis, *Walking with the Wind,* 103; "Negroes Press Protest," *New York Times,* 4 March 1960, 11; "8 Negroes Choose," *New York Times,* 19 March 1960, 8; Patricia Stephens, "Letter from a Jailed Student," *CORE-lator,* April 1960, https://www.crmvet.org/docs/core/core6004.pdf (accessed 18 November 2019).

271. "NAACP Position," n.d., part 21, reel 22, frames 63–67, NAACP Papers; F. DuBose Singleton, interview by the author.

272. "Lunch Counters Mixed," *Columbia (S.C.) State,* 13 October 1960, 13; "Integration Gain," *New York Times,* 18 October 1960, 47; "NAACP Regrets," *Columbia (S.C.) State,* 19 October 1960, 14.

273. "Sitdowners on Trial," *Sumter (S.C.) Daily Item,* 13 October 1960, reel 42, frame 1229, CORE Papers; Clifford Sumer, James Lewis to Wade Kolb, 21 October 1960, reel 42, frame 1228, CORE Papers. Capitalization is CORE's.

274. Charles R. Oldham to Dear Friend, 27 October 1960, reel 42, frame 1220, CORE Papers; Gaither, Sumter, South Carolina, October–November 1960, CORE Papers;

"Five Negroes Convicted," *Columbia (S.C.) State,* 28 October 1960, 37; Report of McCain, Sumter, 2 November–22 November 1960, reel 42, frames 1246–47, CORE Papers; "South Carolina," *Student Voice,* November 1960, 5, http://www.crmvet.org /docs/sv/sv6011.pdf (accessed 18 November 2019).

275. "Six Sumter Negroes," *Columbia (S.C.) State,* 23 November 1960, 7; Oldham, 27 October 1960, CORE Papers; Report of McCain, Sumter, reel 42, frame 1247, CORE Papers.

276. Gaither, Sumter, South Carolina, October–November 1960, CORE Papers; McCain, October–November 1960, CORE Papers; "Please Don't Buy," reel 42, frame 1221, CORE Papers; F. DuBose Singleton, interview by the author.

277. Newman, Annual Report, NAACP, 7 December 1961, 11, South Caroliniana Library. This report covers 1960. "Kneel-Ins," *Student Voice,* August 1960, 2, http://www.crm vet.org/docs/sv/sv6008.pdf (accessed 18 November 2019); "Integrated Services," *New York Times,* 8 August 1960, 25; "Kneel-In Extended," *New York Times,* 15 August 1960, 20; "Negroes Turned Away," *New York Times,* 22 August 1960, 25.

278. "Kneel-In Fails," *Columbia (S.C.) State,* 21 November 1960, 3; McCain, Sumter, 2 November–22 November 1960, reel 42, frame 1247, CORE Papers; Newman, Annual Report; McCain, Sumter, 6 December–24 December 1960, reel 42, frame 1248, CORE Papers.

279. McCain, Sumter, frames 1248–49, CORE Papers

280. Ibid.

281. "Counter Integration Peaceful," *Southern Newsletter,* September–October 1960, Simkins Papers.

282. Gaither, interview by Mosnier, Civil Rights History Project; M. Moultrie Howard, interview by the author, 2003. McDew, interview by the author, 2017.

283. Bess Furman, "President's Yule Message," *New York Times,* 24 December 1960, 1, 13; "Text of Eisenhower," *New York Times,* 24 December 1960, 13; "Time to End Racial Prejudice," *Columbia (S.C.) State,* 24 December 1960, 15.

284. "Strangely Mixed Cup," *Columbia (S.C.) State,* 30 December 1960, 9.

285. Newman to Spearman, 22 November 1960, administrative, general, November–December 1960, SCCHR Papers; "Sacrifices Mark Christmas," *Columbia (S.C.) State,* 25 December 1960, 19; "Christmas Buying Boycott," *Jet,* 15 December 1960, 50; "Southern Stores Feel Boycott," *Student Voice,* December 1960, 1; "Christmas Withholding Campaign," *Student Voice,* December 1960, 1, https://www.crmvet.org/docs/sv /sv6012.pdf (accessed 18 November 2019).

286. "U.S. Negro Gains," *New York Times,* 23 January 1960, 57; "Limited Advances," *New York Times,* 28 January 1961, 16; Lerone Bennett Jr., "What Sitdowns Mean," *Ebony,* June 1960, 35–38, 40; Sitton, "Sit-In Campaigns Spread," *New York Times,* 29 January 1961, 64. Grammar and mechanics are Matthew D. McCollom's and Ruby Hurley's.

287. Newman, Student Protest Activity, 1960–61, reel 30, part 25, frame 479, NAACP Papers; Sitton, "Sit-In Campaigns Spread." Grammar and mechanics are Newman's. In 2019 dollars the state NAACP Conference spent \$360,117; the LDF spent \$1.374 million.

288. McDew, "Remembrances of SNCC," Trinity College SNCC Reunion, April 1988, https://www.crmvet.org/nars/mcdew.htm (accessed 18 November 2019).

289. Henry v. City of Rock Hill, 376 U.S. 776 (1964); Bouie v. City of Columbia, 378 U.S. 347 (1964); Barr v. City of Columbia 378 U.S. 146 (1964); Fields v. South Carolina, 375 U.S. 44 (1963); McAllister et al. v. City of Sumter, 241 S.C. 355 (S.C. 1962). State v. Irene Brown et al., 126 S.E. 2d 1 (S.C. 1962); Hamm v. City of Rock Hill, 379 U.S. 306 (1964); Sullivan, *Lift Every Voice*, 335.

290. *Hamm*, 379 U.S. 306 (1964); "Court Upholds Rights Act's Ban," *New York Times*, 15 December 1964, 1; Edwards v. South Carolina, 372 U.S. 229 (1963). Ivory's appeal ended with his death in 1961.

291. Quarterly Report, administrative staff, December 1959–February 1960, SCCHR Papers; "Complete Freedom Urged," *Greenville (S.C.) News*, 26 October 1959, 1.

292. "Gloster Current to Robert Carter," in Robinson, *First Class Citizenship*, 75–76; "Negroes Stage Demonstration," *Columbia (S.C.) State*, 2 January 1960, 13; Valerie Russ, "Church Honors Pastor," *Philadelphia Inquirer*, 19 November 2016, https://www.inquirer.com/philly/news/20161120_Triumph_Baptist_Church_honors_Pastor_James_S__Hall_Jr__for_65_years_of_preaching_and_activism.html; Patrick Obley, "Jackie Robinson Ignited," *Columbia (S.C.) State*, 6 April 2013, https://www.the state.com/news/local/civil-rights/article14425475.html.

Five: You Thought We'd Say, "Sorry, Boss"

1. Claudia Smith Brinson, "Black Nursing Assistants Find,'" *Columbia (S.C.) State*, 4 March 2003; Fink and Greenberg, *Upheaval in the Quiet Zone*, 143; Mary Moultrie, interview by the author, 15 January 2008; Charron, *Freedom's Teacher*, 5. Septima Clark developed the concept of Citizenship Schools and broadened its reach with support from Highlander Folk School in Grundy County, Tennessee.

2. Moultrie, interview by the author.

3. Ibid.; Ike Ridley, "Strike Leader Tells," *Afro-American*, 24 May 1969, 1.

4. John E. Wise, interview by Leon Fink, February 1980, box 146, Retail, Wholesale and Department Store Union, Local 1199 Drug and Hospital Union, Hospital Division Records, Kheel Center for Labor Management Documentation and Archives, Martin P. Kheel Center, Cornell University; Moultrie, interview by the author.

5. Martha "M. S." Alston, interview by the author, July 2008; Moultrie, interview by the author. Alston named Betty Lawrence, Frances Mack, Bessie Polite, and someone named Myers as the other four.

6. M. S. Alston, interview by the author; "Black Nurses' Aides," *Lowcountry Newsletter*, 5 March 1968, 14–15, William J. Saunders private collection; J. L. Lowder, RN, 27 December 1967, box 3, William Mellon McCord Papers, Waring Historical Library, MUSC; Moultrie, interview by the author.

7. M. S. Alston, interview by the author.

8. "Black Nurses' Aides," *Lowcountry Newsletter*. Capitalization is newsletter's.

9. M. S. Alston, interview by the author; William J. Saunders, interview by the author, July 2008; "Bill Saunders," *Lowcountry Newsletter*, 5 March 1968, 1–4.

10. Saunders, interview by the author; Anne Braden, "SNCC Trends," *Southern Patriot*,

May 1966, Michael J. Miller Civil Rights Collection, University of Southern Missis-sippi; Moultrie, Saunders, and Rosetta Simmons, interview by Taylor, Citadel Oral History Program.

11. The local HEW compliance committee consisted of Reginald C. Barrett Sr., J. Ar-thur Brown, Russell Brown, Rev. B. J. Glover, and Dr. T. C. McFall. William D. Huff, "Compliance," box 1, McCord Papers; Robert Gordon, "Hospital Workers Fight," *Afro-American*, 3 May 1969, 2.

12. Moultrie, interview by the author; Mark R. Arnold, "Civil Rights and Labor," *National Observer*, 16 June 1969, box 2, McCord Papers.

13. Moultrie, interview by the author; Saunders, interview by the author; Arnold, "Civil Rights and Labor."

14. Moultrie, interview by the author; Saunders, interview by the author; Arnold, "Civil Rights and Labor"; Lillie Doster, interview by the author, June 2008; "Martin Luther King at Local 1199," 10 March 1968, YouTube, https://www.youtube.com/watch?v =IBodqhUGoqo (accessed 29 November 2019).

15. Doster, "Lillie Marsh Doster, Interview U-0386."

16. Fink, "Labor Crusade," 59; Charles Hunter, "Hospital Strike Here," *Charleston (S.C.) Evening Post*, 26 March 1969, B1; Moultrie, interview by the author; Henry Nicholas, interview by the author, 22 July 2009.

17. R. Simmons, interview by the author, 2 July 2008.

18. Ibid.

19. McCord to Dear Fellow Employees, 11 October 1968, box 1, McCord Papers; Murray Seeger, "Carolina Strike Unites," *Los Angeles Times*, 14 April 1969, 7.

20. Moultrie, interview by the author; McCord to John Cummings, 14 October 1968, box 1, McCord Papers.

21. James B. McCord, *My Patients Were Zulus*, 51, 166–67; McCord Hospital, "A Few Achievements," GivenGain Foundation; Biographical Note, McCord Papers.

22. Saunders, interview by the author; "1199B Is Here," *1199 Drug and Hospital News*, May 1969, box 144, Local 1199, Kheel Center; Board of Trustees Minutes, 13 Decem-ber 1968, McCord Papers; Moultrie, interview by Germany, "Telling Our Story."

23. Isaiah Bennett to Barrett, 29 November 1968, box 1, McCord Papers; Louise B. Bur-ney, 5 December 1968, box 1, McCord Papers.

24. M. S. Alston, interview by the author; Barbara Williams, "There's Trouble," *Charleston (S.C.) News and Courier*, 3 March 1969, 15; Moultrie, interview by the author; "Case Study," *Southern Hospitals*, March 1971, box 2, McCord Papers.

25. Wise, minutes, 11 December 1968, box 1, McCord Papers.

26. Board of Trustees, minutes, 11 October 1968, box 1, McCord Papers; Board of Trust-ees, minutes, 13 December 1968, box 1, McCord Papers.

27. Belcher, *Greenville County*, 109; Archie Vernon Huff, *Greenville*, 302–5; "1934: South-ern Workers Spark," *American Postal Worker*, September–October 2013.

28. Hodges, "J. P. Stevens and the Union," 54, 56–57; Textile Workers Union v. Darlington Mfg. Co., 380 U.S. 263 (1965).

29. "Case Study"; W. Huff, Medical College of South Carolina Compliance, box 2, McCord Papers; McCord to Board, 3 March 1969, box 1, McCord Papers; Fred Rigsbee and

Jack Leland, "McCord Says Hospital," *Charleston (S.C.) Evening Post,* 6 May 1969, 1.

30. Moultrie, interview by the author; Affidavits on 17 March 1969, box 1, McCord Papers.

31. Rigsbee and Leland, "McCord Says Hospital"; Moultrie, interview by the author; Affidavits on 17 March 1969; Moultrie, interview by the author; Louise Brown, interview by the author, 1 July 2009.

32. Rigsbee and Leland, "McCord Says Hospital"; Moultrie, interview by the author; Affidavits on 17 March 1969.

33. L. Brown, interview by the author; "Efforts to Meet with McCord Fail," box 1, McCord Papers; Moultrie, interview by the author. While Moultrie, Brown, and some MCH narratives place the workers in the president's office, one hospital narrative says McCord was in his office with the door locked. The narrative in *Southern Hospitals* places everyone in the boardroom.

34. Moultrie, interview by the author.

35. Ibid.; Twelve Statements, box 1, McCord Papers; L. Brown, interview by the author. Moultrie remembers twelve being invited to meet with McCord and the same twelve being fired. Hospital papers indicate fifteen workers were invited, not all from the seventh floor, but afterward only seventh-floor workers were fired. Moultrie named herself, Louise Brown, Andrew Daniels, Rosalie Fields, Priscilla Gladden, Mary Grimes, Helen Husser, Margaret Kelly, Annie Morris Lee, Vera Smalls, Virginia Stanley, and Hazel White, who worked on the eighth floor. Hospital statements and affidavits provided the same names with the occasional addition of Juanita White. See also Isaiah Bennett, list of twelve employees, Isaiah Bennett Papers, Avery Research Center, College of Charleston.

36. L. Brown, question and answer, "Black Stories: Two Cities," showing of *I Am Somebody,* Nickelodeon Theatre, Columbia, South Carolina, 19 February 2018; Moultrie to McCord, telegram, 17 March 1969, box 1, McCord Papers; 1199B Executive Committee to Louise Burney, John Wise, Isaiah Bennett Papers; Bennett to J. Palmer Gaillard Jr., telegram, 17 March 1969, Bennett Papers; Bennett to Gov. Robert McNair, Finway Young, Gaillard, telegram, 17 March 1969, Isaiah Bennett Papers.

37. L. Brown, interview by the author; Meeting Notice, 19 March 1969, box 3, McCord Papers.

38. Moultrie, interview by the author; L. Brown, interview by the author; "Hospital Workers," *Charlotte Observer,* 21 March 1969, B1.

39. The Poor People's March ended in Resurrection City in Washington, D.C., a wood-and-canvas tent encampment of three thousand, where residents and temporary mayor Jesse Jackson stayed for forty-two days.

40. Andrew Young, interview by Fink, January 1980, box 146, Local 1199, Kheel Center; Young, *Easy Burden,* 497; Abernathy, *Walls Came Tumbling,* 542–45. On April 16 the Memphis City Council reached an agreement with the American Federation of State, County, and Municipal Employees to recognize the union and improve wages.

41. Young, *Easy Burden,* 138–39; Nicholas, interview by the author. The Highlander Folk School closed in 1961 when the state of Tennessee revoked its charter and seized its land and buildings. Clark moved the Citizenship Schools under the SCLC.

42. Moultrie, interview by the author; Saunders, interview by the author; L Brown, interview by the author; Anonymous, List of Grievances, Septima P. Clark Papers, Avery Research Center. "I Am Somebody" was coined by Rev. Dr. William Holmes Borders Sr., pastor of Atlanta's Wheat Street Baptist Church. Jackson used the statement as a call-and-response. In 1970 Johnnie Taylor recorded the hit "I Am Somebody" for Stax Records.

43. Moultrie, interview by the author; Dora Ann Reaves, "Hospital Workers," *Charleston (S.C.) Evening Post,* 20 March 1969, 1; Elaine S. Stanford, "Workers Picket," *Charleston (S.C.) News and Courier,* 21 March 1969, 1. Lucille Simmons sang a slow gospel song, "I'll Overcome Some Day," changed *I* to *we,* and thus inspired the evolution of "We Shall Overcome."

44. Reaves, "Hospital Workers"; Stanford, "Workers Picket"; Nicholas, interview by the author.

45. Drago, *Charleston's Avery Center,* 257–58; Bedingfield, *Newspaper Wars,* 152, 169.

46. Baker, *Paradoxes of Desegregation,* 150–53.

47. Fink, "Labor Crusade," 60; Stanford and William Walker Jr., "Medical College Injunction Violated," *Charleston (S.C.) News and Courier,* 22 March 1969, 1; Hunter, "Hospital Services," *Charleston (S.C.) Evening Post,* 24 March 1969, 1.

48. Stanford and W. Walker, "Medical College Injunction Violated," *Charleston (S.C.) News and Courier;* Naomi White, interview by the author, 24 July 2008.

49. N. White, interview by the author; Reaves, "State Can't Negotiate," *Charleston (S.C.) Evening Post,* 21 March 1969, 2.

50. Clarence Singletary, interview by Fink, February 1980, box 146, Local 1199, Kheel Center.

51. "20 Pickets Arrested," *Charlotte Observer,* 24 March 1969, D8; Leland and Reaves, "Clergymen Seek," *Charleston (S.C.) Evening Post,* 22 March 1969, 1; Bass and Nelson, *Orangeburg Massacre,* 64–71.

52. Fielding, interview by the author, 11 January 2009; Leland and Reaves, "Clergymen Seek"; Reaves, "Federal Judge Returns," *Charleston (S.C.) Evening Post,* 26 March 1969, 1; L. Brown, question and answer, Nickelodeon Theater.

53. Leland and Reaves, "Clergymen Seek"; "Isaiah Bennett," Bennett Papers; "Dock Men," *Charleston (S.C.) Evening Post,* 21 March 1969, B1; "Case Study."

54. "Negotiators Meet," *Charleston (S.C.) News and Courier,* 23 March 1969, 1; Saunders, interview by the author; "More than 50," *Charleston (S.C.) News and Courier,* 24 March 1969, 1.

55. Nicholas, interview by the author; Bennett to Delbert L. Woods, telegram, 23 March 1969, Bennett Papers; "S.C. NAACP," *Charlotte Observer,* 25 March 1969, B4; "Newman Resigns Post," *Columbia (S.C.) Record,* 12 April 1969, 15.

56. "50 More Strikers Arrested," *Charlotte Observer,* 25 March 1969, B4; Hunter, "Hospital Services," *Charleston (S.C.) Evening Post,* 24 March 1969, 1; "Medical School Strikers," *Charlotte Observer,* 27 March 1969, 9; Reaves, "Federal Judge Returns."

57. Hunter, "Grievances," *Charleston (S.C.) Evening Post,* 25 March 1969, B1; Reaves, "Ralph Abernathy," *Charleston (S.C.) Evening Post,* 27 March 1969, 1; Reaves, "County

Hospital," *Charleston (S.C.) Evening Post,* 28 March 1969, 1; "30 Children Picket," *Charlotte Observer,* 30 March 1969, D1.

58. R. Simmons, interview by the author; Hunter, "Grievances"; Bass, "Strike at Charleston," *New South* 24, no. 3 (Summer 1969): 36.

59. Reaves, "State Can't Negotiate," *Charleston (S.C.) Evening Post,* 21 March 1969, 1; "S.C. NAACP," *Charlotte Observer,* 25 March 1969, B4; Stanford, "Union Says," *Charleston (S.C.) News and Courier,* 27 March 1969, 1.

60. James T. Wooten, "Carolina Affirms," *New York Times,* 16 May 1969, 31.

61. "30 Children Picket"; Moultrie, interview by the author; "Charleston Hospital Strike—Outtakes," MIRC, Digital Video Repository, https://mirc.sc.edu/islandora /object/usc:29838; handbill, memorial service and rally, 31 March 1968, box 3, McCord Papers.

62. Jack Roach and Stanford, "McNair to Name," *Charleston (S.C.) News and Courier,* 28 March 1969, 1; Harriet Rose Lowe, "The History of the Personnel Division in South Carolina: 1949–1973" (paper, University of South Carolina, 1974), 51–66, South Caroliniana Library; "Civil Rights Act of 1964," Enrolled Acts and Resolutions of Congress, 1789–2011, National Archives Catalog; "Equal Employment Opportunity," Executive Order 11246 of September 28, 1965, Equal Employment Opportunity Commission.

63. Moultrie, interview by the author.

64. N. White, interview by the author; M. S. Alston, interview by the author.

65. Wooten, "14 Rights Leaders," *New York Times,* 21 April 1969, 29; Hunter, "Abernathy Promises," *Charleston (S.C.) Evening Post,* 1 April 1969, B1; Stewart R. King, "Abernathy Pledges," *Charleston (S.C.) News and Courier,* 1 April 1969, 1; Wooten, "Racial Overtones," *New York Times,* 5 April 1969, 14. "It's Your Thing," released by the Isley Brothers in February 1969, reached the top of Billboard's charts. The lyrics include, "It's your thing, do what you want to do; / I can't tell you who to sock it to." "Sock it to me!" became popular in comedy shows.

66. Dan North and Dave Prosten, "Hospital Workers," *1199 Drug and Hospital News,* April 1969, 17, box 144, Local 1199, Kheel Center; Hunter, "Abernathy Promises"; Wooten, "Racial Overtones."

67. Seeger, "Carolina Strike Unites"; Moultrie, interview by the author, 2 July 2009; "30 Children Picket."

68. McCord to Beverly T. DeBerry, 18 June 1969, box 1, McCord Papers; Saunders, interview by the author.

69. Rudolph Pyatt Jr., "HEW Report," *Charleston (S.C.) News and Courier,* 18 June 1969, A1; Jack Nelson, "U.S. May Stop," *Los Angeles Times,* 12 June 1969, 4; McCord to DeBerry, McCord Papers; Brimm to McCord, 19 September 1968, box 3, McCord Papers.

70. M. S. Alston, interview by the author; Saunders, interview by the author.

71. Stanford, "Strikers Seek," *Charleston (S.C.) News and Courier,* 1 April 1969, 1; Fink, "Labor Crusade," 73–74; "Bishop Urges," *Charleston (S.C.) Evening Post,* 25 April 1969, B1.

72. Knox Haynsworth to Board, memo, 2 April 1969, box 1, McCord Papers; "Case Study"; Father William Joyce, "Agitation for Equality," *Afro-American,* 31 May 1969, 6.

73. Charleston Area Community Relations Committee, minutes, 10–11 April 1969, box 1, McCord Papers.

74. Stanford, "McCord Rejects," *Charleston (S.C.) News and Courier,* 3 April 1969, B1; Rigsbee, "Service Affected," *Charleston (S.C.) Evening Post,* 31 March 1969, 1.

75. Stanford, "McCord Rejects"; Reaves, "March Is Planned," *Charleston (S.C.) Evening Post,* 3 April 1969, 1; Twelve Statements, box 1, McCord Papers; "HEW Report: McCord Sought," *Charleston (S.C.) Evening Post,* 18 June 1969, 1; Kay Lingle Koonce, "The Political and Social Impact of the Charleston Hospital Strike" (paper, Public Sector Labor Relations, University of South Carolina Law School, 1981), 43.

76. "Graham Says County," *Charleston (S.C.) News and Courier,* 30 April 1969, B10; N. White, interview by the author; Rigsbee, "Service Affected"; Barbara S. Williams, "Possibility Raised," *Charleston (S.C.) News and Courier,* 7 May 1969.

77. N. White, interview by the author.

78. Ibid. "Hell Angels," without the possessive, is correct. According to Naomi White, the Hell Angels included Eva Alston, Georgetta Way, Alberta Rouse, Hermina Traeye, and four others.

79. R. Simmons, interview by the author; Saunders, interview by the author; N. White, interview by the author; Moultrie, interview by the author.

80. R. Simmons, interview by the author; Saunders, interview by the author; N. White, interview by the author; Moultrie, interview by the author.

81. Thomasina Washington, affidavit, 10 April 1969, box 1, McCord Papers; L. Brown, interview by the author.

82. Stanford, "McCord Rejects." Meeting with McNair were the reverends Thomas Duffy, Mark Sharpe, Z. L. Grady, Leo Crogham, William Joyce, and John Enwright.

83. Reaves and Rigsbee, "Striking Hospital Workers," *Charleston (S.C.) Evening Post,* 9 April 1969, 1.

84. Moultrie, memorial service telegram, 28 March 1969, Bennett Papers; Stanford and W. Walker, "Peaceful March," *Charleston (S.C.) News and Courier,* 5 April 1969, 1; "6,000 Guard Troops," *Washington (Pa.) Observer Reporter,* 4 April 1969, 1; "Striking Workers," *Charleston (S.C.) News and Courier,* 7 April 1969, B1.

85. Stanford and W. Walker, "Peaceful March"; R. Simmons, interview by the author.

86. Roach, "Meeting with McNair," *Charleston (S.C.) News and Courier,* 9 April 1969, B1; Bass, "State House Pickets," *Charlotte Observer,* 8 April 1969, B1; Moultrie, interview by the author.

87. C. J. Williams, *Out of-the-Box,* 97–150; Fred Henderson Moore, interview by the author, July 2008; Grose, *South Carolina at the Brink,* 242.

88. Bass, "Striker Threatens," *Charlotte Observer,* 10 April 1969, B1; "Strike Situation," *Charleston (S.C.) News and Courier,* 20 April 1969, 6.

89. Seeger, "Carolina Strike Unites"; Hugh Gibson, "Charleston Bears Brunt," *Charleston (S.C.) News and Courier,* 14 May 1969, 1; Father Leon J. Hubacz, "Letter to Ralph

Abernathy," *Charleston (S.C.) Evening Post,* 7 May 1969, 10. Grammar and mechanics are Hubacz's; Abernathy, *Walls Came Tumbling,* 543.

90. Reaves and Rigsbee, "Striking Hospital Workers Plan," *Charleston (S.C.) Evening Post;* Reaves, "Harassment Shows Increase," *Charleston (S.C.) Evening Post,* 10 April 1969, 1; "Strikers, Police Clash," *Charlotte Observer,* 11 April 1969, B1.

91. W. Walker, "Court Orders Limit," *Charleston (S.C.) News and Courier,* 11 April 1969, 1.

92. Moultrie, interview by the author; Reaves, "31 More Pickets Arrested," *Charleston (S.C.) Evening Post,* 12 April 1969, B1; "Jailed Hospital Workers," *Afro-American,* 19 April 1969, 3.

93. Moultrie, interview by the author; N. White, interview by the author.

94. Moultrie, interview by the author; N. White, interview by the author.

95. W. K. Pillow Jr., "Graham Complains," *Charleston (S.C.) News and Courier,* 16 April 1969, B1; "Threatening Phone Calls," *Charleston (S.C.) News and Courier,* 15 April 1969, B1; "Case Study"; L. Brown, question and answer, Nickelodeon Theater; Nicholas, interview by the author; Moultrie, interview by the author; Fink, "Labor Crusade," 61.

96. Moultrie, interview by the author; "1199B Is Here," *1199 Drug and Hospital News,* 20.

97. Timothy Grant, interview by the author, 14 July 2009; List of Those Arrested, 23 June 1969, Isaiah Bennett Papers; Moultrie, interview by the author; L. Brown, interview by the author; Saunders, interview by the author.

98. Moultrie to Congresswoman Shirley Chisholm, 24 March 1969, Bennett Papers; Chisholm, "Charleston Strike," *New York Times,* 21 April 1969, 46. In 1968 Chisholm became the first African American woman to serve in Congress and, in 1972, the first African American woman to seek the Democratic presidential nomination. Wooten, "14 Leaders," *New York Times,* 21 April 1969, 29.

99. Stewart R. King, "Abernathy Sets," *Charleston (S.C.) News and Courier,* 22 April 1969, B1; Hunter, "Abernathy 'Bears Witness,'" *Charleston (S.C.) Evening Post,* 22 April 1969, 1; Wooten, "Abernathy Leads," *New York Times,* 23 April 1969, 24; "Abernathy Leads 800," *Charleston (S.C.) News and Courier,* 23 April 1969, B1.

100. "Hospital Issue Needs," *Charleston (S.C.) Evening Post,* 23 April 1969, 16; Nicholas, interview by the author; Young, *Easy Burden,* 497; Foner, *Not for Bread Alone,* 70.

101. Williams, "Trustees Reaffirm," *Charleston (S.C.) News and Courier,* 24 April 1969, B1; "400 Youths Urged," *Charleston (S.C.) News and Courier,* 24 April 1969, 6. *Fuzz* was a derogatory term for police.

102. W. Walker and S. R. King, "Guardsmen Ordered," *Charleston (S.C.) News and Courier,* 26 April 1969, 1; Ron Brinson, "Abernathy Leads," *Charleston (S.C.) Evening Post,* 25 April 1969, 1; Wooten, "Abernathy Jailed." Because local march estimates were consistently low, *New York Times* numbers are used.

103. R. Brinson, "Abernathy Leads"; Wooten, "Abernathy Jailed."

104. L. Brown, interview by the author.

105. R. Brinson, "Abernathy Leads"; Wooten, "Abernathy Jailed"; Wooten, "100 Negroes Seized," *New York Times,* 27 April 1969, 60; Robert Ford, interview by the author, 26 July 2009. From 1974 until 1992, Ford served on Charleston County Council; from

1993 until 2013, he represented Charleston's District 42 in the S.C. Senate, resigning during a scandal.

106. Clyde Johnson, "Absentee Students Rally," *Charleston (S.C.) Evening Post,* 28 April 1969, 1; Wooten, "100 Negroes Seized"; "Hospitals Make Offers," *Charleston (S.C.) Evening Post,* 26 April 1969, 1; "Arrest of 30," *Charleston (S.C.) News and Courier,* 27 April 1969, 1.

107. Carl B. "Pedro" Stokes, interview by the author, 28 July 2009. Stokes served in undercover operations, crowd control, forensics, and investigations for SLED. W. Huff, Medical College of South Carolina Compliance, box 2, McCord Papers.

108. S. R. King, "47 Are Arrested," *Charleston (S.C.) News and Courier,* 28 April 1969, 1; "45 More," *New York Times,* 29 April 1969, 29.

109. "Arrests in Charleston," *New York Times,* 29 April 1969, 44; Wooten, "Charleston Armed Camp," *New York Times,* 29 April 1969, 42; S. King, "Police Arrest 128," *Charleston (S.C.) News and Courier,* 29 April 1969, 1; Joyce, "Agitation for Equality."

110. "Firmness and Fairness," *Charleston (S.C.) News and Courier,* 29 April 1969, 10; "Arrests in Charleston," *New York Times;* "Nixon Sending Observers," *New York Times,* 10 May 1969, 51.

111. Edrena Johnson, "Diary from a Charleston Jail," *1199 Drug and Hospital News,* July 1969, 8, Charleston County Public Library.

112. Moultrie, interview by the author; "1199B Is Here to Stay," *1199 Drug and Hospital News,* 15.

113. Charleston Clergy Emergency Fund, 29 April to 12 May 1969, box 3, McCord Papers; M. S. Alston, interview by the author; Rigsbee and Leland, "Tensions Eased," *Charleston (S.C.) Evening Post,* 16 May 1969, 1.

114. Moultrie, interview by the author; Nicholas, interview by the author; L. Brown, question and answer, Nickelodeon.

115. Moultrie, interview by the author; Nicholas, interview by the author; R. Simmons, interview by the author.

116. M. S. Alston, interview by the author.

117. Robert D. McFadden, "Leon Davis," *New York Times,* 15 September 1992, 87; Gibson, "Charleston Bears Brunt"; "An Open Letter," *Charleston (S.C.) Evening Post,* 25 April 1969, 10.

118. Ralph Abernathy, "A Letter from the Charleston County Jail," *Charleston (S.C.) Evening Post,* 29 April 1969, 3.

119. Williams, "SCLC Head Freed," *Charleston (S.C.) News and Courier,* 3 May 1969, 1; Abernathy, *Walls Came Tumbling,* 554; Panetta, *Bring Us Together,* 186; "Abernathy Calls Nixon," *New York Times,* 14 May 1969, 19; "Abernathy Unsuccessful," *Charleston (S.C.) News and Courier,* 14 May 1969, B1; "Abernathy Ends Drive," *New York Times,* 17 May 1969, 40.

120. Foner, *Not for Bread Alone,* 73; "Violence Hits Charleston," *Pittsburgh Post-Gazette,* 2 May 1969, 10; Belvin Horres, "Two Planes, Auto," *Charleston (S.C.) Evening Post,* 29 April 1969, B1; Saunders, interview by the author; Moore, interview by the author.

121. Fink and Greenberg, *Upheaval in the Quiet Zone,* 144; R. Brinson and Clyde Johnson,

"Mrs. King Leads Strike," *Charleston (S.C.) Evening Post*, 30 April 1969; "S.C. Hospital Workers," *Afro-American*, 3 May 1969, 2; "Mrs. King Will Lead," *New York Times*, 30 April 1969, 40; S. King, "Coretta Scott King Pledges," *Charleston (S.C.) News and Courier*, 30 April 1969, 1.

122. Wooten, "Mrs. King Leads," *New York Times*, 1 May 1969, 31; Wooten, "Charleston's Strike," *New York Times*, 4 May 1969, B4; S. King, "Widow of Dr. King," *Charleston (S.C.) News and Courier*, 1 May 1969, B1; R. Brinson, "Mrs. King Leads," *Charleston (S.C.) Evening Courier*, 30 April 1969, 1.

123. Pillow and Betty Walker, "Economy Feeling Pangs," *Charleston (S.C.) News and Courier*, 4 May 1969, D3; Saunders, interview by the author; Lane, "History of Banking"; "Mayor Gaillard Urges," *Charleston (S.C.) Evening Post*, 29 April 1969, 1; "Graham Says County Doors," *Charleston (S.C.) News and Courier*, 7 May 1969, B1; "Graham Standing Firm," *Charleston (S.C.) News and Courier*, 7 May 1969, B1.

124. Ashley Cooper, "Doing the Charleston," *Charleston (S.C.) News and Courier*, 4 May 1969, D1. Under his real name, Gilbreth was coauthor with sister Ernestine Gilbreth Carey of the bestsellers *Cheaper by the Dozen* and *Belles on Their Toes*. Anthony Ashley Cooper, First Earl of Shaftesbury, 1621–83, was among the first eight lords proprietors of Carolina. "Nixon Rejects," *Schenectady Gazette*, 3 May 1969, 2; "S.C. Hospital Workers Fight," *Afro-American*, 3 May 1969, 1.

125. "Negro Leader Urges," *Spokane Daily Chronicle*, 2 May 1969, 2; Saunders, interview by the author; R. Brinson, "Abernathy's Opinion," *Charleston (S.C.) Evening Post*, 2 May 1969, B1; Cooper, "Doing the Charleston," *Charleston (S.C.) News and Courier*, 6 May 1969, B1.

126. Williams and King, "Curfew Is Clamped," *Charleston (S.C.) News and Courier*, 3 May 1969, 1; Abernathy, *Walls Came Tumbling*, 548–49.

127. "Possibility of Solution," *Charleston (S.C.) News and Courier*, 3 May 1969, 1; R. Brinson and Hunter, "Strike Settlement Sought," *Charleston (S.C.) Evening Post*, 8 May 1969, B1; Pyatt, "Charleston—Another Selma?" *Charleston (S.C.) News and Courier*, 4 May 1969, 15; "Nixon Sends Observers," *Washington Post*, 10 May 1969, 3.

128. "Legislature Asked," *Charleston (S.C.) Evening Post*, 29 April 1969, 1; S. King and Roach, "Curfew Imposed," *Charleston (S.C.) News and Courier*, 2 May 1969, 1; Gibson, "McNair Squares Off," *Charleston (S.C.) News and Courier*, 2 May 1969, 1.

129. Gibson, "McNair Squares Off"; Gibson, "State of Siege," *Charleston (S.C.) News and Courier*, 4 May 1969, 15.

130. Pyatt, "Charleston—Another Selma?"

131. "Probe Ordered," *Charleston (S.C.) News and Courier*, 10 May 1969, 7; Ridley, "Charleston Curfew Assailed," *Afro-American*, 24 May 1969, 2; Wooten, "Charleston's Strike," *New York Times*, 4 May 1969, B4; "Strife Leads," *Los Angeles Times*, 2 May 1969, 13.

132. N. White, interview by the author.

133. "Strike Termed First Step," *Charleston (S.C.) News and Courier*, 5 May 1969, B1.

134. T. Grant, interview by the author. Since 1953 Penn Center had served as a safe and somewhat secret location for biracial meetings of organizations such as the SCLC, the Citizenship Schools, CORE, and SNCC.

135. N. White, interview by the author; R. Simmons, interview by the author; T. Grant, interview by the author; Moore, interview by the author; M. S. Alston, interview by the author; Moultrie, interview by the author; "Negotiators Meet," *Charleston (S.C.) News and Courier,* 23 March 1969, 1.

136. S. King and Roach, "Curfew Imposed," *Charleston (S.C.) News and Courier,* 2 May 1969, 1; T. Grant, interview by the author; N. White, interview by the author; Moultrie, interview by the author; Moore, interview by the author; "Chief Conroy," *Charleston (S.C.) Evening Post,* 2 May 1969, B1; Ford, interview by the author.

137. James Coates, "Riots Follow Killing," *Chicago Tribune,* 11 August 2015, chicagotribune .com; Michael Walsh, "Violence in Baltimore," Yahoo News, 28 April 2015, https:// news.yahoo.com/baltimore-riots-freddie-gray-police-violence-maryland-18074 0987.html; "Riots Erupt in Washington, D.C.," World History Project, https://world historyproject.org/1968/4/4/riots-erupt-in-washington-dc-following-martin-luther -king-jr-assassination; Rucker and Upton, *Encyclopedia of American Race Riots,* 332, 368, https://books.google.com/books?id=oLoXHHc_uUkC&printsec=frontcover& dq=Rucker+and+Upton,+Encyclopedia+of+American+Race+Riots,&hl=en& newbks=1&newbks_redir=0&sa=X&ved=2ahUKEwiVyNjExOjoAhVETt8KHaso BMsQ6AEwAHoECAIQAg#v=onepage&q=Rucker%20and%20Upton%2C%20 Encyclopedia%20of%20American%20Race%20Riots%2C&f=false.

138. "Labor Leaders Join," *Palm Beach Post,* 12 May 1969, 16; Wooten, "A Grim Charleston Looks," *New York Times,* 10 May 1969, 64; Roach, "Five Union Chiefs Meet," *Charleston (S.C.) Evening Post,* 9 May 1969, B1; Williams, "McLeod Silent," *Charleston (S.C.) News and Courier,* 10 May 1969, 1.

139. Rigsbee and Leland, "McCord Says Hospital," *Charleston (S.C.) Evening Post,* 6 May 1969, 1; Memorandum, 2 May 1969, box 1, McCord Papers.

140. Wooten, "Grim Charleston Looks"; Williams and S. King, "Talk Ends," *Charleston (S.C.) News and Courier,* 9 May 1969, 1; R. Brinson, "Trustee Discouraged," *Charleston (S.C.) Evening Post,* 9 May 1969, B1; Ridley, "Mass March Backs," *Afro-American,* 17 May 1969, 1; McCord, Grievance Procedure, 5 December 1968, box 1, McCord Papers; "Strife Leads," *Los Angeles Times,* 2 May 1969, 13.

141. John Kifner, "12,000 March," *New York Times,* 12 May 1969, 43; "10,000 Join Abernathy," *Los Angeles Times,* 12 May 1969, 4; Pillow and S. King, "Thousands March," *Charleston (S.C.) News and Courier,* 12 May 1969, 1.

142. Ridley, "6,000 Back Hospital Workers," *Baltimore Afro-American,* 13 May 1969, 20; "Negro Strike Gathers," *St. Petersburg Times,* 12 May 1969, 4; "Labor Leaders Join"; Abernathy, *Walls Came Tumbling,* 553.

143. Hunter, "National Labor Fund," *Charleston (S.C.) Evening Post,* 12 May 1969, 1; Foner, *Not for Bread Alone,* 75. Jackson ran for president in 1984, following Chisholm as the second black candidate to run a national campaign.

144. Foner, "Reminiscences," session 10.

145. Moultrie, interview by the author.

146. Kifner, "12,000 March"; Foner, "Reminiscences," session 10.

147. Leland and Rigsbee, "Strike Pressure," *Charleston (S.C.) Evening Post,* 14 May 1969, 1; Jules Loh, "Gears Meshed," *Daytona Beach (Fla.) Morning Journal,* 24 August 1969,

D1; Nicholas, interview by the author; Stokes, interview by the author; Transcript of Statement by Agent, March 1969, box 3, McCord Papers.

148. "Charleston Coalition," *New York Times*, 14 May 1969, 46; "Charleston Medical Society," *Charleston (S.C.) News and Courier*, 14 May 1969, 2; Gibson, "Charleston Bears Brunt."

149. Ford, interview by the author; Nicholas, interview by the author; Wooten, "Mrs. King and Abernathy," *New York Times*, 31 May 1969, 21.

150. Fink and Greenberg, *Upheaval in the Quiet Zone*, 145.

151. Statements on March 17, box 1, McCord Papers; McCord, Short Resume of Discussion with HEW Team, n.d., box 3, McCord Papers.

152. Murray Seeger, "Racial Inquiry Starts," *Los Angeles Times*, 20 May 1969, 5; "U.S. Probes Bias," *Washington Post*, 20 May 1969, 3; Billy Bowles, "HEW Head Says," *Charleston (S.C.) Evening Post*, 12 June 1969, 1; Foner, "Reminiscences," session 10; Bruce Galphin, "Mrs. King in Charleston," *Washington Post*, 30 May 1969, 2.

153. Lane, "History of Banking"; Saunders, interview by the author.

154. "Strike Termed," *Charleston (S.C.) News and Courier*, 5 May 1969. B1; "Charleston: Blacks," *Michigan Daily*, 29 May 1969, 1; Ford, interview by the author.

155. Leland and Rigsbee, "Strike Pressure," *Charleston (S.C.) Evening Post*, 14 May 1969, 1; "Support the Hospital Workers," handbill, box 3, McCord Papers; "Abernathy's Plan," *Charleston (S.C.) News and Courier*, 24 May 1969, 8; Fink, "Labor Crusade," 74.

156. Moore, interview by the author; Foner, *Not for Bread Alone*, 71; Williams and S. King, "Curfew Is Clamped"; Rigsbee and Leland, "Tensions Eased"; Gibson, "Union 'Victory,'" *Charleston (S.C.) News and Courier*, 18 May 1969, 1; Foner, "Reminiscences," session 9.

157. Ridley, "Leader in Hospital Row," *Baltimore Afro-American*, 17 May 1969, 1, 2.

158. "Troopers Cleared," *Oswosso (Mich.) Argus-Press*, 27 May 1969, 13; "No Indictments," *Afro-American*, 16 November 1968, 1; Proposed Agenda, 8 May 1969, box 1, McCord Papers; J. Edwin Schachte, Schachte to Board, confidential memorandum, 26–27 May 1969, Pinopolis, South Carolina, box 2, McCord Papers; Williams and S. King, "Curfew Is Clamped"; Williams, "Possibility of Solution," *Charleston (S.C.) News and Courier*, 3 May 1969, 1.

159. Schachte to Board, 26 May 1969, box 1, McCord Papers; William D. Huff, 24 May 1969, box 1, McCord Papers; Schachte, chronology, 4 August 1969, box 2, McCord Papers.

160. Wooten, "Mrs. King and Abernathy Vow," *New York Times*, 31 May 1969, 21; King, "Support Growing," *Charleston (S.C.) News and Courier*, 30 May 1969, B1.

161. Panetta, *Bring Us Together*, 124; "Farmer Intends," *Afro- American*, 22 February 1 969, 1.

162. Foner, *Not for Bread Alone*, 77; Foner, "Reminiscences," session 10; Panetta, *Bring Us Together*, 186; "Abernathy Says," *Charleston (S.C.) Evening Post*, 14 May 1969, B1.

163. Brimm to McCord, 5 June 1969, box 1, McCord Papers.

164. Rigsbee, "HEW Recommends," *Charleston (S.C.) Evening Post*, 10 June 1969, 1; Panetta, *Bring Us Together*, 183; Brimm to McCord, 5 June 1969, box 1, McCord Papers; Jack Nelson, "U.S. May Stop," *Los Angeles Times*, 12 June 1969, 4; Galphin, "HEW

Orders 12," *Washington Post,* 12 June 1969, 4; Fink, "Labor Crusade," 75; Meeting of the Board of Trustees, minutes, 5 June 1969, Waring Historical Library; Galphin, "Charleston Pact Seen," *Washington Post,* 10 June 1969, 6; "Graham's Letter Shows," *Charleston (S.C.) News and Courier,* 3 June 1969, B1.

165. Grose, *South Carolina at the Brink,* 253, 255; Various Memoranda, box 1, McCord Papers; Schachte to Board, 6 June 1969, box 1, McCord Papers.

166. Ridley, "Charleston Strike Leader."

167. "Strike in Charleston," *New York Times,* 21 April 1969, 46; "Charleston Coalition," *New York Times,* 14 May 1969, 46; "Charleston Peace Path," *New York Times,* 6 June 1969, 42.

168. Various Memoranda, box 1, McCord Papers; Schachte, box 1, McCord Papers. In an interview with the author, Saunders denied that he and Rev. Henry Grant made such statements, but he also said that the two were convinced that the SCLC and 1199 had made a deal not to pursue setting up a local union office.

169. Meeting of the Board of Trustees, minutes, 8 June 1969, box 1, McCord Papers; McCord to W. Huff, 12 June 1969, box 1, McCord Papers; "Major Obstacle," *Charleston (S.C.) Evening Post,* 11 June 1969, 1; Grose, *South Carolina at the Brink,* 257; Reaves and Leland, "Strikers Begin," *Charleston (S.C.) Evening Post,* 13 June 1969, 1.

170. Moore, interview by the author; Foner, "Reminiscences," session 10.

171. McCord to W. Huff, 12 June 1969, box 1, McCord Papers; "Accord Fails," *New York Times,* 14 June 1969, 26; McCord to Saunders, 12 June 1969, box 1, McCord Papers; Pillow, "Authorization to Rehire," *Charleston (S.C.) News and Courier,* 11 June 1969, B1; "State Voids," *Washington Post,* 13 June 1969, 12; "Intransigence in Charleston," *Time,* 20 June 1969, http://content.time.com/time/magazine/article/0,9171,844860,00.html (accessed 29 November 2019).

172. McCord Responses, press, box 2, McCord Papers; "Dr. McCord," *Charleston (S.C.) Evening Post,* 20 June 1969, 1; Margaret M. Wilcox, 'Hospital Rescinds," *Charleston (S.C.) News and Courier,* 20 June 1969, l; Pillow, "Authorization to Rehire"; "Rehiring Offer Withdrawn," *Charleston (S.C.) News and Courier,* 13 June 1969, 1; Billy E. Bowles, "Thurmond Says," *Charleston (S.C.) News and Courier,* 13 June 1969, 1; "Political Infighting," *Washington Post,* 16 June 1969, 1; "Charleston Strike," *New York Times,* 18 June 1969, 46.

173. Pyatt, "Now Political Football," *Charleston (S.C.) News and Courier,* 15 June 1969, 1; Galphin, "HEW Orders 12," *Washington Post,* 12 June 1969, 4; "Workers Want Backing," *Hendersonville (N.C.) Times-News,* 9 June 1969, 20; Nicholas, interview by the author.

174. Reaves and Leland, "Begin to Regroup," *Charleston (S.C.) Evening Post,* 13 June 1969, 1; "Groups March," *Charleston (S.C.) News and Courier,* 17 June 1969, B1; "Seven Persons Given," *Charleston (S.C.) Evening Post,* 17 June 1969, B1.

175. Fielding, interview by the author; Saunders, interview by the author.

176. William Cotterell, "SCLC 'Wrecking Crew,'" *Hendersonville (N.C.) Times-News,* 5 July 1969, 1.

177. "Curfew Reinstated," *Charleston (S.C.) Evening Post,* 21 June 1969, 1; H. Williams, "Hosea Williams Interview."

178. W. Walker, "Violence Follows," *Charleston (S.C.) News and Courier,* 21 June 1969; "Curfew Reinstated"; Cotterell, "Abernathy Jailed," 21 June 1969, *Lexington (N.C.) Dispatch,* 1; Abernathy, *Walls Came Tumbling,* 558; Ralph D. Abernathy v. John F. Conroy, 429 F.2d 1170 (1970).

179. Abernathy, *Walls Came Tumbling,* 559; N. White, interview by the author; "Violence Flares," *Beaver County (Penn.) Times,* 21 June 1969, 1.

180. "Police Hold Abernathy," *Toledo Blade,* 22 June 1969, 10; S. King and W. Walker, "Curfew Again," *Charleston (S.C.) News and Courier,* 22 June 1969, 1, 2; "Curfew Reinstated."

181. Abernathy, *Walls Came Tumbling,* 556; Wooten, "Abernathy Held," *New York Times,* 22 June 1969, 1; Saunders, interview by the author; Moore, interview by the author; "Strike's 'Fringe Element,'" *Sarasota (Fla.) Herald-Tribune,* 22 June 1969, 16; S. King, "Police Turn Back," *Charleston (S.C.) News and Courier,* 23 June 1969, B1; "Charleston Goes Under," *Gadsden (Ala.) Times,* 22 June 1969, 1; Wooten, "Negroes Visit White," *New York Times,* 23 June 1969, 44; Jane Thornhill, interview by the author, June 2010.

182. Abernathy, *Walls Came Tumbling,* 554, 559–67; "Hospital Expected," *Charleston (S.C.) Evening Post,* 24 June 1969, B1; "Mrs. Abernathy Vows," *Charleston (S.C.) Evening Post,* 23 June 1969; S. King, "Police Turn Back."

183. Wooten, "Tension Is Growing," *New York Times,* 25 June 1969, 25; McCord to Robert H. Finch, 21 June 1969, box 2, McCord Papers; Board Memorandum, 23 June 1969, box 1, McCord Papers; Leland, "Hospital Will Rehire," *Charleston (S.C.) Evening Post,* 28 June 1969, 1; Bass, "Strike at Charleston," 41.

184. N. White, interview by the author; Koonce, "Political and Social Impact," 47; Saunders, interview by the author.

185. Foner, *Not for Bread Alone,* 79; Panetta, *Bring Us Together,* 187; Leland, "Hospital Will Rehire"; "Hospital Strike," *New York Times,* 28 June 1969, 1; Bass, "Strike at Charleston," 41, 43; McCord to *Newsweek,* 9 July 1969, box 1, McCord Papers; T. R. Waring with Lane, summary of a conference, 29 September 1969, private collection of Saunders; "HEW Report," *Charleston (S.C.) Evening Post,* 18 June 1969, 1; "Dr. McCord," *Charleston (S.C.) Evening Post,* 20 June 1969, 1.

186. Young, *Easy Burden,* 499–500; Sybil Fix and Herb Frazier, "Charleston Was Benchmark," *Charleston (S.C.) News and Courier,* 17 April 1994, 8; W. Walker and S. King, "Labor Chiefs Shocked," *Charleston (S.C.) News and Courier,* 26 June 1969, 1.

187. "Dixie Shows Power," *Afro-American,* 21 June 1969, 1; Victor Riesel, "ILA Plans Boycott," *Beaver County (Penn.) Times,* 19 June 1969, 6; U.S. Department of Labor, "Impact of Longshore Strikes," 30 January 1970, 4, Institute of Industrial Relations Library, University of California, Berkeley; Bass, "Strike at Charleston," 43; Leland, "Hospital Will Rehire"; Stoddard, *Re: Gedney Main Howe Jr.,* 149.

188. Wooten, "Abernathy Waits," *New York Times,* 29 June 1969, 22; Rigsbee, "Federal Mediators Meet," *Charleston (S.C.) Evening Post,* 27 June 1969, 1; W. Walker, "Medical College Strike Ends," *Charleston (S.C.) News and Courier,* 28 June 1969, 1; W. Huff, Medical College of South Carolina Compliance, box 2, McCord Papers; "Hospital Dispute Settled," *Sumter (S.C.) Daily Item,* 28 June 1969, 1.

189. Moultrie, interview by the author; Saunders, interview by the author; Leland, "Hospital Will Rehire"; "Hospital Strike," *New York Times,* 28 June 1969, 1.

190. Foner, "Reminiscences," session 10; "Hospital Strike," *New York Times;* Abernathy, *Walls Came Tumbling,* 570–71; Bass, "Strike at Charleston," 38.

191. Graham to County Council, 26 June 1969, box 1, McCord Papers; Young to Graham, 27 June 1969, box 1, McCord Papers; W. Walker, "Rehiring Sole Bar," *Charleston (S.C.) News and Courier,* 29 June 1969, 1; R. Simmons, interview by the author.

192. W. Walker, "Rehiring Sole Bar"; S. King, "Negotiations Deadlocked," *Charleston (S.C.) News and Courier,* 1 July 1969, 1; Williams, "High Hopes," *Charleston (S.C.) News and Courier,* 3 July 1969, 1; "Hospital Strikers Reject," *Charleston (S.C.) Evening Post,* 1 July 1969, B1; Chronology and Outline of Events, 26 June 1969 to 7 July 1969, box 1, McCord Papers.

193. Rigsbee, "Offers Rejected," *Charleston (S.C.) Evening Post,* 2 July 1969, B1; "County Hospital Strikers," *Charleston (S.C.) News and Courier,* 3 July 1969, B1; Wooten, "Abernathy Leaves Jail," *New York Times,* 4 July 1969, 6; Abernathy, *Walls Came Tumbling,* 574–75; "Strike Mediator," *Charleston (S.C.) News and Courier,* 6 July 1969, D1.

194. Young, *Easy Burden,* 499; "Hospital Strike Goes On," *New York Times,* 14 July 1969, 35; "230 Hospital Workers," *Charleston (S.C.) Evening Post,* 5 July 1969, B1; Rigsbee, "Federal Mediator Here," *Charleston (S.C.) Evening Post,* 7 July 1969, B1; "County Pondering," *Charleston (S.C.) Evening Post,* 8 July 1969, B1. In 2019 dollars $13,850.00 is $96,825.84.

195. County Council's Proposal, 11 July 1969, box 1, McCord Papers; "Strikers Reject Offer," *Charleston (S.C.) Evening Post,* 12 July 1969; "Strike Far," *Sumter (S.C.) Daily Item,* 14 July 1969, 1.

196. R. Simmons, interview by the author, 2 July 1969. Included in the strikers' negotiating committee were Stalin Bryant, Alma Harden, Willene Myers, and Hermina Traeye.

197. County Council's Proposal, 18 July 1969, private collection of Rosetta Simmons; "2d Hospital Ends," *New York Times,* 19 July 1969, 1; "Hospital Walkout Ends," *Charleston (S.C.) Evening Post,* 19 July 1969, 1; B. Walker, "Hospital Strike Settled," *Charleston (S.C.) News and Courier,* 19 July 1969, 1; "Charleston Hospital Walkout," *St. Petersburg Times,* 19 July 1969, 1; R. Simmons, interview by the author.

198. Bass, "Strike at Charleston," 37; Young, *Easy Burden,* 500; Koonce, "Political and Social Impact," 67; Riches, *Civil Rights Movement,* 98; Moultrie, "Mary Moultrie, William Saunders, Rosetta Simmons," 5 March 2009, Citadel Oral History Program, The Citadel; "SCLC Leader Visits," *Daytona Beach Morning Journal,* 28 January 1970, 11; "Rev. Abernathy Fasts," *New York Herald-Tribune,* 24 June 1969, 3; R. Simmons, interview by the author.

199. "Strike Aid," *1199 Drug and Hospital News,* September 1969, 11, Charleston County Public Library; Foner, "Reminiscences," sessions 10–11; Foner, *Not for Bread Alone,* 81; Nicholas, interview by the author.

200. "Federal Role Played," *Charleston (S.C.) Evening Post,* 28 June 1969; Leon Davis, "Lesson from Charleston," *1199 Drug and Hospital News,* September 1969, Charleston County Public Library; Young, *Easy Burden,* 495; Abernathy, *Walls Came Tumbling,*

544, 575, 579–83. Young left the SCLC to run for Congress and won; in 1972 he became Georgia's first black representative since Reconstruction and, in 1977, U.S. ambassador to the United Nations. Abernathy continued as president of a fading SCLC until 1976, when he was asked to resign and did so.

201. "2d Hospital Ends"; Kurtz, *Workplace Justice,* 58–59; "Charleston Local 1199B," *1199 Drug and Hospital News,* November 1969, 3, Charleston County Public Library.

202. "SCLC and Hospital Workers Win," *SCLC News,* 1 July 1969, Steve Estes Papers; Moore, interview by the author; Grievance Procedure, 29 July 1969, box 1, McCord Papers; Nicholas, interview by the author; Moultrie, interview by the author; R. Simmons, interview by the author.

203. Moultrie to James W. Colbert Jr., 22 August 1969, box 3, McCord Papers; Douglas Jackson to C. L. Fennessy, 3 September 1969, box 3, McCord Papers; McCord to Brimm, 15 October 1969, box 1, McCord Papers.

204. R. Simmons, interview by the author.

205. Nicholas, interview by the author; Moultrie, interview by the author; R. Simmons, interview by the author; Various Memos, August and September 1969, box 3, McCord Papers; Foner, "Reminiscences," sessions 10–11.

206. Moultrie, interview by the author; L. Brown, interview by the author; N. White, interview by the author.

207. Moultrie, interview by the author.

208. M. S. Alston, interview by the author; L Brown, interview by the author; Moultrie, interview by the author; R. Simmons, interview by the author; N. White, interview by the author.

Bibliography

Abernathy, Ralph David. *And the Walls Came Tumbling Down*. New York: Harper & Row, 1989.

Anderson, Carol Elaine. *Eyes Off the Prize: The United Nations and the African-American Struggle for Human Rights, 1944–1955*. Cambridge: Cambridge University Press, 2003.

Anderson, Madeline, dir. *I Am Somebody*. New York: American Foundation of Nonviolence, 1969.

Arsenault, Ray. *Freedom Riders: 1961 and the Struggle for Racial Justice*. New York: Oxford University Press, 2006.

Ashmore, Harry S. *Hearts and Minds: The Anatomy of Racism from Roosevelt to Reagan*. New York: McGraw-Hill, 1982.

Baker, R. Scott. *Paradoxes of Desegregation: African American Struggles for Educational Equality in Charleston, South Carolina, 1926–1972*. Columbia: University of South Carolina Press, 2006.

Bartels, Virginia B., ed. *The History of South Carolina Schools*. Rock Hill: Center for Educator Recruitment, Retention, and Advancement, Winthrop University, 2004.

Bass, Jack, and Jack Nelson. *The Orangeburg Massacre*. Macon, Ga.: Mercer University Press, 1984.

Bass, Jack, and Marilyn W. Thompson. *Strom: The Complicated Personal and Political Life of Strom Thurmond*. New York: Public Affairs, 2005.

Beacham, Frank. "This Magic Moment: When the Ku Klux Klan Tried to Kill Rhythm and Blues Music in South Carolina." In Moore and Burton, *Toward the Meeting of the Waters*, 119–41.

Bedingfield, Sid. *Newspaper Wars: Civil Rights and White Resistance in South Carolina, 1935–1965*. Urbana: University of Illinois Press, 2017.

Belcher, Ray. *Greenville County, South Carolina*. Charleston: History Press, 2006.

Blair, Ezell A., Jr. "Ezell Blair, Stokely Carmichael, Lucy Thornton, Jean Wheeler." Interview by Robert Penn Warren. In *Robert Penn Warren's Who Speaks for the Negro: An Archival Collection*. Nashville: Robert Penn Warren Center for the Humanities, Vanderbilt University, 1964.

Boulware, Harold R., Sr. "Quest for Civil Rights: Judge Harold R. Boulware Sr." Interview by Grace McFadden. Columbia: Quest for Human/Civil Rights—Oral Recollections of Black South Carolinians, Moving Image Research Collections, University of South Carolina, n.d.

Boyce, Travis D. "I Am Leaving and Not Looking Back: The Life of Benner C. Turner." Ph.D. diss., College of Education, Ohio University, 2009.

Branch, Taylor. *Parting the Waters: America in the King Years 1954–1963.* New York: Simon & Schuster, 1988.

Brinkley, Alan, and Davis Dyer, eds. *The American Presidency.* New York: Houghton Mifflin, 2004.

Brown, Cynthia Stokes, ed. *Ready from Within: Septima Clark and the Civil Rights Movement. A First Person Narrative.* Navarro, Cal.: Wild Trees, 1986.

Brown, Millicent E. "The NAACP Years." In Logan, *Spirit of an Activist,* 63–82.

Burke, W. Lewis. *All for Civil Rights: African American Lawyers in South Carolina, 1868–1968.* Athens: University of Georgia Press, 2017.

Burke, W. Lewis, and Belinda F. Gergel. *Matthew J. Perry: The Man, His Times, and His Legacy.* Columbia: University of South Carolina Press, 2004.

Burke, W. Lewis, and William C. Hine. "The South Carolina State College Law School: Its Roots, Creation, and Legacy." In Burke and Gergel, *Matthew J. Perry,* 17–60.

Butler, Angeline. "What We Were Talking About Was Our Future." In Holsaert et al., *Hands on the Freedom Plow,* 39–45.

Bynum, Thomas. *NAACP Youth and the Fight for Black Freedom, 1936–1965.* Knoxville: University of Tennessee Press, 2014.

Carey, Gordon. Interview by Judith Vecchione. *Eyes on the Prize Interviews.* St. Louis: Washington University Digital Gateway, 1985.

Carter, Robert L. *A Matter of Law: A Memoir of Struggle in the Cause of Equal Rights.* New York: New Press, 2005.

Chafe, William H. *Greensboro, North Carolina and the Black Struggle for Freedom.* New York: Oxford University Press, 1980.

Charron, Katherine Mellon. *Freedom's Teacher: The Life of Septima Clark.* Chapel Hill: University of North Carolina Press, 2009.

Chestnut, Trichita M. *Lynching: Ida B. Wells-Barnett and the Outrage over the Frazier Baker Murder.* Washington, D.C.: Rediscovering Black History, Black History Guide, National Archives and Records Administration, 2008.

Clyburn, James E. *Blessed Experiences: Genuinely Southern, Proudly Black.* Columbia: University of South Carolina Press, 2014.

Cohodas, Nadine. *Strom Thurmond and the Politics of Change.* New York: Simon & Schuster, 1993.

Collins, LeRoy, "Statewide TV-Radio Talk to the People of Florida on Race Relations." In *Rhetoric, Religion and the Civil Rights Movement, 1954–1965,* vol. 1, edited by Davis W. Houck and David E. Dixon, 349–56. Waco, Tex.: Baylor University Press, 2006.

CORE Rules for Action. New York: Congress of Racial Equality, 1963.

Crawford, Vicki L., Jacqueline Anne Rouse, and Barbara Woods, eds. *Women in the Civil Rights Movement: Trailblazers and Torchbearers, 1941–1965.* Bloomington: Indiana University Press, 1993.

Currie, Cameron McGowan. "Before Rosa Parks: The Case of Sarah Mae Flemming." In Burke and Gergel, *Matthew J. Perry,* 81–103.

Curry, Constance. "NSA's Southern Civil Rights Initiative." In *American Students Organize: Founding the U.S. National Student Association after World War II,* edited by Eugene G. Schwartz, 444–55. Santa Barbara, Cal.: Praeger, 2006.

————. "Wild Geese to the Past." In *Deep in Our Hearts: Nine White Women in the Freedom Movement*, edited by Joan C. Browning, 1–36. Athens: University of Georgia Press, 2000.

DeLaine, Mattie. Interview by Grace McFadden. Columbia: Quest for Human/Civil Rights—Oral Recollections of Black South Carolinians, Moving Image Research Collections, University of South Carolina, n.d.

Dobrasko, Rebekah. *South Carolina's Equalization Schools 1951–1960*. Columbia: State Historic Preservation Office, South Carolina Department of Archives and History, 2008.

Doster, Lillie Marsh. "Lillie Marsh Doster, Interview U-0386." Interview by Jennifer Otha Dixon. In *Long Civil Rights Movement: Economic Justice in Charleston, SC*. Chapel Hill: Southern Oral History Program Interview Database, Center for the Study of the American South, University of North Carolina, 2008.

Drago, Edmund L. *Charleston's Avery Center: From Education and Civil Rights to Preserving the African American Experience*. Charleston: History Press, 2006.

DuBose, Sonny. *The Road to Brown: The Leadership of a Soldier of the Cross, Rev. J. A. DeLaine*. Orangeburg, S.C.: Williams Publishing, 2002.

Early, Charity Adams. *One Woman's Army*. College Station: Texas A&M University Press, 1989.

Edgar, Walter. *History of Santee Cooper, 1934–1984*. Moncks Corner: S.C. Public Service Authority, 1984.

Equal Justice Initiative. *Lynching in America: Confronting the Legacy of Racial Terror*. Montgomery, Ala.: Equal Justice Initiative, 2017.

Farmer, James. "James Farmer Oral History Interview 1, Transcript." Interview by Harri Baker. Austin, Tex.: Lyndon Baines Johnson Library Oral History Collection, 1969.

————. *Lay Bare the Heart: An Autobiography of the Civil Rights Movement*. New York: Arbor House, 1985.

Federal Bureau of Investigation (FBI). "Citizens Councils, Savannah Division." In *Citizens Council Movement*. Mobile, Ala.: United States Government, 1956. https://archive.org /stream/CItizensCouncilMovement/CitCouncils-Savannah#page/n3/mode/2up /search/South+Carolina (accessed 18 November 2019).

————. "Klan Infiltration into the Citizens Councils of Alabama." In *Citizens Council Movement*. Mobile, Ala.: United States Government, 1956. https://archive.org/stream /CItizensCouncilMovement/CitCouncils-Alabama-HQ-2_djvu.txt (accessed 18 November 2019).

Fink, Gary, and Merl E. Reed. *Race, Class, and Community in Southern Labor History*. Tuscaloosa: University of Alabama Press, 1994.

Fink, Leon. "A Labor Crusade behind the Magnolia Curtain: Hospital Workers and the Politics of Race and Class." In *Search of the Working Class: Essays in American Labor History and Political Culture*, edited by Leon Fink, 51–85. Chicago: University of Illinois Press, 1994.

Fink, Leon, and Brian Greenberg. *Upheaval in the Quiet Zone: A History of Hospital Workers Union, Local 1199*. Chicago: University of Illinois Press, 1989.

Fischer, Louis. *Gandhi: His Life and Message for the World.* New York: Mentor, 1982.

Foner, Moe. *Not for Bread Alone.* Ithaca, N.Y.: Cornell University Press: 2002.

———. "Reminiscences of Moe Foner." Interview by Robert Master, sessions 9–11. New York: Columbia University Libraries, 1986.

Fordham, Damon L. *True Stories of Black South Carolina.* Charleston: History Press, 2008.

Frederickson, Kari. *The Dixiecrat Revolt and the End of the Solid South: 1932–1968.* Chapel Hill: University of North Carolina Press, 2001.

Gaither, Thomas. "Orangeburg: Behind the Carolina Stockade." In *Sit-Ins: The Students Report,* edited by Jim Peck, 9–11. New York: CORE, 1960.

———. "Students on a Road Gang." In *Freedom Ride,* edited by James Peck, 94–113. New York: Simon & Schuster, 1962.

———. "Thomas Walter Gaither Oral History Interview." Interview by Joseph Mosnier. Washington, D.C.: U.S. Civil Rights History Project, Library of Congress, 2011.

Gandhi, Mohandas K.. *Gandhi: An Autobiography.* Boston: Beacon, 1957.

Gergel, Richard. *Unexampled Courage: The Blinding of Sgt. Isaac Woodard and the Awakening of President Harry S. Truman and Judge J. Waties Waring.* New York: Farrar, Straus & Giroux, 2019.

Gona, Ophelia De Laine. *Dawn of Desegregation: J. A. De Laine and Briggs v. Elliott.* Columbia: University of South Carolina Press, 2011.

Gravely, William B. *They Stole Him Out of Jail: Willie Earle, South Carolina's Last Lynching Victim.* Columbia: University of South Carolina Press, 2019.

Grose, Philip G. *South Carolina at the Brink: Robert McNair and the Politics of Civil Rights.* Columbia: University of South Carolina Press, 2006.

Halberstam, David. *The Children.* New York: Fawcett Books, 1998.

Hine, William C. *South Carolina State University: A Black Land-Grant College in Jim Crow America.* Columbia: University of South Carolina Press, 2018.

Hodges, James A. "J. P. Stevens and the Union: Struggle for the South." In Fink and Reed, *Race, Class, and Community in Southern Labor History,* 53–64.

Holsaert, Faith S., Martha Prescod Norman Noonan, Judy Richardson, Betty Garman Robinson, Jean Smith Young, and Dorothy M. Zellner, eds. *Hands on the Freedom Plow: Personal Accounts by Women in SNCC.* Champaign: University of Illinois Press, 2012.

Houck, Davis W., and David E. Dixon, eds. *Women and the Civil Rights Movement, 1954–1965.* Jackson: University Press of Mississippi, 2011.

Huff, Archie Vernon Jr. *Greenville: The History of the City and the County in the Piedmont,* Columbia: University of South Carolina Press, 1995.

Jones-Branch, Cherisse. "Modjeska Monteith Simkins: I Cannot Be Bought and Will Not Be Sold." In Spruill, Littlefield, and Johnson, *South Carolina Women,* 3:221–39.

Kluger, Richard. *Simple Justice.* New York: Vintage Books, 1975.

Lane, Hugh C., Sr. "The History of Banking in South Carolina in the 20th Century Project." Interview by John G. Sprout. Columbia: South Caroliniana Library Oral History Collections, University of South Carolina.

Lare, Marvin Ira. *Champions of Civil and Human Rights in South Carolina: Dawn of the Movement Era, 1955–1967.* Columbia: University of South Carolina Press, 2016.

———. "Cleveland Sellers, Part 1, From Denmark to Destiny." In Lare, *Champions of Civil and Human Rights,* 134–45.

Lau, Peter. *Democracy Rising: South Carolina and the Fight for Black Equality since 1865.* Lexington: University Press of Kentucky, 2006.

———. "Mr. NAACP: Levi G. Byrd and the Remaking of the NAACP in the State and Nation, 1917–1960." In Moore and Burton, *Toward the Meeting of the Waters,* 146–55.

Lee, Ulysses. *The Employment of Negro Troops: United States Army in World War II.* Washington, D.C.: Center of Military History, United States Army, 2001.

Lewis, John, with Michael D'Orso. *Walking with the Wind: A Memoir of the Movement.* New York: Simon & Schuster, 1998.

Lochbaum, Julie Magruder. "The Word Made Flesh: The Desegregation Leadership of Rev. J. A. DeLaine." Ph.D. diss., College of Education, University of South Carolina, 1993.

Logan, Sadye L. M. "Isaiah DeQuincey Newman: The Servant Leader." In Logan, *Spirit of an Activist,* 8–46.

———, ed. *The Spirit of an Activist: The Life and Work of I. DeQuincey Newman.* Columbia: University of South Carolina Press, 2014.

McCord, James B., with John Scott Douglas. *My Patients Were Zulus.* New York: Rinehart, 1946.

McDew, Charles F. "Charles F. McDew Oral History." Interview by Joseph Mosnier. Civil Rights History Project, 2011.

McMillen, Neil R. *The Citizens' Council: Organized Resistance to the Second Reconstruction. 1954–64.* Champaign: University of Illinois Press, 1994.

Meriwether, Colyer. "History of Higher Education in South Carolina." In Vol. 4 of *Contributions to American Educational History,* edited by Herbert Baxter Adams. Washington, D.C.: Government Printing Office, 1889.

Middleton, Earl M., with Joy W. Barnes. *Knowing Who I Am: A Black Entrepreneur's Struggle and Success in the American South.* Columbia: University of South Carolina Press, 2008.

Montgomery, Eugene A. R. "Quest for Civil Rights: Eugene A. R. Montgomery." Interview by Grace McFadden. Columbia: Quest for Human/Civil Rights—Oral Recollections of Black South Carolinians, Moving Image Research Collections, University of South Carolina, 1980.

Moore, John Hammond. *Carnival of Blood: Dueling, Lynching, and Murder in South Carolina 1880–1920.* Columbia: University of South Carolina Press, 2006.

Moore, Robert J. "The Civil Rights Advocate." In Burke and Gergel, *Matthew J. Perry,* 155–182.

———. "Matthew J. Perry, Part 1, A Pearl of a Case." In Lare, *Champions of Civil and Human Rights,* 129–33.

Moore, Winfred B., Jr., and Orville Vernon Burton, eds. *Toward the Meeting of the Waters:*

Currents in the Civil Rights Movement of South Carolina during the Twentieth Century. Columbia: University of South Carolina Press, 2008.

Motley, Constance Baker. "Memory, History, and Community: The Assimilation of Houstonian Principles in the Career of Matthew J. Perry." In Burke and Gergel, *Matthew J. Perry,* 221–37.

Moultrie, Mary. Interview by Kent Germany. "Telling Our Story, Unsung Heroes and Heroines Conference," Thirty-fifth Anniversary of African American Studies, University of South Carolina, Columbia, October 12–13, 2006.

———. "Mary Moultrie, William Saunders, Rosetta Simmons." Interview by Kerry Taylor. Charleston, SC: Citadel Oral History Program, Citadel Archives and Museum, 2009.

Myers, Andrew H. *Black, White and Olive Drab: Racial Integration at Fort Jackson, South Carolina, and the Civil Rights Movement.* Charlottesville: University of Virginia Press, 2006.

National Association for the Advancement of Colored People (NAACP). "A Program to Implement the Supreme Court's School Desegregation Decision," Emergency Southwide NAACP Conference. In *African-American Political Thought: Confrontation vs. Compromise, from 1945 to the Present,* vol. 4, edited by Marcus Polman, 251–55. London: Routledge, 2003.

Newman, Betsy, dir. *Carolina Stories: Charlie's Place.* Columbia: South Carolina Educational Television, 2018.

Panetta, Leon E. *Bring Us Together.* Philadelphia and New York: Lippincott, 1971.

Patterson, James T. *Brown v Board of Education: A Civil Rights Milestone and Its Troubled Legacy.* New York: Oxford University Press, 2001.

Peck, Jim. *Cracking the Color Line: Non-violent Direct Action Methods of Eliminating Racial Discrimination.* New York: Congress of Racial Equality, 1959.

Quint, Howard H. *Profile in Black and White: A Frank Portrait of South Carolina.* Washington, D.C.: Public Affairs Press, 1958.

Ransby, Barbara. *Ella Baker and the Black Freedom Movement.* Chapel Hill: University of North Carolina Press, 2003.

Riches, William T. Martin. *The Civil Rights Movement: Struggle and Resistance.* New York: Palgrave Macmillan, 2010.

Roberts, Gene, and Hank Klibanoff. *The Race Beat: The Press, the Civil Rights Struggle, and the Awakening of a Nation.* New York: Knopf, 2006.

Robinson, Jackie. *First Class Citizenship: The Civil Rights Letters of Jackie Robinson,* edited by Michael G. Long, 75–76. New York: Times Books, 2007.

Rogers, George C., and C. James Taylor. *A South Carolina Chronology, 1497–1992.* Columbia: University of South Carolina Press, 1994.

Rucker, Walter C., and James C. Upton, eds. *Encyclopedia of American Race Riots, vol. 1.* Westport, Conn.: Greenwood, 2007.

Saunders, William. "Mary Moultrie, William Saunders, and Rosetta Simmons." Interview by Kerry Taylor. Avery Research Center Oral Histories, 2009.

Simkins, Modjeska. "Modjeska M. Simkins." In Houck and Dixon, *Women and the Civil Rights Movement, 1954–1965,* 139–47.

————. "Oral History Interview with Modjeska Simkins, G-0056–2." Interview by Jacquelyn Hall. Chapel Hill: Southern Oral History Program Collection, University of North Carolina at Chapel Hill, 1976.

Smith, Harold L. "Casey Hayden." In Turner, *Texas Women: Their Histories, Their Lives,* 359–87.

Southern Regional Council. *The Student Protest Movement.* Atlanta: Southern Regional Council, 1960.

Spruill, Marjorie, Valinda W. Littlefield, and Joan Marie Johnson. *South Carolina Women: Their Lives and Times,* vol. 3. Athens: University of Georgia Press, 2012.

Stoddard, Belle Howe. *Re: Gedney Main Howe Jr., 1914–1981.* Adamsville, Ala.: Action Printing, 1985.

Student Nonviolent Coordinating Committee (SNCC). Tape 9, Student Nonviolent Coordinating Committee 40th anniversary conference videocassette tapes. Durham, N.C.: David M. Rubenstein Rare Book and Manuscript Library, Duke University, 2000.

Sullivan, Patricia. *Lift Every Voice: The NAACP and the Making of the Civil Rights Movement.* New York: New Press, 2009.

Tracy, James. *Direct Action: Radical Pacifism From the Union Eight to the Chicago Seven.* Chicago: University of Chicago Press, 1996.

Turner, Elizabeth Hayes, ed. *Texas Women: Their Histories, Their Lives.* Athens: University of Georgia Press, 2015.

U.S. Bureau of Education. *Industrial Education in the United States.* Washington, D.C.: Government Printing Office, 1883.

Warren, Earl. *The Memoirs of Chief Justice Earl Warren.* Garden City, N.Y.: Doubleday, 1977.

Wells, Ida B. *Crusade for Justice: The Autobiography of Ida B. Wells,* edited by Alfreda M. Duster. Chicago: University of Chicago Press, 1970.

Wicker, Tom. *Dwight D. Eisenhower.* New York: Holt, 2002.

Williams, Cecil J. *Freedom and Justice: Four Decades of the Civil Rights Struggle as Seen by a Black Photographer of the Deep South.* Macon, Ga.: Mercer University Press, 1995.

————. *Out of-the-Box in Dixie: Cecil Williams' Photography of the South Carolina Events That Changed America.* Orangeburg, S.C.: Cecil J. Williams, 2007.

Williams, Hosea. "Hosea Williams Interview." Interview by Steve Estes. Charleston, S.C.: Steve Estes Papers, Avery Research Center for African American History and Culture, College of Charleston, 1996.

Williams, Juan. *Thurgood Marshall: American Revolutionary.* New York: Three Rivers, 1998.

Willoughby, Lynn. *The Good Town Does Well: Rock Hill, SC, 1852–2002.* Orangeburg, S.C.: Written in Stone, 2002.

Wolff, Miles. *Lunch at the 5 and 10.* Chicago: Ivan R. Dee, 1990.

Woods, Barbara. "Modjeska Simkins and the South Carolina Conference of the NAACP, 1939–1957." In Crawford, Rouse, and Woods, *Women in the Civil Rights Movement,* 99–120.

Yarborough, Tinsley E. *A Passion for Justice: J. Waties Waring and Civil Rights*. New York: Oxford University Press, 1987.

Young, Andrew. *An Easy Burden: The Civil Rights Movement and the Transformation of America*. Waco, Tex.: Baylor University Press, 2008.

Zinn, Howard. *SNCC: The New Abolitionists*. Cambridge, Mass.: South End, 1964.

Index

15; and threats of violence against, 2, 3–4, 20–22, 26; and voting rights, 6, 7, 8, 9, 10

Hinton, Lula, 2, 26

Hinton, Novella, 21

Hinton, Rodney, 26, 50, 61, 67, 69, 75, 78, 79

Holden, Clara, 220

Holland, Wanda, 132

Holliday, Billie, 14, 22

Hollings, Ernest F.: 132, 134, 147, 153–54, 162–63, 180, 184, 188, 190; and the Charleston hospital strike, 264, 265; sit-ins criticism, 124, 127, 128, 148, 153, 155, 158, 179, 186; support for segregation, 86, 93, 187, 197

Holt, Leon, 202

Hoover, J. Edgar, 86, 108

hospital salary inequity, 232, 234, 241, 244, 249, 260, 269

House Un–American Activities Committee (HUAC), 27

Houston, Charles Hamilton, 10, 12, 34, 60

Howard, Mae Frances Moultrie. See Moultrie, Mae Francis

Hubacz, Leon J., 238

Huff, William D., 219, 220, 221, 260, 262

Hughes, Genevieve, 109

hunger strikes, 266

Hunsucker, John, Jr., 106, 132, 134

Hurd, Roosevelt Carlos, Sr., 17

Hurley, Ruby, 161, 208

Husser, Helen, 325n35

I Am Somebody, 275

institutional racism, 215

Interstate Commerce Act, 109

Interstate Commerce Commission, 190, 304n42

invaders/invasion, 27, 124, 177, 191, 192, 194, 238, 251, 316n170, 317n1

Irene Brown et al. v. South Carolina, 209

Ivory, Cecil Augustus, ix, 96–97, 121, 122, 124, 128, 129, 277, 280, 304n44, 323n290; and Local Committee for the Promotion of Human Rights, 99, 102; and lunch-counter protests, 104, 105, 106, 107, 108,

134, 135, 209, 210; and the NAACP, 99, 101, 102, 107, 118, 119, 132; and threats of violence against, 99–100, 102, 126, 127; and transportation activism, 99, 100–101, 103–104, 109, 130–31

Ivory, Cecil, Jr., 102

Ivory, Darnell, 102

Ivory, Emily, 101, 102, 107, 108, 110

Ivory, Titus, 102

J. G. McCrory's, 104, 106–107, 112, 115, 121–23, 125, 126, 134, 135, 173, 191, 203, 209

J. L. Phillips Drugstores, 121

Jackson Street Panthers, 235, 241, 252

Jackson, Jesse, 255

Jackson, Robert Henry, 77

Jones, E. C., 56, 277, 278

James, Frederick Calhoun, 175, 194

Javis, Moses, 186, 188

Jenkins, Esau, 212, 214–15, 216, 233, 236, 238, 249, 269

Jenkins, Lincoln C., 92, 151, 152, 196

Jenkins, Timothy, 163

Johnson C. Smith University, 96, 106, 113, 176

Johnson, Edna, 219, 275

Johnson, Edrena, 245

Johnson, Lyndon B., 230, 250

Johnson, Martin Leroy, 121, 125, 126, 129, 130, 131

Johnston, James Daniel, 23

Johnston, Olin D., 6, 7, 57, 90

Jones, E. C., 277, 278

Jones, J. Charles, 278

Jones, James, 244

Jones, Joseph Charles, 113, 114, 124, 132, 163, 176, 278

Jones, T. B., 97

Jones, W. R., 106

Joyce, William, 240, 245

Keels, Thomas D., 192

Kelly, Margaret, 325n35

Kennedy, Ethel, 261

Kennedy, George, 42

Kennedy, John F., 164, 190, 200, 207, 258

Orangeburg Massacre, 227, 230, 260, 277

Orangeburg Student Movement Association, 142

outside agitators: 124, 176, 184, 192, 232, 255, 278; *see also* agitators

pacifism, 116

Palmer, Robert John, 194

Palmetto State Teachers Association (PSTA), 5, 40, 44

Panetta, Leon E., 261, 264

parades: for Christmas, 90, 104; by Ku Klux Klan, 3, 22, 23, 56; ordinances & permits for, 149, 157, 179, 266

Parents Committee on Action, 46

Parker, John J., 9, 58, 66, 70, 81, 88

Parks, Rosa, 98, 249, 255

Parnell, Ira Byrd, 193, 195, 196, 201, 204

Parson, Bennie, 59, 62

Parson, Celestine, 62

Parson, Plummie, 62

Pate, J. C., 101

paternalism, 262

Patterson, Shirley McDonald, 91

Payton, George, Jr., 237

Pearson v. Clarendon County Board of Education, 43

Pearson, Elijah, 266

Pearson, Ferdinand, 31, 32, 37, 38, 39, 43, 45

Pearson, Hammett, ix, 31, 32, 38, 42, 44, 62, 91, 92

Pearson, James, 42

Pearson, Jesse, 32, 37, 44, 45, 46, 48, 62, 92

Pearson, Levi, ix, 31, 32, 38, 42, 43, 44, 46, 92, 94, 300n200

Pearson, Phynise "Piney," 32, 38, 43

Pearson, Viola, 94

Pearson, Willie, 32

Peck, James, 171

Penn Center, 161, 162, 252, 331n134

Perkins, Joe, 199

Perry, Matthew J., Jr., 98, 132–33, 151, 152, 154, 155, 156, 157, 185, 195, 196, 202, 209, 210, 278, 284n33

Plessy v. Ferguson, 10, 56, 66, 67, 68, 98

Plummer, Abe, 104, 121, 122, 124, 125, 128–29, 130–31, 132, 133

poll taxes, 8, 44

Pough, W. Newton, 151

Progressive Club (Esau Jenkins), 215

Progressive Democratic Party (PDP), 6, 8–9, 177, 178

property damage, 249–50, 251, 253, 267

Prosten, David, 254

protest violence: 176, 179; in Charleston, 248, 249, 250, 251, 253, 257, 263, 266, 267, 268, 272; in Chattanooga, 127, 143; in Greenville, 187, 188

Pryor, Fred, 15–16

Pyatt, Rudolph A., 251

Quarles, H. E., 14

Radke, Marian J., 65

Ragin, Andrew Lee, 33, 51

Ragin, Edward, 46, 59

Ragin, Hazel, 33, 51, 59

Ragin, Henry Jeff, 301n200

Ragin, Leola, 95

Ragin, Lucretia, 95, 301n200

Ragin, William, 53, 59, 92, 301n200

Ragin, Zelia, 33, 51

Rambay School, 32, 49, 64

Ramseur, Charles, 129

Rector, Hendrix, 17

Reeder, James, 160

Reid, Frank Madison, Sr., 68, 87

Republican Party, 77, 162, 188, 190

Reuben, Odell R., 197, 206

Reuther, Walter, 254, 255, 256

Rexall Drug Store, 150

Richardson, Lee, 53, 59, 90, 92

Richardson, Lucrisher, 59, 92

Richburg, Edward Eugene "E. E.," 35, 45, 46, 47, 52, 55, 38, 81, 83, 88

Richburg, Gracie Palmer, 83

Richburg, Helen, 36

Richburg, J. Haskell, 83

Richburg, John Wesley, 51

Richburg, Joseph, 83